Language in

ONE WEEK LOAN

Also by Janet Cotterill

WORKING WITH DIALOGUE (*edited with M. Coulthard and F. Rock*)
LANGUAGE ACROSS BOUNDARIES (*edited with I. Ife*)
LANGUAGE AND POWER IN COURT

Language in the Legal Process

Edited by

Janet Cotterill
Lecturer in Language and Communication at the
Centre for Language and Communication Research
Cardiff University

First published in hardcover 2002
First published in paperback 2004 by
PALGRAVE MACMILLAN
Houndmills, Basingstoke, Hampshire RG21 6XS and
175 Fifth Avenue, New York, N.Y. 10010
Companies and representatives throughout the world

PALGRAVE MACMILLAN is the global academic imprint of the Palgrave
Macmillan division of St Martin's Press, LLC and of Palgrave Macmillan Ltd.
Macmillan® is a registered trademark in the United States, United Kingdom
and other countries. Palgrave is a registered trademark in the European
Union and other countries.

ISBN-13: 978-0-333-96902-1 hardback
ISBN-10: 0-333-96902-2 hardback
ISBN-13: 978-1-4039-3388-1 paperback
ISBN-10: 1-4039-3388-X paperback

This book is printed on paper suitable for recycling and made from fully
managed and sustained forest sources. Logging, pulping and manufacturing
processes are expected to conform to the environmental regulations
of the country of origin.

A catalogue record for this book is available from the British Library.

Library of Congress Cataloging-in-Publication Data
Language in the legal process/edited by Janet Cotterill.
     p.   cm.
Includes bibliographical references and index.
ISBN 0–333–96902–2 (cloth)
ISBN 1–4039–3388–X (pbk)
1. Criminal justice, Administration of—Language.   2. Law enforcement—
Language.   3. Forensic linguistics.   I. Cotterill, Janet, 1968–
K5001 .L36 2002
340′.01′4—dc21
                                                                    2002022017

Transferred to digital print 2007
Printed and bound in Great Britain by
CPI Antony Rowe, Chippenham and Eastbourne

Contents

Preface to Paperback Edition   vii

List of Tables   viii

List of Figures   ix

Acknowledgements   x

Notes on the Contributors   xi

Introduction: Language in the Legal Process   xv
Janet Cotterill

Part I   The Linguist in the Legal Process

1   To Testify or Not to Testify?   3
    Roger W. Shuy

2   Whose Voice Is It? Invented and Concealed Dialogue
    in Written Records of Verbal Evidence Produced by the Police
    Malcolm Coulthard   19

3   Textual Barriers to United States Immigration
    Gail Stygall   35

4   The Language and Law of Product Warnings
    Peter M. Tiersma   54

Part II   The Language of the Police and the Police Interview

5   'I Just Need to Ask Somebody Some Questions': Sensitivities
    in Domestic Dispute Calls
    Karen Tracy and Robert R. Agne   75

6   *So . . . ?*: Pragmatic Implications of *So*-Prefaced Questions
    in Formal Police Interviews
    Alison Johnson   91

7   'Three's a Crowd': Shifting Dynamics in the Interpreted Interview
    Sonia Russell   111

8   The Miranda Warnings and Linguistic Coercion: The Role of
    Footing in the Interrogation of a Limited-English-speaking
    Murder Suspect
    Susan Berk-Seligson   127

Part III   The Language of the Courtroom I: Lawyers and Witnesses

9   'Just One More Time...': Aspects of Intertextuality
    in the Trials of O. J. Simpson
    Janet Cotterill   147

10 'Evidence Given in Unequivocal Terms':
    Gaining Consent of Aboriginal Young People in Court
    Diana Eades   162

11 The Clinton Scandal: Some Legal Lessons from Linguistics
    Lawrence M. Solan   180

12 Understanding the Other: A Case of Mis-Interpreting
    Culture-Specific Utterances during Alternative Dispute Resolution
    Rosemary Moeketsi   196

Part IV   The Language of the Courtroom II: Judges and Juries

13 The Meaning of 'I Go Bankrupt': An Essay in Forensic Linguistics
    Stan Bernstein   213

14 'If you were Standing in Marks and Spencers': Narrativisation
    and Comprehension in the English Summing-up
    Chris Heffer   228

15 Reasonable Doubt about Reasonable Doubt:
    Assessing Jury Instruction Adequacy in a Capital Case
    Bethany K. Dumas   246

16 Discipline and Punishment in the Discourse
    of Legal Decisions on Rape Trials
    Débora de Carvalho Figueiredo   260

Index   275

Preface to Paperback Edition

Since *Language in the Legal Process* was first published in 2002, the field of forensic linguistics/language and law has continued to grow. The number of modules offered at both undergraduate and postgraduate levels has increased, with courses attracting large numbers of students. The field's flagship journal *Forensic Linguistics: The International Journal of Speech, Language and the Law* has received a record number of submissions during 2003, and for the first time, the conference of the International Association of Forensic Linguists (held in 2003 in Sydney, Australia) had to be organised into parallel sessions, due to the large number of submissions. All of this is evidence of a growth in interest in language and the law, not only by linguists but also by members of the legal profession, the police authorities and the judiciary. As the field continues to develop, there is increasing recognition of the importance played by language in the legal process and as a consequence, research which feeds back into the texts and practices of law, or, increasingly, which is commissioned by professionals working in these areas, is becoming more common.

One note of great sadness marks the transition of *Language in the Legal Process* from hardcover to paperback. Dr Sonia Russell, whose contribution '"Three's a Crowd": Shifting Dynamics in the Interpreted Interview' (Chapter 7) deals with the influence of foreign-language interpreters in police interviews, sadly passed away in November 2002. Sonia continues to be missed by all who knew her and her passing is a great loss to the forensic linguistics community. This paperback version of the book is dedicated to her memory.

List of Tables

1.1	Topic analysis in *USA* v. *John DeLorean*	9
1.2	Place references by both speakers	12
3.1	Comparison of number of clauses per sentence	44
6.1	Comparisons of *so* and *so*-preface frequencies across corpora	97
6.2	Comparison of connectives present in interviews with a young child and an adult	100
6.3	Frequency of *so*-prefaced questions in two child interviews	101
6.4	Distribution of *so*-prefaced questions over three phases of the interview	101
14.1	Key tendencies of the narrative and paradigmatic modes	232
14.2	Experiential features in proof directions	234
14.3	Interpersonal features in proof directions	236
14.4	Textual and other features in proof directions	237
14.5	Mode tendencies of proof directions	239

List of Figures

3.1	INS form I-140	42
3.2	INS form I-485	43
3.3	Times Roman and Helvetica font types	44
3.4	I-485 Application Section, part 3, question 1	46
4.1	Biological hazard symbol	62
4.2	FDA label for antidandruff products	67
4.3	Federally-required label for charcoal	68
6.1	Picture of *so*	94
6.2	Picture of *so* + *how*	95
6.3	Concordance of *so* showing *so*-prefaced questions in interviewer turns	98
14.1	Specimen proof directions	231
14.2	Analysis of the specimen proof directions	238

Acknowledgements

I am grateful to many people for their support and assistance in producing this edited collection. Firstly, my sincere thanks are of course due to all of the contributors, who have endured my endless emails, faxes and letters with good humour, and who have responded to each new request with promptness and professionalism. I very much hope they will enjoy the final result. I must also thank my colleagues in the Centre for Language and Communication Research at Cardiff University, for their encouragement and constant supply of caffeine.

I am, as always, most grateful to Malcolm Coulthard, who introduced me to forensic linguistics in the first place, and who continues to be a great inspiration, and to Michael Hoey for his unfailing support and encouragement. I have been greatly assisted by the staff at Palgrave Macmillan, though particular thanks are due to Jill Lake who has guided me through the editorial process with considerable patience.

My final and greatest thanks must be reserved for my family, Jean and Doug, Michaela and Erik. During a difficult year, they have provided both sanity and sanctuary. Without their love, support and friendship, this book would not have been completed.

JANET COTTERILL

Notes on the Contributors

Robert Agne is a doctoral candidate in the Department of Communication at the University of Colorado, Boulder, USA. His research interests include work on discourse, and the management of identities and interaction problems. His dissertation project is focusing on analysing the religious talk in the telephone negotiations during the FBI/Branch Davidian standoff at Waco, Texas.

Stan Bernstein serves as a US Bankruptcy Judge for the Eastern District of New York, USA. He also holds adjunct academic appointments teaching ethics and philosophy of law at Hofstra University, and bankruptcy law at Touro Law School.

Susan Berk-Seligson is an Associate Professor in the Department of Hispanic Languages and Literatures and in the Department of Linguistics of the University of Pittsburgh, Pennsylvania, USA. She has a PhD in linguistics from the University of Arizona, and specialises in sociolinguistics. Within the field of language and the law, she has done most of her research on court interpreting for the non-English speaking. Outside this field, she has done research on language and gender and on phonological variation, specifically in Latin America.

Janet Cotterill is a Lecturer in Language and Communication at Cardiff University, UK, where she teaches forensic linguistics, systemic functional linguistics and language and gender. She has recently completed a doctoral thesis at the University of Birmingham on the discourse structures and strategies of the criminal courtroom. In addition to her research into courtroom language, she is also involved in ongoing work on the comprehensibility of legal language. She is joint editor of *Forensic Linguistics: The International Journal of Speech, Language and the Law*.

Malcolm Coulthard is Professor of English Language and Linguistics in the Department of English, University of Birmingham, UK. He was the founding editor of *Forensic Linguistics: The International Journal of Language and the Law* and was the founding President of the International Association of Forensic Linguists. He has been commissioned to write reports as an expert witness in over 150 cases and has given evidence in three terrorist trials in Northern Ireland and in a case of academic plagiarism in Hong Kong. He has appeared as an expert twice in the Court of Appeal, including the successful

Derek Bentley Appeal when, in 1998, the verdict of guilty was overturned after 46 years.

Bethany K. Dumas is Associate Professor of English and Chair, Linguistics Programme at the University of Tennessee, USA. She received her BA from Lamar University in 1959, her MA from the University of Arkansas, 1961, her PhD also from the University of Arkansas, 1971, and a JD from the University of Tennessee in 1985. She has published widely on topics such as language variation, discourse analysis and language in judicial process, especially jury instructions and product warnings. She teaches courses and workshops in variation and language and law topics.

Diana Eades is Associate Professor in the Department of Second Language Studies at the University of Hawaii, USA. She has been doing sociolinguistic research on language and the law since 1987. Her publications include the 1992 handbook for lawyers titled *Aboriginal English and the Law* (Queensland Law Society), and the 1995 edited book titled *Language in Evidence: Issues Confronting Aboriginal and Multicultural Australia* (University of New South Wales Press). She has also been actively involved in legal applications of sociolinguistic research as consultant, expert witness and advisor to several inquiries. From 1995–99 she was President of the International Association of Forensic Linguists.

Débora de Carvalho Figueiredo lectures at Faculdades Barddal in Southern Brazil. Her research interests include the investigation of issues of gender and power in legal discourse from the perspectives of critical discourse analysis, gender studies and feminist legal studies, as well as the investigation of professional discourses. She has published articles about the discourse of women's magazines, the teaching of reading from the perspective of critical discourse analysis, and the discourse of legal decisions on rape.

Chris Heffer lectures in linguistics at Nottingham Trent University, UK. His doctoral dissertation at the University of Birmingham dealt with the language of legal professionals in the courtroom. For many years he lectured in English Language at the University of Venice. He has also been a professional translator, editor, courtroom interpreter and voiceover artist. He is a member of the Birmingham Forensic Linguistics Group and has presented a number of papers on forensic topics at international conferences.

Alison Johnson is a Lecturer in Linguistics and English Literature at the University of Birmingham, Westhill, UK. She began her working life as a police officer in the West Midlands Police, where she served as a constable for six years. Her interest in forensic linguistics resulted from the combination of professional work and study. She is currently writing-up her doctoral thesis on the effect of questions in police interviews.

Rosemary H. Moeketsi is Assistant Professor in the Department of African Languages at the University of South Africa, Pretoria. She received her DLitt in African languages: forensic linguistics from the University of South Africa in 1992. In 1999, she published *Discourse in the Multilingual and Multicultural Courtroom: A Court Interpreters' Guide* through Van Schaik.

Sonia Russell was a Member of the Institute of Linguists and graduated from Aston University, Birmingham, in 1998, with a MSc in teaching English for specific purposes. She was a French/English legal interpreter based in Dover, England, and worked for Kent Police, the Facilitation Support Unit, Dover and HM Customs & Excise. She received her doctorate from Aston University, Birmingham, UK.

Roger W. Shuy is Distinguished Research Professor of Linguistics, Emeritus, at Georgetown University, USA where he specialised in sociolinguistics and forensic linguistics. After retiring to the mountains of Montana, he continues to consult with attorneys, carry out research and write. His most recent books include *Language Crimes* (Blackwell, 1996), *The Language of Confession, Interrogation and Deception* (Sage, 1999), *Bureaucratic Language* (Georgetown Press, 1999) and *A Few Months to Live: Different Paths to Life's End* (Georgetown Press, 2001). He has consulted on hundreds of criminal and civil law cases and has served as expert witness on 50 occasions.

Lawrence Solan is a Professor of Law at Brooklyn Law School, USA. He holds a PhD in linguistics from the University of Massachusetts, and a law degree from Harvard Law School. After graduating from law school, he clerked for Justice Stewart Pollock of the Supreme Court of New Jersey, after which he practised law in New York. He is the author of *The Language of Judges* (University of Chicago Press, 1993), and a number of articles on the relationship between linguistics and matters of legal interpretation. He has lectured widely on issues of language and law, including to American judges, and has recently taught a course on that subject as a visiting faculty member at Princeton University. He is the current President of the International Association of Forensic Linguists.

Gail Stygall is Associate Professor of English Language and Literature at the University of Washington, USA, where she teaches discourse analysis, rhetoric and legal discourse. She has written *Trial Language* (Benjamins, 1994), as well as articles on legal discourse, narrative, social constructions of minority students in the USA, writing assessment, and language and gender, appearing in collections and journals. She is also the co-editor of *New Directions in*

Portfolio Assessment (Boynton/Cook, 1994) and her co-edited collection with Ellen Barton, *Discourse Studies and Composition* will appear in March 2001 (Hampton Press). She consults on cases ranging from patent and trademark to immigration and criminal confessions. She is currently completing *The Discourse of Divorce and the Foucaudian File*.

Peter Tiersma is Professor of Law and Joseph Scott Fellow at Loyola Law School in Los Angeles, USA, where he has taught for the past ten years. He holds both a doctorate in linguistics (University of California, San Diego) and a JD in law (Boalt Hall, U.C. Berkeley). He is the author of *Legal Language* (University of Chicago Press, 1999) and several articles on language and law published in the *Texas Law Review, Wisconsin Law Review, Southern California Law Review, Rutgers Law Review, Language*, and other venues. Presently, he and Lawrence Solan are writing a book that is tentatively entitled *Language on Trial: Linguistics and the Criminal Law*.

Karen Tracy is Professor of Communication at the University of Colorado, Boulder, USA. She studies problematic exchanges in institutional settings. She has published articles in communication and language/discourse journals examining different kinds of interactional difficulties in citizen calls to the police, and is the author of *Colloquium: Dilemmas of Academic Discourse*. She is currently editor of the journal *Research on Language and Social Interaction*.

Introduction: Language in the Legal Process

The aim of this collection is to bring together into a single volume some of the key researchers currently working in the areas of forensic linguistics and language and the law. A distinctive feature of the book is the range of contributors involved; researchers from six countries and four continents are represented, including North America, the UK, Brazil, Australia and South Africa. Many of the authors, in addition to being academics, are currently or have previously been employed as practitioners in the legal process; thus, the collection includes papers by an ex-police officer, courtroom and police interpreters, lawyers and a bankruptcy judge, as well as academics who are actively involved in language reform in legal contexts or in expert witness work.

Several important issues and concerns permeate this collection of papers. Many of the chapters (Coulthard, Tracy and Agne, Johnson and Cotterill) deal with the communicative difficulties which occur at the legal – layperson interface, in terms of interactional problems faced by victims, witnesses and suspects who come into contact with the legal process. A second group of papers deals with the communicative problems caused by legal texts (Stygall, Tiersma, Heffer and Dumas), with several suggesting practical measures for improving the comprehensibility of legal language. Finally, a number of chapters, including those by Tiersma, Russell, Berk-Seligson, Eades, Moeketsi and Bernstein, address the particular problems faced by non-native-speaker witnesses, suspects and defendants within the legal system.

The first part of the book begins with a pair of papers which analyse the work of the linguist as an expert witness. Two highly experienced linguistic consultants, Shuy and Coulthard, discuss the roles and responsibilities of the linguist as consultant, each illustrating their discussions with high-profile cases with which they have been associated. Shuy outlines some of the types of evidence linguists are able (and, significantly, are *not* able) to present to lawyers and juries, whilst Coulthard's paper discusses three cases referred successfully to the Court of Appeal in the late 1990s. A second pair of papers, by Stygall and Tiersma, focus on immigration documentation and warning labels, respectively, and deal with the role of the linguist as language reformer. They explore the issues of transparency and comprehensibility in documents designed by the legal community but intended ostensibly for a lay end-user.

The next part of the book has a more descriptive orientation. The chapters move through the chain of forensic events from an initial 911 emergency call reporting a crime through to the police interview situation and beyond into the courtroom. Tracy and Agne's paper analyses the interactional dynamics of the emergency call centre. The chapter's concern is to explicate how, where, and in what ways person-description is a morally loaded undertaking in both spontaneous and elicited descriptions. The following papers by Russell and Johnson focus on the UK police interview, both in its monolingual and interpreted forms, and explore some of ways in which the strategic choices in questioning strategies may influence the evidence elicited from native and non-native-speaker witnesses and suspects. This theme is further developed by Berk-Seligson, who studies linguistic coercion in the setting of a US police interrogation which involved the violation of the suspect's Miranda rights. The case discussed demonstrates the dangers of using police officers as foreign language interpreters during interrogations.

The second half of the book takes the courtroom as its setting, and includes coverage of both criminal and civil courtrooms, as well as appeal courts and non-trial routes to justice. Part III includes papers on two of the highest profile US cases of the late 1990s; Cotterill begins with a comparative analysis of testimony from the criminal and civil trials of O.J. Simpson, tracing intertextual echoes in the narratives of the two trials. Solan's chapter explores ex-President Clinton's impeachment trial testimony, and, drawing on speech act theory, pragmatics and lexical semantics, discusses what it means to tell the truth, and what it means to tell a lie in a legal context.

The third and fourth papers in this part discuss some of the linguistic and cultural difficulties faced by witnesses in court. Eades' chapter analyses the trial testimony of three teenage Aboriginal boys in Australia. She illustrates how some of the linguistic strategies used by the cross-examining lawyers succeeded in manipulating and misconstruing the evidence of the three boys. The section concludes with Moeketsi, who presents an analysis of Alternative Dispute Resolution (ADR), a structured alternative to conventional litigation processes. Drawing on data from South African tribunals, she argues that untrained and inexperienced interpreters are being used to facilitate discourse where business and labour almost invariably comes from different language and cultural groups.

The final section of the book focuses on the judge and the jury in the adversarial trial setting and returns to the issue of comprehension and comprehensibility. In the context of a US bankruptcy hearing over which the author presided as judge, Bernstein explores what forensic linguistics can contribute to improving a trial judge's understanding of talk exchanges between parties, and encourages linguists to carry out further research in bankruptcy court settings.

For Heffer and Dumas (reporting on trial data from the UK and the US, respectively) the focus is the jury rather than the judge and the problems faced by jurors in understanding complex and legalistic jury instructions. Heffer argues that different modes of reasoning between legal professionals and laypeople may lead to problems with comprehensibility. Dumas' paper, relating to instructions in capital cases, also raises concerns about comprehension and comprehensibility; she reports a collaborative critique of the *reasonable doubt* standard and argues that jurors in a recent case were confused by the jury instructions presented to them by the trial judge.

The final chapter of the book moves to the appellate stage of trial proceedings. Figueiredo analyses a corpus of appeal decisions in English rape cases. Within a Foucauldian framework, she discusses the judicial discourse surrounding sexual assault and rape, and explores the relationship between trial testimony and legal judgements in reported appellate decisions on rape cases.

In summary, *Language in the Legal Process* represents an attempt to provide an overview of current and ongoing concerns in forensic linguistics and language and the law, and, it is hoped, will serve as an inspiration for further research in this dynamic and important area of applied linguistics.

JANET COTTERILL
Cardiff

Part I

The Linguist in the Legal Process

1

To Testify or Not to Testify?

Roger W. Shuy

Introduction

When attorneys call on a linguist to help them with a criminal case, their first words are usually, 'I need someone to testify'. To me, this signifies one of three things: the attorney has never used a linguist before, the case is so hopeless that desperation has already set in, or the attorney has actually become aware of the importance of linguistic analysis for a case.

I have given expert witness testimony in 50 (10 per cent) of the some 500 cases that I have worked on over the past 30 years. In 20 per cent of these cases in which my testimony was proffered (one in five), judges ruled against linguistic expert witness testimony, based on representations made by attorneys rather than from any *voir dire* of me, because the judges feared that what I had to say might invade the province of the jury. After reviewing the language evidence in the most hopeless cases presented to me (I would estimate that this comes to about 20 per cent), my only advice to the attorneys was that there was no real help that linguistic analysis could do for their cases and that they should take the best plea they could get. In some 40 per cent of the cases that I analysed, the attorneys decided not to use my analysis at trial. There were several reasons for this, including:

- my analysis did not show that their client was innocent;
- new evidence was discovered that cast a different light on the client's guilt or innocence;
- the client was unwilling to provide necessary resources;
- there was a change in attorney;
- there was a change in the criminal charges;
- there was a change from the client's original plea.

The remaining third of these 500 cases were ones in which, from the very outset, the attorneys made it clear that they wanted to use my analysis to understand their case better, to use my information in cross-examination of witnesses, and to bolster their opening and closing arguments.

From the outset, it should be clear that expert witnesses, including linguists, cannot be said to either win or lose cases. There is much more involved, including the evidence itself. Based on my experience, there are three things that a linguist can do when asked to help an attorney in a criminal case: (1) say no, (2) testify at trial, or (3) provide consulting assistance. This chapter analyses advantages and disadvantages for both the expert witness linguist and for the attorney's case, as follows.

Agreeing not to testify

There are several reasons to say 'no' to a request by an attorney. I know one well-known and respected expert who, for personal reasons, will not accept a case against people of her own religious affiliation. I know other experts who cannot and will not deal with certain types of heinous cases, such as child sex abuse. Such preferences are normal and natural and if the expert feels strongly about such matters, the best thing to do is to say 'no' from the very beginning, since personal objectivity is hard enough to maintain in the context of the rampant advocacy of the courtroom. It is crucial for the linguist to remain outside the advocacy that attorneys are, by definition, required to have. Linguists must carry out their analyses in such a way that the same results would occur if they were working for the other side in that case. If linguistic experts join attorneys and their clients in the role of advocate, their credibility is seriously eroded. If one believes that one's objectivity may be compromised in the case, the only thing to do is to tell the attorney that participation is not possible.

A second reason for saying 'no' is simply because linguistic analysis will not help the client. Admittedly, this is difficult, if not impossible to determine before examining the data. My own solution to this problem is to make my involvement a two-step process. Step one is first to review the data and let the attorney know what I believe I can do with it. This offer is usually agreed to since it carries with it a promise of not wasting the client's resources. There are many criminal attorneys who frequently handle tape-recorded narcotics violation cases. When they are unsure about whether or not linguistic analysis might help them, they send me the tapes for preliminary examination. More often than not my review of the tapes leads to the advice of taking the best plea offered, another way of saying 'no'.

From a business point of view, agreeing to take on a case in which there is little or no hope of helping dismiss at least some of the charges seems to me to be less than honest. I have found attorneys very appreciative of an early warning that linguistics cannot offer them a magic fix. For example, a few years ago I was called to work on the money-laundering case against the BCCI bank, a case that included about a thousand tape-recorded conversations between many different bank officials in several different countries. Simply reviewing all the tapes first would have been a monumental task, so the attorneys and I hit on a compromise procedure. I would listen to as many tapes as I could each week, then meet with the attorneys and discuss my findings. After examining about a third of the tapes over a three-month period, it became increasingly apparent to me that the bank was in such deep trouble that it would be prudent for it to admit guilt and seek a plea bargain. The attorneys agreed with me and a plea was eventually offered by the government – a $14 million fine. At first the defence attorneys thought this was too severe, but the bank accepted it anyway. Later, after the separate trials of the individual bank officials found them all guilty with lengthy prison sentences, the defence attorneys agreed that the bank's fine was actually very small. They were extremely pleased with our earlier decision to accept a plea.

Finally, it is easy to say 'no' to an attorney who begins by explaining what he wants the testimony to conclude. The best attorneys don't do this, so when they begin by saying, 'I need you to testify that my client didn't do it', I am almost convinced that I won't get involved. Akin to this situation, but much more difficult to predict in advance, is the attorney who changes the game plan after I have completed the linguistic aspects of my testimony and at trial asks me a concluding question that I have not agreed to address and have no right to answer, such as 'Is it your conclusion that my client is not guilty?' Questions of ultimate guilt or innocence are outside the realm of linguistic expertise. They are the sole province of the trier of the fact. Sometimes the attorney will come close to such a question but not actually ask it, as in, 'What did my client really mean here?' Linguists (or anyone else, for that matter) cannot get inside the mind of anyone. We can point out patterns of language use that may give clues to intentions or clues to agendas, but the conclusions to be drawn from such analysis are the jury's alone.

Agreeing to testify

American courts have been generally agreeable to accepting linguistics expertise about issues of dialect identification, linguistic proficiency, various language issues involved in trademarks, and the comprehensibility and clarity of warning labels in product liability cases (see Tiersma, this volume). Linguistics has also been accepted in cases of defamation, and the language of contracts. Although judges sometimes rule against admitting linguists to offer testimony based on discourse analysis in criminal cases, the rejection rate is actually very low (Wallace, 1986).

On some occasions the most useful way to make use of linguistic expertise is not to have the linguist testify at trial. For those who have never experienced cross-examination, there is no way to emphasise how emotionally draining it can be. It can be quite like taking one's doctoral oral examinations all over again. Testifying is not for the weak at heart. It can also consume vast amounts of time from first contact, analysis of data, preparation to testify, and the actual trial itself. My first trial testimony was in a solicitation to murder case in 1979 (Shuy, 1982a). The defendant was a millionaire oil-man in Fort Worth, Texas and the trial was a huge media event in that area. I was on the witness stand for three days, explaining my linguistic analysis with charts and graphs for the first day, then enduring cross-examination for the next two. In all fairness I must say that none of my following trial experiences were quite as emotionally taxing, but each case has its own ways to be difficult.

In many criminal cases, the defendants are judged by their own attorneys to be potentially poor witnesses for themselves. They may be inarticulate or have mannerisms, reputations, or personalities that will not set well with juries. Or they may be powerful executives who are not willing to answer the questions that are asked them or who are so used to giving orders that they can't deal with the one-down position of being a witness. In any case, very few people have ever experienced giving testimony at trial and are easily trapped by their inexperience.

Somebody has to be the vehicle for putting information into the trial record. When tape-recorded evidence is presented, the prosecution has not only the tape as its witness, but also the agent making the tape as well as other agents who were involved in other ways. If possible, the defence has to provide somebody to counter government testimony. And if the attorney thinks it unwise for the defendant to testify, a linguist is a possible option.

The thought of being the representative of a defendant, especially an allegedly (or actually) unsavoury one, is a daunting thought to many experts. Early in my work in criminal cases, more than one linguist colleague asked me how I could possibly defend a criminal. My answer then (and still today) is that I do not defend anybody. The expert witness is not an advocate – that's the attorney's defined job. The expert's role is to analyse the taped conversations and, if it is deemed prudent, to present this analysis at trial, which analysis should be the same whether carried out for the defence or the prosecution. On occasions when my analysis turns up both good and bad points for the defence, it is the attorney's call as to whether or not to use me as an expert witness. During my direct examination the defence attorney may choose to ask me questions that show only the most favour-able side of his client's case. But, in cross-examination, if the prosecutor asks me questions about the unfavourable aspects of the tapes, I am honour-bound to answer truthfully about what I found, whether or not it hurts the client. By making this very clear to the defence attorney from the outset, the defence sometimes decides not to use me as an expert witness. This decision does not mean that my analysis has been useless or even unhelpful to the defence. It typically provides the attorney with insights to use in cross-examining prosecution witnesses or in helping the defendant decide to take whatever plea may be offered.

In cases where my analysis has revealed only that the defendant was headed for certain conviction, attorneys have asked me to meet with their clients and go through every step of my findings as a way of convincing the defendant(s) that it was in their best interests to plead guilty. In another case that had many wiretap videotapes of a bar where drug deals were being made, my analysis showed that one defendant was not involved in either buying or selling drugs, although he was clearly very busy illegally making book on the phone. The defence attorney decided to have me testify to this, which I did, using charts of all of that defendant's verbal exchanges. The chart showed three columns, one marked 'buying drugs', one marked 'selling drugs', and the third labelled 'making bets'. There were many instances of conversations marked 'making bets' but the other two columns, the only ones for which he was indicted, were completely empty. Since the defendant was not charged with bookmaking, he was acquitted of the more serious drug charges. Thus by admitting the crime, for which he was never charged, the strategy worked to his benefit.

Agreeing to consult

Solan (1998) argues that one of the most useful ways for an attorney to use linguistic analysis is as a 'tour guide' for the trier of fact, especially when issues of meaning are in question. Here I extend his meaning of 'tour guide' for the trier of the fact to 'tour guide consultant' for the defence attorney or prosecutor trying the case. As noted earlier, a major contribution of the linguist in a criminal case is often as a consultant to attorneys for the defence. But it is sometimes the case, though not often, that the prosecution also consults with linguists. I have provided such consultation to US District Attorneys and other Department of Justice officials on numerous occasions.

Three such instances involved impeachment procedures against federal judges. In the cases of the two judges that in previous trials had been convicted of felonies, my role was to analyse the tape recording used in the criminal proceedings to determine whether or not the evidence used to convict them would hold up in the impeachment hearings. I was also told that the government wanted to co-opt my services so that I would not be used in a similar role in the defence of those two judges. As it turned out, the defence employed no linguist on their side and my government consultation helped impeach both of them without requiring my testimony.

In the third impeachment proceeding, in which the federal judge had not been convicted at his previous criminal trial, the US House of Representatives called on me to reexamine the tape recording used at the criminal trial. I did so and testified both before the US House of Representatives and, later, before a subcommittee of the US Senate, both of which found the judge guilty and removed him from the bench (Shuy, 1997).

On three other occasions I was asked by District Attorneys to analyse tapes used at criminal trials in New Hampshire and District of Columbia. In none of these did the District Attorneys call me as an expert witness. They claimed that my analysis helped them in cross-examination of various witnesses but further observed that if they were to use my expert-witness testimony, this would legitimise linguistic testimony when used by defendants. It is noteworthy that one of the standard questions a prosecutor asks me when I testify for the defence is, 'Haven't all of the times you have testified been for the defence?' It is no secret that the reason for such a question is to impeach my testimony by implying that I am not impartial since I only serve the defence. This is, of course, nonsense, but the fact remains that at criminal trial (not impeachment cases) I have still never been called by the prosecution.

Most of my consultation, however, has been for the defence in criminal cases. One reason for this is that even after decades of the law-enforcement practice of tape recording, many defence attorneys are still either unaccustomed to such evidence or overwhelmed by it when it is presented to them. For example, the government may spend months or even years building its evidence through taped conversations. Then, after the indictment, when the discovery process gradually reveals these tapes to the defence, they have to be sorted through and defended. In the process, defence attorneys often make several errors. They may listen to the tapes only once. Being accustomed to working with paper, they may incorrectly assume that the prosecution's transcript of the tape is accurate. They may passively accept the prosecution's interpretation of ambiguous passages, as in different meanings of pronoun references, such as 'it' (the investigator's, 'We know you did it,' cannot be fully understood by the suspect if the reference to 'it' is left unclear). They may not be familiar with the special techniques and conversational strategies used by undercover agents and cooperating witnesses. They may not know what linguists know about how the structure of conversation can give clues to the intentions of the participants. Once defence attorneys realise what they don't know and how much work it will be to organise and work their way through massive amounts of language data, they may call on a professional to help them do this, even on a consultation basis.

Several defence attorneys that I have worked with over the years state from the outset that they want linguistic consultation, but not expert-witness testimony. They prefer to take my analysis and use it themselves in several ways. For one thing, it may help them determine what to stay away from as they try to make their case. Some use my analysis as part of their opening and closing statements at trial, but the most common use of linguistic consultation is for cross-examination of prosecution witnesses.

The following are some examples of how defence attorneys have used linguistic analysis in their cross-examination of agents and cooperating witnesses.

Topic analysis

There is probably no better clue to the agenda of a speaker than the topics that person introduces to a conversation. We talk because we have something we want to say. Topic introductions are somewhat like a team's offence in an American football game. We try to get our points across in a manner akin to trying to score a goal. We try to overcome the detours offered by the other person's defence by holding the floor, retaking it as soon as we can, and recycling our agenda topics until we get the satisfaction we are after in the first place.

In the case of a speaker who is accused of a language crime, it is usually instructive to carry out a topic analysis of the entire conversation or set of conversations (Shuy, 1993). Topic introductions are marked by obvious semantic shifts from the previous topic, by structural clues indicated by pauses and intonation changes, by discourse markers such as 'well', and by performative topic-changing phrases such as 'not to change the subject but...', 'let's move on to something else', or 'let me tell you something here'. Combinations of these ways to mark topic shifts are reasonably clear. Topic analysis provides attorneys with a skeletal view of the event, a kind of index of where to place their attention. This skeletal picture is usually presented in chart form, with the topic number and transcript page reference as the left column, followed by separate columns for each speaker. In order to be as objective as possible, the exact words of the speakers are used to represent the topics introduced, as the columnar model of Table 1.1, used as part of the trial of *USA* v. *John DeLorean* illustrates; only the first 13 topics in one of the taped conversations are presented.

Table 1.1   Topic analysis in *USA* v. *John DeLorean*

Topic	Page	Agent	Defendant
1	1	Hi John (greeting)	
2	1	Did you get the money?	
3	2	I'd like to help you	
4	2		I've been busy
5	2	Gordon looks like a good prospect	
6	3		My sales have been up
7	3	Want him to do it?	
8	3		I sold stock to Smith
9	4	He's ready for you	
10	4		Prices have fluctuated
11	4	He'll keep it quiet	
12	5		Think I'll buy Cisco
13	5	He does good work	

The reason for the created topic analysis presented here is to display its form. Notice especially that the words of the two speakers are set apart from each other physically, somewhat like cartoon figures with balloons over their heads to indicate what they are saying. One of the problems with transcripts is that it is more difficult to separate and remember who said what to whom. The obvious different agendas of the two speakers is set off more clearly than it would be in the common play-script approach. In this fictional conversation, the topics that each speaker introduces make it obvious that they have very different agendas, something that the inclusion of elaborations of one speaker and the responses to that topic by the other would make less easy to follow.

If attorneys happen to be able to think this way, focusing only on the topics introduced as a guide to speaker agendas, they might be able to come to similar conclusions on their own. Two things militate against such a possibility, however. For one thing, the vast majority of lawyers are not trained to think this way or to do this. Second, although they are perfectly able to see more obvious meaning clues, they are normally not able to see the ones that are indicated by subtle linguistic clues such as topic changing or recycling. But once such analysis is presented to them by a linguist, they have a tool available to them for cross-examination as well as for their opening and closing statements.

Response analysis

An analysis of the responses given by the target to topics introduced by the agent throughout several tape-recorded conversations enabled one attorney to structure his cross-examination of the man who wore the mike as follows:

> Q   With the transcript of this conversation in front of you, will you point out the place where you feel the defendant said that he wanted his wife killed?
>
> A   Okay, on page 27.
>
> Q   I see that in this passage the defendant says 'Uh-huh' there. Did this 'Uh-huh' ask you to kill his wife?
>
> A   That's how I saw it.
>
> Q   Did he bring up that topic or did you?
>
> A   Well, he was answering my question, 'When do you want me to hire someone to do her?'
>
> Q   And does 'Uh-huh' answer your question about when?
>
> A   To me it did.

In this cross-examination, the attorney made use of my analysis of the many, many times the defendant's responses used the feedback marker, 'uh-huh', to acknowledge that the confidential informant had the floor, but was not agreeing with that topic. His response, 'uh-huh', could not be interpreted the way the prosecution interpreted it. This cross-examination exchange also gave the attorney the opportunity to bring in another major point of my analysis, that it was always the confidential informant who introduced the topic of 'doing' the wife. The defendant never brought this up, an odd thing for a man who is accused of wanting someone to do it. Finally, this exchange highlighted the prosecution's use of inferencing rather than basing their case on explicit statements.

Other response types can be equally useful to the attorney. For example, if the target changes the subject after a potentially incriminating observation made by the agent, it is a rather clear sign that he is at least uncomfortable with that topic, or that he was not sufficiently interested in the issue to respond to it if, indeed, he even heard it at all.

Ambiguity and inferencing analysis

Likewise, it is common for attorneys to use my analysis to cross-examine agents or cooperating witnesses about why they chose to be ambiguous in their representation of the illegal act to which they are trying to get the target to agree. A common cross-examination sequence is as follows:

Q   Why weren't you more explicit about the source of the money? Why didn't you tell him 'my friends are using drug money' instead of 'my friends are from Columbia?'
A   He knew what I meant. Anyway, if I ever said 'drug money' he would have walked away.
Q   I agree. In all of your conversations you use the reference, 'Colombian', seven times. Is it your experience that everyone from Columbia is a drug dealer?
A   No, but these were.
Q   I notice that you referred to the source of the money as coming from 'down south' Is everyone from down south a drug dealer?
A   No, but these guys were.
Q   And did Richards ever use the expressions, 'Colombians', or 'drug dealers?'
A   I think so.
Q   You may think so but would it surprise you to know that he never used these expressions?
A   Yeah.
Q   The tape speaks for itself. I assure you, there are none. But did Richards ever refer to a possible source of the money?
A   I don't know.
Q   Look at page 17 and at page 24. What does he say there?
A   Mexico.
Q   And what does he say about Mexico?
A   That he thought the guy had flight capital money.
Q   And wouldn't it have been perfectly legal for him to have dealt with a Mexican man who has flight capital money?
A   I don't know.

My analysis had charted all references to the alleged source of the money in question here. It showed the cooperating witness saying 'these guys are

Table 1.2   Place references by both speakers

Place references	Agent	Richards
Mexico	0	8
Columbia(n)	7	0
Down south	5	0
Down there	1	4

Colombians' and 'from down south'. On Richards' side of the chart it showed only 'in Mexico', and 'down there', both consistent with his belief that they were dealing with flight capital. In this instance, my chart (Table 1.2) was used by the defense attorney in his cross-examination. Obviously, the two speakers were on different tracks. The prosecution wanted it to appear that whatever the cooperating witness said registered as illegality in Richards' mind. But it was apparent from the words used by Richards that he thought it was something else. My proposed testimony about inferencing was made unnecessary here by the manner in which the attorney used it with the agent.

The linguistic ambiguity of these tape-recorded conversations was also used by the attorney to show that the cooperating witness did not follow the FBI's own safeguards and guidelines for undercover operations. These guidelines are not often known to defence attorneys; they exist in an obscure report of the Subcommittee on Civil and Constitutional Rights of the Committee on the Judiciary, House of Representatives, 98th Congress, published in April 1984. The then Assistant Attorney General, Philip Heymann, described these guidelines to that subcommittee. Perhaps the only reason I knew about them was that I was also subpoenaed to appear before that subcommittee and present my observations about the previous FBI undercover sting cases for which I had made linguistic analyses. The Assistant Attorney General's testimony revealed these guidelines to the public, one of which follows:

> Most important, however, is the second major safeguard followed in every undercover operation, of making clear and unambiguous to all concerned the illegal nature of any opportunity used as a decoy. (FBI Undercover Operations, 1984, p. 36)

A few years after this subcommittee report was published, I was asked to conduct a one-day seminar for US drug enforcement undercover agents in Miami. After presenting this guideline to them and showing them how their case could be destroyed if they did not follow such practice, I was dismayed to hear many of the agents tell me exactly the same thing that the cooperating witness in this case said: 'If we were clear and unambiguous, the target would walk away.' The linguist's task is to determine the extent to which the tapes reveal clear and unambiguous representations of illegality. When they fail to do this, the defence has a much stronger case.

The point here is that the linguist's job was to inform the attorney of the FBI's own guideline, then find the passages in the text that fall short of its fulfilment. Perhaps attorneys could do this on their own, but I have found that in most cases they simply have never thought of this or don't have the time and skills to do it themselves. More important, they don't have the linguistic framework and expertise to identify the nuances of ambiguous conversation. But if the linguist's consultation is effective enough, the attorney can use it to advantage.

Identifying conversation strategies

In most criminal cases involving tapes, the focus of the trial is on the language of the defendants. Did they incriminate themselves by what they themselves introduced or by what they explicitly and unambiguously agreed to in their responses to the agents' topics.

But there is also another linguistic analysis available to the defence attorney: the conversational strategies used by the agent. One of the things lawyers love to do is to shift the issue away from their client and onto the prosecution, putting them on trial instead. The way undercover operations work often provides the opportunity to examine such strategies, especially if the person doing the taping is a cooperating witness trying to endear himself to the government by netting another victim for them (Shuy, 1982b).

Camouflaging

One common undercover strategy is to camouflage something illegal or important by making it look legal or unimportant. One strategy used by the FBI in its Abscam operation in the 1980s was to declare conversations 'unofficial', in much the same way as some interviewees tell reporters that their comments are 'off the record'. No conversation in undercover operations is ever 'unofficial'. In a bribery case against Texas State Representative Billy Clayton in the early 1980s the agents tried to make the conversation appear to be about giving Clayton a campaign contribution while their real goal was to get him to accept a bribe (Shuy, 1993). They first defined the money as a contribution, then later tried to redefine it, although ambiguously, by implying that that it was a *quid pro quo* for Clayton to open up the state's insurance contract bidding. When Clayton replied that he would report the campaign contribution, the agents tried to discourage him from doing so, leading to Clayton's statement that neither he nor they wanted to do anything illegal. Clayton was indicted, despite this denial, and was eventually acquitted by the evidence on the government's own tape.

Contaminating

Another strategy is what I refer to as the contamination principle. Later listeners to taped conversations get general, overall pictures of what went on. This is well and good, but it is not enough. The first time I ever listened to a conversation in which the topic of killing someone occurred, I was deeply disturbed. Since the defendant's attorney had asked me to help him, I was ready to conclude that our defendant had a serious problem. But as I listened to the tape over and over again, I finally concluded that the defendant was not the one speaking about killing. The agent did this alone. I had been contaminated by the topic and had not listened carefully enough to realise how one-sided this was.

The contamination principle is at work in everyone's daily lives. You overhear a dirty joke being told and you conclude that 'they' were telling dirty jokes, even if the listener was appalled, said nothing, or didn't even smile. At the US Senate impeachment hearings of Senator Harrison A. Williams, Jr of New Jersey, I was talking with the Senator during a break when Senator Mark O. Hatfield of Oregon came up to us and asked Senator Williams why he had to swear all the time in the video recordings just reviewed by the Senate. Senator Hatfield had been contaminated by the fact that it was the FBI agents who were swearing, not Senator Williams.

In a more recent case, a telemarketer, as part of his plea agreement, tape recorded another telemarketer, our client. Among other things, the cooperating witness kept referring to still another telemarketer who had been caught and was now serving a prison sentence. Our client didn't even know this man, but the contamination damage was done. The prosecution associated the man in prison with our client, much to his disadvantage.

Most attorneys are vaguely familiar with the concept of contamination but are usually unable to use it effectively as a common discourse strategy. The linguist can not only inform attorneys of its power in how later listeners interpret a conversation, but also point out the places it happens and how it occurs. But once the attorney is aware of the strategy and how it works, he can use this information in his briefs and cross-examinations very effectively.

Blocking exculpatory statements

Interruption is common in conversation. In some contexts, it is even considered cooperative (Tannen, 1993), but in many other cases it is not. The pursuit of justice, like the pursuit of science, is not well-served by the incomplete information that interruption creates. When the target begins an utterance and is cut off by the agent before he can get it out, we can never know what that utterance might have been. I have worked on many cases in which the tape of a defendant begins something like, 'I don't want...', but is interrupted by the agent or cooperating witness. If such an utterance occurs immediately after a hint of something illegal, we can be doubly troubled. By analysing the interruption patterns in a conversation, the linguist can offer considerable help to the defending attorney. The attorney may not present such information in the same way that the linguist would, but the result, if done well, can be almost equally effective. If it turns out that the agent blocked every effort by the defendant to make an exculpatory statement, this linguistic fact deserves to come out at trial, whether done by the attorney alone or by expert testimony of the linguist.

Using cultural differences to advantage

It is not uncommon for agents in undercover sting operations to use language that is generally thought to be more common in the lower socio-economic levels of society (Shuy, 1995). Alternatively, the agent affects the broken English assumed to be used by a foreigner. What defending attorneys need to know is how this asymmetric language and culture can affect their clients' responses. Most of us make certain allowances for those who are in a one-down position. Thus, the native speaker tends to forgive the mispronunciation of a foreigner, the educated tend to accept the fact that the less-educated use words imprecisely or even erroneously. I have worked on several cases in which the targets were indicted for responding with such forgiveness and tolerance when the prosecution felt that they should have been indignant.

In Senator Williams' criminal trial, for example, he was presented with an FBI agent dressed as a sheik from the United Arab Emirates. He spoke a very broken English, one that a linguist could easily spot as inauthentic but which fooled the Senator completely (Shuy, 1993). When the 'sheik' offered Williams money for helping him get American citizenship, the senator said 'no, no, no', but did not appear to be deeply offended and did not tell the man that this was a very dishonest thing to do. Williams was criticised first by the prosecutor and later by the US Senate for not registering his indignance and horror at an offer which, in his mind, may have been culturally acceptable in the sheik's country but illegal and despicable in America. The context called for a rejection, but did it also call for a sermon on ethics, especially to an alleged foreign dignitary?

In another case, an undercover agent pretending to be a semi-literate, uneducated victim of an alleged automobile accident gave false information to an attorney about the accident. The tape recording gave evidence that the agent's sentences were garbled and her knowledge of proper procedure was limited. If later listeners could not tell exactly what she was saying, how is it that the prosecution could figure it out? The attorney was charged with aiding her making a false claim, but was acquitted once the tape was played in court.

Coaching or scripting the target

Undercover agents know exactly what is necessary to obtain a conviction. When targets fail to self-generate their own guilt, agents are tempted to help them along by telling them what to say, especially when there will be a follow-up meeting when such things could be captured on tape.

A classic example of how the agents coached, even scripted, the target about what to say next is the case of Senator Williams (Shuy, 1993), discussed above. In preparation for a meeting with the alleged Arab sheik, the Senator was told over and over again that he should puff about his power in the US Senate in order to impress the sheik to agree to flee his country and invest his vast wealth in US companies. The videotape of this coaching session shows Senator Williams sitting silently while the FBI agent and cooperating witness list some 30 or 40 things he should tell the sheik.

The subsequent videotape shows Williams' actual meeting with the sheik and the agents. For the defence, I made a chart of all the words used by the agents as a script for the Senator. I also made a companion chart of who used these words in the actual meeting with the sheik. The column with the Senator's name above it was empty. It was the FBI doing the puffing, not the Senator. Such analysis might have been done by the defence attorneys without the help of a linguist, but it is rare that attorneys have the patience or linguistic skill to even think about such things. But they can use this analysis very effectively, once it is given them, especially when cross-examining the agents at trial.

Confusing with conflicting information

Almost invariably, undercover sting operations begin with a broad proposal which has all the marks of legitimacy, then gradually try to shift the focus to something more narrowly illegal. This is somewhat similar to the tactic used in car sales, in which the salesperson begins broadly, noting all the advantages the products have, only narrowing down the pitch once the customer expresses some preferences.

The FBI investigation of John Z. DeLorean began in such a manner. DeLorean Motors was in financial trouble and needed a quick influx of capital, either by investors to buy stock in the company or from a large loan (Shuy, 1993). Knowing this, the government began its discussion with him by having an agent pose as a bank loan officer trying to help him secure funding. Discussions went on for several months, coming to a head when the agent explained that he could not work out a loan from the bank after all. Instead, he proposed that he would continue to look for investors but, in addition, he added new information – that he had access to money generated from drug sales from Thailand.

DeLorean did not withdraw from the discussions for, after all, the old information of locating investors for his company was still open. The FBI took this lack of withdrawal as DeLorean's tacit agreement to invest his remaining capital in their new drug scheme and began to offer conflicting information about the nature of their drug business. The problem was that there were still two old information options on the table, a loan or a capital investment.

There were over 60 tape-recorded conversations used as evidence against DeLorean and the defence task of keeping the various strands straight was difficult but necessary. DeLorean continued to back off from any investment in the drug business, causing the government to continue to pursue him until they could get convincing evidence of his willingness to invest in the illegal scheme.

Finally, the agents taped a conversation in which they believed they had finally secured DeLorean's agreement to invest his remaining company resources in a way that would net him a quick turnaround with enough money to save his company from bankruptcy. DeLorean's topics at that meeting were about whether or not they had found investors. To this the agent described in detail how their drug scheme would work. DeLorean commented that this sounded dangerous. The agent tried to be more explicit about how DeLorean could be involved in their drug operation. DeLorean then told him that he had powerful Irish allies (clearly referring to the IRA) who would never permit this, a negative signal that the agent could not have missed. At this point both men agree that 'investment' would be a good thing. The government took this to mean that DeLorean would invest in the drug business, which was enough for them to bring an indictment. The fact that DeLorean took 'investment' to indicate that these men would continue to look for investors in DeLorean Motors was lost on, or overlooked by, the prosecution.

The core of the defence case, then, was the two different meanings of 'investment' as a 'good thing'. The agents had presented conflicting information and used it ambiguously to give the impression to the jury that DeLorean understood what they understood these words to mean. For a jury to comprehend this, it would be necessary to take the hundreds of hours of taped evidence and point out the threads of meaning that came and went. Juries can be swamped with information in virtually any case, including those without taped conversations, but when tapes are presented their task of tracing meaning, conflicting or not, is even more difficult.

The linguist's task here was to take the 60-plus conversations and trace the three themes (drug scheme, find investors, get a loan) throughout, showing how they are presented, ignored, resolved or left ambiguous. By pulling out the exact words used in the texts and associating them with these three shifting topics between several people over almost a year, linguistic analysis assisted the defence attorneys in their approach to the various agents on the witness stand. Again, it is perhaps possible that an attorney, given time, patience and considerable understanding about how discourse works, might have accomplished similar things. Lawyers are, in at least one sense of the term, specialists in language, but not the kind of specialisation in language that linguists are trained in. The DeLorean case is a good example of what attorneys can do with a linguist's analysis in front of them, while not using the testimony of an expert witness at trial.

Conclusions

There are good reasons to not agree to testify as an expert witness in linguistics and there are times when such testimony is quite appropriate. In my experience, however, in the majority of the cases simply consulting with attorneys is the most useful service a linguist can offer. Besides, many attorneys prefer this approach, since it gives them the opportunity to star on their client's behalf. Some attorneys have told me that they prefer to use this approach to avoid whatever disadvantages might come from the cross-examination of their experts. Others explain that it can look bad for their client to have to bring in an expert to speak for them. Whatever the reason, being a consultant can be far more comfortable than appearing on the witness stand.

References

FBI Undercover Operations (1984) Report of the Subcommittee on Civil and Constitutional Rights of the Committee on the Judiciary, House of Representatives, 98th Congress, second session. April, 1984. Washington, DC: US Government Printing Office.

Shuy, R. W. (1982a) 'Topic as the Unit of Analysis in a Criminal Law Case', in D. Tannen (ed.), *Analyzing Discourse: Text and Talk*. Washington, DC: Georgetown University Press, pp. 113–26.

Shuy, R. W. (1982b) 'Entrapment and the Linguistic Analysis of Tapes', *Studies in Language*, vol. 8(2), pp. 215–34.

Shuy, R. W. (1993) *Language Crimes*. Oxford: Blackwell (reprinted in paperback, 1996).

Shuy, R. W. (1995) 'Dialect as Evidence in Law Cases', *Journal of English Linguistics*, vol. 23(1/2), pp. 195–208.

Shuy, R. W. (1997) 'Discourse Clues to Coded Language in an Impeachment Hearing', in G. Guy, C. Feagin, D. Schiffrin and J. Baugh (eds), *Towards a Social Science of Language: Papers in Honor of William Labov*. Amsterdam: John Benjamin, pp. 121–38.

Solan, L. (1998) 'Linguistic Experts as Semantic Tour Guides', *Forensic Linguistics*, vol. 5(2), pp. 87–106.

Tannen, D. (1993) *Gender and Conversational Interaction*. Oxford: Oxford University Press.

Wallace, W. D. (1986) 'The Admissibility of Expert Testimony on the Discourse Analysis of Recorded Conversations', *University of Florida Law Review*, vol. 38(1), pp. 69–115.

2
Whose Voice Is It? Invented and Concealed Dialogue in Written Records of Verbal Evidence Produced by the Police

Malcolm Coulthard

Introduction

One major type of evidence presented by the police at trial is their record of what the accused said. This evidence comes in two forms – records of interviews *with* suspects and records of statements made *by* suspects. Since the Police and Criminal Evidence Act (PACE, 1984) which was introduced following a spate of claims that those accused of crimes were frequently 'verballed' (that is, verbal evidence was fabricated by police officers), the police in England have been required, whenever possible, to make a contemporaneous audio or video recording of verbal evidence. However, the three cases that I will discuss in this chapter predate PACE and come from a time when it was customary to record what was said in interviews laboriously in longhand. I was commissioned as an expert in all three cases when they were referred, successfully, to the Court of Appeal in the late 1990s.

English courts have long insisted that, as far as possible, a record of what was said by and to the accused should be presented in direct speech rather than indirect or summary form. This was because, in the terms of Austin (1962), they wanted to receive the uninterpreted *locution* and saw it as their role to determine the *illocutionary* force of the words of the witness or accused. I will not expand on the linguistic assumptions underlying this stance, but merely give a famous example of it at work. In one of the cases I discuss below one of the two accused, Derek Bentley, was said to have shouted the words 'Let him have it, Chris' after which his companion, Chris Craig, shot and killed a policeman. At trial the lawyers discussed at length the two possible illocutionary forces of the phrase – 'give him the gun' and 'shoot him'. However, of more significance was the fact that both sides gave scant attention to the claims of the defendant that he had not even uttered the words – no-one at all questioned the accuracy of the wording, although even the police officers themselves admitted that the words had not been recorded contemporaneously.

In the days before tape-recording police officers were very much in control of the verbal evidence. Not only did they control the topics covered in interviews, they also controlled what was recorded and what not recorded and, even more significantly, the form in which it was recorded. Of course, anyone who has tried to make a verbatim record, whether in real time or with the assistance of repeated listenings to a tape-recording, knows that it is literally impossible to do so. The police were never given any explicit guidelines as to what did and did not constitute a 'verbatim' record nor what they could and could not legitimately omit, but then neither did the courts seriously question whether their records were actually verbatim (see Blackwell, 1996, and Eades, 1996, on the problems of verbatim transcription). It was, apparently, generally accepted unchallenged that police officers could record what was said with sufficient accuracy for the *wording* of utterances rather than just their *content* to be used in evidence. It was even believed that officers could *remember* substantial chunks of conversation for several hours and then write them down verbatim.

Before being questioned suspects were cautioned that 'anything you say will be taken down and may be used in evidence against you', but only the police records were presented in Court as evidence and there was no provision for the accused to make, and then to present in court, his own written version of what was said. If he disputed the accuracy of the record, his only option was to refuse to sign, but that did not prevent the record being taken as true provided it was countersigned by a second police officer.

These pre-PACE records are fascinating because they are, on the one hand, factual records of interaction, but on the other texts whose function is to represent this interaction at a later time to a different audience for a different purpose. So they have not only an evidential, but also a persuasive function. Indeed, the police participants were certainly aware, at the time of the primary interaction, that the record was intended for, and therefore could be specifically designed for, another audience – and certainly some of these records appear to be consciously constructed with the future audience in mind. In an earlier paper (Coulthard, 1996) I drew attention to a number of these design features; in what follows I will mention but two of them.

The metalinguistic validation of an interview record

The two extracts below come from an armed robbery case, where the accused strongly denied ever having uttered any of the 'recorded' incriminating items (which are not reproduced in the extracts quoted below), let alone having been offered the chance to emend the text. Even so, he was subsequently convicted on the basis of this interview record:[1]

> DS Smith said 'Listen Roy, we keep true records of what you've said. I speak for my colleague here Mr Jones when I say that we will be completely honest and truthful ... but to allay your suspicions I could write down in question and answer form what is said and you can read it and then sign it, that way you would know it was a true record of what you have said, is that fair?'

After this preamble there follows a record of an incriminating interview which concludes with:

> DS Smith 'Right now Roy, DC Jones will read this over to you, then you can read it yourself. You can make any alterations you wish. Is that being fair with you?'
> MORLEY replied 'Yes'.
> DS Jones then read over to MORLEY the contemporaneous notes ... MORLEY read them and was invited to sign them.
> MORLEY then said 'No I can't ... Nothing personal lads'.
> DS Jones said 'Look Roy, have we put anything down in these notes that you didn't say?'
> MORLEY replied 'No, I can't sign the notes, but at least you know the truth'.

These extracts display several devices frequently used to reinforce an unsigned confession: the police officers are lexically constructed as reasonable, yea honourable, men: they make 'true records', they are 'completely honest and truthful', they want to 'allay suspicions', and produce a 'true record' which is also 'fair'. The text conveys an apparently friendly, non-threatening atmosphere through the repeated and reciprocal use of familiar terms of address, 'Roy' and 'lads', and a situation in which Morley is 'invited' to sign, feels sufficiently at ease with and linked to the officers to apologise for not signing – 'nothing personal lads' – and wants them to 'know the truth', which he openly admits he will later deny.

The metalinguistic creation of police character

Some records go further in the creation of a positive police image, probably because ultimately a witness statement has value and credibility only insofar as the witness himself has value and credibility. The following extracts, taken from separate cases, are simply more extreme examples of a general technique:

> I believe that you were there and I think the strain of having to carry that knowledge of what you did and what you saw happen was so horrible that you almost convinced yourself it never happened, you would feel very much better in yourself if you got rid of that burden that you've carried for so long.

> All that points to the fact that you committed this robbery and I must tell you that you have shown no remorse, you've shown no feelings and you have offered me no help in bringing these matters to a satisfactory conclusion. I feel very sorry that you have that dreadful disease of being a gambler and you stole that money to feed your habit.

In this chapter I propose to examine texts from three murder cases tried in the English Courts – each resulted in a conviction which depended crucially on a disputed confession. In the Court of Appeal, in each case linguistic evidence was fundamental to the defence who claimed that, in some of the incriminating texts attributed to the accused, the police had unfairly concealed their own voice and/or represented what they had said as having been said by the accused. In all three cases the original verdict was eventually overturned.

A case of persuasive dialogue

The first case I will discuss is that of Ashley King who was accused and convicted of battering an old lady to death in 1985. The police presented as evidence typed versions of handwritten records of 10 interviews with King. In the early interviews King admits having known the deceased and having visited her to ask for money on the day she was murdered, while in a later interview he admits to having hit her on the head, although this admission was immediately withdrawn in the next interview and never made again. Text 1a below is the first page of the first interview exactly as it was read out in court, except that I have highlighted some words in bold in order to be able to refer back to them in the discussion which follows:

Text 1a   Extract from the record of an early interview with Ashley King

KING was then transported to Houghton-le-Spring Police Office where at 11.35 am that day he was interviewed in the following manner by myself and DC Simpson:

Q   When we saw you last Saturday you told us that you didn't go out at all on the evening of Monday 4th November. Are you still saying that's true?
A   Yes, I'm sure that's right.
Q   It can be difficult thinking back Ash, so think very carefully, it's very important.
A   Aye, I'm sure about that. I never left the house.
Q   We've interviewed some people who say you were out that night? [*sic*]
A   I don't think so.
Q   Think very carefully about it, it's important.
A   I think that was the night we got the tyres, is that what you mean?
Q   Tell us about it.
A   **Billy, Berti and Melley called for** us and we went up the bank and got some tyres.
Q   What time was this?
A   They came for us about **six o'clock**.
Q   Who's Berti?
A   I don't know his second name but he's **from Shiney**.
Q   When you say you got some tyres, do you mean you stole them?
A   Aye, I think so

I then cautioned KING.

Q   Where did you get the tyres from?
A   It's a place next to the garage, its **near the pit**.
Q   Do you know the name of the premises?
A   **Tyre Services** I think, but I'm not sure.

[This interview record continues for a further three pages.]

There are several points which immediately strike the reader, and which would have similarly struck the members of the jury, because this would have been their first contact with King. Firstly, following the prose introduction, we are presented with a verbatim account of what was said by King and the interviewing officer. Secondly, King is seen to not tell the truth when first questioned – the interview begins with three denials that he had been out on the night of 4 November, followed by a grudging admission – 'I think that was the night we got the tyres, is that what you mean?' Shortly afterwards he admits that, although he used the word 'got', he knew he was in fact 'stealing' the tyres. Thirdly, the police officer is apparently very patient and good-natured in his questioning – he offers a let-out after the first denial 'It can be difficult thinking back Ash, so think very carefully', and doesn't directly contradict King, but rather coaxes the truth out of him.

Although cases are decided on evidence, the value of that evidence often depends on the credibility of the witness, and juries are repeatedly reminded to evaluate witnesses when considering their evidence. In these early exchanges we can see King being created as untrustworthy, as someone who needs to have the truth gradually drawn out of him, whereas the police officer is presented as a kindly patient character. This was of tremendous value to the prosecution, because their major problem was that King only confessed once and then only in the eighth interview and the defense would deny the confession and argue that there was undue police pressure on their client. In this context the importance of this first page of the first interview is that it shows a very different picture – a sympathetic interrogator who is able to coax the truth out of a shifty suspect.

It is therefore something of a surprise to discover that this text is not a verbatim record at all, but rather a persuasive dramatisation based on minimal trigger notes, which were only written up several hours later – a fact which was not conveyed to the jury. The actual trigger notes, on which the interview record is based, are presented below in their original layout:

Text 1b   Police trigger notes

6pm   Left house called for Billy Waugh & Melvin Waugh + (Berty) [*sic*] from
Shiney Row
TO TYRES Place BY PIT (TYRE SERVICES?)

[The notes continue for 15 more lines.]

I have highlighted in bold in Text 1a above those items which are based directly on the trigger notes and this emphasises just how little basis there was and how much has been (re)created by the police from either memory or imagination. A reading of the monologue or indirect speech expansion presented below, which I offer as an alternative way of presenting the information to the jury, emphasises just how much of the persuasiveness of the text comes from the police dramatisation:

Text 1c   A monologue expansion

King said he left home at 6pm and called for Billy Waugh, Melvin Waugh and Berty from Shiney Row. They went to the tyres place near the pit, which he thought was called Tyre Services.

Gone are the two contrasting characters, the shifty King and the kindly policeman, and all that remains is an uninteresting short narrative of events, with none of the evaluation of character and action which makes the dramatisation so persuasive.

A case of supportive dialogue

The second case concerns the 1978 murder of a teenage boy who was delivering newspapers to a remote farmhouse in the Birmingham area. Four men were arrested in connection with the murder and one of them, Patrick Molloy, confessed to being involved in the murder and incriminated the other three. He later withdrew his confession, claiming that in the period leading up to making the confession he had been physically and verbally abused and, more significantly, had been shown another confession dictated and signed by one of his co-accused, which incriminated him in the murder. The police, along with the supposed author, subsequently denied the existence of this other confession and it was never produced at trial.

Molloy did not deny making his 'confession', but said he had merely been repeating what one of the police officers had dictated into his ear. In other words, his claim was that he was merely the *mouthpiece* and not the *author* of the confession. Nevertheless, on the basis of this confession – there was no forensic evidence to link them with the killing – all four of the accused were convicted of the murder.

One of the reasons that the confession was believed by the jury was that it was supported by a record of an interview, timed as occurring immediately before the confession, which contained essentially the same material. Molloy insisted that this interview had never occurred and that this text was a total fabrication.

I present below the first two-thirds of the confession statement – I will concentrate on sentences 17 onwards which constitute the incriminating part:

Text 2a   Extract from Molloy's statement

(1) I need to tell you the truth, you wouldn't understand the pressure that I have been under. (2) I am terrified of the others, I have been threatened with personal injury. (3) I know they will do it but even so I must tell you the truth. (4) I was at the farm when that lad, the paper boy was killed. (5) I was upstairs searching for something of value, anything, money or coins.

(6) Four of us had gone to the farm. (7) There were two motors, a blue Cortina Estate, which I went in with Vinny Hickey who was driving and his relation Micky. (8) I sat in the back. (9) Jimmy Robinson drove a Van I think it had a white top, it belonged to someone in the Dog and Partridge, he borrowed it for the job. (10) We arrived at the farm first and waited for Jimmy who arrived shortly afterwards. (11) We parked both motors away from the farm and walked down to the farm. (12) We didn't all go together, me and Vinny walked down first. (13) We waited and the others joined us. (14) Jimmy broke in through a window and loosed us in. (15) They went downstairs and I went upstairs by myself. (16) I searched the bedrooms I remember taking the drawers from some furniture and after searching them I stacked them one on top of the other. (17) I had been drinking and cannot remember the exact time I was there but whilst I was upstairs I heard someone downstairs say be careful someone is coming [*sic*]. (18) I hid for a while and after a while I heard a bang come from downstairs. (19) I knew that it was a gun being fired. (20) I went downstairs and the three of them were still in the room. (21) They all looked shocked and were shouting at each other. (22) I heard Jimmy say, 'It went off by accident'. (23) I looked and on the settee I saw the body of the boy. (24) He had been shot in the head. (25) I was appalled and felt sick.

Below is the corresponding part of the disputed interview. What is immediately evident is that not only are the content and sequencing remarkably similar, but so also is the wording of the numbered utterances attributed to Molloy – I have highlighted in italic words and phrases that are identical to parts of the statement:

Text 2b Extract from the police interview with Molloy

P   How long were you in there Pat?
(17) *I had been drinking and cannot remember the exact time that I was there, but whilst I was upstairs I heard someone downstairs say 'be careful someone is coming'.*
P   Did you hide?
(18) Yes *I hid for a while* and then *I heard* the *bang* I have told you about.
P   Carry on Pat.
(19) I ran out.
P   What were the others doing?
(20) *The three of them were still in the room.*
P   What were they doing?
(21) *They all looked shocked and were shouting at each other.*
P   Who said what?
(22) *I heard Jimmy say 'it went off by accident'.*
P   Pat, I know this is upsetting but you appreciate that we must get to the bottom of this. Did you see the boy's body?
(23) Yes sir, he was *on the settee.*
P   Did you see any injury to him?
(24) Yes sir, *he had been shot in the head.*
P   What happened then?
(25) *I was appalled and felt sick.*

Apparently, the persuasive effect, or the 'meta-message', of the close textual similarity on the court was to reinforce the credibility of both texts, whereas the same phenomenon would have had just the opposite of effect on linguists, who, very conscious of the uniqueness of utterance, would be very suspicious of such similarity. In arguing against the independent production of the two texts, it was necessary not simply to assert linguists' views on uniqueness, but also to demonstrate how one text had indeed been derived from the other.

Obviously the two texts do not share the overt presence of the police interviewer as interlocutor and some of the content of the police utterances. If Molloy was right in asserting that it was the interview which was a fabrication, then one would expect some signs of this in the interview record – in essence what we have again is the 'policeman as dramatist' constructing a dialogue from a monologue. This is not as simple a task as it might seem. It involves first dividing up the monologue text into candidate answers and then devising questions for the pre-existing answers. One would expect, and we do indeed find, problems with cohesion:

(i)   an inability to create the appropriate question form:

P   What were the others **doing**?
(20)   The three of them **were** still in the room.
P   What were they **doing**?
(21)   They all **looked** shocked and were shouting at each other.

Here we can see two successive examples of a 'doing' question apparently receiving a 'being' response.

(ii)   a tendency to link forward to the already known answer rather than backward to the preceding answer. We can see this in the pair of exchanges (21/22):

(21)   They all looked shocked and were **shouting** at each other.
P   Who **said** what?
(22)   I heard Jimmy **say** 'it went off by accident'.

Following (21) one would expect 'Who shouted what' or 'What were they shouting?'; there is no reason to at all ask 'who **said** what?' – except that 'say' is already in the pre-existing 'answer' which follows.

(iii)   problems with grammatical cohesion:

P   . . . Did you see **the boy's body**?
(23)   Yes sir, **he** was on the settee.

In this instance we would expect to find the pronoun 'it' referring back to the body, not 'he'. It looks as if the 'he' has been borrowed from the statement, where the sequence is:

I saw **the body of the boy**. (24) **He** had been shot

and therefore where 'he' is a perfectly acceptable referent.

Thus the evidence suggests, as Molloy had always asserted, that a complete interview record was created by dialogising the original monologue statement and that again the persuasive power of contemporaneously recorded dialogue had been used to help convict the innocent. It was, sadly, never possible to test the persuasiveness of this discourse evidence in court as, shortly before the date fixed for the hearing of the appeal, an ESDA test[2] was conducted on the original handwritten version of Molloy's statement and it revealed traces of the confession statement Molloy claimed he had been shown and the forged signature of the supposed author. The three surviving men were released within 24 hours of this discovery being made public and their convictions were subsequently quashed. Molloy, sadly, had long since died in prison.

A case of concealed dialogue

One November evening in 1952 two teenagers, Derek Bentley aged 19 and Chris Craig aged 16, tried to break into a warehouse. They were seen, as they climbed up onto the roof, by a woman who was putting her daughter to bed. She called the police, who arrived soon afterwards and surrounded the building. Three unarmed officers, two in uniform the other in plain clothes, went up onto the roof to arrest the boys. Bentley immediately gave himself up. Craig drew a gun, started shooting and eventually killed a police officer.

Bentley was jointly charged with murder, even though he had been under arrest for some considerable time when the officer was shot. At the trial, which lasted only two days, both boys were found guilty. Craig, because he was legally a minor, was sentenced to life imprisonment; Bentley was sentenced to death and executed shortly afterwards. Bentley's family fought for a generation to overturn the guilty verdict and they were eventually successful 46 years later in the summer of 1998. The evidence which was the basis for both Bentley's conviction and the successful appeal was in large part linguistic and will be the focus of the rest of this chapter.

In the original trial the problem for the prosecution, in making the case against Bentley, was to demonstrate that he could indeed be guilty despite being under arrest when the murder was committed. At this point it would be useful to read the statement which the police claimed Bentley had dictated shortly after his arrest. It is presented in full below – the only changes I have introduced are to number the sentences for ease of reference and to highlight in bold for subsequent comment a series of negative clauses:

(1) I have known Craig since I went to school. (2) We were stopped by our parents going out together, but we still continued going out with each other – I mean **we have not gone out** together until tonight. (3) I was watching television tonight (2 November 1952) and between

8 pm and 9 pm Craig called for me. (4) My mother answered the door and I heard her say that I was out. (5) I had been out earlier to the pictures and got home just after 7 pm. (6) A little later Norman Parsley and Frank Fasey [*sic*] called. (7) **I did not answer the door or speak to them.** (8) My mother told me that they had called and I then ran out after them. (9) I walked up the road with them to the paper shop where I saw Craig standing. (10) We all talked together and then Norman Parsley and Frank Fazey left. (11) Chris Craig and I then caught a bus to Croydon. (12) We got off at West Croydon and then walked down the road where the toilets are – I think it is Tamworth Road.

(13) When we came to the place where you found me, Chris looked in the window. (14) There was a little iron gate at the side. (15) Chris then jumped over and I followed. (16) Chris then climbed up the drainpipe to the roof and I followed. (17) Up to then **Chris had not said anything**. (18) We both got out on to the flat roof at the top. (19) Then someone in a garden on the opposite side shone a torch up towards us. (20) Chris said: 'It's a copper, hide behind here.' (21) We hid behind a shelter arrangement on the roof. (22) We were there waiting for about ten minutes. (23) **I did not know** he was going to use the gun. (24) A plain clothes man climbed up the drainpipe and on to the roof. (25) The man said: 'I am a police officer – the place is surrounded.' (26) He caught hold of me and as we walked away Chris fired. (27) **There was nobody else** there at the time. (28) The policeman and I then went round a corner by a door. (29) A little later the door opened and a policeman in uniform came out. (30) Chris fired again then and this policeman fell down. (31) I could see that he was hurt as a lot of blood came from his forehead just above his nose. (32) The policeman dragged him round the corner behind the brickwork entrance to the door. (33) I remember I shouted something but I forgot what it was. (34) **I could not see** Chris when I shouted to him – he was behind a wall. (35) I heard some more policemen behind the door and the policeman with me said: '**I don't think** he has many more bullets left.' (36) Chris shouted 'Oh yes I have' and he fired again. (37) I think I heard him fire three times altogether. (38) The policeman then pushed me down the stairs and **I did not see** any more. (39) I knew we were going to break into the place. (40) **I did not know** what we were going to get – just anything that was going. (41) **I did not have** a gun and **I did not know** Chris had one until he shot. (42) I now know that the policeman in uniform that was shot is dead. (43) I should have mentioned that after the plain clothes policeman got up the drainpipe and arrested me, another policeman in uniform followed and I heard someone call him 'Mac'. (44) He was with us when the other policeman was killed.

Bentley's barrister spelled out for the jury the two necessary preconditions for them to convict him: they must be 'satisfied and sure'

(i)   that [Bentley] knew Craig had a gun and
(ii)   that he instigated or incited Craig to use it.

(Trow, 1992, p. 179)

The evidence adduced by the prosecution to satisfy the jury on both points was essentially linguistic. To support point (i) it was observed that in his statement, which purported to give his unaided account of the night's events, Bentley had said 'I did not know he was going to use the gun', (sentence 23). In his summing up, the judge, Lord Chief Justice Goddard, made great play of this sentence arguing both that its positioning in the narrative of events, before the time when there was any policeman on the roof and also the choice of '*the* gun' (as opposed to '*a* gun') must imply that Bentley knew that Craig had a gun well before it was used – in other words 'the gun' at that position in the statement must be taken to mean 'the gun I already knew at this point in the narrative that Craig had'. In addition, the judge argued, this sentence also showed Bentley to be an unreliable witness, because he then contradicted himself later, in sentence 41, by saying 'I *did not know* Chris had [a gun] until he shot'.

The evidence to support point (ii), that Bentley had incited Craig to shoot, was that the police officers in their statements and in their evidence given in court, asserted that Bentley had uttered the words 'Let him have it, Chris' immediately before Craig had shot and killed the policeman. Bentley, supported by Craig, had denied uttering these words – a claim also supported years later by a fourth policeman, who was never called to give evidence at the trial.

Bentley's defence, in the words of the judge in his summing-up, was:

> 'I didn't know he had a gun and I deny I said "Let him have it, Chris". I never knew he was going to shoot and I didn't think he would.' Against that denial (which, of course, is the denial of a man in grievous peril), you will consider the evidence of the three main officers who have sworn to you positively that those words were said.
>
> (Quoted in Trow, *op. cit.*, p. 109)

So, as the judge emphasised, the strength of the linguistic evidence depended essentially on the credibility of the police officers who had collected it and then sworn to its accuracy. When the case came to Appeal in 1998, one of the defence strategies was to challenge the reliability of the statement. They felt that if they could throw doubt on the veracity of the police, they could mitigate the incriminating force of both the statement and the phrase 'Let him have it, Chris'.

The linguistic evidence

At the original trial three police officers swore on oath that Bentley's statement was the product of unaided monologue dictation, whereas Bentley asserted that it was, in part at least, the product of dialogue – in other words that police questions and his replies had been converted into a monologue attributed to him:

> Q Did you in fact dictate that statement as it is written down.
> A No Sir.
> Q How was it taken from you.
> A In questions sir.
>
> (Trial transcript, pp. 100–1)

There is no doubt that this was a recognised procedure for producing statements at the time – a senior police officer, Chief Inspector Hannam, in another murder case, that of Alfred Charles Whiteway one year later, explained to the Court how he had elicited a statement from the accused in exactly this way:

> I would say 'Do you say on that Sunday you wore your shoes?' and he would say 'Yes' and it would go down as 'On that Sunday I wore my shoes'.
>
> (Trial transcript, p. 156)

There are, in fact, many linguistic features which suggest that Bentley's statement is not, as claimed by the police, a verbatim record of what he dictated, and I have written about these elsewhere (Coulthard, 1993); here I will confine myself simply to evidence that the statement was indeed, at least in part, dialogue converted into monologue. One of the first things that strikes one on reading the statement is that for most of the text the narrative of events is fairly coherent. However, this narrative seems to end with utterance (38) 'The policeman then pushed me down the stairs and I did not see any more'. What follows in sentences 39–42:

> (39) I knew we were going to break into the place. (40) I did not know what we were going to get – just anything that was going. (41) I did not have a gun and I did not know Chris had one until he shot. (42) I now know that the policeman in uniform that was shot is dead.

appears to be some kind of meta-narrative whose presence and form are most easily explained as the result of a series of clarificatory questions about Bentley's knowledge at particular points in the narrative, information which the police knew would be very important later at the trial.

At first one might not attach too much importance to these post-narrative questions – they certainly do not materially change the narrative which Bentley has already told – on the contrary, they allow him to clarify what he knew and did not know and also give him a chance to assert his lack of any pre-knowledge of Craig having a gun. Indeed, the fact that these may have been elicited, rather than spontaneously offered, did not seem to trouble the prosecution at trial. When Bentley was asked specifically about the sentence sequence (39–40) he replied 'That was [*sic*] an answer, Sir, to a question', to which the prosecution barrister replied 'I daresay it was in reply to a question' and then moved on immediately to a new topic.

However, this passing acknowledgement does reinforce Bentley's claim and prompts us to look for evidence of multiple voices elsewhere in the statement. We do so, of course, in the knowledge that there will always be some transformations of Q–A which will be indistinguishable from authentic dictated monologue. In the example quoted above, had we not been told that 'On that Sunday I wore my shoes' was a reduction from a Q–A we would have had some difficulty in deducing it, although the pre-posed adverbial, 'On that Sunday', certainly sounds a little odd.

We can begin our search with the initial observation that narratives, particularly narratives of murder, are essentially accounts of what happened and to a lesser extent what was known or perceived and thus reports of what did *not* happen or was *not* known are rare and special – there is an infinite number of things that did not happen and thus the teller needs to have some special justification for reporting any of them to the listener, in other words there must be some evident or stated reason for them being newsworthy.

We can see typical examples of 'normal' usage of negative reports in the sentences below taken from Molloy's confession statement already referred to above:

(a) Micky dumped the property but I **didn't** know where.
(b) Micky Hickey drove the van away, I **don't** know where he went to.
(c) We **didn't** all go together, me and Vinny walked down first.

(Molloy's statement)

In the first two examples, (a) and (b), the second negative clause functions as a *denial* of an inference which the listener could otherwise have reasonably derived from the first clause. Example (c) is similar, but this time it is a denial of an inference which the narrator guesses the listener might have made, as there is no preceding textual basis for the inference.[3] In other words, such negatives are an integral part of the ongoing narrative. We find examples of negatives being used in a similar way in Bentley's statement:

(6) A little later Norman Parsley and Frank Fasey called.
(7) I **did not** answer the door or speak to them.

When Bentley reported that his friends had called, the listener would reasonably expect him at least to have talked to them and therefore here there is a quite natural denial of a reasonable expectation.

However, there are, in Bentley's statement, some negatives which have no such narrative justification, like sentence (17) below:

(16) Chris then climbed up the drainpipe to the roof and I followed.
(17) Up to then Chris **had not said anything**.
(18) We both got out on to the flat roof at the top.

Chris is not reported as beginning to talk once they got out onto the roof, nor is his silence contrasted with anyone else's talking, nor is it made significant in any other way later in the narrative. A similarly unwarranted example is:

(26) He caught hold of me and as we walked away Chris fired.
(27) There **was nobody else** there at the time.
(28) The policeman and I then went round a corner by a door.

None of the possible inferences from the denial seem to make narrative sense here – for example, 'that as a result of there being no one else there…'

(a) it must be the policeman that Craig was firing at,
(b) that it must be Craig who was doing the firing,
(c) that immediately afterwards there would be more people on the roof.

So the most reasonable conclusion is that at this point in the statement-taking a policeman, trying to clarify what happened, asked a question to which the answer was negative and the whole sequence was then recorded as a negative statement. The fact that, like (27), other sentences in the statement may have been elicited in this way, becomes particularly important in relation to sentence (23):

(23) I **did not know** he was going to use the gun.

which is the one singled out by Lord Chief Justice Goddard as incriminating. This sentence, too, would only make narrative sense if it were linked backwards or forwards to the use of a gun – in other words if it were placed immediately following or preceding the report of a shot. However, the actual context is:

(22) We were there waiting for about ten minutes.
(23) I **did not know** he was going to use the gun.
(24) A plain clothes man climbed up the drainpipe and on to the roof.

If it is accepted that there were question/answer sequences underlying Bentley's statement, then the logic and the sequencing of the information were not under his direct control. Thus, the placing of the reporting of some of the events depends on a decision by the police questioner to ask his question at that point, rather than on Bentley's reconstruction of the narrative sequence and this, crucially, means that the inference drawn by the judge in his summing-up is unjustified. If one were able to assume that the confession statement was Bentley's unaided narrative, then the positioning of 'I didn't know he was going to use the gun' would be significant, because there is no timing adverbial and so the observation would have to take its time from its position in the narrative. In that view Bentley appears to be reporting that, well before the gun was used, he knew about its existence. However, if this sentence is in fact the product of a response to a question with its placing determined by the interrogating police officers, there is no longer any conflict with his later denial 'I did not know Chris had one [a gun] until he shot'. Nor is there any significance either in Bentley being reported as saying '*the* gun' – all interaction uses language loosely and cooperatively. If the policeman had asked Bentley about '*the* gun' Bentley would assume they both knew which gun they were talking about and the sensible interpretation would be 'the gun that had been used earlier that evening' and not 'the gun that was going to be used later in the sequence of events that made up Bentley's narrative'.

By a remarkable coincidence a parallel sequence occurred during the trial itself. Bentley's barrister, whilst eliciting a narrative of the evening's events from him, produced the following set of questions:

Q   Well, after some difficulty did you then get on the roof and find Craig?
A   Yes sir, I went on Craig's drainpipe and got up.
Q   Up to that time did you know that Craig had a loaded revolver?
A   No Sir.
Q   When you got on to the roof what happened then?
A   Some lights in the garden; someone shone a light in the garden.

(Trial transcript, p. 97)

If this sequence of Q–A exchanges were to be turned into a monologue narrative, the 'knowledge' about the loaded gun would similarly be reported well in advance of its use, with a similarly misleading effect.

The judgement

Demonstrating that the statement was indeed a jointly produced document, in part authored by the police officers who wrote it down, both removed the incriminating value of the phrase 'I didn't know he was going to use the gun' and undermined the credibility of the police officers on whose word depended the evidential value of the utterance 'Let him have it, Chris'. In August 1998, 46 years after the event, the then Lord Chief Justice, sitting with two senior colleagues, criticised his predecessor's summing-up and allowed the Appeal against conviction.

Conclusion

In focusing in detail on these three cases of invented and concealed dialogue I hope that I have shown how the medium is part of the message. In other words how, by being in control of the written form in which the original interaction was to be subsequently presented to the Court, the police were able to create a misrepresentation which would significantly influence the outcome of the case and help to secure a conviction. Examples like these confirm the wisdom of the 1984 PACE decision to introduce the tape-recording of police interviews and statement-taking; at the same time they reinforce concerns about judicial systems where both the police and the judiciary are still allowed to make written records of interactions with no taped record to consult in case of a later dispute.

Notes

1   All names occurring in examples in this section have been anonymised.
2   ESDA is an acronym for Electro-Static Detection Apparatus, a machine which enables the trained user to read the indentations on a piece of paper which were

created as a consequence of someone writing on a sheet of paper resting at the time on top of the paper under examination. For further information see Davis (1994).
3   See Pagano (1994) for a discussion of the function of negative clauses in texts.

References

Austin, J. L. (1962) *How to do Things with Words.* Oxford: Oxford University, Press.

Blackwell, S. (1996) 'Corrective Measures: Some Aspects of Transcription in the British Legal System', in H. Kniffka, S. Blackwell and R. M. Coulthard (eds), *Recent Developments in Forensic Linguistics.* Frankfurt, Peter Lang, pp. 255–76.

Coulthard, R. M. (1993) 'On Beginning the Study of Forensic Texts: Corpus, Concordance, Collocation', in M. Hoey (ed.), *Data, Description, Discourse.* London: HarperCollins, pp. 86–114.

Coulthard, R. M. (1996) 'The Official Version: Audience Manipulation in Police Reports of Interviews with Suspects', in C. R. Caldas-Coulthard and R. M. Coulthard (eds), *Texts and Practices: Readings in Critical Discourse Analysis.* London: Routledge, pp. 164–76.

Davis, T. R. (1994) 'ESDA and the Analysis of Contested Contemporaneous Notes of Police Interviews', *Forensic Linguistics,* vol. 1(1), pp. 71–89.

Eades, D. (1996) 'Verbatim Courtroom Transcripts and Discourse Analysis', in H. Kniffka, S. Blackwell and R. M. Coulthard (eds), *Recent Developments in Forensic Linguistics.* Frankfurt, Peter Lang, pp. 241–54.

Pagano, A. (1994) 'Negatives in Written Text', in R. M. Coulthard (ed.), *Advances in Written Text Analysis.* London: Routledge, pp. 250–75.

Trow, M. J. (1992) *'Let him have it Chris'.* London: HarperCollins.

3

Textual Barriers to United States Immigration

Gail Stygall

Introduction: the politics of immigration and the processing of documents

The ideological project of keeping the USA free from illegal aliens is often captured in images of an actual physical border to be defended, asserting bounded, nationalist space. We see and read news accounts of the border patrol holding back the 'flood' of illegal immigrants from Latin America. Accounts of these Latin Americans trying to reach the USA – sometimes dying of heat or cold in the desert-like land of the south-western states or chased out by vigilante ranchers protecting their property – appear frequently in US newspapers and news magazines. If they are still alive when found, they are 'processed' back out of the country. Alternatively on both coasts, media reports warn of the dangers of attempting to enter the USA without formal application, when yet another container ship from East Asia filled with weakened, dying or dead bodies of illegal immigrants is discovered. They, too, are processed out as soon as they are physically able. The Coast Guard patrols the waters off the coast of Florida, too, keeping Haitians at bay. The Immigration and Naturalization Service maintains these images in their own in-house publication, occasionally publishing graphs and pie charts extolling their abilities to meet the quotas on 'alien removal' for the year.

Moreover, the threat is also perceived as *within*, the border already being breached. As cultural studies scholar Stacy Takacs suggests, even when illegal immigrant communities attempted to oppose xenophobic attempts to control illegal immigration, such as California's Proposition 187, designed to deny basic social services to illegal aliens, their work in joining mass political movements may have the opposite effect. Takacs (1999, p. 609) describes the reactions of the public to a mass demonstration of patriotism by both legal and illegal immigrants and citizens thus: 'the march made the problem of (illegal) immigration materially manifest for a mainstream public conditioned by the mass media to receive such activities as always already chaotic and threatening'. The ways in which the media portrayed the event made it seem as if the public was being overwhelmed by alien bodies. It is thus the physical aspect of the border and the alien body that dominate public associations with immigration.

To the US Immigration and Naturalization Service (INS), physical barriers are only one part of keeping 'the hordes' away. The textual barriers are every bit as significant. In order to become a legal immigrant to the USA, to attain permanent residency status and to become a naturalised citizen, the immigrant must become a better, more savvy reader of the US legal process and documents than the average native-born citizen. Applicants must apply for an entry visa at a US consulate in their country of residence, work through whatever application forms and interviews are required at that point and present the appropriate documents at the border or port of entry. They then begin a whole new application procedure for 'adjusting status' – that is, applying for permanent residence – and must apply for special documents to leave the USA and return while the application is pending, and begin the process yet again in applying to become a US citizen. If the immigrant makes a mistake on the form, fails to recognise US legal terms for a variety of criminal or even civil offences, or lacks a necessary document, permanent immigration or citizenship will be denied and the applicant can be deported. The forms themselves – both the instructions and the questions – seem to be designed to impede practically any reader's comprehension.

One of the most important documents an immigrant must file is INS Form I-485, the Application to Register Permanent Residence or Adjust Status. The INS Form I-485 is the document required for an immigrant to become a permanent resident, that is, a person who has a 'green' card (though the cards are no longer green) and is able to work in the United States. Two years ago, I was asked, as a forensic linguist, to assess the comprehensibility of Form I-485 for a case in which the immigrant's answers to several questions on the application was at issue. This essay reports my findings in that case and discusses their implications. I concluded that both the instructions and the application are extraordinarily difficult to understand, even for the native speaker of English, and much more so for applicants whose first language in not English. The barriers to comprehension in Form I-485 are multiple. Unlike citizens, immigrants, even legal permanent residents, have no vote, yet they number more than 10 million. Because they are not considered an identifiable voting constituency to elected officials, the INS, unlike other federal agencies, is under no pressure to revise documents for comprehensibility unless under court order.

Thus, the role of the forensic linguist here is to describe the comprehension issues, and in doing so perhaps help speak for the unrepresented, unfranchised immigrants. In what follows, I first discuss the legal background of comprehension issues, then move to document design, syntax and referencing the textual world of the INS administrative law. I then move to a brief analysis of the speech acts represented by the document. In the final section, I discuss the possibilities of improving the documents with an eye towards these immigrants' lack of the voting franchise.

Legal framework

The following comments made by the 9th Circuit Court of Appeals about the comprehensibility of INS documents could be equally applied to INS Form I-485:

> Moreover, we conclude that the documents are so bureaucratic and cumbersome and in some respects so uninformative and in others so misleading that even those aliens with a reasonable command of the English language would not receive adequate notice from them.
>
> *Walters* v. *Reno* 145 F.3d 1032, 1041 (9th Cir. 1998)

In *Walters* v. *Reno* the court reviewed the trial court's issuing of permanent injunctive relief and certifying of a class of 4000 immigrants who were contesting the means of notifying them of their 'document fraud'. The central issue was whether the immigrants had received actual notice of their rights and the consequences when they were charged. Document fraud refers to false answers on various INS forms. In these cases of document fraud, the alien discovers the charges against him or her through legally-served INS forms. As the 9th Circuit describes the problem, aliens who commit civil document fraud are subject to immediate deportation. Aliens typically receive three forms at once:

- a fine notice for the penalty of document fraud;
- a rights/waiver notice; and
- an Order to Show Cause.

The fine notice gives the specific charge and notifies the alien that he or she may file a written request for a hearing. The rights/waiver notice informs the alien of his or her rights and asks that the alien waive rights to a hearing. As the court notes, it isn't clear in the rights/waiver document that the immigrant is also waiving rights to challenge the deportation and permanent bar to entering the USA. The Order to Show Cause notice indicates that a hearing will be scheduled, but doesn't indicate that it is not possible to contest deportation at the hearing. If the immigrant hasn't made the written request required in the fine notice, he or she cannot challenge the accusation of document fraud.

The trial court heard evidence on the difficulties of comprehension presented by the language of the documents, based primarily on surveys of the class members rather than a linguistic analysis. It also heard evidence on non-citizens' lack of understanding of the actions required to secure their rights to a hearing. As the 9th Circuit reports on the trial court's action, they said:

> [i]ndeed, the district court observed that the forms are so obscure and confusing with respect to this point (that a written request for a hearing on the fine notice must be made) that even some of the INS agents who administer them are unable to explain adequately the immigration consequences of a final order on document fraud charges . . . Given that most recipients of the forms are noncitizen immigrants whose primary language is one other than English, the court concluded there is very little chance that they, in particular, would be able to plow through the legalistic language in order to figure out what steps to take so as to contest their deportation.
>
> (Ibid., pp. 1049–50)

As such, these forms then could not be providing adequate legal notice to the immigrants so that they could protect their rights. Thus, the 9th Circuit agreed with the trial court that for this certified class of defendants, the forms needed to be revised. The court stopped short of requiring that the forms be available in both English and Spanish, something the trial court's order had included.

Walters v. *Reno* is unusual in its emphasis on the extreme difficulties defendants had in comprehending the INS forms. But various commentators are aware of other well-known problems with INS administrative adjudication. As the Chief Judge of the 7th Circuit, Richard Posner, commented in *Salameda* v. *INS*, 70 F.3d 447 (7th Cir. 1995):

> The proceedings of the Immigration and Naturalization Service are notorious for delay, and the opinions rendered by its judicial officers, including the members of the Board of Immigration Appeals, often flunk minimum standards of adjudicative rationality. [citations omitted] The lodgment of this troubled Service in the Department of *Justice* [italics in original] of a nation that was built by immigrants and continues to be enriched by a flow of immigration is an irony that should not escape notice.
>
> (Ibid., p. 449)

Yet even with such criticism from the judiciary, INS practices have changed very little.

Moreover, US law in other areas – especially jury instructions and the understanding of criminal defendants – suggests that lay comprehension of rights and notices is often not a central issue for courts. In my own earlier work and that of Tiersma and Dumas, it is clear that standard-pattern jury instructions are difficult for jurors to understand.[1] Yet almost every state has case law that concludes that juror comprehension is not as important as a correct statement of the law. Dumas (2000, p. 54) suggests that reform has been difficult in the face of judges who wish to retain control, in spite of 30 years of research indicating that jury instructions 'are not understandable to most jurors'. Moreover, she questions whether jurors are in fact treated as experts in the facts of the case, their designated role in trials. If jurors do not understand what they are being asked to do, then their verdicts become questionable. Yet as many US linguists have learned, appellate courts rarely reverse trial court decisions on the failure of jury instructions, with state courts affirming on appeal instructions that correctly state the law, even if comprehension is poor.

Criminal proceedings are another arena in which correct statements of law prevail over actual comprehension. Philips' (1985) analysis of pleas in an Arizona court indicates that much of the exchange between judges and defendants is formulaic rather than substantive. Recently in *Davis* v. *United States*, 512 US 452 (1994), the Supreme Court declared that ambiguous reference to an attorney – 'Maybe I should talk to a lawyer' – did not mean that interrogation by the police must halt. While some legal scholars argued that the police should have limited further questioning to clarifying whether the suspect actually wanted a lawyer, the Court disagreed. Justice Souter's dissent, while concurring in the judgment, agreed that clarification should have been the appropriate response, and is remarkably well-informed in the discourse dynamics of differing cultural responses to making direct requests and to the power dynamics of the interrogation context. He was, of course, in the minority in *Davis*.

Moreover, when the issue of English as a second language surfaces in immigration cases, the courts have not always been concerned with defendants' understanding of the legal proceedings. In *El Rescate* v. *Executive Office of Immigration Review*, 941 F.2d 950 (9th Cir. 1991), the court upheld the Board of Immigration Appeals policy that the defendant is entitled to a interpreter only for his or her own testimony, while 'arguments presented by counsel and the rulings of the immigration judge are primarily legal matters, the translation of which would not be required where the alien is represented and the protection of his interests is assured by counsel's presence' (*ibid.*, p. 952). The proceedings themselves, then, outside of the immigrants' own testimony, may be entirely beyond the comprehension of the immigrant-defendant. Thus comprehension of non-legal participants in trials and hearings may not surface until the distance between the discourse and the comprehension is extreme.

INS form I-485

The specific document addressed in this paper is the Application to Register Permanent Residence or Adjust Status. It consists of seven pages, divided into two parts. The first three pages are the instructions for the form, although they are not labelled as such. The information in the instructions is presented in a two-column form and consists of 112 sentences with 309 clauses. The second part, the application itself, is four pages long. It consists of 47 sentences with 76 clauses. A minor revision of the form took place in February 2000.

Document design of I-485

With the visual component of texts increasingly important to discourse analysts (see Kress and van Leeuwen, 1996), forensic linguists in cases involving forms may want to consider document design in their analysis. This attention to written presentation may mirror a similar concern with the oral presentation of jury instructions (Dumas, 2000, pp. 65–6) which are fully given only at the end of trials and usually delivered in a formal, oral monotone. Yet research on document design has, like research on the difficulties of jury instructions, been available for more than 30 years. Research on document design – in technical reports, insurance and credit documents, and government forms – gathered impetus during the Carter presidency. Researchers at the Document Design Center at the American Institutes for Research and the Carnegie Mellon University Communications Design Center put together interdisciplinary groups to study communication problems, as well as ways to meet Carter's 'plain language' policy. Researchers on both of these projects, as well as those working at Georgetown University's Applied Linguistics Center and other document designers, worked – and some continue to work – with government agencies such as the Veterans Administration, the Social Security Administration, including the section administering Medicare, the Internal Revenue Service, and the Federal Communications Commission. The Immigration and Naturalization Service participated in a Document Design Project during the Carter administration,[2] and it is likely that the 'you' language referring to the applicant dates from that period, but their contemporary forms demonstrate little impact of that research. The Reagan administration rescinded the 'plain language' policy, substituting the Paperwork Reduction Act – which focused on loss of business and citizen time on forms.

Standard document-design principles have emerged, the most important of which emphasises the reading audience of the document. Other corollary principles are that good design helps readers locate information, that good design emphasises the most important content, and that the best test of good design involves readers' comprehension and satisfaction after reading the document. Design principles also include organisational patterns, such as aligning related elements to one another, providing contrasts in looks – typeface and size, placement on page, white space-establishing hierarchy, placing related items in proximity to one another, and repeating design elements to establish document coherence.[3]

The design elements of the current I-485 violate many of these principles. One way of examining this issue is to compare forms written for two different audiences, the I-485, written for immigrant applicants, and the I-140, written for a US employer who is supporting the application of a worker. The I-140, Immigrant Petition for Alien Worker, is used for example by universities to hire faculty from other countries. Figure 3.1 shows the first page of the instructions of the I-140, while Figure 3.2 is the first page of instructions for the I-485. (See pp. 42–3.)

Several differences are immediately apparent in the design. First, the amount of white space in the I-140 is greater, including a large 'gutter', the white space between columns, contributing to ease of reading. In the I-485, the gutter is 0.2 inch, making the column separation nearly indistinguishable. White space is little used. Second, the typeface in the I-485 is 8-point Times Roman, a *serif* typeface, while the typeface in the I-140 is 10-point Helvetica, a *sans serif* typeface, also thought to contribute to reader comprehension.[4] The Helvetica type also appears slightly larger as letter height, what typographers call 'x-height,' is greater in the Helvetica than in the Times Roman. Figure 3.3 on page 44 illustrates the two font types.

Third, the I-485 contains line lengths as long as 90 characters, violating the standard rule of 50–70 characters per line for readers' ease. The I-140 does not violate this standard rule and additionally I-140 uses slightly more space between the lines. Fourth, the hierarchical divisions among topics are problematic in the I-485, with different level categories appearing with the same bold-faced type. It also contains no overview statements, found to be important for increased comprehension by reading researchers (Spyridakis and Standal, 1987) and by researchers examining jury instructions in the late 1970s and early 1980s (Elwork, Alfini and Sales, 1982), and more recent research by Dumas and Johnson (1999, cited in Dumas, 2000) indicating that roadmap statements help jurors by previewing the information that follows. Comparatively, the I-140 is enhanced by better spacing, larger-point type, and setting-off subsection information with bold italics.

The logic of using very poor document design for the non-native-speaker of English, decreasing reader comprehension, while producing better document design for the proficient native speaker of English seems backwards even in the most generous interpretation. What the comparison does establish, however, is that the INS can produce better-designed forms than the I-485, perhaps when the intended audience changes to people with votes and political representation.

Syntax: clauses and sentence complexity

One of the most important measures of a document's comprehensibility by readers is the complexity of the sentences in the document. While readability formulas typically count sentence length, sentence complexity is a more accurate measure of likely reader difficulty. Linguists are likely to prefer methods that count the number of clauses embedded into a single sentence, comparing that document to other types of documents, as well as comparing it to spoken conversation. As we know, the more clauses a sentence has, the more difficult it is for readers to comprehend and the longer it takes to do so. Psycholinguistic researchers established as early as the 1970s that processing time increased with each clause embedded into a sentence (Holmes, Kennedy and Murray, 1987; Larkin and Burns, 1977; Irwin, 1980; Matthews

42

U.S.Department of Justice
Immigration and Naturalization Service

10 & 14 pt.
Helvetica

OMB No. 1115-0061
Immigrant Petition for Alien Worker

Purpose Of This Form.
This form is used to petition for an immigrant based on employment.

Adequate space between sections

Who May File.
Any person may file this petition on behalf of an alien who:
- has extraordinary ability in the sciences, arts, education, business, or athletics, demonstrated by sustained national or international acclaim, whose achievements have been recognized in the field; or
- is a member of the profession holding an advanced degr[ee] Subsection marked [o]ptional ability in the Science[s] by Bold Italic type [a]nd is seeking an exemption of the requirement of a job offer in the national interest.

A U.S employer may file this petition who wishes to employ:
- an outstanding professor or researcher, with at least 3 years of experience in teaching or research in the academic areas, who is recognized internationally as outstansing,
  - in a tenured or tenur-track position at a university or institution of higher educati[on] academic area,
  - in a comparable position at [an] institution of higher education to conduct research in the area, or
  - in a comparable position to conduct research for a private employer who employs at least 3 persons in full-time research activities and has achieved documented accomplishments in an academic field,

Parallel sized subset entries

- an alien who, in the 3 years preceding the fi[ling] petition, has been employed for at least 1 year by a firm or corporation or other legal entity and who seeks to enter the U.S. to continue to render services to the same employer or to a subsidiary or affiliate in a capacity that is managerial or executive;

Greater space between lines

- a member of the professions holding an advanced degree or an alien with exceptional ability in the sciences, arts, or business who will substantially benefit the national economy, cultural or educational interests, or welfare of the U.S.;
- a skilled worker (requiring at least 2 years of specialized training or experience in the skill)- to perform labor for which qualified workers are not available in the U.S.;
- a member of the professions with a baccalaureate degree; or
- an unskilled worker to perform labor for which qualified workers are not available in the U.S.

General Filing Instructions.
please answer all questions by typing o[r printi]ng in black ink. Indicate that an item is not applicable with "N/A." If an answer to a question is "none." write "none." If you need extra space to answer any item, attach a sheet of [paper] with your name and your A# if any, and indicate the number of the item to which the answer refers. You must file your petition with the required Initial Evidence. Your petition must be properly signed and filed with the correct fee.

59 character line

Wider Gutter

More White Space

Initial Evidence.
If you are filing for an alien of extraordinary ability in the sciences, arts, education, business, or athletics, you must file your petition with:
- evidence of a one-time achievement (i.e., a major, internationally-recognized award), or
- at least three of the following:
  - receipt of lesser nationally or internationally recognized prizes or awards for excellence in the field of endeavor,
  - membership in associations in the field which require outstanding achievements as judged by recognized national or international experts.
  - Published material about the alien in professional or major trade publications or other major media.
  - participation on a panel or individually as a judge of the work of others in the field or an allied field,
  - original scientific, scholarly, artistic, athletic, or business-related contributions of major significance in the field,
  - authorship of scholarly articles in the field, in professional or major trade publications or other major media.
  - display of the alien's work at artistic exhibitions or showcases,
  - evidence that the alien has performed in a leading or critical role for organizations or establishments that have a distinguished reputation,
  - evidence that the alien has commanded a high salary or other high remuneration for services, or evidence of commercial successess in the performing arts, as shown by box office receipts of record, cassette, compact disk, or video sales.
  - If the above standards do not readily apply to the alien's occupation, you may submit comparable evidence to establish the alien's eligibility; and
- evidence that the alien is coming to the U.S. to continue work in the area of expertise. Such evidence may include letter(s) from prospective employer(s), evidence or prearranged commitments such as contracts, or a statement from the alien detailing plans on how he or she intends to continue his or her work in the U.S.

Form I-140 (Rev. 10/13/98)N

Figure 3.1   INS form I-140

Figure 3.2 is an annotated reproduction of an INS form. The form text and the annotation callouts read as follows:

OMB No. 1115-0061

Department [of] ... Immigration ...

Form I-485, Application to Register permanent Residence or Adjust Status

Annotation callouts on the figure:
- *No distinction between major category and subcategory*
- *8 pt. Font Times Roman*
- *90 character line*
- *White space emphasizes less important material*
- *Narrow Gutter*
- *General Instruction section doesn't provide specific information.*
- *No organizational overview of all 10 documents to be produced*
- *No distinction between major categories*
- *82 character line*
- *Subset sizes not parallel*

Purpose [of this form].
This form is [used by persons in] the United States to apply to the Immigration and Naturalization Service (INS) to adjust to permanent resident status or register for permanent residence. It may also be used by certain Cuban nationals to request a [change] in the date their permanent residence began.

Who May File.
Based on an immigrant petition. You may apply to adjust your status if:
- an immigrant visa number is immediately available to you based on an approved immigrant petition; or
- You are filing this application with a complete relative, special immigrant juvenile or special immigrant military petition, which if approved, [would make an immigran]t visa number immediately available [to you.]

Based on being th[e spouse or child (deriv]ative) at the time another adjustment applica[nt is granted perm to ad]just status or at a person is granted permar[ent residence] in immigrant category that allows derivatives [to apply for spouses and] children.
- **If the spouse or child is in the United states,** the individuals derivatives may file their Form I-485 adjustment of status applications concurrently with the Form I-485 for the Principal beneficiary, or file the form I-485 at anytime after the principal is approved, if a visa number is available.
- **If the spouse or child is residing abroad,** the person adjusting status in the United States should file the **Form I-824, Application for Action on an Approved Application or petition, concurrently** with the principal's adjustment of status application to allow the derivatives to immigrate to the United States without delay, if the principal's adjustment of status application is approved. **No I-824 fee will be refunded if the principal's adjustment is not granted.**

Based on admission as the fiancé(e) of a U. S. citizen and subsequent marriage to that citizen. You may apply to adjust status if you were admitted as the K-1 fiancé(e) and you married that citizen within days your entry. If you still qualify as am asylee or as the spouse or child of a refugee.

Based on asylum status. You may apply to adjust status if you have been granted asylum in the U. S. after being physically present in the U. S. for one year after the grant of asylum, if you still qualify as an asylee or as the spouse or child of a refugee.

Based on Cuban citizenship or nationality. You may apply to adjust status if:
- you are a native or citizen of Cuba, were admitted or paroled into the U. S. after January 1, 1959, and thereafter have been physically present in te U. S. for at least one year; or
- you are the spouse or unmarried child of Cuban described above, and regardless of your nationality, you were admitted or paroled after January 1, 1959, and thereafter have been physically present in the U. S. for at least one year.

Based on continuous residence since before January 1, 1972. You may apply for permanent residence if you have continuously resided in the U. S. since before January 1,1972.

Applying to change the date your permanent residence began. If you were granted permanent residence in the U. S. prior to November 6, 1966, and are a native or citizen of Cuba, his or her spouse or unmarried minor child, you may ask to change date your lawful permanent residence began to your date of arrival in the U. S. or May 2, 1964, whichever is later.

Other basis of eligibility. If you are not [in any of the above categories,] but believe you may be eligible for a[djustment of] permanent residence, contact your loc[al INS office.]

Persons who are ineligible.
Unless you are applying for creation of record based on continuous residence since before January 1, 1972, or adjustment of status under a category in which special rules apply (such as asylum adjustment, Cuban adjustment, Special immigrant juvenile adjustment or special immigrant military personnel adjustment), **You are not eligible for adjustment of status if any of the following apply to you:**
- you entered the U. S. in transit without a visa;
- you entered the U. S. as a nonimmigrant crewman;
- you were not admitted or paroled following inspection by an immigration officer;
- your authorized stay expired before you filed this application; you were employed in the U. S. prior to filing this application, without INS authorization; or you otherwise failed to maintain your nonimmigrant status, other than through no fault of your own or for technical reasons, unless you are applying because you are an immediate relative of a U. S. citizen (parent, spouse, widow, widower or unmarried child under 21 years old), a K-1 fiancé(e) or K-2 fiance(e) dependent who married the U. S. petitioner within 90 days of admission or an"H" or "I" or special

immigrant (foreign medical graduates, international organization employees or their derivative family members);
- you are or were a J-1 or J-2 exchange visitor, are subject to the two-year foreign residence requirement and have not complied with or been granted a waiver of the requirement;
- [you have or had a J-1] or G nonimmigrant status, or have an [A or G status that would] allow you to have this status, unless you complete Form I-508 (I-508F for French nationals) to wave diplomatic rights, privileges and immunities, and if you are an A or G nonimmigrant, unless you submit a complete Form I-566;
- you are admitted to Guama a visitor under the Guam visa waiver program;
- you were admitted to the U. S. as a visitor under the Visa Waiver Pilot Program, unless you are applying because you are an immediate relative of a U. S. citizen (parent, spouse, widow, widower or unmarried child under 21 years old);
- you are already a conditional permanent resident;
- you we[re admitted as a K-]1 fiancé(e) but did not marry the U. S. citizen [who filed the petitio]n for you, or were admitted as theK-2 child of a fiance(e) and your parent did not marry te U. S. citizen who filed the petition.

General Filing Instructions

Please answer all questions by typing or clearly printing in black ink. Indicate that an item is not applicable with "N/A." If the answer is "none," write "none." If you need extra space to answer any item, attach a sheet of paper with your name and you[r] alien registration number (A#), if any, and indicate the n[umber of the item the] answer refers. You must file your a[pplication with the requ]ired **Initial Evidence** described below, b[efore it is accepted.] Your application must be properly signed a[nd accompanied by the] fee. If you are under 14 years of age, your [parent or guardian may] sign your application.

Translations. Any foreign language document must be accompanied by a full English translation which the translator has certified as complete and correct, and by the translator's certification that he or she is competent to translate the foreign language into English.

Copies. If these instructions state that a copy of a document may be filed with this application, and you choose to send us the original, we may keep the original for our needs.

Initial Evidence.
you [must] file your application with the following evidence:
- **Birth certificate.** Submit a copy of you foreign birth certificate or other record of your birth that meets the provisions of secondary evidence found in 8 CFR 103.2(b)(2).
- [Passport page] with nonimmigrant visa. If you have [a visa(s)] from an American consulate [abroad,] submit a photocopy(ies) of you[r visa(s).]
- **Photos.** Submit two (2) identical natural color photographs of yourself, taken within 30 days of the application. Photos must have a white background, be unmounted, printed on thin paper and be glossy and unretouched. They must show a three-quarter frontal profile showing the right side of your face, with your right ear visible and with your head bare. You may wear a headdress if required by a religious order of which you are a member. The photos must be no larger than 2×2 inches, with the distance from the top of the head to just below the chin about 1 and 1/4 inches. Lightly print your A# (or your name if you have no A#) on the back of each photo, using a pencil.
- [You will be notified to] be[tween the ages of 14 and 75, you] [must appear to be fingerprinte]d. After filing this application, INS will notify [you of the t]ime and location where you must go to be fingerprinte[d.] Failure to appear to be fingerprinted may result in denial of your application.
- **Police clearances.** I you are filing for adjustment of status as a member of a special class described in an I-485 supplement form, please read the instructions on the supplement form to see if you need to obtain and submit police clearances, in addition to the required fingerprints, with your application.
- **Medical examination (section 232 of the Act).** When required, submit a medical examination report on the form you have obtained from INS.

Form I-485 (Rev. 10/13/98)N

Figure 3.2 INS form I-485

Here is Times Roman in the 8 point size. It is difficult to read at this size along with its *serif* characteristic.

Here is Arial, 8 point, the word processing form of Helvetica. It is a 10 point in the 1-140, but even in 8, it appears larger.

Figure 3.3   Times Roman and Helvetica font types

and Chodorow, 1988). Additionally, clauses without their own immediately visible subjects, such as infinitive clauses, present additional processing difficulties as readers search for the proper subject. Clauses of this type appear throughout the I-485. An example of this type of embedding is found in the I-485 instructions:

> If you were granted permanent residence status in the US prior to November 6, 1966, and are a native or citizen of Cuba, his or her spouse, or unmarried child, you may ask *to change the date your lawful permanent residence began to the date of your arrival in the US or May 2, 1964,* whichever is later.

The infinitive clause here is deeply embedded into the sentence and the grammatical agent able to change the date of lawful permanent residence, presumably the INS, is deleted altogether. Such sentences are even more difficult to process.

Form I-485 contains an extraordinarily high number of sentences with multiple clause embeddings. Fully 47 per cent of the sentences contain three or more clauses. Using data from the *Longman Grammar of Spoken and Written English* (1999), which is based on their 40-million-word corpus, some useful comparisons can be made between the I-485 text, spoken conversation, and news-reporting texts. The *Longman Grammar* employs a smaller subset of texts to produce the percentages used for this comparison. Table 3.1 sets out the percentages for each level of embedding from each type of source.

In the I-485, only 28 per cent of the sentences are single clauses, in contrast to conversation's 74 per cent and news reporting's 37 per cent. For two-clause sentences, the I-485 is 25 per cent of the total, conversation 22 per cent and

Table 3.1   Comparison of number of clauses per sentence

Number of clauses per sentence	I-485	Conversation	News reporting
1	28%	74%	37%
2	25%	22%	43%
3	25%	4%	15%
4 or more	22%	0%	5%

news reporting 43 per cent. Thus, with both conversation and news reporting, one- and two-clause sentences comprise 96 per cent and 80 per cent of the total sentences, respectively. The I-485, however, offers the reader 47 per cent of its sentences at three or more clauses, while conversation presents three or more clause sentences as 4 per cent of the total and news reporting 20 per cent of the total. On clause embedding alone, the I-485 presents a much higher level of difficulty, even for the native-English-speaking, highly proficient and educated reader.

In addition to the difficulty of embedded clauses, the type of clause and task of identifying the agent of these sentences increase the difficulty. The *unless* and *if* clauses are examples of the types of clause that create additional reading difficulties. In these clauses, the reader must hold either the exception (*unless*) or the condition (*if*) in mind as he or she processes the rest of the sentence. Moreover, *unless*-type clauses require that the reader keep a negative in mind, further adding to processing time, especially when the negative precedes the main clause, as in the **Persons Whox Are Ineligible** section of the I-485 instructions. This sentence reads as follows:

> Unless you are applying for creation of record based on continuous residence since before January 1, 1972, or adjustment of status under a category in which special rules apply (such as asylum adjustment, Cuban adjustment, special juvenile immigrant adjustment or special immigrant military personnel adjustment), you are not eligible for adjustment of status if any of the following apply to you.

A bulleted list follows, filled with immigration categories, such as being a K–1, H, I, J–1, J–2, A, E or G immigrant or non-immigrant. Add these difficulties to the number of embeddings cited above and the reading difficulties increase along multiple lines. Readers can and do become confused by the embeddings and the exceptions.

A second type of problem involves agency in these sentences; that is, figuring out who is doing the acting. One example of the problem with agency can be found in Part 3 of the application section in the first numbered question. This question, with four separate questions embedded, switches the agent over the four subquestions. The question is shown in Figure 3.4.

In Part 3, question 1(a), the agent is the person filling out the form, yet in the very next subquestion, (b), the agent is someone in an agency with police powers, who can arrest, cite or charge, or someone with judicial powers who can indict, fine or imprison. Agency switches again in 1(c) and 1(d); in (c) the agency is someone who can grant pardons, amnesties, rehabilitation decrees and other forms of clemency, with the agency returning to the applicant in (d). The effect of shifting agency across subsections of the question is to disrupt coherence, that sense that readers have of sentences belonging together. In this case, the reader is forced to reconsider why these items are presented as if they belong together. All that actually binds them together is the lead clause, 'Have you ever, in or outside the US:' and mere

1. Have you ever, in or outside the US:

    a. knowingly committed any crime of moral turpitude or drug-related offense for
        which you have not been arrested?

    b. been arrested, cited, charged, indicted, fined or imprisoned for breaking or
        violating any law or ordinance, excluding traffic violations?

    c. been the beneficiary of a pardon, amnesty, rehabilitiation decree, other act of
        clemency or similar action?

    d. exercised diplomatic immunity to avoid prosecution for a criminal offense in
        the US?

Figure 3.4   I-485 Application Section, part 3, question 1

physical proximity to one another. In addition, shifting agency away from
the applicant means that the applicant is now responsible for identifying
and correctly assessing someone else's agency. So the applicant becomes
responsible for knowledge about someone else's actions, what the correct
categories are for those actions and not for his or her own actions.

Text world: reference and vocabulary

Reference and vocabulary present other problems for the reader of Form I-485.
By reference, I mean those words and phrases referring to other texts and
documents outside the text in question. By vocabulary, here I mean the
presence of rarely used vocabulary or vocabulary that has a specialised technical meaning within a particular community, such as that of lawyers, or
that of people who work for the Immigration and Naturalization Service.

The I-485 is full of references to other texts and documents – a total of
28 – a handful of which are multiple references to the same text. The I-94,
Arrival/Departure Record, possibly familiar to applicants, is mentioned four
times, but so, too, is Section 212 (a)(9)(B)(i) of the Immigration Act, something much less likely to be a well-known text to the immigrant applicant.
Ten other INS forms, some of which would be familiar to applicants at this
point in the process, and four other sections of the Act are mentioned.
Perhaps the most bizarre reference for the immigrant applicant is to 8 CFR
103.2(b)(2), the text that the applicant is, in theory, supposed to read to
find out if he or she has the acceptable secondary documentation of birth,
in lieu of a birth certificate. The likelihood of the average applicant for
immigration 'benefit' of permanent resident status to have access to the *Code
of Federal Regulations* is small indeed. Even if the applicant could find it, it is
unlikely that the *Code* would be clarifying, given the relevant section's
emphasis on denying the benefit without the documents the INS requires.
The ideal reader for this document, then, is not the applicant; instead, the

ideal reader is an intra-agency professional with the next-best reader an attorney specialising in immigration law.

The vocabulary used in the document presents another set of problems, slightly different in each of the two sections, the instructions and the application. In the instructions unusual formations and infrequently-used vocabulary appear. The most unusual formations are 'derivates' and 'derivatives,' used to refer to biological relatives. While the idea of derivative rights is familiar to attorneys, the practice of calling a human being a 'derivate' or a 'derivative' is highly unusual, in any layperson's usage. One needs to go deep into the references in the *Oxford English Dictionary* to find usages that approximate the INS uses of derivative, and most of the demonstrative entries are dated 1500–1700. No widely available US dictionary has an entry for derivates that applies to human beings. In conducting my original analysis, I found the *Collins COBUILD English Dictionary* (1995) useful as it is designed for learners of English. The *Collins COBUILD* is based on a corpus of 200 million words ('Preface': viii), and it includes frequency bands to indicate how typically the word in question is used. Many words that highly literate speakers of English find unproblematic are words that learners of English will not encounter in speech. Words fitting that category in the I-485 include the following: *adjustment, concurrently, certified, supplement, jurisdiction, deficiency, registry, waiver, termination, discretion*, and a number of others. Because *Collins COBUILD* also includes frequency bands, assigning words to one of five bands representing the most frequently used English vocabulary, we find that all of the words in the above list are usages outside the 75 per cent of the most frequently used spoken and written English words. Words outside those bands, that is outside 95 per cent of the most frequently used English vocabulary, include *inadmissability, paroled, collude* and *turpitude*, all appearing in the I-485.

In addition, a significant number of words and phrases are legal in origin and usage. The difficulties with laypeople reading legal language are well-documented and include problems ranging from the use of archaisms to terms of art, generally unknown to the lay reader. An additional problem is the use of vocabulary which has both a legal definition and an ordinary one.[5] These types of difficulties are well-illustrated in Part 3, found on page 3 of the I-485. The average immigrant is unlikely to know the criminal law import of the phrase 'knowingly and willfully', nor is he or she likely to know the differences among 'arrested, cited, charged', and 'indicted', particularly if applicants come from nations with dissimilar legal systems. With the word 'turpitude', the immigrant reader is also unlikely to know that the phrase 'moral turpitude' has a particular meaning in law. Likewise, the series 'encouraged, induced, assisted, abetted or aided' refers to specific legal acts as does the phrase 'controlled substances', all of which appear in the same sentence. The terminology of criminal law and especially crimes against the US government is threaded through the questions in Part 3, collectively making even minimal reader comprehension highly unlikely. Only an immigrant who has been processed through a criminal proceeding or a lawyer will be familiar with the terms.

Speech acts: offerings and warnings and their consequences

Speech acts provide another means to assess the comprehensibility of the INS document. The primary speech act of the I-485 document is that of 'offering'. The INS offers to process the application for what they call a 'benefit', but the offering is deeply conditional. The applicant must collect and copy all of the relevant documents and forms, and if the applicant does not file all of the required 'Initial Evidence', then he or she has not 'establish[ed] a basis for eligibility', and the INS can deny the application. The written application is also only a preliminary, as the applicant must go to an INS office 'to answer questions about the application' and 'will be required to answer these questions under oath or affirmation'.

Tucked near the end of the instructions section of the I-485 are two warnings, one of which reads as follows:

> Travel outside the US may trigger the 3- and 10-year bars to admission under section 212(a)(9)(B)(i) of the Act for adjustment applicants, but not registry applicants. This ground of inadmissability is triggered if you were unlawfully present in the US (i.e., you remained in the United States beyond the period of stay authorized by the Attorney General) for more than 180 days before you applied for adjustment of status, and you travel outside of the US while your adjustment of status application is pending.

If the applicant leaves the United States for any reason while the application is pending and has not filed INS Form I-131 and received the 'advance parole document', the applicant may be denied reentry into the United States or the application for permanent residence status denied. It would be difficult for any reader to correctly identify the procedure necessary to travel outside the United States – even just across the border to Mexico or Canada – by reading this warning. The necessary form, the I-131, the Application for Travel Document, is not mentioned. Nor is the actual penalty for not filing the document mentioned. It is, in a sense, an empty warning, but one with severe consequences.

The second 'warning' is actually empty as well. This subsection is called 'Penalties' and relates the following information:

> If you knowingly and willfully falsify or conceal a material fact or submit a false document with this request, we will deny the benefit you are filing for and may deny any other immigration benefit. In addition you will face severe penalties and may be subject to criminal prosecution.

The actual penalty for document fraud, which is what 'knowingly and willfully falsify or conceal a material fact' means, is deportation. That is what denying an immigration benefit means. Rather than simply indicating that the INS will not process the forms or make the applicant start again, it is a serious penalty, and is unlikely to be reversed. Moreover, the connection between filling out the application and this abstract statement of penalties is difficult to make. No actual mention is made of the term 'document fraud' nor of the specific consequences of document fraud in the instructions, nor is there any information on the application itself. At the top of page 3 of the actual application, the instructions note that 'Answering "Yes" does not automatically mean that you are not entitled to adjust your status or register for permanent residence', another multiple clause sentence actually hidden in parentheses. That sentence hardly qualifies as a warning about the penalties for false (or poorly understood) statements. Yet it is those very questions that are likely to produce document fraud at this stage in applicant's movement towards citizenship. We have to wonder if a speech act of warning meets sincerity conditions when the warning itself is perhaps deliberately ambiguous.

The questions themselves in Part 3, page 3, could easily be misunderstood as well. The presentation of the questions suggests that all the questions (and possible 'yes' answers) are equal. Answering 'yes' to question 5 (b), 'Do you intend to engage in the US in any activity a purpose of which is opposition to, or the control or overthrow of, the government of the United States, by force, violence or other lawful means?' will earn the immigrant an almost automatic exit. One wonders what the purpose of such a question might be or who would answer yes if he or she intended to do so. So it would appear that question's purpose might be to pursue 'document fraud' in addition to US criminal prosecution should the applicant turn out to 'oppose' the US government. If answering 'yes' to 5 (b) means the applicant will be refused, question 1 (a) appears to offer the INS an opportunity at any point to discover evidence of a crime of moral turpitude, for which the applicant has never been arrested. If such evidence is discovered, then the applicant has committed document fraud.

There is an additional logical problem with these questions. Though the February, 2000 revision now provides separate yes/no boxes for the a–d parts of questions 1, 3 and the a–c parts of question 5, the fundamental problem for applicants is not resolved. If the answer is 'yes,' let's say, to having 'been arrested', but 'no' to being 'cited, charged, indicted, fined or imprisoned', how is the applicant to respond? Neither yes nor no as presented on the form is an adequate response. Neither response is correct for all of the things in the question. Yes/no questions about singular acts prevent this logical problem. Combined with the facts discussed above – poor document design and difficult sentence structure and vocabulary – it would be something of a wonder than any applicant actually comprehends what is at stake. If a highly-proficient, well-educated, native speaker of English has difficulties with the document, then the audience for I-485, alien applicants, will have even greater comprehension difficulties.

Moreover, the alien applicant faces significant consequences for such a misunderstanding.

Conclusion

As it turned out, my declaration in the appeal had little effect, as the case was decided on other issues. I don't think, however, that means the forensic linguist can have no impact on these problems with the INS documents and the barrier they represent to immigrants. While in the particular case I worked on, comprehension was not the key issue, the 9th Circuit finding in *Walters* v. *Reno* certainly did make comprehension central. Moreover, linguists have already amassed a great deal of information about how to improve these documents. The lack of political representation for immigrants is ultimately a grave problem, but the interest of academic and forensic linguists in the problem issue provide an alternative pathway towards better documents. I address each of these points briefly in these concluding remarks.

While it is usually through litigation that document changes have occurred, the litigation itself does provide a vehicle for improving the documents. Without being an outright advocate for a 'side', (the importance of which Shuy in this volume underlines) the linguist can and should provide a descriptive framework for assessing the ways in which the documents block an applicant's understanding of what he or she is being asked. Moreover, once the litigation is concluded and the agency involved is attempting to respond to court direction, the linguist can also play a role. Shuy's (1998) book, *Bureaucratic Language in Government and Business* provides ample evidence of the usefulness of linguistic input into improving documents. In chapter 2, 'Training a Bureaucracy to Write Clearly: A Case Study of the Social Security Administration', Shuy describes a training programme, deeply informed by applied linguistics and discourse analysis, for agency writers of notices to the agency's constituents. In defining bureaucratic language, he notes that '[t]he real forces are, of course, the law and regulations that government bureaucrats begin with' (Shuy, 1998, p. 180), and in the case of the Immigration and Naturalization Service, the 'law' is imported straight into documents that allege to communicate with immigrant applicants. Shuy argues for an active role of linguists in the process of change, whether through agency consultation or participation as an expert in litigation.

Yet the issues with the documents of the Immigration and Naturalization Service are caught in a wider discourse about immigration to the USA in general. As I suggested in the introduction, the imagery of immigrants overwhelming the citizens sends a powerful and xenophobic message. Congressional legislation has confirmed to the Service that keeping the barriers high is of critical importance. The relatively recent legislation requiring removal of legal permanent residents who had committed a crime at any point in the past have produced poignant stories of people torn from their work, their families and their communities over relatively minor offences that the INS did not contest at the time of their original 'adjustment of status' to permanent residence. If the agency's primary purpose is to 'alien removal', then improving documents for those same aliens to increase their movement towards citizenship will not be a priority. Thus, Shuy's (1998) observation that litigation is critical remains relevant with INS documents.

Recent agency statistics demonstrate a most interesting anomaly. In an estimation of the number of permanent residents eligible to apply for naturalization, the INS estimates that there are 5.8 million who are eligible and have not applied for citizenship (www.ins.usdoj.gov/graphics/aboutins/statistics/lprest.htm). Moreover, the INS estimates that another 687 000 children would become citizens if their parents proceeded through naturalization. But it is easy to imagine that going through the process of applying is hardly a welcome invitation. The INS cautions:

> Immigrants must meet other requirements to become a US citizen such as demonstrating good moral character and knowledge of English and US civics. These qualifications, which would tend to lower the number of persons eligible for naturalization, have not been taken into account in the estimates.
>
> Ibid.

Whatever their reasons for not applying, there are 5.8 million legal permanent residents in the USA who work, who pay taxes, who send their children to state schools, who are under obligations of military service, and who contribute to their communities, but who also cannot vote. And without voting, they can have very little impact on government policies.

I want to suggest a small role for linguists in the process. As I suggested above, linguists can and should involve themselves in the litigation process. But as concerned citizens, we can also be a part of providing both the agency and our own US government representatives with evidence of the comprehension problems with INS documents. Any changes in the documents are announced and followed by a public comment period. Moreover, the Office of Management and Budget reviews all government forms as a part of the Paperwork Reduction Act, so there is an additional agency involved as well. We can and should be a part of these two processes as well. Ninety-four of the INS forms are available online, so I invite you to select any form directed at an immigrant applicant and use your linguistic expertise in breaking down the textual barriers.

Notes

1 See my 'Texts in Oral Context: The "Transmission" of Jury Instructions in an Indiana Court', in C. Bazerman and J. Paradis (eds) (1991) *Textual Dynamics of the Professions*, Madison, WI: University of Wisconsin Press; Dumas, B. (2000) 'US Pattern Jury Instructions: Problems and Proposals' in *Forensic Linguistics* vol. 7(1), pp. 49–71;

and Tiersma, P. (1993) 'Reforming the Language of Jury Instructions', 22 *Hofstra Law Review* 37, pp. 42–52. Both Dumas and Tiersma have served or are currently serving on either bar or statewide court committees to reform pattern jury instructions.

2   See the report from the American Institutes for Research, Siegel & Gale, Inc., and Carnegie-Mellon University, 'Technical Assistance and Training from the Document Design Project', Final Report, ERIC ED 221868 (1981), in which the project examined the INS forms, among those of a number of federal agencies. A scan of INS forms available online shows a number of forms last revised in the early 1980s.

3   These design principles are found in a large number of technical communications textbooks, the most widely used and cited being Paul Anderson's (1998) *Technical Communication: A Reader Centered Approach*, 4th edn, Fort Worth, TX: Harcourt; and Karen Schriver's (1997) *Dynamics of Document Design: Creating Texts for Readers*, New York: Wiley.

4   *Serif* type has projections from the top or bottom of the main stroke of the letter. Times Roman or Times New Roman are commonly-used *serif* types. *Sans serif* types do not have the projections and are more contemporary typefaces. *Serif* types are thought by some graphic designers to promote horizontal flow for the reader. However, most contemporary adult readers have experienced *sans serif* throughout their educational experiences. *Sans serif* types are preferable for readers at small type sizes.

5   David Mellinkoff's (1963) classic, *The Language of the Law*, Boston: Little, Brown, devotes considerable space to these issues, especially in terms of legal vocabulary. More recently, Peter Tiersma's (1999) book *Legal Language*, Chicago: University of Chicago Press, considers legal vocabulary in the larger context of legal discourse practices.

References

Biber, D., Johansson, S., Leech, G., Conrad, S. and Finegan, E. (1999) *Longman Grammar of Spoken and Written English*. Essex. England: Pearson Education.

Collins COBUILD English Dictionary (1995). London: HarperCollins.

Dixon, P. (1987) 'The Processing of Organizational Information in Written Directions', *Journal of Memory and Language*, vol. 26, pp. 24–35.

Dumas, B. (2000) 'US Pattern Jury Instructions: Problems and Proposals', *Forensic Linguistics*, vol. 7(1), pp. 49–71.

Elwork, A., Sales, B. D. and Alfini, J. J. (1982) *Making Jury Instructions Understandable.* Charlottesville, VA: Michie.

Fuqua, R. W. and Phye, G. D. (1978) 'The Effects of Physical Structure and Semantic Organization on the Recall of Prose', *Contemporary Educational Psychology*, vol. 3, pp. 105–17.

Holmes, V. M., Kennedy, A. and Murray, W. S. (1987) 'Syntactic Structure and the Garden Path', *Quarterly Journal of Experimental Psychology*, vol. 39, pp. 277–93.

Immigration and Naturalization Service, 'State Population Estimates: Legal Permanent Residents and Aliens Eligible to Apply for Naturalization' <http://www.ins.usdoj.gov/aboutins/statistics/lprest.htm>

Irwin, J. W. (1980) 'The Effects of Explicitness and Clause Order on the Comprehension of Reversible Causal Relations', *Reading Research Quarterly*, vol. 14, pp. 477–89.

Kress, G. and van Leeuwen, T. (1996) *Reading Images: The Grammar of Visual Design.* London: Routledge.

Larkin, W. and Burns, D. (1977) 'Sentence Comprehension and Memory for Embedded Structure', *Memory and Cognition*, vol. 5(1), pp. 17–22.

Loman, N. L. and Mayer, R. E. (1980) 'Signaling Techniques that Increase the Readability of Expository Prose', *Journal of Educational Psychology*, vol. 75(3), pp. 402–12.

Matthews, A. and Chodorow, M. S. (1988) 'Pronoun Ambiguity in Two-Clause Sentences: Effects of Ambiguity, Antecedent Location, and Depth of Embedding', *Journal of Memory and Language*, vol. 27, pp. 245–60.

Oxford English Dictionary (1998). Oxford: Oxford University Press.

Philips, S. U. (1985) 'Strategies of Clarification in Judges' Use of Language: From the Written to the Spoken', *Discourse Processes*, vol. 8, pp. 421–36.

Shuy, R. W. (1998) *Bureaucratic Language in Government and Business*. Washington, DC: Georgetown University Press.

Spryridakis, J. H. and Wenger, M. J. (1992) 'Writing for Human Performance: Relating Reading Research to Document Design', *Technical Communication*, vol. 39(2), pp. 202–15.

Spyridakis, J. H. and Standal, T. C. (1987) 'Signals in Expository Prose: Effects on Reading Comprehension', *Reading Research Quarterly*, vol. 22(3), pp. 285–98.

Takacs, S. (1999) 'Alien-Nation: Immigration, National Identity and Transnationalism', *Cultural Studies*, vol. 13(4), pp. 591–620.

Tiersma, P. M. (1999) *Legal Language*. Chicago: University of Chicago Press.

Cases cited

Davis v. *United States*, 114 S.Ct. 2350 (1994).

El Rescate v. *Executive Office of Immigration Review*, 941 F.2d 950 (9th Cir. 1991).

Salameda v. *Immigration and Naturalization Service*, 70 F.3d 447 (7th Cir. 1995).

Walters v. *Reno*, 145 F.3d 1032 (9th Cir. 1998).

4

The Language and Law of Product Warnings[1]

Peter M. Tiersma

Product liability is a relatively recent development in the law. Products can be dangerous – and thus lead to liability by the manufacturer or seller – for a variety of reasons. Sometimes they are poorly designed; or they might be defectively manufactured. Increasingly, however, manufacturers and sellers of products are held liable because they failed to warn consumers of potential risks or dangers associated with their use.

If a product is inherently dangerous, it should probably not be sold to the public at all. There are many products, however, that serve a useful function but nonetheless can pose a risk to users under certain circumstances, even if the product is designed and manufactured as carefully as possible. In such cases, it makes sense to allow the product to be sold, but there obviously needs to be an adequate warning given to users. Thus, rubbing alcohol (isopropyl alcohol) has many beneficial applications, but drinking it is not one of them. In light of the temptation that some people might have to do so, purchasers of such alcohol should be clearly warned not to drink it.

To be effective and to render safe a product that might otherwise be overly dangerous, a warning must clearly communicate all relevant risks to the consumer. All too often, warnings are not particularly effective; that is the topic of this article. Although the focus will be on American law, the problems and solutions apply to any legal system in an industrialised nation.

The legal standard

Although it might seem self-evident that product warnings are good and that the legal system should generally require more of them rather than fewer, this has never been the law. Some risks or dangers might be relatively rare, for example, and arguably a manufacturer cannot be expected to warn against every conceivable risk. According to the highly respected Restatement of Torts, a manufacturer or supplier therefore has a duty to warn users or consumers only if it knows or should have known of the danger.[2] Moreover, there is no duty to warn of dangers that are obvious or widely known to users.[3] An example is that a manufacturer does not have to warn professional electricians about the dangers of using standard electrical equipment.[4]

Yet, on many other occasions, a risk posed by a product is sufficiently likely and non-obvious that the manufacturer has a duty to warn. According to the proposed new Restatement of Torts:

> a product is defective because of inadequate instructions when the foreseeable risk of harm posed by the product could have been reduced by the provision of reasonable instructions or warnings by the seller...and the omission of the instructions or warnings renders the product not reasonably safe.[5]

Nonetheless, we will probably never occupy a utopia in which every object that we use in our daily lives is completely safe for all users. Indeed, I imagine that most of us would not want to live in a sanitised world completely devoid of risk and danger. And as long as risk and danger exist, we will need warnings.

What constitutes an adequate warning?

Where someone has a duty to warn, the legal standard is that it must be 'adequate'.[6] One court has explained this standard as depending 'on the language used and the impression that the language is calculated to make upon the mind of the average user of the product'.[7] In the words of another court: an adequate warning is one 'in such form that could reasonably be expected to catch the attention of a reasonably prudent man in the circumstances of its use' and whose content is understandable and conveys 'a fair indication of the nature and extent of the danger' to that person.[8]

One of the basic features of an adequate warning is that it must be calculated to come to the attention of the user. Thus, one court held that a jury could properly conclude that a warning about leaking gas in a motorcycle, placed in ordinary print on page 13 of the user's manual, was not sufficiently prominent to draw the attention of the user.[9] Phrased differently, this is simply not an effective way to communicate a potentially serious danger. The same point has been made in the context of consumer documents like promissory notes, credit purchase agreements, and releases of liability, where the most important provisions from the consumer's perspective are often found in tiny type on the back of the document or other out-of-the-way location (Tiersma, 1999, pp. 220–7).

Not only must a warning attract the attention of the user, but its message must be understandable, and of course what it means for a message to be comprehensible depends on the audience. Consider jury instructions, which constitute another example of communication by professionals to a lay audience. There, the standard is normally that the charge should be understandable to the *average* juror. This means that some jurors will not be able to understand all aspects of the instructions, but most of them should have acquired a good idea of the legal standard after hearing arguments by the lawyers and deliberating with other jurors. The standard regarding comprehensibility of warnings is less clear. The few cases that mention it require a warning to be understandable to the 'ordinarily intelligent person' or the 'average person'.[10] It seems to me that this standard fails to properly account for the differing audiences for warnings. The law does generally recognise that warnings on prescription medicine may be directed to an audience of medical professionals, who are sometimes known as 'learned intermediaries'.[11] Such warnings can therefore be communicated in 'medicalese' rather than ordinary language, because the prescribing doctor is expected to administer the drugs correctly and explain any risks to the patient.

But with most products, where the warning is communicated directly to the end user, we should do better than just warn consumers who are average or above average in terms of language and literacy skills. Surely below average consumers also have the right to safe products! Remember that here – unlike jury instructions – there is no deliberation among the jurors or argument of counsel to explain difficult language.

Research reveals that comprehension is a significant problem with safety warnings. One study found that many warnings on labels of over-the-counter drugs require 11th or 12th-grade reading skills, and in some cases a college education (Pryczak and Roth, 1976, p. 243). Other experts have observed that words such as *accidental, contact, consult* and *persist*, all common in warnings, caused comprehension difficulties (Lehto and Miller, 1988, p. 236). Studies on literacy confirm that a large number of people do not have the reading skills needed to understand warnings and directions on the products they use every day (Marsa, 2000).

Clearly, any standard of comprehensibility aimed at the 'average' or 'reasonable' user will fail to adequately warn a substantial portion of the population. At the least, it seems to me, the standard should be that a warning should be understandable to a substantial majority of users. Consider some actual examples. The following warning is printed on the label of a bottle of isopropyl rubbing alcohol, readily available in American drug stores:

FOR EXTERNAL USE ONLY
Will produce serious gastric disturbances if taken internally.

Anything labeled *alcohol* is likely to seem attractive to some members of our society. The average person probably understands that the phrase *for external use only*, if placed on a bottle of liquid, means 'do not drink'. Yet people who have lesser levels of education might very well think that rubbing alcohol, which is quite cheap, is safe if taken outdoors and drunk in the open air.

The warning continues by stating that if the alcohol is *ingested*, the user should seek medical attention. In other words, 'if someone drinks this, call a doctor immediately'. Why the makers of this substance avoid the perfectly understandable word 'drink', in place of highly formal and obscure terminology like *take internally* and *ingest*, is simply baffling.

Technical terminology also has no place in warnings on products sold to the public. For example, labels on many medical products contain the term *indications*, which explains when the product can or should be used. This is fine when communicating with doctors, but for the general public this usage is quite odd. *Contraindications* – situations in which a medication should not be used – is even worse.

Warnings, further, should not be too weak or indirect. In a case from New Mexico, a medication stated in very small letters that it *may* damage the kidneys. The court held this language too equivocal; it should have said that it *will* damage the kidneys. The warning also used the phrase *in large amounts* but did not specify further, leaving the consumer to guess how much of the medication could be taken before the damage began to occur. Consequently, the court held that the jury could properly have found the warning inadequate.[12]

Linguists have made similar points about overly weak warnings. Dumas (1992), for example, analysed cautionary language on cigarette packages mandated by the federal government, which at one time advised purchasers that smoking *may* be hazardous to your health. It is obviously more effective to state, as did subsequent warnings, that it *is* hazardous to your health. Her study also revealed that the phrase *Cigarette Smoke Contains Carbon Monoxide* was not very effective. Note that it presupposes knowledge that is not provided by the warning, namely, that carbon monoxide is bad for you. The warning also depends on an inferential chain of reasoning: that carbon monoxide is bad for you, that you should therefore not breathe it in, that cigarette smoke contains carbon monoxide, and that therefore you should not smoke cigarettes. As Shuy (1990, p. 296) has observed in the context of warnings on tampons, '[t]he good writer does not provide information about X, then information about Y, and then expect the reader to infer the connection between X and Y'. If smoking is bad for your health, the warning should say so.

Indirection is the problem of saying too little. Equally problematic are warnings that say too much. As the philosopher Grice (1989, p. 26) observed, a general rule of conversation – the 'maxim of quantity' – is that speakers should say enough for purposes of a particular exchange, but not too much.

This principle applies to product liability. Pointing out too many dangers, especially those that are less serious or likely to occur, has the effect of diluting or trivialising more important warnings. Information overload is not the only drawback of listing many risks. On a more practical level, the product may not have space for a label listing all dangers. At least one court has held that listing all the 10 or more hazards associated with use of a drill would have undermined the warning's effectiveness. In such situations, the following language was adequate:

CAUTION: For Safe Operation See Owner's Manual.[13]

Of course, if the owner's manual is full of marginally relevant warnings, information overload remains a problem.

Perhaps a more serious issue is that many manufacturers provide a mixed message that undermines clear communication. One case involved a cleaning product called *Safety Kleen*. The name was prominently displayed on all four sides of the can in which it was sold. The can had a label – in much smaller letters – that warned of the danger of using it in a poorly ventilated area. That label might have been adequate under other circumstances, but here the product name arguably diluted the warning and rendered it inadequate.[14] A similar result was reached with safety glasses called *Sure-Guard* and *Super Armorplate*; the court upheld a jury verdict finding inadequate a warning in very small letters that *lenses are impact resistant but not unbreakable*.[15]

Several linguistic factors may be at play here. One is that typesize is a way of emphasising or downplaying information. Important or urgent messages are spoken loudly or shouted for emphasis in speech. In a written text, large letters carry out that function. Faced with an apparent contradiction between the name of a product in large print (*Sure-Guard*) and a warning in much smaller letters that the product is not unbreakable, we tend to give more credence to the emphasised message. We also read messages in context and assume – barring indications to the contrary – that a speaker is rational and is providing relevant information. This relates to another of Grice's maxims of conversation: that a speaker's contribution should be relevant – the 'maxim of relation'. Faced with apparently conflicting messages from the same speaker, we try to treat each as relevant to what the speaker is trying to communicate. We might therefore conclude that Sure-Guard glasses will guard the eyes under all normal conditions and break only in highly unusual circumstances, perhaps after intentional abuse.

Overall, the legal standards imposed on warnings by court decisions are a mixed bag. Courts have shown concern for issues such as type size, the location of the warning, the problem of mixed messages, overly weak warnings, and information overload. Most courts have not, however, given any substance to the requirement that the warning be adequate in a linguistic sense. Few published judicial opinions have explicitly considered whether a specific warning really is comprehensible, even though it should be clear from this discussion that many warnings are not. Moreover, by adhering to the overall standard that the warnings must be understandable to the 'average' user, courts have allowed manufacturers to provide warnings that are almost surely not comprehensible to vast numbers of adult Americans.

Bilingual warnings

The legal standard requiring adequate warnings is even more difficult to apply when users of a product speak limited English. We have seen that, to be effective, warnings must take their audience into account. Warnings to doctors or other specialists can be made in technical language or jargon of the trade, and the doctors will 'translate' the warning to the end users of the product. Warnings to ordinary consumers should at least be understandable to most potential users; ideally, they should comprehensible to *any* anticipated user.

The situation is complicated when anticipated or foreseeable users are not speakers of English. In the United States warnings must obviously be provided in English, but whether they must also be given in one or more of the hundreds of other languages spoken there is less clear. *Stanley Industries, Inc.* v. *W.M. Barr and Co., Inc.* involved a fire that was allegedly caused by the use of linseed oil, which can apparently cause rags to spontaneously burst into flames. The injured workers primarily spoke Spanish, but the label on the product was only in English and contained no symbols or graphics warning of danger. The plaintiffs contended that the manufacturer had a duty to warn of the danger in Spanish because it advertised and promoted its products in that language. The defendant manufacturer, on the other hand, claimed that the English warning was sufficient. The court ultimately ruled against the defendant, holding that it was up to the jury to decide whether the manufacturer should reasonably have foreseen that Spanish-speaking workers would use the product.[16] Other cases have followed this rule as well, basically stating that an English warning may be insufficient if the manufacturer could have foreseen that non-English-speaking users would not understand the warning.[17]

A different approach was taken recently by the California Supreme Court in *Ramirez* v. *Plough*. When he was a few months old, Jorge Ramirez had a viral infection, for which his mother gave him St Josephs Aspirin for Children. Not long after, his condition worsened and at the time of trial Jorge suffered from serious brain damage. The manufacturer warned users not to give its aspirin to children with viral infections like colds or the flu, but his mother, originally from Mexico, did not read English. The issue was whether the manufacturer had a duty to provide a similar warning in Spanish. The manufacturer sometimes advertised in that language, and it was surely foreseeable that the aspirin would be used by Spanish speakers, especially in California with its millions of Spanish speakers.[18]

The California Supreme Court rejected use of the foreseeability test in this context. It noted that federal regulations do not require warnings in languages other than English, and it also alluded to the burden of warning in the many languages spoken in the state.

A concurring opinion by Justice Mosk pointed to the fact that the manufacturer advertised its product in Spanish. He suggested that manufacturers should have a duty to warn in a particular language if they advertise in it. This approach seems fair enough for speakers of major languages, such as Spanish speakers in the United States where advertising in the language has become fairly common, but it does nothing to help millions of people who speak other languages. It is arguably an improvement over the present situation, but would still leave a substantial number of people unwarned.

A possible solution is the use of symbols, which, to some extent, can transcend language and be understood by just about anyone. Consider traffic signs in Europe, which make heavy use of symbols in place of words. In the same way, a skull and crossbones is a fairly commonly recognised symbol for poison.

More useful, perhaps, are pictograms, which visually represent an action or object (as opposed to more abstract symbols like the skull and crossbones). A pictogram that commonly appears on labels attached to ladders, at least in Europe, is a picture of a person standing on the top rung but who is clearly losing his balance. In Australia one sometimes sees the silhouette of a kangaroo on signs along the road to warn motorists to watch out for these animals. Arguably, even pictograms are culturally determined to some extent, but generally their message is more recognisable to untrained viewers than abstract symbols.

Some courts have endorsed symbolic or pictographic warnings when a product is likely to be used by speakers of languages other than English.[19] Judges have at times specifically suggested that pictograms or symbols could be used instead of bilingual warnings.[20] In a case involving non-English-speaking farmworkers injured by pesticides, the court observed that the label was in English only and lacked 'skull and bones, or other comparable symbols or hieroglyphics.'[21] Moreover, governmental regulations sometimes encourage or require the use of certain symbols. Thus, federal law requires products with a certain percentage of benzene to display a skull and crossbones symbol (16 CFR § 1500.14 (b)(3)).

Despite their utility, symbols and pictograms – like all non-verbal communication – have several limitations. Compared to language, gestures or symbols typically communicate only a narrow range of messages. How should an aspirin manufacturer communicate via symbols or pictograms that aspirin should not be given to young children who have a viral infection? Moreover, symbols and gestures differ from culture to culture (Birdwhistell, 1970); consequently, the meaning of such symbols must be learned and there is no guarantee that speakers of Spanish, Hmong or Tamil will understand them. A European or American would realise that a circle with a diagonal line through it means that a specified activity is prohibited, but a Mayan immigrant from rural Guatemala might not.

Colour can also be given significance in warning schemes. For example, federal regulations regarding accident-prevention signs in the workplace mandate that 'danger' signs be black, red and white, while 'caution' signs (for less immediate hazards) be black and yellow (29 CFR§ 1910.145). Yet colour, likewise, has its limitations as a means of communication. Obviously, once a colour scheme is learned it can be very helpful in quick and effective communication. Anyone who has ever driven an automobile knows the significance of red, green and yellow on a traffic signal, but generally the meaning attributed to a colour is something that must be acquired. Colours do have certain associations, of course. In many western cultures, red signifies anger, green is associated with envy, white with goodness and purity, and black with evil and death. These cultural associations do little to explain why, on traffic signals, red means 'stop' and green means 'go.' Moreover, these associations are not universal. In some Asian cultures, the colour white is identified with death. To the extent that colours on warning labels or signs are viewed, like symbols or emblems, as a means of overcoming the problems of multilingualism, the effort can only succeed if the colour schemes are adopted and learned throughout the world.

Research confirms these conclusions. Experts have found that safety symbols related to hazards, especially those dealing with unfamiliar or abstract topics, are not well-understood – often by fewer than 50 per cent of the test subjects. Pictograms, as opposed to abstract symbols, do quite a bit better. Additionally, many warning symbols are not understood across cultures. One study found that Vietnamese immigrants had 'profound misunderstanding' of symbols understood by Europeans. Even within Anglo-American culture, studies have shown that people often poorly understand the meaning of safety symbols and pictograms (Lehto and Miller, 1988, pp. 238–45); consider, for instance, the biological hazard symbol reproduced in Figure 4.1.

A case that illustrates the problem of using symbols and colours is *Tarshis v. Lahaina Investment Corporation.*[22] Tarshis was a guest at a seaside hotel in Hawaii. She saw red flags along the beach, apparently thought little of them, and entered the water; she was injured when a large wave knocked her down and later sued the hotel for her injuries. Let us assume that the hotel had a duty to warn her if water conditions were dangerous (the hotel apparently advertised that 'the sea is safe and exhilarating for swimming'). Did the red flags on the beach constitute an understandable warning? After all, red does mean 'stop' on traffic signals. But it can also symbolise communism or anarchism, or it can be purely decorative. The hotel must have recognised this problem because it placed warning signs near the beach explaining that red flags meant the surf was dangerous. The issue for the jury would thus have boiled down to whether Tarshis should have seen those signs. For us, the lesson is that if symbols need written signs explaining what they mean, then those symbols by themselves are not very effective; they are certainly not going to warn vacationers who cannot read the English on the sign.

Perhaps the lesson is that in a multilingual and multicultural country like the United States (and, to an increasing extent, all industrialised nations), there is no single way to communicate an effective warning. Depending on

Figure 4.1   Biological hazard symbol
Source: 29 CFR § 1910.145.

the type of product, where it is advertised and sold, and who is likely to use it, warnings will have to reach the attention of the broadest possible audience without becoming so long and convoluted that consumers begin to ignore them.

Better warnings

Every year, according to the American Society of Orthopedic Surgeons, over half a million Americans are injured and 300 of them die while using ladders.[23] Many other people are harmed or killed while using other products at work, in the household or during recreation. Quite a few of these 'accidents' no doubt would have happened even with the best of product designs, production and warnings. Still, effective warnings play an important role in educating consumers and reducing injuries and fatalities, and it is therefore worth considering how to produce better warnings.

First, let us step back and consider what it means to warn someone. An analysis by Fraser (1998, p. 164) concludes that a warning involves the speaker expressing to the addressee:

1   the belief that some unfavorable state of the world exists (*The ice is thin*) or will exist (*I'm going to turn on the sprinklers*);
2   the belief that this state of the world is unfavorable to the addressee's best interests;
3   the intent to inform the addressee before a harmful effect can ensue.

Fraser was not concerned with product warnings, so it may not be entirely appropriate to use his definition in this context. Nonetheless, his approach seems correct as far as it goes and is a good starting point for our analysis. There are many examples of statements intended to inform the addressee of an unfavourable state of affairs that clearly count as warnings. Thus, a warning might inform a hiker that there are dangerous cliffs ahead, or the user of a product that it is harmful if swallowed. Notice that we can say that I 'warned' her that there were dangerous cliffs ahead, or I 'warned' her that swallowing the product was harmful.

Yet there is another way of commonly warning people that does not fall within Fraser's definition. We often warn by using an imperative construction that directs the addressee not to engage in some dangerous activity, or to do something that will avoid the harm. *Stay on the trail* can function as a warning. The same is true for *don't swallow this product*. Note that I can again say that I 'warned' her to stay on the trail, or that I 'warned' her not to drink the product. Also noteworthy is that often these two types of warnings are combined. I could warn the hiker by saying: *dangerous cliffs ahead – stay on the trail*. Or I could tell the consumer of a product containing methanol: *do not drink – this product is harmful if swallowed*.

One way of making sense of this issue is to suggest that Fraser is correct after all and that the prototypical warning is indeed informational rather than imperative. The imperative style can constitute a warning under this approach, but only indirectly. Thus, *do not drink this product* would be a command or suggestion that indirectly warns the addressee (via the maxim of relevance) that drinking the product is dangerous.

Ultimately, however, I am inclined to agree with Vanderveken (1990, p. 174) that the speech act of warning is 'systematically ambiguous between an assertive and directive use'. In other words, warnings can be in either an informational or imperative style. Every warning does a bit of both. An imperative warning (*stay on the trail*) not only orders or advises the hiker, but indirectly communicates that there is some danger lurking off the trail. An informational warning (*dangerous cliffs ahead*) informs the hiker of the danger, but also indirectly suggests or directs the hiker to avoid the danger by staying on the trail.

The fact that all warnings have both an imperative and an informational element does not mean that these two styles of warning are equivalent, however. An imperative warning is generally clearer about how to avoid a danger (*do not drink*) but typically provides less information on the exact nature of the danger. Conversely, an informational warning is generally more specific on the nature of the hazard (*dangerous cliffs ahead*), but leaves it up to the addressee to figure out how to avoid it.

Which approach is more effective? The aim of the legal system, after all, is – or should be – to encourage the most effective warnings, those that best reduce the number and seriousness of injuries. In some cases, an informational warning may be the best possible because there may be no single way to avoid the danger. For instance, a drug manufacturer might warn that a medication may damage the kidneys. An imperative warning may be inappropriate here because there may be no way of predicting whose kidneys will be affected. Elsewhere, an imperative warning may be practically or politically problematic. An effective warning on cigarettes would be both imperative and informational: *do not smoke cigarettes; smoking can kill you.* Many governments will balk at the imperative element, however, given the tax revenues that derive from smoking.

In the area of product liability, it is my view that the goal of harm avoidance is best served by requiring imperative warnings, when feasible. The most important thing that consumers must know is how to avoid a danger. Imperative warnings tell users of a product what they need to know: *do not drink this product* or *use only in a well-ventilated area.* At the same time, an informational warning can be a useful backup. Moreover, by understanding the nature and potential severity of a risk, consumers are more likely to heed critical warnings. The ideal, therefore, would be to have both an informational and imperative warning. When that is not possible, or when it would be entirely redundant, the imperative warning should be preferred. I hasten to add that this question is open to empirical testing, which is ltimately how the issue should be resolved.

Now that we have a better idea of the nature of warnings, we can compare the above analysis with theory and practice in the real world. It turns out that not only the legal system, but also government regulators and product manufacturers themselves have devoted quite a bit of attention to the problem. For example, the American National Standards Institute (ANSI) has developed guidelines for product warnings, and recommends that warnings begin with consistent signal words (*danger, caution,* etc.), followed by a pictogram or symbol.[24] They also recommend that the colour of the label should be correlated to the seriousness of the warning. As discussed previously, symbols and colours have the disadvantage that their meaning generally has to be learned, but once this has been accomplished, they can help users readily identify the nature of a danger.

Probably most important for consumers is the content of the warning itself. According to ANSI, the hazard should be identified, followed by the result of ignoring the warning, and finally instructions on how to avoid hazards. Shuy (1998, p. 171), discussing these standards, suggests a slightly different list of elements in an effective product warning:

1 Tell what the hazard is;
2 Tell how to avoid the hazard;
3 Tell what to do if a person is injured by the hazard.

Both of these lists seem to recognise, at least implicitly, the dual nature of warnings. Each requires that the warning inform the user of the danger or hazard, and that it direct the user how to avoid being harmed. What is not entirely evident, and therefore bears emphasising, is that the directive aspect of the warning should normally be in the form of an imperative; this is the most common and direct way of instructing the user on how to steer clear of harm.

Most products should not be sold to consumers unless there is a reasonable way to prevent foreseeable risks from happening and the manufacturer communicates this information to users. It should not suffice to simply inform users that a certain dishwashing soap may cause blindness. The manufacturer should also tell users to wear safety goggles, or to use it only in certain sorts of dishwashing machines. In other words, *this soap can cause blindness* might constitute a warning, linguistically speaking, but should not be considered effective in legal terms.

Another difference between the ordinary understanding of warnings and legal requirements is that normally a warning is not expected to inform users of what to do when a risk becomes reality. Often enough, of course, people will know what to do. Most folks should have the good sense to call paramedics if someone falls off a ladder and is seriously injured. On other occasions, however, the best course of action may not be self-evident. A legally adequate warning will not only direct users not to swallow a substance, but should also tell them how to react if they do. Thus, a heavy-duty cleaner in my house advises users who accidentally swallow it not to induce vomiting, but to call a physician, drink large quantities of water, and take several tablespoons of milk of magnesia.

Of course, the description of the risks and directions on how to avoid them should be in plain, ordinary language typified by active constructions, concrete nouns, action verbs, strong auxiliary verbs such as *can* or *will*, and other characteristics of comprehensible language. Consider again the warning on my bottle of isopropyl rubbing alcohol:

FOR EXTERNAL USE ONLY
Will produce serious gastric disturbances if taken internally.

It also advises users that *[i]n case of accidental ingestion, seek professional assistance or contact a Poison Control Center immediately*.

In plain English, the warning should begin with the most important message in imperative form: *do not drink*. As noted previously, some users may think that *external use* means that it is fine to drink it outside. The explanation that follows about *gastric disturbances* (an informational warning) is appropriate, but would be more comprehensible if it told users that *you will get severe stomach problems*, or something along those lines. The term *accidental ingestion* will also not be understood by a substantial number of users, and in any event it does not matter if the ingestion is accidental or on purpose; in either event, it must be promptly treated. Thus, *if you drink this product, go to a doctor or get other medical help immediately.*

One of the reasons that items like rubbing alcohol still have warnings that are less than ideal is that they are not subject to intense governmental regulation. With most products, the manufacturer is responsible for the wording of the warning, subject to the legal rules laid out at the beginning of this chapter. We have seen that the courts, though adhering to the principle that a warning must be adequate, tend to be rather lax in practice. Indirect warnings, information overload, and the requirement that the warning be understandable to 'average' users all undercut that standard. Finally, the adequacy of the language of a warning is typically a jury question, which is not always conducive to consistent decision-making. It is therefore not all that surprising that the legal standard for warnings is not particularly clear.

One way to improve the situation would be for lawyers who bring product liability lawsuits to become better informed about the linguistic issues posed by warnings. The legal profession has until now been mainly concerned with *whether* a warning should be required and, if so, the *content* of the warning. It has given relatively little attention to the issue of *how* the content is conveyed. And even then, most of the emphasis, to judge from the published legal decisions discussed above, has been on factors like type size and placement of the warning rather than on whether the message is comprehensible.

This is an area in which linguists could provide a useful service. If enough lawyers involved in product liability were aware of the problem and raised it in litigation, with the assistance of linguistic experts, the issue would eventually reach the appellate courts. Because the published opinions of courts of appeal establish binding precedent, a few opinions emphasising that warnings should truly be comprehensible for the great majority of consumers could reach the attention of manufacturers and lead to improvement in this area of the law.

The other main route towards obtaining more effective and understandable warnings is through governmental regulation. For example, the Food and Drug Administration (FDA) has for some time had fairly specific rules relating to the labelling of drugs. Interestingly, as opposed to the common law standard, the FDA requires that warning labels must be 'likely to be read and understood by the ordinary individual, including individuals of low comprehension, under ordinary conditions of purchase and use' (21 CFR § 330.10(a)(4)(v) (1993)).

In the late 1990s the FDA undertook a revision of its labelling requirements for over-the-counter drug products (that is, medications that can be bought without a prescription). Motivated by studies and its own experience, the FDA decided that warnings on such labels should be made more readable and 'user-friendly'. Specifically, the agency proposed the use of less complex terminology, shorter sentences, improved organisation, and a reduction in the 'cognitive load' of the label (64 Federal Register 13,254 (1999)).

Many of the FDA's new labelling rules relate more to readability than to linguistic comprehension, although the two are obviously closely related. Thus, labels must begin with *Drug Facts*, which lists the active ingredients (for example, selenium sulfide 1 per cent) and explains the purpose of the drug (as in *antidandruff*). This is followed by *Uses*, which replaces the obscure but oft-used medicalese term *indications*. Next comes the *Warnings* section, followed by *Directions* and a list of *Inactive Ingredients*. Figure 4.2 illustrates this. Concentrating on the linguistic aspects of the label, there is no doubt that the example in Figure 4.2 is a great improvement over former practice. For example, it straightforwardly tells users: *do not get into eyes*, which is more comprehensible than statements like *avoid contact with eyes*. Rather than being told to *consult a physician*, users are now informed to *ask a doctor*.

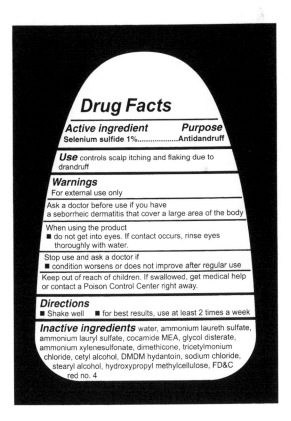

Figure 4.2 FDA label for antidandruff products
Source: 21 CFR § 201.66.

At the same time, the warning still contains the critical language *for external use only*, which – as explained previously – is not particularly clear. And external to what? *External* might refer to the outside of the body, or to the outside of a building. The difficulty lies in the fact that this is a nicely compact phrase that is hard to translate into more ordinary language. *Do not swallow* may not always be an adequate substitute because there are other ways to get substances into the body. Perhaps *use only on the skin* would work in most cases. Although it is somewhat longer, the phrase *use only on the outside of the body* may be the most accurate rendition in plain language.

Perhaps the most interesting feature of the FDA's regulations is that they allow for a large number of terms to be used interchangeably, as long as the meaning of the warning does not change. A few examples (21 CFR § 330.1(i)) follow:

abdominal or *stomach*
administer or *give*
aggravate or *make worse*
assistance or *help*
avoid contact with eyes or *do not get into eyes*.

Because the FDA mandates the specific content of warnings on a large number of drugs and related products, this provision allows manufacturers to substitute more comprehensible language when it can be done without affecting the meaning. Whether such a voluntary approach will work is hard to predict.

The FDA is not the only federal agency promoting more understandable product warnings. As a final illustration, consider Figure 4.3 which reproduces a label now required on charcoal. Burning charcoal in an enclosed area can be deadly because it produces carbon monoxide fumes. This label clearly proclaims that it contains an important warning. However, the pictograms require some cultural knowledge to interpret, especially the significance of placing a large X through an activity. Yet they will undoubtedly be helpful to many people who do not read English. As for those who do read English, the language of the warning seems about as clear as possible.

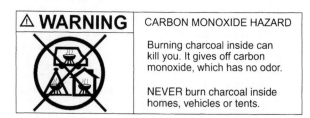

Figure 4.3   Federally-required label for charcoal
Source: 16 CFR § 1500.14(b)(6).

Conclusion

We will probably always use products that can injure us in some way. Even though product safety is, for the most part, continually improving, there will inevitably be useful items that are dangerous in certain situations, and warnings are an essential means of trying to reduce the risks posed by such products. There is no doubt that, overall, warnings are becoming more comprehensible to a larger part of the speech community, and, as we have seen, federal regulatory agencies have definitely been making progress. Unfortunately, such agencies are subject to political pressure. It is worth noting that the changes that have taken place recently were made under President Clinton, whose administration took several initiatives promoting plain language (Tiersma, 1999, p. 221). It remains to be seen whether President Bush and subsequent administrations will sustain these efforts, or possibly even reverse them.

Moreover, the evidence from published appellate opinions reveals a rather mixed picture. This is significant because the warnings on many products are not regulated by the government. Some manufacturers do seem to be making an effort to provide more understandable warnings, yet they often fear that overly ominous-sounding warnings will scare away customers, leading them to downplay the dangers. The history of cigarette warnings is an obvious example. Consider also the notice that I recently saw at a local gasoline station:

Long-term exposure to vapors has caused cancer in laboratory animals
Avoid prolonged breathing of vapors

What the oil company does not want to say is that *breathing gasoline fumes may cause cancer* and *try not to breathe any fumes*. A straightforward message to that effect might frighten customers.

For these reasons we will always need an independent legal system to monitor the effectiveness of warnings. Government regulators are often beholden to special interests; and manufacturers may not want to give adequate warnings because customers might decide not to buy the product. Of course, the legal system moves slowly, and judges and lawyers may not even be aware that a problem exists or how to address it. Further research into this issue, published in accessible places, may make the difference.

Notes

1 Thanks to Richard Haren and Roger Shuy for comments, and to Scott Bishop, a graduate of Loyola Law School, for research assistance.
2 Restatement (Second) of Torts § 402A cmt. j (1965). The Restatement is a type of summary or compilation of American law. See also *Lindsay* v. *Ortho Pharma. Corp.*, 637 F.2d 87, 91 (2d Cir. 1980).

3　See, for example, *Jonescue* v. *Jewel Home Shopping Serv.*, 306 N.E.2d 312, 316 (Ill. Ct. App. 1973); *Hagans* v. *Oliver Mach. Co.*, 576 F.2d 97, 102 (5th Cir. 1978).
4　*DuCote* v. *Liberty Mut. Ins. Co.*, 451 So. 2d 1211, 1215 (La. Ct. App. 1984); *Mackowick* v. *Westinghouse Elec. Corp.*, 575 A.2d 100 (Pa. 1990).
5　See *American Law Institute, Restatement of the Law Third, Torts: Product Liability* § 2 (Tentative Draft No. 1, 1994).
6　*Shell Oil Co.* v. *Gutierrez*, 581 P.2d 271, 277 (Ariz. 1978).
7　*Ortho Pharma. Corp.* v. *Chapman*, 388 N.E.2d 541 (Ind. Ct. App. 1979).
8　*Bituminous Cas. Corp.* v. *Black and Decker Mfg. Co.*, 518 S.W.2d 868, 872–3 (Tex. 1974).
9　*Stapleton* v. *Kawasaki Heavy Industries, Ltd.*, 608 F.2d 571, 573 (5th Cir. 1979). See also *Gordon* v. *Niagara Mach. and Tool Works*, 574 F.2d 1182 (5th Cir. 1978).
10　*Tarshis* v. *Lahaina Investment Corp.*, 480 F.2d 1019, 1020–1 (9th Cir. 1973); *Walton* v. *Sherwin Williams Co.*, 191 F.2d 277, 286 (8th Cir. 1951). See also Jacobs (1992: 127), who comments that warnings must convey their message in a manner intelligible to the average consumer and be adequate with respect to the consumer's experience and his or her literacy level.
11　*Northern Trust Co.* v. *Upjohn Co.*, 572 N.E.2d 1030, 1036 (Ill. Ct. App. 1991); *Incollingo* v. *Ewing*, 282 A.2d 206, 220 (Pa. 1971); *Pierluisi* v. *E. R. Squibb and Sons, Inc.*, 440 F. Supp. 691, 694 (DC Puerto Rico 1977).
12　*Michael* v. *Warner/Chilcott*, 579 P.2d 183, 187 (N.M. Ct. App. 1978).
13　*Broussard* v. *Continental Oil Co.*, 433 So. 2d 354, 358 (La. Ct. App. 1983).
14　*Maize* v. *Atlantic Refining Co.*, 41 A.2d 850, 852 (Pa. 1945). The court held that the adequacy of the warning in this situation could go to the jury.
15　*American Optical Co.* v. *Weidenhamer*, 404 N.E.2d 606, 616–617 (Ind. Ct. App. 1980).
16　784 F. Supp. 1570, 1576 (S.D. Fla. 1992).
17　*Hubbard-Hall Chemical Co.* v. *Silverman*, 340 F.2d 402, 405 (1st Cir. 1965). See also *Building and Const. Trades Dept., AFL-CIO* v. *Brock*, 838 F.2d 1258, 1277 (D.C. Cir. 1988).
18　*Ramirez* v. *Plough, Inc.*, 863 P.2d 167, 175 (Cal. 1993).
19　*Campos* v. *Firestone Tire and Rubber Co*, 485 A.2d 305 (N.J. 1984) (superseded by statute); *Hubbard-Hall Chemical Co.*, 340 F.2d at 405; *Stanley Indus., Inc.*, 784 F. Supp. at 1576; *Torres-Rios* v. *LPS Laboratories*, 152 F.3d 11, 14 (1st Cir. 1998).
20　*Building and Const. Trades Dept.*, 838 F.2d at 1277.
21　*Hubbard-Hall Chemical Co.*, 340 F.2d at 405.
22　480 F.2d 1019 (9th Cir. 1973).
23　U.C. Berkeley Wellness Letter, April 1999, at 8.
24　See Kenneth Ross, 'Legal and Practical Considerations for the Creation of Warning Labels and Instruction Books', in K. Ross and B. Wrubel (eds) (1989), *Product Liability 1989: Warnings, Instructions and Recalls* p. 103. Attachment A contains a draft ANSI standard (ANSI Z535.4), which deals with warning labels. Id. at 119.

References

Birdwhistell, R. (1970) *Kinesics and Context: Essays on Body Motion Communication*. Philadelphia: University of Pennsylvania Press.
Dumas, B. K. (1992) 'Adequacy of Cigarette Package Warnings: An Analysis of the Adequacy of Federally Mandated Cigarette Package Warnings', *Tennessee Law Review*, vol. 59, pp. 261–304.

Fraser, B. (1998) 'Threatening Revisited', *Journal of Forensic Linguistics*, vol. 5, pp. 159–173.

Grice, P. (1989) *Studies in the Way of Words*. Cambridge, MA: Harvard University Press.

Jacobs, M. S. (1992) 'Toward a Process-Based Approach to Failure-to-Warn Law', *N.C. Law Review*, vol. 71, p. 121.

Latin, H. (1994) '"Good" Warnings, Bad Products, and Cognitive Limitations', *UCLA Law Review*, vol. 41, pp. 1193–295.

Lehto, M. R. and Miller, J. M. (1988) 'The Effectiveness of Warning Labels', *Journal of Product Liability*, vol. 11, pp. 225–70.

Marsa, L. (2000) 'Illiteracy can be Hazardous to your Health', *Los Angeles Times*, 31 July, section S1.

Pryczak, F. and Roth D. (1976) 'The Readability of Directions on Non-Prescription Drugs', *Journal of the American Pharmaceutical Association*, vol. 16, pp. 242–51.

Shuy, R. W. (1990) 'Warning Labels: Language, Law and Comprehensibility', *American Speech*, vol. 65, pp. 291–303.

Shuy, R. W. (1998) *Bureaucratic Language in Government and Business*. Washington, DC: Georgetown University Press.

Tiersma, P. M. (1999) *Legal Language*. Chicago: University of Chicago Press.

Vanderveken, D. (1990) *Meaning and Speech Acts, Volume 1: Principles of Language Use*. Cambridge: Cambridge University Press.

Part II

The Language of the Police and the Police Interview

5
'I Just Need to Ask Somebody Some Questions': Sensitivities in Domestic Dispute Calls

Karen Tracy and Robert R. Agne

Introduction

Call 1

A call comes in on 911. A man is hollering saying that a woman needs to be arrested. He states that he was arrested last time and it's her turn. She is downstairs and has 'my baby'. The caller notes that there is a restraining order on him but she has come to his place of work. The man is mad. The call-taker says that he can explain it to the officer. The caller seems to expect that since he requested that she be arrested that she will be. The call-taker informs him that the officer will decide what to do when he arrives. The man ends the conversation after this exchange by saying sarcastically, 'I'll call you back to chat.'

Call 2

A man begins a call to the regular police line by asking, 'Who would I need to speak to? I'm worried about my wife. She needs help for drugs.' The caller mentions that 'there's white stuff in her jewellery box'. He mentions that he tasted it. He goes on to say that she is having an affair, and that the man she is having the affair with has been in their home. The caller notes that they have two kids. He states that at first he didn't do anything about 'it'. He goes on to say that a week ago, 'he lost it'. His wife was attacking him and he hit her back. Because of this, she got a warrant for him. The call-taker keeps asking questions that suggest that the caller has a counselling need; she asks if he wants a referral number to call. The man persists in telling his story. He resists the call-taker's attempt to frame his problem as a request for information about what telephone number to call.[1]

Citizen calls to the police to report disputes they are having with close others often involve communicative trouble: shouting, convoluted accounts, and disparaging remarks are frequent. Simply put, calls about domestic disputes are common sites for interactional trouble between citizens and police call-takers. One reason for this, identified three decades ago (Reiss, 1971), is that citizens lack an adequate understanding of the distinction between criminal, civil and private matters. Citizens expect the police to intervene and do whatever a caller regards as morally right. From the police point of view, however, that is not their job. Only certain kinds of complaints are legitimately within their jurisdiction.

A police call-taker's first job, then, is to determine if a citizen's complaint concerns something about which police action may be taken. By no means, though, is this an easy assessment to make. Determining what exactly is being requested may present a challenge; shaping a caller's complaint so that it may be put into a relevant police category is another. Informing a caller that help cannot be provided is yet another. For the most part, police call-takers recognise that citizen expectations may not match what the institution can provide. In the training manual at Citywest Police, the site for this chapter's discourse analysis, call-takers were warned that, 'frequently people [will] call us with a non-police problem'. In these kinds of situations in which 'no department action may be initiated', call-takers are instructed that they should 'always attempt to provide the caller with acceptable alternatives' (APCO, 1992).

Callers, too, face a delicate communicative task. Describing police-relevant trouble in a close relationship, whether a speaker is the 'victim' or the 'instigator' makes inferable an array of identity-negative implications about the kind of person that a speaker may be. As Bergmann (1998, p. 280) notes, 'When talking about other people it is hardly possible to avoid expressions that do not somehow or other carry a moral meaning ... [M]orality is omnipresent in everyday life.' A citizen, then, could be expected to do conversational work to display the self as a person of reasonable character and/or morality given the situation faced.

Our purpose in this chapter is twofold: (1) to identify key sites of interactional sensitivity in citizen – police calls about domestic trouble, and (2) to describe the conversational practices that reveal and manage these sensitivities. By domestic trouble we mean verbal disagreements and/or physical fighting that occurs between intimates, most often, although not exclusively, family members and lovers. After reviewing past studies about citizen – police calls, we describe the Citywest site, the telephone call base, and our discourse analytic approach. Then, using excerpts from selected telephone calls, we identify three communicatively delicate tasks and discuss how these tasks are managed conversationally.

Past research on citizen – police calls

Studies of emergency communications can be divided into three traditions. A first strand studies police centres and their communicative work in order to address issues of organisational communication. A good example of this tradition is seen in Manning's (1988) ethnographic study of the communications centres in two police departments in Britain and the United States which serve the public. More recent work has sought to understand the emotional demands of call-taking and how call-takers communicatively manage these demands (Shuler, 2001; Tracy and Tracy, 1998).

A second strand of research on citizen – police calls, conversation analytic work, seeks to describe how 911 calls are interactionally structured. We know from this work, for instance, that the most typical emergency call sequence is one that begins with an opening that involves identification and acknowledgment, with greetings usually omitted. Then, there is a request phase with a series of interrogatives to elicit the information needed. Finally there is an announcement of the institutional response, and then calls conclude with a closing exchange (Zimmerman, 1984, 1992). In addition to studies of sequential structures, conversation analytic research has also described the structure of participants' sense-making.

One example of this work is Sharrock and Turner's (1978) notion of conversational equivocality. Complaints by certain categories of persons in particular environments are the grounds for 'equivocality', a conversational phenomenon in which an utterance points to a double interpretation, a literal one and an alternate. Some relationships are common sites for spite (for example, landlord/tenant, homeowner/neighbourhood teens) such that when complaints are offered by one party about the other, there is simultaneously hearable an alternate version. Callers' complaints display awareness of this possible alternate reading.

In the third camp, of which this chapter is an example, Tracy and her colleagues have taken the interactional trouble in citizen–police phone calls as their focal interest. In one study (Tracy, 1997b), the different expectations citizens and the police had regarding appropriate questioning, and decisions about service delivery related to time and geography were described. The difference in expectations, Tracy argued, were the concrete manifestations of a frame mismatch; an event that accounts for much routine interactional trouble (for example, raised voices, hang ups) that occurs in calls. In another study (Tracy and Tracy, 1998), two 'rude' 911 calls were analysed to identify the conversational practices that comprised face attack (Goffman, 1955).

In a further study (Tracy and Anderson, 1999), the difficulties citizens face when they want to get help from the police to deal with a non-serious problem involving someone with whom they have a connection was investigated. Because there is a cultural expectation that one should avoid getting known others in trouble with the police – unless it is serious – citizens do conversational work to minimise or mask their degree of relationship closeness with the complained-about other. Four relational positioning strategies were identified that citizens use to do this.

In this chapter we seek to unpack a different kind of trouble: the interactional sensitivities faced by callers and call-takers in managing reports about domestic disputes. First, some background on materials and method.

Citywest Emergency Center and the telephone calls

Citywest Center is located in a major Western city in the United States and coordinates dispatch of police, fire and paramedic services for the entire city. At the centre, civilian call-takers, trained by and working for the police department, answer 911 calls and calls to the regular police dispatch number. While on a shift, call-takers are assigned to either regular police dispatch lines or 911; should 911 call volume become heavy, call-takers on police dispatch will also take 911 calls. With computer-aided dispatch, call-takers forward key information gleaned in the calls to police dispatchers (all civilians), or in calls in which paramedic or fire services are required forward the call itself and its accompanying ANI/ALI information (automatic telephone number and location information) to fire and paramedic dispatchers.

The analysis in this chapter draws on several kinds of materials collected by a two-person[2] research team over a 10-month time period. For each call, the research team constructed a written record in which the content of the call, its time of occurrence and several other details were identified. Interactional features that seemed communicatively interesting were noted. Approximately 60 calls from this data set have been transcribed using a simplified version of the Jeffersonian transcription system (Atkinson and Heritage, 1984).[3] In addition to the recorded telephone calls, this analysis draws on field observation notes and training and policy manuals (see Tracy, 1997a, for details).

Action-implicative discourse analysis (AIDA)

The selection of calls, analytic focus and reasoning procedures for assessing claims uses action-implicative discourse analysis (Tracy, 1995, 2001). AIDA is a type of discourse analysis that builds upon a variety of traditions, including pragmatics (Brown and Levinson, 1987), conversation analytic studies of institutional discourse (Drew and Heritage, 1992), discursive psychology (Edwards and Potter, 1992) and critical discourse approaches (Fairclough and Wodak, 1997), and combines them to address an intellectual agenda distinctive to the field of communication (Craig, 1989, 1995, 1996; Craig and Tracy, 1995). In particular, AIDA is interested in identifying problems of communicative practices (from multiple participants' viewpoints), conversational techniques for managing the problems, and participants' beliefs about how conduct in this practice ought to proceed. No single study need address all concerns but an action-implicative discourse analysis will take at least one as a central concern. In this chapter, our focus is on describing the conversational practices that reveal and attempt to manage the interactional sensitivities in domestic dispute calls.

Practices that mark call sensitivity

Sensitivity 1: callers license a long and complex narrative

In emergency telephone calls, callers' openings typically provide some reason for the call, and Zimmerman (1992a) described a range of openings that callers use. Citizens may open with a request for what they need (for example, 'would you send the police to...') or they may formulate a report or a description of the problem in which the call-taker must translate whatever is said to the type of dispatch required (if any). Narratives are also common openings. Callers describe mundane events around them or activities they were doing before the trouble began and then the trouble that implies what is needed (for example, 'I was just sitting in my living room watching TV when I heard gunshots in the alley').

In domestic disputes, calls to the police often have openings that do not immediately give a reason for calling. Rather, callers' openings function to license the telling of a complicated, not-straightforward narrative. Domestic disputes, by definition, involve trouble in close relationships. That initiating a call about domestic trouble is regarded as sensitive by callers is cued in the opening moment of citizen calls. Rather than the relatively straightforward approaches that are most common in emergency calls (Zimmerman, 1992a), a set of conversational practices are used that cue that an explanatory story is needed before the citizen can make the request. Features in telephone openings vary somewhat depending on whether the call is to the 911 or the non-emergency police dispatch line, but in each case callers do conversational work to license a narrative.

A first practice, seen primarily on the 911 line, is to problematise the assumed precondition for making an emergency call. Excerpt 1 illustrates how this may be done:

Excerpt 1
Tape 2, call 117, female C, male CT

1 CT Citywest police do you have an emergency?
2 C   Well, I don't know if it's an emergency.
3 CT S'okay, go ahead.
4 C   Um I just got in a fight with my fiancé an:: the wedding got broken off, and
5   he's smashing things all over the apartment, So I would ( ) that he leave my
6   place and he's not leaving.

Callers in non-domestic dispute situations (calling the 911 line) also open by denying that the situation they are calling about is an emergency. For example, a citizen may say, 'No, this is not an emergency but I wanta make a noise complaint.' Excerpt 1, however, is slightly different. The caller (C) does not merely deny that the category of emergency applies, rather her comment points to some difficulty of categorising the event about which she is calling. By saying, 'Well, I don't know if it's an emergency' (line 2), she makes visible a degree of complexity in her upcoming event report. This remark, in turn, prompts the call-taker (CT) to invite an explanation at a greater level of detail. The call-taker's 'S'okay' and 'go ahead' licenses the caller to provide a more extended narrative before identifying what she wants.

In Excerpt 2, the caller also licenses a narrative by denying that his situation is an emergency; consider, though, how he does this:

Excerpt 2
Tape 4, call 218, male C, female CT

1	CT	911 emergency.
2	C	um not really ma'am not l – life threatening.
3	CT	may I help you?
4	C	um yes um I believe my girlfriend probably called in I'm not sure if she did
5		um but maybe the last ten minutes ago?
		[Caller proceeds to tell a lengthy story about a fight he had with his girlfriend.]

'Not really . . . life threatening' (line 2) does deny that the call is an emergency, at least the most serious kind. At the same time, in hesitating (um) and non-fluently (l – life threatening) asserting what the situation *is not*, the caller implies that the event to be described may be just on the other side of the emergency/non-emergency divide. That is, the event is serious, but not life threatening; and it is an event that is not easy to classify. Similar to Excerpt 1, Excerpt 2 also licenses the caller's launching into a long story.

Perhaps the most straightforward way to license a complex narrative is to forecast it at the start. This is illustrated in Excerpt 3 where the caller bypasses answering the call-taker's question about whether her situation is an emergency, and labels what she has to tell as 'a long story'.[4]

Excerpt 3
Tape 4, call 240, female C, female CT

1	CT	Citywest 911 how may I help you?
2	C	Um, my name is Sally Hall, and I have a long story to tell you. I was
3		supposed to m- um get my friend from her apartment at 11:15 this morning
4		'cause she has a flight that she's supposed to catch at 12:30?
5	CT	Yeah?

A subtler way of marking the coming of a long story is found in the following opening:

Excerpt 4
Tape 8, call 359, female C, female CT

1	CT	Citywest police Agent Phillips.
2	C	uh yes I just need to ask somebody some questions.
3	CT	uh huh.
4	C	u::m I'm like in, like a domestic thing here?

Line 4 indicates that the caller's questions relate to her 'domestic thing'. Her saying 'I just need to ask somebody some questions' does not by itself indicate that a story is forthcoming. After such a statement, and the call-taker's acknowledgment ('uh huh'), it is conceivable for a caller to start asking questions (First, I wanted to know who I would talk to about...) but the caller does not do this. In formulating her trouble as, 'I'm like in a domestic *thing* here' the caller's vague label ('thing') where a more explicit one would be expected, cue that the situation is too complicated to give a straight-forward name. Her vocal emphasis on '*thing*' further highlights this. As the paper discusses later, the domestic thing is a dilemma the caller is facing about what is the best way to deal with her drinking husband.

A final conversational practice that citizens used to license a narrative is to open the emergency call with a friendly greeting. Consider how (and why) a greeting performs this function:

Excerpt 5
Tape 9, call 562 male C, male CT

1 CT   Citywest 911, Agent Geltner.
2 C   Hi how are you?
3 CT   I'm well sir, how can I help?
4 C   I had a uh theft in my family house, my uh ex-wife.

By opening a 911 call with 'hi how are you', the purpose of the call is implicitly framed as not serious. Moreover, this kind of opening also fore-casts that what is to come next is likely to be at odds with the kinds of reports usually expected. Greetings, as noted earlier, are usually absent in emergency calls, and hence are noticeable when present. Personal inquires about the call-taker's well-being, even in a ritualised way such as seen above, cue that whatever is coming up may not fit the expected 'police call' form.

In sum, from the opening moments of an exchange, callers cue that what they are about to say is not police business as usual – it will involve sensitiv-ities. Citizens do this at the call's outset by forecasting a not-brief narrative. These forecasting or narrative-licensing moves project that something com-plicated, not usual or easy-to-classify is on its way. Consider, then, the inter-actional sensitivities faced as callers tell their stories.

Sensitivity 2: callers' managing the moral implications of their stories

Having licensed a long and/or complicated narrative, citizens must now tell their story. These tellings challenge callers to show themselves to be morally reasonable actors, or at least not highly unreasonable. What exactly the challenges will be depends on a whole set of particularities related to the event being reported and features of the disputants. In telling their stories two discursive choices are especially crucial: (a) the problematic act or event needs to be named, and (b) a sense of its normalcy or unusualness needs to be conveyed. Each of these choices is consequential as it sets in motion different inferences about the degree of goodness/badness (and related judgments) of the speaker. These inferences will be shaped not only by the language and discourse practices selected, but by the group identities (including sex and age) of the speaker and the spoken-about. Consider how this process works when callers report instances of fighting that involve bodily contact of some type.

In Excerpt 6 a male caller is telling a story about a fight that he had with his girlfriend of four years that involved mutual 'slaps'. The caller had begun his call by mentioning that his girlfriend had probably already called the police about him (see Excerpt 2). Following a question from the call-taker about where his girlfriend was likely to be calling from, the caller tags onto his answer the following story:

Excerpt 6
Call 218, lines 9–19 (see Excerpt 2 for the call opening)

Yes Tenth and Schwartz. And fr- the thing is I'm calling because, I be- basically she slapped me twice and I, I did slap her, I've never hit a girl in my life and I *did* slap her. And then she slapped me again and I did slap her again . . . And what I did then was, becau- she said uh, she was calling the police. And I said well and, and what happened was I stayed over her hou- her n- her house and what I did was I, I drove her car away and about three blocks aw*ay*. So what I'm, I guess, well what I'm saying is, I guess I just want to re- report also her, I wanna report her and I, I, I really don't know what to do hh I've never been in this kind of situation thing.

In this excerpt the caller labels his problematic act 'a slap', a name that minimises its physical violence. The name implies an impulsive reaction, mostly probably provoked and involving little physical damage. Contrast what is likely to be inferred by describing an act as 'a slap' versus 'a hit' or 'a beating'. The significance of act description is implicitly oriented to by a woman calling to seek advice about how to deal with her husband, a call we focus on in Excerpts 8–10, below. At one point she says, ' I mean he he *slap*ped me or hit me whatever the hell you wanna call it.' In problematising how the husband's acts should be labelled, the caller makes visible the non-transparent nature of all descriptions. The woman's difficulty in selecting a label may be tied to the narrow implicative path she must walk if she is to avoid creating a picture of herself as an unreasonable person. If her husband's actions toward her are highly violent (that is, he hits and beats her) and she is unwilling to do anything about it then she will appear unreasonable, being a 'victim', putting up with violence. On the other hand, if her husband has done no more than 'slap' her, the likely physical danger is not that great. To call the police if these milder circumstances apply may suggest she is the kind of wife willing to get her husband in trouble with the police for 'little stuff'. Naming of an act is a caller's first rhetorical choice.

A second choice concerns conveying whether the act being described is normal and unremarkable, or quite unusual. Then, depending on the culturally-understood evaluation of the reported act – Would most people regard the act as a good or bad, normal or bizarre? – implications about a speaker's character and morality are set in motion. Three conversational practices provide evidence that the caller in Excerpt 6 sees his slapping of his girlfriend as an unusual event.

The most obvious are the explicit statements that the caller makes that this is the case – 'I've never hit a girl in my life' and 'I've never been in this kind of situation thing'. In addition, though, are two more subtle practices. The second practice is the phrase, 'situation thing' to describe the event – 'I've never been in this kind of situation thing'. Using this phrase implies that the speaker is having a difficult time knowing what to call the situation he is in. This phrase is a throw-up-your-hands kind of phrase. In this context, the occurrence of this kind of labelling difficulty makes the most sense if a speaker is in an unusual situation; referring to an event as a 'situation thing', therefore, implies that the situation is an unusual one for the speaker. The final way the slap is marked as unusual in this excerpt is through the story-teller's non-fluent style. In recounting the slap incident the story is produced with a large number of restarts, repetitions and word searches. This high level of non-fluency marks the caller as telling about an act that is hard to talk about, that is out of the ordinary and atypical for him.

Contrast his telling about the slap to a woman caller's recounting of a chair throwing:

Excerpt 7
Call 159, lines 126–36

Recently I was in court an my cousin he threw a chair at me? And it was just me and him outside. She came outside after I was walking away and said I have a restraining order against you, well my re-, her restraining order against me is I can go to the front door. She comes to me. She calls me, she pages me, she does all this stuff, and she made a false report saying that I had been, didn't tell her one thing. I didn't say her name, nothin. She called the cops on me saying that I threatened to kill her and her baby, she was pregnant at the time, and *I* didn' do that and now I hafta go to court for somethin I didn't do, I don't have any witnesses, she has his family to witness for him.

Of note in the above story, is that the caller includes the details about her cousin's chair throwing in a straightforward manner, merely to set the physical scene in which to describe a confrontation been herself and her ex-husband's soon-to-be wife. No markers are included in the caller's talk that evidence that the caller sees the chair-throwing event as anything out of the ordinary, as would have been the case if she had prefaced her scene-setting with comments such as, 'It was in a strange scene to begin with', or 'I was in court because my cousin threw a chair. That's another story. Anyway . . . '

Thus in narrating a story, speakers treat some events as normal and undeserving of comment, and others as unusual and in need of marking. What a speaker chooses to mark or leave unmarked generates character-related inferences. The caller who treated chair-throwing as a normal event, for instance, implicated that she is probably living a non-middle-class life in which violent encounters are not unusual. Because the caller in Excerpt 6 treated his 'slapping' as so highly unusual, it becomes possible to see him as a 'reasonable' man who did an isolated and relatively small act that was wrong. This picture of what his act should count as is further justified through the way the caller describes the event. He works to frame his slap as 'provoked', and not just by words: his girlfriend slapped first. In these multiple ways, then, the caller works to present himself and his actions in a way that will offset the taken-for-granted cultural view that a man who hits a woman is a bad person, violent and brutal.

Sensitivity 3: call-takers responding in a helpful and institutionally appropriate manner

How do call-takers respond when citizens present complaints that do not readily fit into a police category? For certain kinds of complaints, call-takers may give citizens a telephone number to obtain appropriate assistance. If the citizen's problem involves the non-human environment – dead or live animals, gas or electric outages, water, street or housing problems – referrals are relatively straightforward. Person-linked complaints of any type, but especially in domestic situations, are more complicated. In this final section we highlight how these stories about hard-to-categorise person problems challenge police call-takers' responding skills.

One important goal of police departments is to be (and to be regarded as) helpful to citizens. A challenge, though, well-recognised in 911 operator training manuals, is that 'the community expectation is that you will be able to handle the problem [whatever the citizen calls about]. Failure on the part of the telecommunicator to provide acceptable alternatives generates frustration and belligerence on the part of the citizen' (APCO, 1992). The training manual at Citywest implied, albeit indirectly, that failure may occur because a call-taker is less than ideally knowledgeable or skilled. Undoubtedly this is true. However, this assessment does not recognise the complexity of the situation that call-takers routinely face.

In domestic dispute calls police call-takers face a dilemma (Tracy, 1997b) involving both contrary values about what is an institutionally desirable kind of response, and a set of conversational options that connect back, albeit in a loose fashion, to the espoused values. The police mandate is to be helpful – to get citizens the help they desire, either directly by sending an officer or by referral. 'Helpful', however, is not determined by the intention of a speaker, but is an assessment that recipients of 'help' get to make. If a party judges what another said as 'not helpful', that is the judgement that stands. Helpfulness, then, is a judgement that citizens make about the institution, a judgement we could expect to be related to call-takers' actions but not determined by them.

At the same time the police are a complex institution, one agency in a web of social services that is legally accountable for not overstepping its institutional boundaries. Repeatedly, Citywest manuals document the importance of call-takers not overstepping boundaries as they talk with citizens. Immediately following the instructions to provide alternative actions for citizens, the policy manual concludes the sentence with the clause, 'but NEVER give legal advice to the caller' (APCO, 1992). In the Citywest policy notebook, the section on telephone protocol, states, 'DO NOT quote civil or criminal law or otherwise give advice in matters of civil or criminal law. Wrong advice is worse than no advice at all.' In addition, there is another constraint on being helpful that comes into play in all police calls, especially those made to 911. Help, whatever it may be, is to be given quickly; telephone lines should not be tied up for long periods of time.[5] Thus, although call-takers are expected to be helpful, they are expected to do so quickly and not to give advice that could be construed as 'legal'. This communicative ideal is a difficult one to accomplish.

Consider a call in which a man complains about his 'ex-wife' (in fact, the woman he had been living with for five years who had left two weeks ago and returned the previous night) stealing his wallet, identification and food stamps. After the caller states, ' I just figured I'd call the police officers and see what, if they could make her give me my money and stuff back', the call-taker highlights how the wife's actions do not meet the legal definition of 'theft'. Over several exchange rounds the caller continues to express disbelief that the police cannot help. Finally, the call-taker concludes the conversation with the following statement, one hard to imagine the caller regarded as helpful:

> What you need to do is cancel those documents if you don't want her to use them, get new ones. Call the bank, go to motor vehicle, get some new ID, get some new checks, get a lawyer. You need to have a property settlement.

To tell a man living on the financial edge – using food stamps, having no more money at his disposal other than what was in his wallet – to get an attorney to settle a financial dispute with his wife seems transparently unhelpful. On the other hand, the piece of advice does respect the institutional constraint of not offering legal advice. And it is accomplished relatively quickly. Contrast this call-taker's response to what is done in a call made by a woman to get advice about whether she should return to her home where her drinking and sometimes violent husband is. The caller initially describes her problem as a 'domestic thing' about which she has questions (see Excerpt 4). She then describes her quandary as follows:

Excerpt 8
Call 359, lines 6–13

C   and um I'm just uh (.) calling to, like get some information. U:m my problem I'm having is (.) last night we had uh a problem the night before and I talked to his mom and everything was fine last night but he's been drinking today. And I'm not at home but I *wanna* go home but I'm like *afraid* to go home because I don't know how's he's gonna react because

> he's still really mad. And somebody told me to call and talk to somebody who has experience in that so
>
> CT   And you're *wanting* to go home?

There are a number of features in this call that show that the call-taker is seeking to be helpful, as the caller might define it, and at the same time avoid taking institutionally inappropriate action. First, although calls to the police vary enormously in length, this call by almost any measure is long (7 mins and 10 secs, 146 lines). The call's length in itself points to the call-taker's sustained efforts to be helpful.

More telling than the length, though, is the content of the call-taker's response. In contrast to some exchanges in which a call-taker cuts off a long-winded caller with directed questions such as 'what is it that you want the police to do?', this call-taker allows the caller to tell her story in the kind of complexity that the caller wishes. In addition, over long stretches the caller's story is encouraged with frequent continuers (13 instances of mhm), including occasional tokens that indicate marked appreciation of the difficulty of the caller's situation ('it's a hard one', 'wow').

Why is this citizen calling the police? What does she want from them? An answer to that question is suggested later:

Excerpt 9
lines 71–6

C   you know I'm tryin to, what I'm really trying to do is find somebody that can talk to him.
CT   mhm.
C   you know I'm thinking maybe I could find someone to go and talk to him.
CT   mhm.
C   A:nd straighten this situation out.

The caller would like someone to intervene with her husband. She would like someone to 'talk to him' and 'straighten this situation out' presumably before another round of slapping and hitting or 'whatever the hell you wanna call it' (line 47) occurs. The citizen's request, however, is not something that the police can act upon. The police are not benevolent community elders who step into domestic scenes and help a couple sort things out before it escalates to something worse. For the police to step in is consequential: it is a public announcement for many to see of a marital relationship gone seriously awry. Police intervention transforms a spouse who hits into a person with a 'criminal' record, and, for the initiating party, it is an action that she (or he) knows the other may see as 'unreasonable, 'overreacting' 'airing family conflicts where they shouldn't be'. Moreover, the caller appears to recognise that the kind of 'help' she wants is not the kind that police will be able to provide. This recognition is made visible though repeated use of 'I'm trying', a phrase that conveys a speaker's good intention but her expected lack of success.

From the call-taker's point of view, she is faced with a needy citizen who cannot be offered institutional help of the kind the citizen seeks. Not only can she not commit the police, the call-taker needs to be careful not to offer advice that could have a bad outcome for which the police department could be legally liable. That the call-taker knows that she needs to attend to this important institutional constraint is displayed through her repeated comments about not giving advice:

- 'the only thing I can say is the police ... ' (line 33).
- 'but as far as, I mean I can't really give you advice on (.) going home' (line 37).
- 'cause we can't give any advice out like that um' (line 60).
- 'I mean you are putting yourself into a danger and if you go back and he's drunk, I can say that' (line 62).

In addition, where the call-taker does offer a suggestion (lines 54, 57) it is couched in the form of what she 'wouldn't recommend'. This formulation is interesting in that it permits the giving of advice while framing what is being offered as 'not advising'. The caller, in fact, in the next response (line 59) explicitly affirms that the call-taker may be in a difficult spot ('it's hard for you, huh?'), a response triggered, we suggest, by the call-taker's halting, multiply restarted, non-recommendation:

Excerpt 10
lines 57–60

CT   I wouldn't recommend, I mean, if you're (.) if he's gonna (3.0) he's been that way in the past hh I mean.
C   I don't know, it's hard for you huh?
CT   yeah cause we really can't give any advice out like than um.

In sum, the call-taker displays a high level of discomfort thoughout the call. This is marked not only in Excerpt 10 above, but by multiple long pauses within turns where the call-taker is engaging in talk most people would hear as advice, albeit perhaps not 'legal' advice.

Conclusion

When citizens call the police to report domestic trouble, these calls are likely to be interactionally difficult for both parties. Domestic disputes, perhaps more than other kinds of police call, are bad fits for institutional categories. Domestic disputes involve complex, messy dramas that poorly match the 'police intervention' script, with its presumed clear categories of 'victim', 'wrongdoer' and 'crime'. In domestic disputes, category lines are especially blurry. Callers and call-takers recognise this, and the mismatch gets played out over and over in citizen–police exchanges about domestic matters. From the opening moments, through a caller's narrating of the event, to the police call-taker's response, domestic dispute calls are enacted as interactively challenging, morally loaded conversational events.

There is no easy 'fix' for this problem, no piece of advice that will lead to the disappearance of the difficulty. Nonetheless, we envision this discourse-analytic study being useful in two ways. First, our analysis makes clear the character of police call-takers' competing institutional commitments – the interactional problem that they face. As Dewey (1989, p. 123) argued many years ago, 'the nature of the problem fixes the end of thought'. We assume that a helpful problem formulation – one that captures the competing concerns in operation – will enable thoughtful, experienced practitioners to develop reasonable conversational responses. Second, call-taker training that involved listening to a category of calls along with transcripts could aid call-takers in 'seeing' more discourse particulars (such as wordings, pauses, question forms) as resources (talk options) that are available for use in the call-taking moment as they deal with this kind of two-headed problem.

Notes

1 Both of these notes come from a field observation that the senior author carried out with a police call-taker at Citywest Emergency Center on 25 July 1995. Note-taking procedures combined gist summary of talk with marking verbatim phrases. Phrases in quotes are the verbatim parts.
2 Doctoral student Sarah Tracy was the other person on the team. She assisted in downloading calls and was responsible for more than half of the observations. Our thanks to her.
3 Modifications included simplifying information about pause time; (.) marks a short roughly 0.2 of a second pause and (pause) is used for anything longer. Separated capital letters (e.g., E S T indicate that a person is spelling a name or address). Italics indicate a stressed word or syllable.
4 This call is not a domestic dispute but one friend calling about another. Field observations of the call-taking suggest that this was a practice that occurred in domestic disputes as well.
5 There are exceptions to this. On suicide calls, for instance, the call-taker's job is to keep the person talking on the telephone until the police arrive.

References

APCO (1992) *Basic Telecommunicator Training Course*. South Daytona, FL: APCO Institute.

Atkinson, J. M. and Heritage, J. (eds) (1984) *Structure of Social Action: Studies in Conversation Analysis*. Cambridge: Cambridge University Press.

Bergmann, J. R. (1998) 'Introduction: Morality in Discourse', *Research on Language and Social Interaction*, vol. 31, pp. 279–94.

Brown, P. and Levinson, S. C. (1987) *Universals in Language Usage: Politeness Phenomena*. Cambridge: Cambridge University Press.

Craig, R. T. (1989) 'Communication as a Practical Discipline', in B. Dervin, L. Grossberg, B. J. O'Keefe and E. Wartella (eds), *Rethinking Communication: Vol. 1. Paradigm issues*). Newbury Park, CA: Sage, pp. 97–122.

Craig, R. T. (1995) 'Applied Communication Research in a Practical Discipline', in K. Cissna (ed.), *Applied Communication in the Twentieth Century*. Norwood, NJ: Lawrence Erlbaum, pp. 147–56.

Craig, R. T. (1996) 'Practical–Theoretical Argumentation', *Argumentation*, vol. 10, pp. 461–74.

Craig, R. T. and Tracy, K. (1995). 'Grounded Practical Theory: The Case of Intellectual Discussion', *Communication Theory*, vol. 5, pp. 248–72.

Dewey, J. (1989) *John Dewey: The Later Works 1925–1953, Volume 8: 1933* (J. A. Boydston, ed.), Carbondale, IL: Southern Illinois Press.

Drew, P. and Heritage, J. (eds) (1992), *Talk at Work: Interaction in Institutional Settings*. Cambridge: Cambridge University Press.

Edwards, D. and Potter, J. (1992) *Discursive Psychology*. London: Sage.

Fairclough, N. and Wodak, R. (1997) 'Critical Discourse Analysis', in T. A. van Dijk (ed.), *Discourse as Social Interaction*. London: Sage, pp. 258–84.

Goffman, E. (1955) 'On Facework: An Analysis of Ritual Elements in Social Interaction', *Psychiatry*, vol. 18, pp. 213–31.

Manning, P. K. (1988) *Symbolic Communication: Signifying Calls and the Police Response*. Cambridge, MA: MIT Press.

Reiss, Jr, A. J. (1971) *The Police and the Public*. New Haven: Yale University Press.

Sharrock, W. W. and Turner, R. (1978) 'On a Conversational Environment for Equivocality', in J. Schenkein (ed.), *Studies in the Organization of Conversational Interaction*. NY: Academic Press, pp. 173–97.

Shuler, S. (2001) 'Talking Community at 911: The Centrality of Communication in Coping with Emotional Labor', in G. J. Shephered and E. W. Rothenbuhler (eds), *Communication and Community*, Mahwah, NJ: Lawrence Erlbaum, pp. 53–77.

Tracy, K. (1995) 'Action-Implicative Discourse Analysis', *Journal of Language and Social Psychology*, vol. 14, pp. 195–215.

Tracy, K. (1997a) *Colloquium: Dilemmas of Academic Discourse*. Norwood, NJ: Ablex.

Tracy, K. (1997b) 'Interactional Trouble in Emergency Service Requests: A Problem of Frames', *Research on Language and Social Interaction*, vol. 30, pp. 315–43.

Tracy, K. (2001) 'Discourse Analysis in Communication', in D. Schiffrin, D. Tannen and H. Hamilton (eds), *Handbook of Discourse Analysis*. Oxford, UK: Blackwell, pp. 725–49.

Tracy, K. and Anderson, D. L. (1999) 'Relational Positioning Strategies in Calls to the Police: A Dilemma', *Discourse Studies*, vol. 1, pp. 201–26.

Tracy, K. and Tracy, S. J. (1998) 'Rudeness at 911: Reconceptualizing Face and Face-Attack', *Human Communication Research*, vol. 25, pp. 225–51.

Tracy, S. J. and Tracy, K. (1998) 'Emotion Labor at 911: A Case Study and Theoretical Critique', *Journal of Applied Communication*, vol. 26, pp. 390–411.

Whalen, M. R. and Zimmerman, D. H. (1987) 'Sequential and Institutional Contexts in Calls for Help', *Social Psychology Quarterly*, vol. 50, pp. 172–85.

Whalen, M. R. and Zimmerman, D. H. (1990) 'Describing Trouble: Practical Epistemology in Citizen Calls to the Police', *Language in Society*, vol. 19, pp. 465–92.

Zimmerman, D. H. (1984) 'Talk and its Occasion: The Case of Calling the Police', in D. Schiffrin (ed.), *Meaning, Form, and Use in Context*. Georgetown: Georgetown University Press, pp. 210–28.

Zimmerman, D. H. (1992) 'Achieving Context: Openings in Emergency Calls', in G. Watson and R. M. Seiler (eds), *Text in Context: Contributions to Ethnomethodology*. Newbury Park, CA: Sage, pp. 35–51.

Zimmerman, D. H. (1992b) 'The Interactional Organization of Calls for Emergency Assistance', in P. Drew and J. Heritage (eds), *Talk at Work*. Cambridge: Cambridge University Press, pp. 418–69.

6
So...?: Pragmatic Implications of *So*-Prefaced Questions in Formal Police Interviews

Alison Johnson

Introduction: questioning in institutional settings

In recent years there has been great interest in the linguistic study of inter-actional processes in occupational and institutional settings. In addition to early important studies of classroom interaction (Sinclair and Coulthard, 1975) and therapeutic discourse (Labov and Fanshel, 1977), Drew and Heritage (1992) and Dillon (1990) have considered interaction in the professions of the media, medicine and employment, focusing on the importance of questioning across a range of contexts. In the forensic domain, Walker (1994) and Aldridge and Wood (1998) devote major attention to questioning strategies with children in criminal cases, from both linguistic and developmental perspectives.

What the studies mentioned have in common is their concern with dyadic asymmetrical institutional interaction, and in particular question and response patterns. I shall examine Drew and Heritage's (1992) assertion that this form of interaction effectively allows the professional to 'gain a measure of control over the introduction of topics and hence of the "agenda" for the occasion' (p. 49). I will concentrate on the distinctive use of *so*-prefaced questions in police interviews with child witnesses and adult defendants and the role of these questions in topic-marking and movement within a narrative agenda. I will argue that *so*-prefaced questions have an important narrative sequencing function in the interview. Together with *and*-prefaced questions, which are discussed elsewhere (Heritage and Sorjonen, 1994; Matsumoto, 1999; Johnson, 2001), they help to construct narrative sequence through interviewer turns. In this way, it is often the interviewer who tells the story.

Although this can lead to an analysis of asymmetry, we should be circumspect in consigning the interviewee's asymmetrical position to one of power-lessness. In interviews with children, for example, the process can be seen as empowering for the child in terms of the collaborative development of a difficult narrative from the child's often unsubstantial contributions, through the expertise of a skilled interviewer. I will focus on the need for the interviewer to maintain control of the topic movement to ensure relevance in relation to the interview's goal. This will inevitably involve moving the questions into areas where the witness or defendant would prefer not to go, because these are likely to involve events that the interviewee would rather not recall because of their disturbing nature or because they might implicate him or her.

In addition to looking at the role of these questions, I will consider the pragmatic implications of *so* as a specialised discourse marker in the narrative setting of the police interview. Before looking at the function and use of *so* in conversation and interviews, however, it is first important to consider its various meanings.

Meanings of *so*

As a frequent function word of English, *so* has many senses and uses. Dictionaries tend to define it in terms of its adverbial (*I am so happy*) and conjunctive uses (*I was hungry, so I made a sandwich*), and then in terms of the regular expressions in which it is found (*so far so good*). Amongst the 18 senses offered by the *Collins COBUILD English Dictionary* (1995, pp. 1581–2), the sense I am focusing on is numbered nine, indicating its significant but infrequent general usage:

> 9 Adverb. You can use **so** in conversations to introduce a new topic, or to introduce a question or comment about something that has been said. *So how was your day? So as for your question, Miles, the answer still has to be no.*

However, none of the senses offered in this dictionary, or in any of the others I have consulted (Chambers; Websters) defines its specialised usage in question-and-answer sequences. This can be accounted for by the emphasis on general rather than specialised corpora and an emphasis on semantics. This chapter argues from the viewpoint of 'complementarism' (Leech, 1983, pp. 6–7), a view that sees semantics and pragmatics as 'complementary and interrelated fields of study' (*op. cit.*, p. 6). It also considers evidence from a specialised corpus of police interviews.

In addition, I will be arguing that meaning is 'associative' (Leech, 1974). When *so* is used in an utterance, speakers and listeners do not necessarily separate its meaning from other meanings of *so*. For example, when *so* is used as an adverb as in *So how was your day?* additional meanings associated with its two conjunctive senses related to result (*therefore*):

> People are living longer than ever before, so even people who are 65 or 70 have a surprising amount of time left.

or reason (*in order to*):

> Come to my suite so I can tell you all about this wonderful play I saw in Boston.

may be produced. In this case the 'result' meaning is associated with the adverbial use of *so* in a way that appears to combine the adverbial and conjunctive uses. I will argue here that as a preface to a question, *so* has a communicative force of simultaneously serving the topic and narrative movement and the causal link made between the discourse and its antecedents.

Data and method

The anonymised data referred to in this chapter are from two corpora: the *COBUILD* Direct Corpus of The Bank of English, and a set of interviews with children and adults collected by the author. The examples from *COBUILD* are from its 9.3 million word sub-corpus of UK spoken English. My own corpus contains a number of interviews amounting to almost 100 000 words, from which I have selected a sub-corpus of five interviews with children and five with adults totalling 82 016 words (46 466 with children and 35 550 with adults). Interviews were carried out in many parts of England by different police officers. The children are witnesses in abuse cases and the adults are defendants accused of a range of serious criminal offences. The analysis is intended to provide an indication of differences in the distribution and function of *so*-prefaced questions between adults and children in the interviews.

The analysis combines the methodologies of conversational analysis, discourse analysis, corpus linguistics and a semantic-pragmatic approach to language in the specialised setting of the police interview. Conversational analysis is concerned not only with the analysis of ordinary conversation in everyday contexts, but also with sequential talk and has moved into 'conversations' in specialised settings such as institutional interactions. The discourse analysis approach analyses talk in terms of exchanges, moves and acts (Sinclair and Coulthard, 1975; Stenström, 1994) and functional units. The corpus approach is based on the belief that the data collected represent a specific and lesser-studied variety of interaction. As such any study of the contents of the corpus may be 'generalised to a larger hypothetical corpus' (Aijmer and Altenberg, 1991, p. 27) and can be seen as a sample of the kind of talk performed in these institutional domains in general. In addition, the analyst is easily able to search the electronic corpus to examine and statistically account for its lexical usage. I used *COBUILD*'s Lookup and corpus tools, Longman's *Mini-Concordancer* and an unpublished file-splitting program (Woolls, unpublished) that splits the dyadic exchange of the interview into two separate files. The pragmatic approach reveals 'meaning in relation to speech situation' (Leech, 1983, p. 15). Here, the analyst considers word use in relation to its domain-specific function.

So in 'ordinary conversation'

In order to consider the significant use of *so*-prefacing in formal interviews, I will first examine this use in 'ordinary conversation'. This will serve to define the conversational functions of *so* as a question preface, so that the institutional setting can be contrasted with the conversational one.

I first analysed which interrogative forms typically co-occur with *so*. Figure 6.1 illustrates the most frequent collocates, in the form of a collocate 'picture'. It reveals four potential interrogative forms as frequent immediate right-hand collocates, that is those words which most commonly appear following *so*; these are highlighted in **bold**.

The 'picture', compiled from the 57 007 occurrences of *so*, confirms the significance of interrogative forms as frequent collocates of *so*. A small but significant proportion of these occurrences in the Bank of English sub-

and	SO	i
erm	SO	that
right	SO	you
think	SO	it
yeah	SO	we
it	SO	they
okay	SO	on
er	SO	much
s	SO	**what**
that	SO	the
know	SO	er
not	SO	erm
was	SO	if
mm	SO	there
or	SO	he
is	SO	many
yes	SO	she
see	SO	and
well	SO	in
you	SO	far
there	SO	**when**
are	SO	**do**
do	SO	**how**

Figure 6.1   Picture of *so*

corpus of UK speech form question prefaces. In a random sample of 100 lines of the possible 57 007, 13 were found to be question prefaces. These formed four classes:

1 Declarative questions (seven occurrences).
   These are questions in function, but declarative in form:
   So that's six altogether?
2 The *So what?* question (two occurrences).
3 *So* with a non-polar question (two occurrences):
   So how do you work it?
4 *So* with a polar question (two occurrences):
   So was that a lot of coursework?

Although the 'picture' confirmed the frequent collocation of *so* with interrogative forms (*what, when, how*), closer examination of examples added to the picture through the presence of declarative questions. We can therefore say that in conversation around 10 per cent of the use of *so* may be connected with questions.

An analysis of the corpus of UK speech revealed that *so*-prefaced questions frequently contain distal deictics. Such deictics create anaphoric cohesive ties between the previous utterance and the current utterance, for example: *that, this, it*, as in '*So how often does this happen?*'. We can see this demonstrated in Figure 6.2, a picture of *so* + *how* (where *how* is the node). The deictics (in the right-hand collocates of *how*) are emboldened.

yeah	right	SO	HOW	do	**you**	**You**
mm	mm		HOW	did	**they**	feel
erm	yeah		HOW	long	is	**that**
right	erm		HOW	many	**that**	get
so	er		HOW	much	did	the
and	if		HOW	would	do	do
yes	and		HOW	can	have	know
it	okay		HOW	are	we	did
s	well		HOW	old	**it**	**it**
t	i		HOW	often	the	work
that	you		HOW	does	are	make
you	think		HOW	s	were	erm
i	yes		HOW	about	would	how
the	t		HOW	come	does	think
way	see		HOW	was	**i**	going
of	a		HOW	have	of	have
on	to		HOW	you	was	deal
know	out		HOW	d	how	be
for	more		HOW	is	people	say
now	but		HOW	on	**this**	**they**
there	like		HOW	were	**she**	go
thing	how		HOW	could	ago	all
good	problem		HOW	i	what	like

Figure 6.2 Picture of *so* + *how*

It follows that the left-hand collocates are chiefly in the prior utterance, sometimes occurring in the previous speaker's turn. The picture reveals that this turn frequently contains discourse markers and backchannels such as *yeah* (or *yes*), *right*, *mm*, *erm*, *er*, *okay* and *well* (shown in italics in Figure 6.2). These collocates all signal either movement or continuation of the current topic, indicating that *so* clearly sits at an important boundary in the interaction. In the following examples (from *COBUILD* UK speech) we can see this in action:

Example 1

A   Businessmen are are tired of politicians talking the economy down. Now isn't the time to be knocking the economy now is the time to talk it up and to look at the positive side.

B   **So how do you do that?** Come on convince me.

A   Well well <laughs> I mean you just have to look around at a number of the businesses.

Example 2

A   We feed this in and then that will that will develop it wash it off and dry it ready for going down for the plate making.

B   Right. **So how long does that process take?**

A   It takes about er two minutes. So in about two minutes it will be coming out the other end of

A   Right.

B   the er machine.

The function of *so* appears to be more closely related to the negotiation and marking of the discourse sequence than the semantic relation where one event is the result of another. It marks 'participation transition' (Schiffrin, 1987, p. 318) and topic movement combining the discourse marker and conjunctive functions of *so*. *So* also marks a challenge to the participant (Example 1) emphasised by the metastatement: *Come on convince me*. The cohesive and connective function of the interrogative is underlined by the fact that it collocates with deictics such as *that* as well as the 'labelling noun' (Francis, 1994), *process*, and the substitute, *do*.

So-prefacing in conversation is discourse-organisational and therefore moves its use beyond a semantic one, related to its conjunctive meanings of reason and result, to a pragmatic function marking the discourse as transitional between stages and between speakers. Discoursally, the meaning and function of *so* is 'Let's move the discourse on from X to Y' or 'It follows that...'. As Schiffrin (1987, p. 316) states, there are several 'planes of talk' and in conversation, discourse markers can function on the semantic, discoursal and pragmatic planes of discourse.

So as a question preface in formal police interviews

In this section I discuss the function and use of *so*-prefaced questions with examples from my corpus, contrasting these with each other and with the conversational data. I look particularly at the use of *so*-prefaced questions to construct discourse and to *evaluate and label* (Francis, 1994) previous utterances on the part of the interviewee. Also, countering the powerless asymmetry analysis in the literature, I will argue that these questions have a vital function in the goal-focused nature of these interviews. The goal for the interviewer, with child witnesses, is to present the evidence as fully as possible using the child's testimony and to elicit as much relevant narrative as possible. Since children may be unwilling and/or unable to produce large stretches of spontaneous narrative, *so*- and *and*-prefaced questions have an important positive role here. They construct, 'scaffold', support, arrange and rearrange the discourse into a narrative that empowers the abused child. Aldridge and Wood (1998, p. 94) discuss the importance of supporting children's narratives during the interview process and cite Foster (1990, p. 127) who notes the role of adults who 'scaffold early stories, allowing children to produce a more complex sequence of ideas than they are unable to convey unaided'. In the unfamiliar setting of the police interview this kind of support is vital. I suggest that *so*- and *and*-prefacing has an important part to play here.

For adults who are suspected of being involved in serious criminal offences, the interviewer has a similar narrative goal. Here, though, the interviewee is largely able, but unwilling to produce an extensive account of something that may incriminate. *So*- and *and*-prefaced questions perform a key role here, too. With adults, though, the evaluation and labelling of previous discourse in these questions is most evident. The interviewer signals and marks the significance of a previous utterance in the developing narrative, producing weighted evidence.

A first task is to make some comparisons between how *so* is used in conversation and in the police interviews as indicated in Table 6.1.

Table 6.1 Comparisons of *so* and *so*-preface frequencies across corpora

	COBUILD corpus of UK speech	Child corpus	Adult corpus
Total words	9 272 579	46 466	35 550
Total *so*	57 007	423	282
No. of *so* per 1000	6	9	8
So-prefaced Q	Not counted	275	111
% of *so*-prefaces	(approx.) 10%	65%	39%

We can make a number of observations based on these comparisons:

1   The frequency of *so* per 1000 words is greater in the police interviews –
    8 and 9 words per thousand compared with 6 per thousand in UK speech.
2   The frequency of *so* per 1000 words is greatest in the child interviews.
3   While there is only a small variation in the occurrence of *so* per 1000 words,
    there is a wide variation in the occurrence of *so*-prefaced questions among
    the three corpora – approximately 10 per cent for UK speech compared
    with 39 per cent and 65 per cent for the adult and child interviews.
4   The frequency of *so*-prefaced questions is very high in the interviews
    with children; 65 per cent of the uses of *so* are to preface questions, com-
    pared with around 10 per cent in UK speech.

These statistics suggest that police interviews produce a specialised and frequent use of *so*-prefacing. It is likely that this also extends to other kinds of
interviews, such as those in the media. Some casual observation of radio and
television interviews (Jeremy Paxman on the UK current affairs programne
Newsnight, for example) bears this out. In addition, *so*-prefaced questions
seem to be a particular feature of child interviews. However, the apparent
sharp contrast in the frequency of *so*-prefaced questions between the child
and adult interviews deserves more detailed discussion. When we look at
the distribution of the use of *so* in the child and adult interviews, there is, in
fact, much more similarity in the distribution of *so*-prefaced questions than
the statistics might indicate. Firstly, the *so*-prefaced questions are exclusively found in the domain of the interviewer (identified as DC, DS or WPC
in Figure 6.3). In the data I found only one example of a *so*-prefaced question used by an interviewee (in the first line of Figure 6.3).

DC Right.NR	So what is there now? We want t repay this money as early
DS E	So what other conversation was there about T then?
DS E	So what pressure were they putting you under
	So what time did you arrive there on the Friday, first off?
WPC Yeah.	So when did you know it wasn't that money?
DC L	So when he was having this done to him did he cry more?
	So when I know - I had nothing to do because I had no money a
DC	So when was you married?
DC	So when - when did you know for sure-
DC	So when you first - when you first opened the account?
DS E	So when you went from - you left the Oxford, where did you go
DS E Okay.	So when you were leaving what was the general impression about
DC D	So when you were stopped by the police then-

Figure 6.3   Concordance of *so* showing *so*-prefaced questions in interviewer turns

By contrast, the way *so* is used both by adult and child interviewees is very different from the overwhelmingly adverbial and question-prefacing use seen with the interviewers. Interviewees chiefly use *so* as a conjunction. In Extract 1 from an adult interview, we can see the conjunctive uses of *so* by the interviewee (B) and the adverbial *so*-prefaces of the interviewer (DCG):

Extract 1: TrfBurn.txt

DCG   ... What- what happened?

B   Well, he- he were stood at bar for ages and he were like staring over ... So I looked, I turned round and he said what are you fucking looking at to me, so I thought, oh, I'm not going to cause no trouble, you know. I didn't want to know, so I turned away then he w- he kept doing it for ages, he was saying stuff like slagging us. So my brother then turned round and said to him what's up with you, you miserable cunt, ... So the bloke automatically just stood up and walked round and, like, picked up a stool.

DCG   **So, this is the same bloke who's been assaulted?**

B   Yeah.

Secondly, in the adult interviews, the interviewee uses *so* more frequently, since he or she is generally able to produce a greater quantity of spontaneous narrative. Therefore, due to the greater amount of narrative, there are, correspondingly, more uses of *so* as a conjunction. This proportionately reduces the number of *so*-prefaced questions in the total uses of *so*. The contrast is apparent in Extract 1 and in Extract 2, where we can also see the range of conjunctions used by the interviewee (DD) in his narrative:

Extract 2: Trard1am.txt

DCR   And you put them to bed.

DD   Yes, they won't sleep for L ... **because** as soon as she goes out of the room they start screaming, **so** I have to put them to bed **and**, like, see to them on a night **or** whatever **if** they wake up.

Thirdly, since young children use fewer complex conjunctions in their narratives (Liles, 1987), this may account for a further reduction in the use of *so* in the child interviews making the interviewer's questioning use more apparent and the proportion greater. By separating speaker A and speaker B's turns we can compare the frequency of *so* in the turns of two interviewees: an adolescent of 14 years and a very young child of five:

Traejacfc.txt	aged 14	interviewee: *so* = 14
Tralcfc.txt	aged 5	interviewee: *so* = 0

Although this is only one comparison, it does seem to suggest the absence of *so* in the turns of very young children. On further examination, this child had the kind of limited profile of connectives expected in the speech of a child of this age. Applebee (1978) suggests that young children first develop 'centring' strategies (generally, simple sentences) in their recounts, only later developing 'chaining' strategies using longer utterances linked by conjunctions such as *and* and *but*. Table 6.2 compares the five-year-old's limited, but developing use of conjunctions with the wider range shown in the adult in Extracts 1 and 2. We can see the limited range of connectives and therefore limited cohesion in the child's account. The interviewer compensates for this in the pragmatic narrative use of *and-* and *so*-prefacing.

So, although on first examination of the statistics in Table 6.2 there appears to be a sharp contrast between the percentage of *so*-prefaced questions in relation to the total occurrences of *so* for children and adults, there are some good reasons for this. In the data it is apparent that very young children produce less spontaneous narrative containing *so* and also use a limited range of conjunctions, thereby excluding *so* in favour of the more general *and*. This results in a difference in the distribution of *so* in the two speakers and therefore in the proportion of *so*-prefaced questions in relation to the total occurrences of *so* in the child and adult corpora. The proportion of *so*-prefaced questions used in child interviews is, however, still higher than in interviews with adults, suggesting overcompensation.

The interviewer compensates for the child's limited ability to produce complex and extensive narrative through the use of *so*-prefaced questions by making the questions highly content and substance-concentrated. This has the effect of making the child's response easier, since the child can agree with, adapt or expand the interviewer's utterance. This form of questioning thereby supports and opens up the narrative and is apparent in the frequency and differential distribution of *so*-prefaced questions. If we compare the adolescent and young child interviews again, though focusing this time on the *inter-*

Table 6.2 Comparison of connectives present in interviews with a young child and an adult

Connectives	Tralcfc.txt (child aged 5) (total words: 1440)	TrFBurnc.txt (adult) (total words: 2764)
Although	0	1
and	20	19
as	6	12
but	4	16
'coz	4	17
if	0	12
or	0	13
so	0	29
then	5	20
though	1	1
when	3	13
Total	43/1440 = 2.9% connectives	153/2764 = 5.5% connectives

viewers' turns, we can see that the number of turns taken by *so*-prefaced questions over the whole of the interview is not significantly different (Table 6.3).

Table 6.3 Frequency of *so*-prefaced questions in two child interviews

Interview	Age of child	No. of interviewer turns	No. of so-prefaced questions	% of turns taken by so-prefaced questions
Traejacfa.txt	14	245	33	13%
Tralcfa.txt	5	519	52	10%

If anything, there are slightly more *so*-prefaced questions in the interview of the adolescent. However, an examination of the distribution of the *so*-prefaced questions over the phases of the interview reveals an important pattern of use. I am using the phases identified in the Home Office's (1992) *Memorandum of Good Practice* (MOGP) for interviewing child witnesses involved in criminal proceedings. This suggests four phases in the interview process: (1) Rapport; (2) Free narrative account; (3) Questioning; (4) Close. The interview ideally moves from establishing rapport through informal talk and play to listening to a child's freely-given account of the event and then to asking questions (Table 6.4).

Table 6.4 Distribution of *so*-prefaced questions over three phases of the interview

Interview	Age of child	Turns	Phase of interview	No. of so questions	% of turns taken by so questions
Traejacfa.txt	14	1–65	Rapport	10	15%
		66–103	Free narrative	1	3%
		104–240	Questioning	12	9%
		240–245	Close	0	0%
Tralcfa.txt	5	1–87	Rapport	5	7%
		88–458	Questioning	57	15%
		459–519	Close	0	

The figures in the right-hand columns of the table show a clear difference in distribution of the *so*-prefaced questions between the 14-year-old and the five-year-old. The adolescent's interview follows the standard process of four phases, but the very young child is unable to achieve free and spontaneous narrative; it has to be induced through questioning. During the free narrative stage of the adolescent interview, the interviewer uses hardly any questions and only one *so*-preface, the interviewer's turns mainly consisting of minimal responses and encouragement. In the questioning phase the tables turn and the interviewer's turns become lengthier and predominantly questioning with a high proportion of *so*-prefaced questions. This pattern of use is also found in interviews with adult defendants.

In the interview of the five-year-old, questioning is the main form of interviewer turn, with no free narrative phase since the child is too young and nervous to be able to do this. However, questioning is only begun after a lengthy rapport phase, where *so*-prefaced questions are frequently used to introduce new topics, much like the conversational uses described above. Here in the rapport phase the interviewer uses questions such as:

{A21}   Right **so** are D and G your brothers?
{A36}   Three. Right. **So** can you tell me who sleeps in what bedroom then?
{A52}   Ah. Right. **So** does he work away from home a lot?
{A53}   Oh. Right. **So** was he at your birthday?

We could describe the function of these questions as *topic-opening and focusing*. Here, though, unlike in conversation, since it is an asymmetrical dyadic interaction, one speaker, the interviewer, introduces the topics. Topic shift is logical and more sequential, and therefore more consistent than in conversation (where inconsistency is tolerated and even valued for its variety), since one of the goals of the interview is to produce coherence. We can see that, as in the conversational setting, these questions have organisational and procedural properties, signalled through the use of *so*. Fraser (1999, p. 950) suggests that discourse markers (such as *so* in question prefaces) 'signal a relationship between the segment they introduce, S2, and the prior segment, S1' and 'have a core meaning which is procedural, not conceptual'. Van Dijk (1981, p. 166) emphasises the pragmatic rather than the semantic properties of connectives, too, stating that 'pragmatic connectives express relations between speech acts, whereas semantic connectives express relations between denoted facts'. He makes a useful distinction between 'semantic *so*' and 'pragmatic *so*' (*op. cit.*, p. 171). I suggest that the use of *so*, here, is primarily pragmatic and most strongly related to the development of the narrative rather than semantic result.

In the questioning phase, the aim is to lead the child or adult back through the narrative and the *so*-prefaced questions are an important feature of the questioning. Alongside *and*-prefaced questions, which are used to develop a section of the narrative, the *so*-prefaced questions are used to lead the narrative on from one logical stage to another and are boundary markers between one topic and its cognitive sequence (indicated with a dashed line in Extract 3, below). *So* marks the focus on a new topic and *and* continues it, as we can see in Extract 3, where DC is the interviewer and N is the interviewee:

Extract 3: Tralcf.txt

DC   **Right so are D and G your brothers?**

N   Yeah.

DC   **And** how old are they?

N   G's two and D's eight.

DC   That's right. **And** you're the middle one then aren't you at five?

N   (Nods head).

DC   Right. **And** can you tell me what your house is like? Can you describe your house to me?

N   Erm.

DC   What's it look like? Could you draw it?

N   (Nods head).

DC   Do you want to draw the house then?

(. . . Dialogue continues prompting the drawing of the house and its rooms.)

- -

DC   **Right. So can you tell me who sleeps in what bedroom then?**

N   My mum and my dad sleep together, and D and G sleep together and I sleep on my own.

From Extract 3, it is apparent that the use of *so*-prefaced questions to focus on a topic and *and*-prefaced questions to continue it have a narrative-structuring function. The use of *so* and *and* in these questions, although adverbial, is simultaneously conjunctive, because it mirrors the use of *and* and *so* in the narrative sections of the interviewee's storytelling, as seen in Extracts 1 and 2, above.

We could describe the function of the *so*-prefaced questions as *topic developers* or *topic sequencers* whilst at the same time *marking* the discoursal act and topic boundary. It is not insignificant that *so*-questions are often preceded by the boundary marker *right*, which underlines the transition from one event to the next and makes these 'boundary exchanges' (Sinclair and Coulthard, 1975), as noted in conversation. We can see this as a combination of discourse markers: acceptance followed by movement, or as Sinclair and Coulthard (1975) and Stenström (1994, pp. 85–6) describe it, as frame and focus in an exchange opening. Frame signals that 'a message is on the way and that there will be a change of topics' and focus is concerned with 'focusing on what is to come'. However, Stenström's analysis is chiefly in relation to conversation, and though it deals with prefacing in the focusing act, it doesn't include question prefacing. These questions do not have a conversational tone, as do the *so*-prefaced questions in the rapport phase, or the *so*-prefaced questions in everyday conversation. It is not a case of '*What shall we talk about next?*' – they are goal and discourse focused. It is important for the interviewer to establish the facts and sequence of the narrative; the *and*-prefaced questions develop the facts in a topic and the *so*-prefaced questions mark the event and develop its (con)sequence. Sequence is underlined through the use of *then* as a frequent adverbial initiator or end-focus in these questions, as in:

> **So** can you tell me who sleeps in what bedroom **then**?   (Extract 5)
> **So** what does he do when he comes into your bedroom **then**? (Tralcf.txt)
> **So, then, then** what happens?   (Tralcf.txt)

The function of these questions is different from the semantic reason or result. It is a pragmatic function that marks stages of the narrative discourse in a way that makes the interviewer the compiler and (re)constructor of the significant events leading up to and including the criminal act, in the case of the two children here, sexual assault. The reconstructive function of the questions is underlined by the presence of metalanguage items such as *you said* or *you say*:

> DC   Right. So, what I'm trying to get is a picture of ho- what he actually did, okay. **So you said** you were wearing boots, how did he take those off? (Tralcf.txt)
>
> DC   Right. **So you say** you actually ran away on Friday night? (Traejacf.txt)

The metalinguistic verb *say* collocating with the *so*-preface contributes to the pragmatic force of the *so*-prefaced question giving it a discourse structural function. In this way the lexical and discoursal planes of talk are united through semantic, discoursal and pragmatic aspects of the interaction.

The boundary-marking function of *so*-prefacing is further emphasised by its use at phase boundaries. The phases of child and adult interviews are clearly marked by the interviewer, often with *so* used as a starter (Extract 4) or with a *so*-prefaced question (Extract 5):

Extract 4: Traejacfa.txt

> {A65}   Right. Okay you said that you're up here today to ... to catch this person who raped you. Yeah? What I need you to do is tell me what happened ... Tell me from Friday four o'clock, all right, evening time. Until Sunday morning ... Give me as much detail as you can ... and I'll just let you talk. All right, **so** off you go.

Extract 5: Traejacfa.txt

> {A104}   Right. Okay. **So you've told me quite a lot there, haven't you?** But I need to know a little bit more detail, okay. **So what we're going to do is go back to the beginning again and I'll just ask you a few questions about what's actually happened. Right?** You say that you left the house at four o'clock. What- which- four o'clock was it you left the house?

Extract 4 marks the end of the rapport phase and beginning of the free narrative phase, and Extract 5 marks the end of the free narrative and the start of the questioning phase.

This structural and reconstructive function is important in interviews with both children and adults. However, with adults, these questions are also used to summarise, evaluate and label the previous answers in order to focus the questioning on a particularly important evidential detail. In the following extract from an interview with a defendant (labelled J) in an interview for an alleged rape, there are five *so*-prefaced questions of this kind. This is just a sample of these kinds of questions that are found throughout my data and in other parts of this interview. In the extract bold indicates the evaluative items:

Extract 6: Tramfam.txt

```
 1  DS   And how many drinks did you have in the Indian restaurant?
 2  J    One.
 3  DS   So are you saying that all evening you had four pints?
 4  J    Mm.
 5       . . .
 6  DS   What time do you think you got there?
 7  J    I'm not really sure cos I didn't have a watch, erm I thi-
 8       eleven I think or near enough coming up to eleven o'clock.
 9  DS   So nearly eleven o'clock in the evening. Did you -
10  J    Or earlier.
11  DS   Or earlier?
12  J    Mm.
13       . . .
14  DS   . . . What did he say?
15  J    Nothing.
16  DS   So what other conversation was there about T [the rape complainant]
17       then?
18  J    That was about it.
19  DS   What he, him suggesting that you and K had sex with her in her r-
20  J    Mm.
21  DS   A .. and with or without her consent?
22  J    No. With her consent.
23       . . .
24  DS   Did T tell you to go in there and uhh speak to her?
25  J    Yeah
26  DS   And did K tell you to go in there and shag her? You're nodding your
27       head.
28  J    Yes.
29  DS   And did D tell you to go in there and shag her as well?
30  J    Yeah.
31  DS   So you were a bit under pressure really to go in there and – have sex
32       with her weren't you?
33  J    Mm.
34       . . .
35  DS   - at that stage she was obviously saying to you she didn't want you to
36       have sex with her otherwise you wouldn't have said those words would
37       you?
38  J    No.
```

39	DS	D'you see? You're nodding your head.
40	J	Yes.
41	DS	So is it **fair to say** then that before you had sex with her she was
42		**certainly** saying to you she didn't want to have sex with you?
43	J	She says she don't know I think.
44	DS	You think?
45	J	As far as I can remember.

The examples in Extract 6 illustrate the kind of evaluation that is carried out through these questions in the data. In the five *so*-prefaced questions in this extract (lines 3, 9, 16, 31 and 41, respectively) the interviewer is evaluating the extent of each event. It is the extent:

1 of the drinking that is in question (line 3);
2 to which the precise time of the alleged rape can be ascertained and the extent to which the drinking and the reliability of the defendant can be relied on, by comparison with the complainant (line 9);
3 to which the alleged rape was planned and discussed with others (line 16);
4 to which the defendant was acting on the persuasion of others in an act that he knew was wrong (line 31);
5 to which the defendant knew that the complainant did not want sex (line 41).

This is signalled through the use of evaluative adjectives and adverbs, *all*, *other*, *a bit*, *nearly* and *certainly*, and through the labelling noun *under pressure*.

In addition, we can see that these questions can help the interviewer to get the interviewee to reformulate an earlier position. In line 14 the interviewer asks *'What did he say?'* to which the interviewee replies *'Nothing'*. However, when he asks the *so*-prefaced question, *'So what **other** conversation was there about T* [the rape complainant] *then?'*, based on previous replies, the interviewee starts to indicate that 'nothing' is not the whole story. He says, 'That was about it', which invites the interviewer to probe further. Similarly in lines 31–40 the interviewee is less secure in his original claim that the victim agreed to sex. Although he avoids direct agreement with the interviewer, after the *so*-question (lines 38–40), he gives indirect agreement, as he has already conceded that the complainant's words amounted to saying that she didn't want to have sex with him. *So*-prefaced questions therefore have an important function in evaluatory summary and are effective in challenging the interviewee's account, to such an extent that they may be forced to reformulate it in a way that is evidentially more significant.

The effect of *so* in these questions is to focus on the status of the talk, as in the conversation and the child-witness interviews. But in addition to the narrative focus, in defendant interviews the focus for the interviewee is on a particular aspect of the narrative that requires precision for evidential purposes. It is, in the words of the interviewing detective at the start of the interview, a response to 'somebody else's perception of what happened during that evening'. This means that these questions mark challenges to the defendant from the witness's perception, a complaint of rape. *So*, combined with the evaluation and question function, marks the challenge to the interviewee. In the conversational use of these questions the challenge was merely conversational; here it is evidential. It is constructed by the interviewer from the contributions of the interviewee and means 'I legitimately challenge you to agree because this is what you said'.

This kind of *so*-prefaced question also assumes agreement, since it consists of a summary of the interviewee's own discourse. If the defendant does not agree with the statement contained in the question, he is challenged to provide a rebuttal which will induce a series of follow-up questions to examine it. Drew (1992, p. 507), although not directly discussing *so*-prefacing, talks about the power of the attorney in the courtroom to question in a such a way that it provides 'the opportunity to bring together pieces of information to make a point'. He quotes Sacks (1992), who says that 'the person who is asking the questions seems to have first rights to perform an operation on the set of answers' (cited in Drew, 1992, p. 507). The operation that is performed on the set of answers in the alleged rape interview, through the use of evaluatory *so*-prefaced questions, is one of summative evaluation. Here, pragmatic (evaluatory and narrative) and semantic (causal) *so* are used. Whereas the child was empowered and enabled to tell a story through the use of *so*-prefaced questions, the defendant is, at times, challenged by them. In conversation, we saw that a speaker could challenge another through *so*-prefacing (as in Extract 1), but in interviews with defendants the challenge is more significant.

These questions are particularly important in the interrogation of the defendant's story. Here the asymmetry could be described as powerlessness for the defendant, but, in terms of establishing weighted evidence that may help to establish the burden of proof, these questions can be seen to play an important part in advancing the presentation of key narrative facts. Important aspects of denial and defence will be established but these questions are not without their dangers. It can be seen that they constitute assumptions; however, these assumptions are based on the narrative of the interviewee and are backed up by other questions for clarification.

Conclusions

This chapter has examined the function and use of *so*-prefaced questions across corpora. Using such small corpora one could argue that the density

of *so*-prefaced questions could be a stylistic feature of a particular interviewer. However, the interviewers are all different police officers, of both
sexes, and are from different parts of England. For that reason, I believe
that institutional context is more influential on the formal and pragmatic
properties of talk than interviewer style. Whilst there were similarities in
the function and use of these questions between the conversational and
institutional data – in both settings *so*-prefaced questions were used to
mark, sequence and even challenge – the pragmatic effects and implications
rendered by the asymmetrical institutional setting were more summative
and evaluatory. Furthermore, a comparison of the child witness and adult
defendant interviews revealed that there were fluctuating asymmetries in
operation.

In interviews with very young child witnesses the asymmetrical relationship between interviewer and interviewee should not be equated with
power over the powerless. *So*-prefaced questions, in association with *and*-
prefaced questions and other eliciting acts, enable the interviewer to
construct, summarise and organise the child's narrative, at times becoming the principal storyteller. This is supportive and scaffolds the child's
storytelling in a way that is natural in parent and child interaction (Foster,
1990).

In an adolescent witness, we saw the narrative and story-telling focus
starting with the interviewee in the free narrative. Here the witness is
the controlling speaker, with the interviewer making a minimal contribution. *So*-prefaced questions are infrequent and are used to support and
stimulate further narrative. The locus of control then moves back to the
interviewer in the questioning phase, in order to direct the examination
of the narrative. It is at this point that *so*-prefaced questions become
more frequent as they take on a narrative sequence and organisational
importance.

In adult interviews, too, the interviewee is invited to produce free and
spontaneous narrative, which gives narrative control to the defendant. Here,
because of age and experience, as with older children, the interviewee
is capable of producing considerable stretches of narrative, where the
occurrences of *so* are almost exclusively of the conjunctive kind, meaning
'therefore' and 'in order to'. It is in the questioning of adults, though,
that the asymmetry produces *so*-prefaced questions that challenge defendants in specialised ways. Whilst in conversation, challenges through
so-prefaced questions are at most face-threatening, in police interviews
with defendants they recapitulate, summarise and evaluate the interviewee's previous responses in a way that expects or assumes agreement.
Any rebuttal of the assumptions will involve challenging the interviewer's words and may necessitate the interviewee reforming an earlier
position.

This analysis contributes to a better understanding of the function, use and effect of *so*-prefaced questions in a specialised institutional setting, questions that unite the semantic, discoursal and pragmatic planes of talk.

References

Aijmer, K. and Altenberg, B. (1991) *English Corpus Linguistics*. Harlow: Longman.

Aldridge, M. and Wood, J. (1998) *Interviewing Children: A Guide for Child Care and Forensic Practitioners*. Chichester: John Wiley.

Applebee, A. (1978) *The Child's Concept of Story*. Chicago: Chicago University Press.

Collins COBUILD English Dictionary (1995). London: HarperCollins.

Dillon, J. T. (1990) *The Practice of Questioning*. London: Routledge.

Drew, P. (1992) 'Contested Evidence in a Courtroom Examination: The Case of a Trial for Rape', in P. Drew and J. Heritage (eds), *Talk at Work*. Cambridge: Cambridge University Press, pp. 470–520.

Drew, P. and Heritage, J. (eds) (1992) *Talk at Work*. Cambridge: Cambridge University Press.

Foster, S. H. (1990) *The Communicative Competence of Young Children*. London: Longman.

Francis, G. (1994) 'Labelling Discourse: An Aspect of Nominal-Group Lexical Cohesion', in M. Coulthard (ed.), *Advances in Written Text Analysis*. London: Routledge, pp. 83–101.

Fraser, B. (1999) 'What are Discourse Markers?' *Journal of Pragmatics*, vol. 31(7), pp. 931–52.

Heritage, J. and Sorjonen, M-L. (1994) 'Constituting and Maintaining Activities across Sequences: *And*-Prefacing as a Feature of Question Design', *Language in Society*, vol. 23, pp. 1–29.

Home Office and the Department of Health (1992) *Memorandum of Good Practice on Video-recorded Interviews with Child Witnesses for Criminal Proceedings*. London: HMSO.

Johnson, A. J. (2001) 'Ask Me a Story – the Narrative Effect of *And*-Prefaced Questions in Formal Interviews', unpublished manuscript.

Labov, W. and Fanshel, D (1977) *Therapeutic Discourse: Psychotherapy as Conversation*. New York: Academic Press.

Leech, G. (1974) *Semantics*. Harmondsworth: Penguin.

Leech, G. (1983) *Principles of Pragmatics*. London: Longman.

Liles, B. Z. (1987) 'Episode Organisation and Cohesive Conjunctives in Narratives in Children With and Without Language Disorder', *Journal of Speech and Hearing Research*, vol. 30, pp. 185–96.

Matsumoto, K. (1999) '*And*-Prefaced Questions in Institutional Discourse', *Linguistics*, vol. 37(2), pp. 251–74.

Sacks, H. (1992) (1964–72) *Lectures on Conversation*, 2 vols, edited by G. Jefferson. Oxford: Blackwell.

Schiffrin, D. (1987) *Discourse Markers*. Cambridge: Cambridge University Press.

Sinclair, J. McH. and Coulthard, R. M. (1975) *Towards an Analysis of Discourse*. Oxford: Oxford University Press.

Stenström, A.-B. (1994) *An Introduction to Spoken Interaction*. London: Longman.

van Dijk, T. A. (1981) *Studies in the Pragmatics of Discourse*. The Hague: Mouton Publishers.

Walker, A. G. (1994) *Handbook on Questioning Children: A Linguistic Perspective*. Washington: ABA Center on Children and the Law.

Software

Chandler, B. (1989) *Longman Mini-Concordancer* (version 1.01), Longman UK Ltd.

Collins COBUILD, *COBUILD Direct. Lookup* <http://www.cobuild.collins.co.uk/>

Woolls, D. (unpublished) Text cleaning software.

7
'Three's a Crowd': Shifting Dynamics in the Interpreted Interview

Sonia Russell

Introduction

Much recent research (Berk-Seligson, 1990, 2000; Morris, 1995, 1999; Hale, 1999; Mikkelson, 2000) has been directed towards demonstrating how interpreting alters the processes and, possibly, the outcomes of trials. However, long before a case comes to trial, an arrest is made and the suspect is interviewed. It is this interview that is the 'upstream' event that sets in motion everything that leads to the trial, months later and miles 'downstream'. Just as at court, a non-English-speaking suspect has the right to be 'linguistically present' at his or her interview, particularly as this is considered to be their first opportunity to set out their explanation of events. However, the insertion of interpreting between the primary participants constitutes a radical shift from the dynamics of the monolingual interview and consequently affects the linguistic processes. This chapter situates the investigative interview within the UK legal system and, using tape-recorded data from Police and Customs interviews, discusses the interpreted interview as a linguistic event, before examining some of the effects which the presence and participation of the interpreter has/may have upon the turn-taking system.

The investigative interview as a situated activity

When a crime is alleged to have been committed, the suspect is arrested and cautioned and may then be taken to a Police or Customs Custody area to be interviewed. The interview is recorded simultaneously on two audio cassettes. One of these is sealed and may only be opened upon the order of a judge, or in the presence of a representative of the Crown Prosecution Service. The other is kept open as a working copy. From this, the Police or Customs can make further copies and typewritten transcripts for use both by prosecution and defence.

In the event of a trial, in cases of serious offences, the transcript of interview which constitutes the main plank of the prosecution's case is almost always read out in full. It can thus be seen that the interview, which took place in the first hours of the case, maintains a position of primary importance right through to the final minutes of the trial, where it constitutes a major piece of evidence for consideration by the jury in reaching their verdict.

In the case of non-English-speaking suspects, the decision as to whether an interpreter is required is normally taken jointly by the interviewing and/or arresting officer and the Custody Sergeant at the police station. This decision is governed by section 13C(b) of the PACE Codes of Practice, which states that:

> . . . a person must not be interviewed in the absence of a person capable of acting as interpreter if:
>
> (a) he has difficulty in understanding English;
>
> (b) the interviewing officer cannot speak the person's own language;
>
> (c) and the person wishes an interpreter to be present.

In the case of a police interview, the interviewing officer begins the proceedings by announcing that: 'This interview is being tape-recorded'. There follows a sequence of formalities which includes presentation of all persons present, a reminder of the right to free and independent legal advice (whether or not a solicitor is present), and the formal Caution.

Before proceeding to linguistic aspects of the interview, and presentation and analysis of the data, it may be useful to consider, in general terms, the way in which interviews are conducted. Personal communication with police officers has revealed broad agreement that the aims of interview are to give and obtain information and to 'get at the truth' in a manner which is robust, challenging and effective, as well as lawful and ethical.

Leaving aside philosophical questions as to what constitutes 'the truth', one of the interviewing officer's principal objectives is to discover whether the suspect was *knowingly concerned* in the committal of the particular offence. In cases of illegal importation of drugs, for example, the discovery of drugs upon the person constitutes *actus reus* (the guilty deed). However, in the UK, both *mens rea* (the guilty mind), and *actus reus* must generally be proved before a person can be convicted of an offence.

The requirement to establish whether or not there was *mens rea* informs the training of police and customs officers. With this objective, police training in interviewing skills is based on a mnemonic of PEACE:

P   Plan and prepare;

E   Engage and explain;

A   Account – obtain a first account of events, suspending belief and disbelief. Review the account, picking a topic, probing and summarising it. Attempt to uncover any anomalies or inconsistencies and get the DP to commit to or compound any apparent lies he may have told. Move on to the next topic and repeat the process, finally challenging the first account;

C   Closure, in a polite and positive manner;

E   Evaluate.

The above mnemonic is self-explanatory, and provides an indication of the overall framework within which police officers conduct interviews. Certainly, the gloss in section A (Account) makes explicit the quest for *mens rea*. Although police training has moved a long way from the overt intention to obtain admissions, or to prove certain points, A = Account demonstrates that the underlying aim is nonetheless to seek evidence of guilt, if guilt there is.

If PEACE is a model for investigative interviewing, PACE (the Police and Criminal Evidence Act 1984) is the law under which such interviews are carried out. More specifically, Code C of the PACE Codes of Practice governs the way in which the police handle the detention, treatment and *questioning* of suspects. This accounts for the admonishments to 'Engage and Explain' and to 'Close in a Polite and Positive manner' in the PEACE mnemonic, as PACE states that 'No police officer may try to obtain answers to questions or elicit a statement by use of oppression' (Code C 11.3). Further:

> As soon as [the officer] ... believes that a prosecution should be brought against him [the detained person] and that there is sufficient evidence for it to succeed, he shall ask the person if he has anything further to say. If the person indicates that he has nothing more to say the officer shall without delay cease to question him about that offence.
>
> (Code C 11.4)

It can be seen that one participant in this institutional event, the officer, has a role which may be unique in the extent to which it is overtly defined. Not only is the role minutely defined, the officer himself has been selected following certain strict criteria, trained in investigative interviewing skills, inculcated with the laws which govern them and constantly monitored in the performance of his duties. He is, to a certain extent, a predictable entity, one-half of a 'situated activity system' (Goffman, 1981, p. 96), the other half of which, the detained person, is almost entirely unpredictable.

The detained person is neither selected nor trained in any conventional sense, although of course sociologists may argue that his birth and background constitute 'training', or at least preconditioning to certain modes of behaviour. Criminologists, too, would invoke the 'profile' of the likely offender; his aims are diametrically opposed to those of the officer. At both a linguistic and a sociological level, this opposition of aims constitutes the defining feature of the interview. Put simply, the officer seeks to demonstrate *mens rea*, the detained person seeks to deny it.

In this sense, investigative interviews constitute a genre that differentiates them from other dialogue, whether everyday talk-in-interaction, or institutional dialogue. Although there are, of course, differences between Police and Customs interviews, for the purposes of this chapter they may be treated as one sub-genre of investigative interviews among others, ranging from, for example, a school head interviewing a pupil suspected of some misdemeanour, to torture aimed at extracting a 'confession'. In every case there is something at stake, whether it is the interviewee's freedom, embarrassment among peers or life itself. In every case, the interviewee's 'story' is tested to destruction.

Tape-recording (mandatory since the Police and Criminal Evidence Act 1984), has dramatically altered the dynamics of the interview as a speech event. Unlike the courtroom where its presence goes largely unremarked, it is here accorded a *persona* by all of those present. Physically, the interviewing officer and detained person sit closest to the microphone. The detained person's attention is explicitly drawn to the fact that new tapes are being unsealed before him. Mention is also usually made of the microphone on the wall and the necessity for giving verbal answers rather than head nods and shakes. The tape buzzer, marking the start and finish of the interview, provides a further indicator of physical presence.

Psychologically, the tape is a strong incentive to participants to orient towards their 'institutional identities' (Drew and Sorjonen, 1997, p. 97). The interviewing officer is aware of the tape's prime importance as evidence in court, and will formulate and reformulate questions until either an explicit answer has been recorded, or until the detained person's answers become patently evasive.

Further, non-verbal activity such as showing of documents, or a non-verbal response by the detained person, will entail explicit reference by a turn prefaced: 'For the benefit of the tape . . . ', as in the following extract:

O   'For the benefit of the tape, I am showing Mr. X a photocopy of passport . . . '

Finally, part 3 of the formal Caution draws the detained person's attention to the fact that 'Anything you do say may be used in evidence'. This means specifically that the interview is being tape recorded and that the tape constitutes part of the evidence.

From an interactional point of view, at least at a superficial level, investigative interviews appear to be a series of questions and answers. Indeed at the grossest of macro levels, the interview consists of one question: 'Did you?' and one answer: 'No I didn't/yes I did' (or of course, 'No comment'). However, closer inspection reveals that:

(a)   not all of the officer's turns are questions. Speech acts include informing, challenging, agreeing, commenting and encouraging, with both narrative and evaluating moves;
(b)   not all of the detained person's turns are answers. They include informing, challenging, agreeing, commenting, narrative, evaluative and even questioning moves.

Some of these are apparent in Extract 1 below using the transcription conventions and abbreviations:

[ ]	Simultaneous or overlapping speech	DP	Detained person
=	Latched utterances	O	Officer
(.)	Pause, less than 0.5 seconds	I	Interpreter
(1.5)	Pause timed in seconds	la::	Preceding syllable
°fine°	Spoken more quietly than		lengthened
	surrounding speech		

Extract 1

```
1   DP   u:hm (3.0) .hh well 'cos the date on the ticket was for later on I went to (.)
2        When we got into the port I saw a (name) kind of a (1.0) ca- you know a
3        place=
4   O    =a kiosk?=
5   DP   =yeah a little kiosk sort [of place ]
6   O                              [yeah ?  ]
7   DP   [and I went in there        ] yeah I went in there and said (.) can I
8   O    [and you drive up to it don't you]
9   DP   go home please 'cos you know the time on this is different is can I (.) get on
10       the next ferry please=
11  O    =mm
12  DP   he said yeah (.) gave me another ticket
13  O    yeah .hh gave you duty free passes didn't they. (1.5) I've got them here
14       actually=
15  DP   =yeah probably
16  O    how many?
17  DP   I don't know (.) I mean literally I was looking forward to going to sleep,
18  O    they gave you two=
19  DP   =yeah?
```

The officer (O) is here *eliciting* an account of the detained person's (DP) journey immediately prior to his arrest. From this macro perspective, the extract is part of a prolonged questioning sequence.

However, it can be seen that the detained person is able to set up a *narrative* in lines 1–3, in which the officer collaborates by offering the suggestion 'kiosk?' in line 4 with rising intonation. DP takes up the suggestion, eliciting an *encouraging* 'yeah?' from O (line 6) before he has finished. With his simultaneous declarative tag question in line 8, O attempts to move the story on, but is unsuccessful. DP simply *acknowledges* the attempt, but continues with his story. O's next turn in line 11 is merely back-channelling. He does not succeed in taking back the turn until line 13. Here, 'yeah .hh' announces another declarative question, with a question tag, followed by an *informing* move 'I've got them here actually', thus precluding any denial by the detained person. Nonetheless, DP's turn in line 15 'yeah probably' resembles a *comment* on the officer's information that he has the tickets, rather than an answer to the first part question. He also deflects the next question, 'I don't know', before attempting to change the topic back to his tiredness, which had been mentioned at an earlier stage. The officer's turn in line 18 is framed as an *informing* move which does not take up the detained person's attempted change of topic and the DP's next-turn 'yeah', with rising intonation merely *comments*, with the intonation of 'oh really?'

Thus it can be seen that, except in the grossest possible terms, it would be wrong to categorise the investigative interview as a series of simple questions and answers. It is a complex dialogue of opposing aims, realised by a variety of means. The participants orientate to a mechanical third party, the tape, which represents a future 'referee group' (Mason, 2000, p. 6), the judge and jury.

In cases where the detained person is a non-English speaker, the dynamics of the interview are altered radically with the addition of an interpreter, transforming the oppositional dyad into a triadic mixture of opposition, cooperation and shifting alignments. The next sections define the *mode* of interpreting used in investigative interviews, review some of the current work in the field of legal interpreting and provide an analysis of the effects of interpreting upon turn-taking, drawing on data from a corpus of interpreted interviews.

The interpreted interview

Alexieva (1997, pp. 156–7) identifies two 'prototype' modes of interpreting:

1 *Simultaneous*: characterised by 'non-stop delivery of the source text and parallel production of the target text'; and
2 *Consecutive*: '... delivery of the source text in chunks of varying lengths followed by the production of the target text'.

Liaison interpreting is classified as a 'peripheral member' of consecutive interpreting, (*ibid.*, p. 159), which tends to take place in more intimate settings, with fewer participants than in conference or large meeting situations. It is generally used in face-to-face interaction, where participants are directly involved in co-constructing the dialogue.

In the investigative interview, where both principal participants are directly involved and where communication is dyadic, liaison interpreting is used almost exclusively. That is, a primary participant will speak in 'chunks' of, say, 10 seconds, wait until the interpreter has translated, then speak for a further 10 seconds and so on.

Communication through a liaison interpreter is perhaps the most difficult mode for primary participants. Arbitrary chunking of text in one language can leave the interpreter unable to even begin her interpretation into another, since a vital syntactic or contextual element may be missing from the first chunk. Further, turn-taking, as discussed in the following section requires strict discipline which cannot always be imposed by the interpreter.

Echoing Bakhtin's (1981) view of all language as *dialogic*, recent research has put forward a *dialogic* model of interpreting (Linell, 1996; Wadensjö,

1998). This asserts that participants co-construct the text, as opposed to the *monologic* view which sees it as a one-way transfer of the speaker's intentions, with the interpreter as an uninvolved conduit. Wadensjö (1998) also suggests that the interpreter has two equally important roles, that of translating, and that of coordinating. Her extracts from immigration interviews do show a quite extraordinary level of intervention on the part of the interpreter, which might best be termed *community interpreting*, since the interpreter also serves, to some extent, as a mediator.

However, this apparent tolerance of intervention does highlight one of the principal dilemmas of liaison interpreting and, more specifically, that of interviews with suspects. It is a question of how much license the interpreter should accord herself in order to facilitate comprehension between primary participants. In an interview with a suspect she is, it must be remembered, facilitating interaction not only between two languages and two cultures, but also between two social spheres. The scope for miscommunication is tremendous, and the consequences are potentially grave.

On the other hand, besides avoiding any alteration of illocutionary force of the primary participants' utterances, the interpreter is barred from any intervention that might alter the *legal* implications of what is said. Viewed against a background of dissimilar legal systems in different countries and the consequent impossibility of assigning terminological equivalence, it can be seen that here is a major dilemma. The interpreter is caught between the extremes of translating for 'skopos', or purpose/aim envisaged (Vermeer, 1998, p. 44) and the legal requirement for a 'faithful' rendering of the original.

Problems of register are also inherent in the difference between social spheres of the primary participants, the '...clash of world perspectives' (Hale, 1997, p. 197) between the officer as institutional representative and suspect as lay person. Hale (*ibid.*), for example, notes a tendency for interpreters (in court) to raise the register when interpreting the defendant's utterances into English for the barrister, and to lower it when interpreting the barrister's utterances into Spanish for the defendant.

Shlesinger (1991) notes that interpreters tend to clean up the disfluencies and false starts of primary participants, and attributes this, in part, to a desire not to be seen as unprofessional or incompetent. Morris (1995, pp. 31–2) adds that, like court reporters, interpreters are expected to clean up utterances from the judiciary, but to reproduce all of the disfluencies from witnesses, thus indicating that '...the "translate, don't interpret" admonition turns out to be relativist in philosophical and practical terms'. In her study of interpreters' treatment of leading questions, Berk-Seligson (1999, pp. 48–9) deduces that their reduction in coerciveness may simply mean that interpreters are not 'keenly aware' of question form, or that they are trying to protect the witness from feelings of discomfort. Rigney (1999) also examines changes in register and pragmatic force in interpreting of questions in court, although she does not hypothesise as to possible reasons for these changes.

In theory, interpreters should adhere rigidly to primary participants' choice of register, leaving them to sort out resultant miscommunication as best they can. This applies both in court and in interview, where certain ambiguities, both from officer/lawyer and suspect/defendant may well be strategic and therefore vulnerable to 'divergent rendition' (Wadensjö, 1998, p. 106) by the interpreter. The interpreter's perception of a successful communicative act may diverge from that of the primary participants in a specific context. However, this does not take into account instances of genuine cultural or linguistic misunderstanding, where a judicious intervention by the interpreter may prevent the interview from becoming 'bogged down' in extraneous and irrelevant exchanges.

It would seem that the solution to the dilemma lies somewhere along the continuum between interventionist and non-interventionist policies. This leaves the legal interpreter to exercise her own judgment to achieve the delicate balance in what she perceives as her normative role.

From their experience, both officer and interpreter adopt a common frame (Goffman, 1974) for the 'interview with suspect' event. It includes not only 'what it is that is going on here' (*ibid.*, p. 8), but also the physical and spatial elements involved (Kendon, 1992). At the start of the interview, they move to predesignated places and carry out the preliminary formalities with very little reference to the detained person. This means that, for the first few minutes, his role in relation to 'role others' is ill-defined. The frame, or schema of a dyadic interaction that he might have carried into the room is rendered void by the presence of a third party who controls all of his speaking rights. His prototypical 'police interview' has acquired an extra node.

The next section will use examples from the data to highlight one feature, turn-taking, with particular reference to overlapping talk, where the presence of an interpreter alters the dynamics of the interaction.

Turn-taking

Following Sacks, Schegloff and Jefferson's (1974) seminal work on the local management of turns, Roy (2000, p. 347) cites more recent work (Bennett, 1981; Edelsky, 1981; Tannen, 1984) which has shown that turns are less rule-governed than originally posited by Sacks *et al.* (*ibid.*). Specifically, that conversation contains overlapping talk, which is acceptable and is not considered as interruption. Indeed Tannen (1984) found that the overlapping talk of some of the interactants in her data signalled involvement and encouragement.

Despite the apparently rigid Q/A format of interviews, both interruptions and overlapping talk happen. The primary participants may both begin to speak at once, one may join in whilst the other is in mid-turn, or may start to speak again, having apparently finished a turn. However, as Roy (2000, p. 84) succinctly puts it, 'An interpreter cannot interpret two speakers at the same time', and it is the interpreter's strategies for dealing with this that bring into focus one aspect of the specific dynamics of the interpreted interview. Using Roy (2000) as a baseline, I shall present sections of data that appear to support this view.

The tape recording of interviews with suspects magnifies this interactional dilemma. Not only can the interpreter not interpret overlapping talk, the tape recorder cannot distinguish it and the transcriber cannot transcribe it. Thus, the record of the interview may be still further degraded before its arrival as a piece of evidence in court.

All three participants orient in some way to the presence of the tape. The officer and interpreter know from experience how to 'do' tape-recorded interviews and the officer explains the recording procedure before switching on the tape recorder. However, taking turns to speak through an interpreter requires a rigid discipline that is not always enforceable, particularly where one participant is from a culture where overlapping talk is acceptable or even desirable (see Tannen, 1984).

Extract 2 below shows an occurrence of DP-initiated overlap, where he has failed to allow time for within-turn interpreting and where the end of the interpreter's rendering in line 4 becomes unclear:

Extract 2

```
1   O    but you're saying you- i- in your m- own mind (1.0) you (.) thought there
2        was nothing wrong with any of this.=
3   I    =vous êtes en train de dire donc que vous dans votre tête il n'y avait rien de
4        mal [unclear              ]
         (you're saying then that in your own mind there was nothing wrong)
5   DP       [non 'y avait rien de mal]
              (no there was nothing wrong)
6   I    No there w- yes there was nothing wrong
```

The end of the interpreter's utterance in line 4 becomes untranscribable as DP's utterance covers her voice. Presumably the interpreter was finishing her rendering of 'with any of this', but this cannot be recovered from the tape. (It is also interesting to note that, following DP's stressed 'non', the interpreter matches her rendering to this negative confirmation, before changing to confirm the positive part of O's utterance, 'but you're saying...'.)

Participants can initiate overlap with each other, or with the interpreter. Indeed, in extreme cases it is not uncommon for the interpreter to initiate overlap, that is, to interpret part of a segment simultaneously. This can occur where she is beginning to tire, or where, in spite of her best efforts at control, the participants continually deny her space to complete her interpretation. Further, many detained persons using an interpreter have at least a rudimentary knowledge of English, and may attempt to reply directly to a question from the officer, without waiting for the interpretation.

Experienced officers will preempt this problem by saying during the preliminary formalities, 'The questions will be put to you in English and will be translated into French. You will reply in French and your replies will be translated into English'.

Interpreting strategies

According to Roy (2000, p. 85) the interpreter has four options for dealing with overlapping talk. She can:

1 stop one (or both) speakers and allow the other speaker to continue;
2 momentarily ignore one speaker's overlapping talk, hold the segment of talk in memory, continue interpreting the other speaker, and then produce the 'held' talk immediately following the end of a speaker's turn;
3 ignore overlapping talk completely;
4 momentarily ignore overlapping talk and upon finishing the interpretation of one speaker, offer the next turn to the other speaker, or indicate in some way that a turn was attempted.

In interviews, it is undesirable for the interpreter's voice to be heard on tape as a primary participant. That is, she should avoid taking a turn, except in extreme circumstances, such as a complete breakdown in communication caused by a cultural or linguistic equivalence problem. She should then identify herself by prefacing her turn with 'interpreter speaking'. This means that the first option of stopping one or both speakers can only be achieved by gesture.

Extract 3 shows an example of Roy's second option, where the interpreter holds a segment in memory and delivers it in a subsequent turn. The officer in this exchange has taken over the interview from a preceding officer and is reconfirming information. The held segment appears in bold type:

Extract 3

```
1   O    I understand the keys were in the battery compartment or near the
2        battery and the vehicle was er: collected by (DP name)
3   I    Et si je comprends bien les clés étaient dans la batterie ou près de la
4        batterie [et-  ]
         (and if I understand rightly the keys were in the battery or near the
         battery and-)
5   DP           [non ]non sous le cache de la batterie=
                 (no no under the battery cover)
6   I    =yes underneath the battery- battery [compartment (.) and you needed
7   DP                                         [fallait ouvrir le cache °et les clés
                                               (you had to open the cover and the keys
8   I    to open the] battery compartment and the keys were there .hh et que
9   DP   étaient là° ]
         were there)
```

10　I　**c'est vous qui avez été donc chercher** [**le camion sur ce parking**　　　]
　　　　(*and that it's you who went to collect the lorry on the carpark*)
11　DP　　　　　　　　　　　　　　　　　　[le camion à pied oui exacte oui]
　　　　　　　　　　　　　　　　　　　　　(*the lorry on foot yes that's right*)
12　I　yes on foot yes

DP overlaps in line 5 to correct O's assertion that the keys were *in* the battery compartment. At this point, I suspends her interpretation of the last part of O's turn (in bold), acknowledges and interprets DP's correction. In line 7, DP again does not wait for her to finish interpreting; he starts to expand his description of the keys' location whilst she is saying 'compartment'. This time, the interpreter holds on to her own turn and switches to simultaneous mode to render the expanded description. There are several possible reasons for this switch into a mode not normally allowable in an interview:

(a) DP's final segment '°et les clés étaient là°' was spoken quietly, so she was sure of her voice being clear on the tape-recording;
(b) she needed to keep the turn because of the uninterpreted segment that she was still holding from the officer's turn in lines 1/2;
(c) the conversational style of that particular DP involved a great deal of overlapping talk, which at times obliged her to interpret simultaneously to keep up. (This strategy is particularly noticeable towards the end of this four-tape interview, as the interpreter began to tire.)

Roy (*ibid.*) posits that (among other reasons) the interpreter may predict that the overlapping talk is going to be short and therefore she will not have to hold the suspended segment in memory for long. This may also be true of Extract 3, since DP's turns are clearly an insertion sequence consisting only of repair and expansion.

Finally, in line 8, having interpreted the complete insertion sequence of DP's repair and expansion, I takes a quick breath and renders the segment that she had been holding from line 2 (in bold).

There are few instances of overlapping talk instigated by officers in the data. However, Extract 4 below shows an example of overlapping talk by all three participants apparently caused by a misplaced pause from the interpreter:

Extract 4

1　O　remind me did you visit mister:: (name) in hospital
2　I　rappelez-moi est-ce que vous êtes allé rendre visite à (name) à l'hôpital
　　　　(*remind me did you go and visit (name) at the hospital*)
3　DP　oui Dimanche.=
　　　　(*yes on Sunday*)
4　I　=yes.(1.0) [yes on Sunday]
5　O　　　　　　　[did you vis. . . .]
6　DP　　　　　　[Dimanche　　] après son (.) son accident
　　　　　　　　　(*Sunday　　　　after his accident*)

```
7    I    after his (.) accident
8    O    OK
9    DP   en réanimation
          (in intensive care)
          (1.0)
10   I    when he was:: (1.0.) er in intensive care
11   O    °fine° .hh did you visit him (2.0) alone?
```

DP appears to have finished his utterance in line 3. However, I's utterance-final intonation on 'yes.' and the one-second pause in line 4 lead both DP and O to think that she has finished. Consequently, at the same time as she adds 'yes on Sunday' as an afterthought, both O and DP attempt to take the next turn, O as a question turn and DP to expand on his own response. O gives up the turn, contenting himself with a receipt marker in line 8 and allows DP to expand further, before finally managing to place his question in line 11.

Generally, experienced officers allow space both for detained persons to give complete answers and for interpreters to interpret. The only exceptions in my data are those where the detained person is 'rambling' or repeating himself and the officer wishes to bring him back to the point. These instantiations, however, are definitely classifiable as interruptions and are treated as such by the interpreter. She then switches from interpreting DP to interpreting O, as in Extract 5 below, where I abandons DP's turn in favour of a new question by O:

Extract 5

```
1    DP   et ils ont chargé du papier
          (and they loaded paper)
2    I    and they loaded [paper      ]
3    DP                   [les bobines ]
4    I    the rolls
5    DP   ils ont ramené le camion à (place)
          (they brought the lorry back to (place))
6    O    [and you saw paper ]
7    I    [they brought-    ] (.) et vous avez vu (.) ce papier
                             (and you saw this paper)
8    DP   oui parce-que m-même euh le (company name) parce-que ça =
          (yes because even er the (company name) because that =)
9    I    =yes=
10   DP   =ça c-c'est moi qui l'ai déchargé
          =(that was me that unloaded it)
11   I    even at (company name) it was me that unloaded
```

Interpreters' decisions concerning turn allocation in overlapping talk may be based upon immediate contextual considerations. In this extract, the officer's line of questioning seeks to establish the driver's awareness of various loads.

The interpreter may have perceived the importance of the officer's question in line 6, leading her to abandon DP's unsolicited utterance, (he has not been asked whether they brought the lorry back.). This is possible because the overlapping speech in lines 6/7 is exactly simultaneous. By the time the interpreter had said 'they brought-', she had heard the whole of the officer's question 'and you saw paper'. The ongoing-agenda nature of the *and*-prefaced question may also have been a factor in the interpreter's decision to prioritise the officer's next question.

Interpreters do not always give preference to the more powerful participant. Also, contrary to other findings (Berk-Seligson, 1990) there is no evidence in the data that foreign national interpreters align with detained persons of their own nationality, or that English interpreters align with English officers. In Extract 6 below, the interpreter, who was English, 'protected' the speaking rights of the detained person by interpreting first the utterance that he had begun simultaneously with that of the officer:

Extract 6

```
1   O   I see so you had a curtain trailer from (town A) to (town B)
2   I   c'était donc une remorque à bâches de (town A) jusqu'à (town B)=
        (so it was a curtain trailer from (town A) to (town B))
3   DP  =voilà
        (that's right)
4   I   yes that's [ right      ]
5   DP             [une verte ]
                   (a green one)
6   O             [you le-  ] you left the curtain trailer at (town B),
7   I   it was green (.) .hh vous avez laissé la:: la remorque à bâches à (town B),
                   (you left the the curtain trailer in (town B))
8   DP  voilà [j'ai écouté moi c'est] ce qu'ils m'ont dit
        (that's right I listened that's what they told me)
9   O         [and you picked . . . .]
10  I   yes that's right I listened that's what they told me to do
11  O   and then you picked up the tipper trailer at (town B) and brought that to
12      England
```

Here, both O and DP overlap the end of I's turn in line 4. DP expands upon his answer and O begins a new question. In line 7, I chooses to render DP's expansion 'it was green' *before* switching to French in the same turn, to interpret O's question. In the next overlap (lines 8–9), I also gives precedence to DP's turn, ignoring O's beginning of a question, causing him to start it again in line 11.

Finally, on the question of interpreters' decisions concerning overlap, it must be noted that these can have serious implications for the outcome of the interview. Although the admonition to 'just translate and translate everything', is unrealistic in real-life interviewing, it is self-evident that an interpreter's opinion as to what is important and what can be ignored is extremely unsafe.

Further, where an interpreter perceives that the detained person's turn is continuing beyond the storage capacity of her short-term memory, she is faced with an impossible dilemma. She can:

(a) stop the DP while she translates his turn so far, signalling for him to begin again when she has finished, or
(b) allow him to continue to the end, knowing that she will not remember all that he has said and that some of it will be lost.

In either case, she influences the process by interfering with spontaneity. In the former case, she may prevent him from either inculpating or disculpating himself with the rest of his turn, since he now has more time to think before continuing. In the latter option, elements of his turn which she forgets may, in fact, be vital.

Conclusion

The investigative interview constitutes a significant, yet largely unexplored area in the judicial process. The dynamics of the *monolingual* interview are, of themselves, worthy of study, in particular, the ways in which speaking rights are negotiated between the two primary participants, with the tape recorder representing a future audience. However, in the *interpreted* interview, the dynamics are radically altered by the presence of the interpreter who, in theory at least, is empowered to allocate interactional space through manipulation of the turn-taking system. This power may be challenged inadvertently by primary participants (Extract 4), as a result of interactional style (Extract 2), or with strategic intent (Extract 5). The interpreter's strategies to coordinate the interaction (Extracts 3, 5 and 6, respectively) result at times in overlapping talk, which has a negative effect upon the production of a clear tape-recording for transcription.

Troubles with turn-taking are a manifestation of just one of the judiciary interpreter's many dilemmas, as outlined above. However, the attention that must necessarily be paid to recording quality means that it may figure more prominently among the interpreter's priorities than other linguistic considerations. Further, the decisions that the interpreter makes in terms of turn allocation mean that her interventions can have far-reaching effects on both the processes and the outcomes of the investigative interview. For these reasons, interpreters must strive to achieve a fine balance between what is possible, given the nature and dynamics of the interview, and what is desirable in terms of the context of the event and the aims of its participants.

References

Alexieva, B. (1997) 'A Typology of Interpreter-Mediated Events', *The Translator*, vol. 3(2), pp. 153–74.

Bakhtin, M. (1981) *The Dialogic Imagination: Four Essays by M.M. Bakhtin*, M. Holquist (ed.), translated by C. Emerson and M. Holquist. Austin: University of Texas Press.

Bennett, A. (1981) 'Interruptions and the Interruption of Conversation', *Discourse Processes*, vol. 4(2), pp. 171–88, and in C. Roy (1993) 'A Sociolinguistic Analysis of the Interpreter's Role in Simultaneous Talk in Interpreted Interaction', *Multilingua*, vol. 12–4 (1993), pp. 341–63.

Berk-Seligson, S. (1990) *The Bilingual Courtroom: Court Interpreters in the Judicial Process*. Chicago: University of Chicago Press.

Berk-Seligson, S. (1999) 'The Impact of Court Interpreting on the Coerciveness of Leading Questions', *Forensic Linguistics*, vol. 6(1), pp. 30–56.

Berk-Seligson, S. (2000) 'Interpreting for the Police: Issues in Pre-Trial Phases of the Judicial Process', *Forensic Linguistics*, vol. 7(2), pp. 212–37.

Drew, P. and Sorjonen, M-L (1997) 'Institutional Dialogue', in Teun A. Van Dijk (ed.), *Discourse as Social Interaction*. London: Sage Publications, pp. 92–118.

Edelsky, C. (1981) 'Who's Got the Floor?', *Language and Society*, in C. Roy (1993) 'A Sociolinguistic Analysis of the Interpreter's Role in Simultaneous Talk in Interpreted Interaction', *Multilingua*, vol. 12–4, pp. 341–63.

Goffman, I. (1974) *Frame Analysis: An Essay on the Organization of Experience*. New York: Harper & Row.

Goffman, E. (1981) *Forms of Talk*. Oxford: Blackwell.

Hale, S. (1997) 'Clash of World Perspectives: The Discursive Practices of the Law, the Witness and the Interpreter', *Forensic Linguistics*, vol. 4(2), pp. 196–209.

Hale, S. (1999) 'Interpreters' Treatment of Discourse Markers in Courtroom Questions', *Forensic Linguistics*, vol. 6(1), pp. 57–82.

Kendon, A. (1992) 'The Negotiation of Context in Face-to-Face Interaction', in A. Duranti and C. Goodwin (eds), *Rethinking Context*. Cambridge: Cambridge University Press, pp. 326–34.

Linell, P. (1996) 'Approaching Dialogue: On Monological and Dialogical Models of Talk and Interaction', *Working Papers from the Department of Communication Studies*, 7, Linköping: Department of Communication Studies.

Mason, I. (2000) 'Audience Design in Translating', *The Translator*, vol. 6(1), pp. 1–22.

Mikkelson, H. *Verbatim Interpretation: An Oxymoron* <http://www.acebo.com/papers/verbatim.htm> (1 November 2000).

Morris, R. (1995) 'The Moral Dilemmas of Court Interpreting', *The Translator*, vol. 1(1), pp. 25–46.

Morris, R. (1999) 'The Gum Syndrome: Predicaments in Court Interpreting', *Forensic Linguistics*, vol. 6(1), pp. 6–29.

Police and Criminal Evidence Act 1984 (s.60(1)(a) and s.66), Codes of Practice A–E. London: The Stationery Office, 1997.

Rigney, A.C. (1999) 'Questioning in Interpreted Testimony', *Forensic Linguistics* vol. 6(1), pp. 83–108.

Roy, C. (2000) *Interpreting as a Discourse Process*. Oxford: Oxford University Press.

Sacks, H., Schegloff, E. and Jefferson, G. (1974) 'A Simplest Systematics for the Organization of Turn-Taking in Conversation', *Language*, vol. 50, pp. 696–736.

Shlesinger, M. (1991) 'Interpreter Latitude vs. Due Process: Simultaneous and Consecutive Interpreting in Multi-Lingual Trials', in S. Tirkonnen-Condit (ed.), *Empirical*

Research in Translation and Intercultural Studies. Tubingen: Gunther Narr Verlag, pp. 147–55.

Tannen, D. (1984) *Conversational Style: Analyzing Talk Among Friends.* Norwood, NJ: Ablex Publishing Co.

Vermeer, H. (1998) 'Starting to Unask what Translatology is About', *Target,* vol. 10(1), pp. 41–68.

Wadensjö, C. (1998) *Interpreting as Interaction.* Harlow: Addison Wesley Longman.

8

The Miranda Warnings and Linguistic Coercion: The Role of Footing in the Interrogation of a Limited-English-Speaking Murder Suspect

Susan Berk-Seligson

The courtroom and even more informal courtroom-like settings have been found to be coercive contexts for those placed in the position of answering questions. Yet the speech situation of the police interview or police interrogation is perhaps a more coercive one from the standpoint of asymmetrical power relationships between interlocutors, since there is no judge present to control the behaviour of the interrogators. It is not by chance that interrogation manuals written by the police for police interrogators specifically advise them not to handcuff or shackle the suspect during the interrogation (Inbau, Reid and Buckley, 1986, p. 40; Van Meter and Bopp, 1973, p. 41), or be armed in the interrogation room (Inbau *et al.* 1986, p. 41), or 'deny him the human comforts he is entitled to', including the right 'to use the bathroom occasionally, eat at regular times, drink water occasionally...' (Van Meter and Bopp, 1973, p. 51). Such manuals go out of their way to make these points because, as they themselves acknowledge, police brutality toward detainees has been common in the past and continues to exist in the present.[1]

This study examines the process by which linguistic coercion by the police is effectuated, and demonstrates how it affected the outcome of a case involving a limited-English-speaking murder suspect.[2] It shows how the rights against self-incrimination were systematically denied the suspect, and reveals the ambiguous role played by a police officer designated as 'interpreter' for the interview. It will be shown as well why this speech event was in fact an 'interrogation' and not an 'interview', and that the police officer assigned the task of interpreting for the interrogating police detective and the detainee moved half-heartedly into this interpreter 'footing', in Goffman's words, and kept sliding back into police detective mode.[3] It will be shown that the police detective/interpreter used the dual role to his advantage, to give himself extra leverage in manipulating the detainee into producing a confession to the crimes with which he was charged.

The Miranda rights

In 1966, the US Supreme Court decided in the case of *Miranda* v. *Arizona* that before interrogating suspects, the police were required to warn them of their constitutional rights. Specifically, the Fifth Amendment to the Constitution provides, that 'no person shall be compelled in any criminal case to be a witness against himself', and the Sixth Amendment states that 'in all criminal prosecutions, the accused . . . shall have the assistance of counsel for the defense'. Thus, a suspect must be warned:

1   that he has a right to remain silent, and that he need not answer any questions;
2   that if he does answer questions, his answers can be used as evidence against him;
3   that he has the right to consult with a lawyer before or during the questioning of him by the police; and
4   that if he cannot afford to hire a lawyer, one will be provided for him without cost to him.

Furthermore, according to *Miranda*, ' . . . if the suspect indicates, at any time or in any manner whatsoever, that he does not want to talk, the interrogation must cease. The interrogator is not privileged to "talk him out of" his refusal to talk' (Inbau, Reid and Buckley, 1986, p. 220). In other words, only the suspect can initiate further talk once he has expressed his unwillingness to talk at some point in the interrogation.

Inbau *et al.* (1986, p. 222) point out that the Supreme Court did not specify that the fifth warning had to be read aloud to the suspect, merely that the police had to honour the wishes of the suspect if he changed his mind about answering their questions during an interrogation. And to proceed with an interrogation required that the suspect 'waive' his Miranda rights. A waiver is some sort of verbal statement by the suspect to the effect that he is willing to answer the questions of the police. Furthermore, the police have to be assured that suspects 'knowingly and intelligently waive those rights and agree to answer questions or make a statement'.

Whereas police officers routinely carry plastic cards with the Miranda rights printed on them, they do not necessarily have to read the rights from the card. They are permitted to paraphrase them. The danger here, as Cotterill (2000) has recently shown in her analysis of the 'police caution', the United Kingdom's equivalent of the Miranda warnings, is that there is great variability in the way that different police officers paraphrase the warnings, and that in the process of paraphrasing, the police often make the warnings less comprehensible than they are in the printed version that appears on the 'caution card'. Shuy (1998, p. 53) demonstrates that even when the police read directly from the card, their performance as readers is often so poor that comprehension of the Miranda warnings is adversely affected.

Comprehensibility is just one of many linguistic issues that need to be considered when one examines the Miranda warnings, as Shuy (1997) notes. Another problematic aspect of the Miranda warnings, according to Shuy (*Ibid.*, p. 179) is that coercion of a suspect can come in the form of verbal dominance or control:

> Intimidation can result both from physical force and from verbal force. If suspects are dominated by verbal force without regard for their individual desire or volition, the result is coercion as much as it would be from physical force.

Van Meter and Bopp (1973, p. 50) concur, advising police interrogators to refrain from using 'duress'. They define duress as a 'state of mind', or 'emotional strain', or 'emotion distress'. They warn that 'anything the interrogator says or does which affects or influences the mind of the suspect to the degree that he is beyond his own choice of complying or denying, can be construed to be duress', and that if duress was considered to have been used, it would vitiate the suspect's confession because the courts would consider it to be unreliable (*Ibid.*).

Despite the fact that the Miranda rights have been in place and have been routinely read to suspects since 1966, seasoned trial lawyers comment that they do not have the intended effect since many suspects tend to ignore them. One criminal defense lawyer with the Legal Aid Society of New York (Perl, 2000) goes so far as to say that:

> Miranda has become meaningless. In the age of Oprah,[4] everyone wants to confess. . . . The Miranda warnings – intended to protect the accused from unwittingly providing the best evidence against himself – have become so much a part of our culture, so familiar, that no one who receives them pays any attention.

Similarly, a lawyer who at one time served as Inspector General of the US Justice Department in the 1990s says that, 'even with the Miranda safeguards, criminal suspects still make incriminating statements and confess to crimes with surprising frequency' (Bromwich, 1999). Statistics support this generalisation: it is estimated that 80 to 90 per cent of suspects waive their Miranda rights and talk to the police (Greenhouse, 2000).

The observations of criminal attorneys such as the ones referred to above are confirmed in a highly lauded book, *Troubling Confessions*, by Peter Brooks (2000). Brooks adds to the voices of those who question the truth of many of the confessions that are made by suspects in custody, despite the fact that these suspects had been given their Miranda rights. As Brooks (2000, p. 31) explains:

> The courts, including the Supreme Court, have been lenient in interpreting the rules imposed on interrogators, so that many forms of trickery are permitted – including lies about evidence inculpating the suspect, fake confessions by confederates – and statements made before the suspect is 'Mirandized' are often allowed on the grounds that the suspect was not yet subject to custodial interrogation...and even statements clearly taken in violation of *Miranda* rules may lead to 'fruits' that are admissible into evidence. Suspects continue to talk, to give confessions (including some later discovered to be wholly false) because the pressure to talk is too great to resist.

Shuy (1998, p. 15) concurs, explaining that one reason why so many suspects confess to crimes, despite being given the Miranda warnings, is that 'the laws regarding police interrogation permit the police to lie, to flatter, to adduce, to ask questions roughly, to play act, to trick, and to cajole'. One such law is the 1969 Supreme Court decision that gives tacit recognition to the necessity for trickery and deceit during police interrogations (Yeschke, 1997, p. 84).

A further factor emasculates Miranda; Brooks (2000, p. 31) argues that most people believe that to remain silent in the face of questions by the police gives the impression that they are guilty, that suspects willingly enter into an interlocutionary relationship with the police interrogator, which in turn results in continued talk. This relationship is a bond, an affective bond instigated by the interrogator which 'contains, and activates, elements of dependency, subjugation, fear, the desire for propitiation, the wish to appease and to please' (*ibid.*, p. 35).

If there is often an affective bond between interrogator and suspect it is not there by chance. Police officers are trained to establish rapport with the person they are interrogating, evidence of this being the advice to this effect that police interrogation manuals offer. Aubry and Caputo (1980, p. 200), for example, recommend 'the sympathetic approach' as 'an excellent all-around approach' to police interrogation. Inbau *et al.* (1986, p. 78) advise the sympathetic approach in interrogating the emotional suspect, the individual who 'has a strong sense of moral guilt – in other words, a "troubled conscience"'; for such suspects they recommend the use of 'expressions of understanding and compassion with regard to the commission of the offense as well as the suspect's present difficulty'. Van Meter and Bopp (1973, p. 79) emphasise that before an interrogator begins to discuss specific facts related to the crime, he should establish rapport with the suspect, that is, 'a harmonious or sympathetic relationship'. Yeschke (1997, p. 84) recommends that the interrogator 'empathize with and help the subject rationalize his or her participation and save face when talking about it'. It is interesting that Yeschke, a former FBI agent not trained in linguistics, has independently discovered the theory of Brown and Levinson (1979) and its notion of positive face wants.

Subversion of the Miranda rights of a limited-English speaker

The case that is analysed here deals with a suspect who tried to invoke his Miranda rights, and did so repeatedly. On 14 occasions during his first interrogation by the police, the detainee expressed the desire not to talk about the details of the crime for which he was being held in custody. As the transcripts of the interrogation show, the police ignored his wishes time and time again. Most interestingly from the vantage point of those who study interpreting in legal settings, the person assigned to interpret for him and for the interrogating police detective, himself a police officer, was as guilty as the official interrogator, if not more so, of violating the suspect's Miranda rights. The case brings to light a problem largely ignored by the courts, namely, that a police officer who is taking on the role of interpreter may subvert that role, and use it to help seduce a suspect into confessing to a crime.

From a discourse-analytic perspective, this chapter will provide evidence to show that in fact both police officers, including the one assigned the role of interpreter, were engaged in the speech event of interrogation throughout the course of their interaction with the suspect, despite his repeated statements indicating that he wished not to talk about the topics that they brought up. In fact, the speech behaviour of the police detectives was at the heart of the arguments made by the appeals judges in their decision on the case.

The Case: *The People* v. *Montano*

In 1987, in the San Francisco Bay area of California, an 18-year-old Mexican man was arrested by the police and charged with first-degree murder and attempted rape. He had been caught running away from the scene of the crime, a row of hedges dividing a parking lot, where the semi-nude body of a young woman was found. Behind the hedge, the defendant 'began a stabbing frenzy', according to Judge Poche (Court of Appeal 1991, p. 2), who wrote the opinion for the appellate court that was considering the appeal of his conviction.

According to Judge Poche, two police officers began interrogating Manuel Hernández Montano: Officer Breuker, a monolingual English speaker, and Officer Kincannon, a bilingual English/Spanish speaker of European descent. Kincannon spoke Spanish with a heavy English accent, and evidenced numerous grammatical and lexical deficiencies in his ability to speak Spanish. It was clear that he was not of Hispanic ethnicity, from his surname and from his English-influenced Spanish, and yet he was assigned the role of interpreter.

The interrogation began at 4:03 in the morning, and ended one and a half hours later. However, it was split into two sessions: the first conducted by

Officer Breuker, and the second led by Officer Kincannon, who was temporarily left alone with the suspect, and who continued the interrogation. The defendant had not eaten anything on the evening of the murder, but had drunk eight or nine beers.

The linguistic achievement of coercion

How did Officers Breuker and Kincannon successfully obtain what the appellate court considered to amount to a confession during their first interrogation of him? It is worthwhile presenting the appellate court's view on what it was about the interrogation that it found coercive. First of all, the interrogation sequence cited by the judges in their ruling constitutes strong evidence of the coercive tactics of the police officers. While some specifics of the questioning strategies are mentioned, it is primarily the repetition by the suspect of his desire not to talk about the crime that the appellate court singles out. The judges do note, however, that each time the defendant expressed this wish, . . .

> the officers ostensibly agreed to talk about other matters, but they soon resumed questioning him about aspects of the incident. The officers' conduct conveyed the unmistakable message that defendant's rights were meaningless. (Court of Appeal 1991, p. 15)

The court characterised the police officers as therefore having a 'callous attitude' toward the defendant.

In addition to presenting the text of what for them was the most damaging aspect of the interrogation, the appellate judges mentioned some of the objectionable points in the interrogation that immediately preceded that phase. What follows are the portions of the defendant's answers, which in their totality inculpate him, as highlighted by Judge Poche (Court of Appeal 1991, p. 3):

> Asked by Officer Breuker to '[e]xplain to me how you feel,' defendant answered: 'I feel badly. I feel . . . I feel that I am bad with myself.' Defendant acknowledged that he had a 'quite serious' problem, and that that problem was why the police had stopped him. Defendant had never had 'a problem like this before,' and had never had problems with the police. After he got defendant to admit having carried a large knife that night, Officer Breuker asked: 'I know you met a lady tonight. . . . True?' Defendant responded that 'I feel bad answering the question.' Officer Breuker stated: 'I can see the tears in your eyes. I know what happened tonight made you very, very bad feeling. Okay, feel bad about that. I know it's in your mouth. What you want to tell me is right in your mouth. It just needs a little pushing to get it out. . . . But we take it a, a little at a time.'

What is it about these questions and answers that the appellate court found objectionable and evidence of coercion? While the appellate judges did not say it, it is clear from a look at police interrogation manuals that the police officers are following tried and true interrogating strategies.

First of all, police interrogators are advised not to refer to the crime itself at the outset of an interrogation, but to call it the 'business' or 'situation' or 'problem' (Van Meter and Bopp, 1973, p. 75, 87–8). The strategy is for the interrogator to keep to him/herself the facts of the crime, withhold as much information from the suspect as s/he can, so as to be able to obtain the version of the story provided by the suspect with whatever is known by the interrogator to be true.

Officer Breuker succeeds in getting Montano to admit that he was carrying a lethal weapon on the night of the murder – a foot-long knife. He also appeals to the suspect's emotions. The suspect conforms to what Inbau *et al.* (1986, p. 77) refer to as 'emotional offenders'. According to these professional interrogators, an emotional offender is one 'who ordinarily experiences a considerable feeling of remorse, mental anguish, or compunction as a result of his offense. This individual has a strong sense of moral guilt – in other words, a "troubled conscience"' (Inbau *et al.* 1986, p. 78). Breuker capitalises on the emotional state of Montano, telling him he sees tears in his eyes, and agreeing with him that he must feel bad. He also is cajoling him into confessing what he did. The words just need a little pushing for them to come out of his mouth.

Breuker follows standard interrogation procedure in making the suspect believe that he and Kincannon 'pretty much know what happened' (page 43, lines 10–11); in other words, that they know the facts of the crime and Montano's role in it. When Montano insists that he does not want to talk about it, Breuker, in typical police interrogator fashion, refers to specific incriminating evidence that he now has against him (finding the knife in the bushes, the presence of blood on the knife, on the suspect's shoes, and pants pocket), implying that it is no use denying his actions in the crime, that he might as well confess since the police have all the evidence they need (although at this point we do not know if the police had in fact found the knife). He prefaces the list of damaging evidence with a motive he has figured out for Montano: that he had wanted to hurt the victim a little, had wanted to scare her (page 43, lines 18–19). There is no question that Officer Breuker is conducting an interrogation, judging by the tape-recording and its transcription. Of greater interest, however, is the behaviour of Officer Kincannon.

Coercion by the police interpreter

It is the thesis of this chapter that Officer Kincannon, in serving as interpreter for Officer Breuker and the suspect, Montano, never saw himself as primarily or even secondarily an 'interpreter'. And neither did Breuker consider him fundamentally to be an interpreter at the interrogation. Nevertheless, the court reporting service that typed the transcript of the interrogation designates the officers as 'Sergeant Breuker: Interrogator' and 'Detective Kincannon:

Interpreter'. Furthermore, the title that appears on the cover page of the transcript is 'Interview with Manuel Montano aka Jose Gonzales', indicating that the trial court had classified the speech event as an 'interview' rather than an interrogation. Despite this, all references to the questioning of the defendant by Breuker and Kincannon in the appellate court's judgment are to the two 'interrogation sessions' that they had led. Thus, while the first questioning of the suspect should have been merely an interview, it was in reality an interrogation.

Despite the fact that Kincannon was supposed to be the 'interpreter' in the interrogation of Montano, he behaved as an interrogator, performing interpreting services in a faulty and half-hearted way, principally to help Breuker carry out his part in the interrogation. As will be demonstrated below, Kincannon's unwillingness to remain in the 'footing' of interpreter is evidenced in three ways:

1   he aligns himself with Breuker as a co-interrogator, making references to both of them in his interpretations of Breuker's questions, when in fact Breuker refers only to himself;
2   he behaves in classic interrogator mode when left alone with the suspect;
3   he fails to interpret many of the questions and statements of Breuker, and the responses of Montano, thereby violating the basic norms of legal interpreting.

Footing as co-interrogator

Upon interpreting the questions and statements of Breuker, Kincannon often inaccurately interprets the latter's use of first-person singular reference, rendering it in Spanish as first-person plural. As can be seen in the extracts below, Kincannon's rendition of Breuker's utterance refers to the two of them, even though Breuker is speaking only for himself. This indicates that Kincannon is not satisfied with simply being an interpreter in this event; he wants to be a member of an interrogating team.

In each of the textual extracts the words highlighted in bold represent the discrepancies between source language and target language first-person pronouns. Note that while interpreting discrepancies abound, they will not be commented on here. The English rendition of Kincannon's Spanish utterances are those of the official court interpreter.

Early on in the interrogation, Breuker tries to get Montano to tell him why he feels bad about himself. Playing on the suspect's sense of guilt and remorse, he tries to bring him to the point of admitting his guilt in the murder by saying, 'Explain to **me** how you feel'. Kincannon renders 'me' as 'us', saying, 'Díga**nos** cómo se ... ' ('Tell *us* how you ... ').

At a pivotal moment in the questioning, Breuker tries to convince Montano that he knows that Montano had met the murder victim that night. In Extract 1, he makes one of the most sensitive, and specific statements thus far in the interrogation.

Extract 1

1	Breuker	Now I . . . I know you met a lady tonight. A young lady
2		tonight.
3	Kincannon	**Sabemos** que conoció a una muchacha esta noche.
4		(We know that you met a girl tonight.)

The rendition of 'I' as 'we' is evidence of Kincannon's attempts to define himself as a police detective rather than as an interpreter.

Kincannon is not alone in seeing his role as one of detective/interrogator: Breuker, too, demonstrates an ambivalence with respect to Kincannon's role in the speech event. He alternates between referring to himself, only, as interrogator and referring to the two of them. One of the most striking examples of Breuker's inclusive pronominal usage, where 'we' refers to himself and Kincannon, and possibly even to 'the police department' with all of its forensic experts, is his listing of the evidence that they have against Montano:

Extract 2

1	Breuker	Okay. (Pause) **We** found a knife . . . in the bushes. There was
2		blood on the knife. It was your knife and **we** will be able to tell
3		because of your fingerprints . . .
4	Breuker	There was blood on the knife. **We** will be able to tell whose
5		blood it is. If it was yours from if you cut yourself, or if it was
6		from somebody else . . .
7	Breuker	**We** know that there's blood on your clothes . . .
8	Breuker	And **we** will also know if that's from him or from somebody
9		else . . .
10	Breuker	**We** know that there's blood on your shoes, and **we** will be able
11		to tell if that blood is yours or from somebody else . . .
12	Breuker	There was blood in your pants pocket from when you put your
13		hand in your pants. **We** will be able to tell if that blood was
14		yours or somebody else's, because **we** took your blood sample . . .
15		
16	Breuker	**We'll** be able to take trace evidence from your hands and match
17		it to other evidence . . .
18	Breuker	I would simply like for him, if he can, to tell **me** why.
19	Kincannon	**Nosotros** simplemente **quisiéramos** que usted **nos** diga por qué.
20		(We would simply like for you to tell us why.)

After listing the pieces of key evidence that 'they' have, Breuker ends his implicit accusation with first-person reference (line 18), addressing Kincannon directly, and Montano only indirectly. Kincannon, hearing the litany of forensic pieces of evidence the police have against the suspect, changes the first-person singular 'I' and 'me' to plural 'we' and 'us', thereby including himself among those who possess all of this evidence against the detainee. This puts him in a more powerful position relative to the detainee than if he were merely an interpreter.

Moving into interrogator footing

Intruding himself into Breuker's self-references as a police officer is one thing; behaving in interrogator mode is another. Kincannon minimises his role as interpreter and insists on establishing a police interrogator footing both in the presence of Breuker and in his absence. His behaviour when Breuker is away is considered by the appeals court to be particularly 'egregious', not because he is out of role, but because he so flagrantly violates the suspect's Miranda right to halt the questioning when the latter no longer wishes to speak. Taking on the role of interrogator while he is purportedly an interpreter for another police officer would be unimaginable in a comparable situation where an interpreter is working with a lawyer and a witness who is undergoing cross-examination on the witness stand. But this is not a courtroom; this is a police interrogation room.

Evidence of the attempts by Kincannon to preserve his status as police detective/interrogator, even while he is supposed to be serving as interpreter for Breuker and Montano, can be found in the fact that he often asks the suspect questions of his own accord. This generally happens whenever he feels that Breuker is not being successful in getting adequate responses from Montano. Other evidence of Kincannon's interrogator footing while being on interpreter duty is his regular challenging of the suspect's answers. By repeating Montano's answers, usually with a question intonation, he indicates a lack of acceptance of these answers, and an attitude of incredulity. Extract 3 below demonstrates both of these phenomena.

Another instance of the police interpreter acting as interrogator comes after Hernández Montano has in effect admitted to stabbing the young woman he followed from the subway station, although at this point he still has not made a full, formal confession. For this reason Breuker continues to pressure him psychologically, recycling a topic (Shuy, 1998) that he has brought up numerous times already, namely that something very bad happened to Montano that night. In Extract 3, Kincannon on his own initiative asks Montano if he knew before Breuker's announcing to him, that the young woman had died. The purpose of the question is not to elicit any new factual information, but to make him even more psychologically vulnerable to confessing. It is meant to wear him down.

Extract 3

1	Breuker	I'm sorry for you Jose. A very bad thing that happened to you
2		here. (Pause) You didn't want to hurt her, did you?
3	Montano	No entiendo lo que dice.
4		(I don't understand what he is saying.)

5	Kincannon	¿Usted no quiso hacerle tanto daño?
6		(You didn't want to hurt her so much?)
7	Montano	No quiero hablar más. No quiero hablar más de nada.
8		(I don't want to talk more. I don't want to talk more about
9		anything.)
10	Kincannon	¿No sabía que estaba muerta?
11		(You didn't know that she was dead?)
12	Montano	No. No quiero hablar más. No quiero saber nada más.
13		(No. I don't want to talk more. I don't want to know anything
14		more.)
15	Kincannon	¿No quiere saber nada más?
16		(You don't want to know anything more?)
17	Montano	No, no quiero (u). No sé.
18		(No, I don't want (u). I don't know.)

Kincannon's repetition (in line 15 of Extract 3) of the suspect's statement about not wanting to know anything else, which immediately follows his unmotivated question regarding Montano's knowledge that the victim had died, can only be interpreted as an additional move to make him look blameworthy. It gives the suspect the clear message that there is more that they, the police, know about the crime and, by implication, about Montano's involvement in it. One gets the impression that Montano feels that if he heard more of the details of the murder, he would be drawn more deeply into the police net. He seems to know intuitively, even without a lawyer present, that to answer the substantive questions about the crime would be to implicate himself in it. His fear is warranted since there was overwhelming evidence that he was guilty of the murder.

Kincannon's discourse strategy of repeating Montano's answers whenever he wants to cast doubt on their veracity or genuineness of feeling is one he uses frequently. It is the equivalent of saying to someone, 'Are you sure about that?' 'Is that what you really feel?' 'Is that what really happened?' Note the repetition sequences involving Kincannon, in the extract below.

Extract 4 follows a question from Breuker about Montano's being stopped by a police officer as he was running near the place where the victim's body was found:

Extract 4

1	Breuker	Do you know where you were running to?
2	Kincannon	¿Sabía adónde , adónde iba a, a correr?
3		(Did you know to where, to where you were going to, to run?)
4	Montano	No.
5	Kincannon	¿No sabía, no?
6		(You didn't know, no?)
7	Montano	No.

It is clear from the pattern of Montano's 'No sé' ('I don't know') answers that he uses them whenever he is unwilling to admit damaging evidence to the police. For example, he answers 'No sé' to Breuker's question about whether he met a girl that night, or why he had leaves in his hair, or whether he had been in some bushes that night. And each time he answers 'No sé' Kincannon questions him with, '¿No sabe?' ('You don't know?').

Kincannon's pattern of questioning Montano's 'I don't know' answers should be interpreted as an unwillingness to accept them. He knows that they could not be true, since he and Breuker are relatively sure that they have the right person in custody for this crime. The constant refusal to accept 'I don't know' for an answer is a form of coercion. It represents a way of pressuring Montano into divulging incriminating information. In fact, at one point Breuker asks Montano to clarify whether these 'I don't know' answers mean that he doesn't understand the question, or that he doesn't know the answer to it. When Breuker asks this question in reference to whether Montano had met a girl that night, the latter answers, 'Pues, (pause) pues, cuando digo que no sé, es que me siento mal contestar a la pregunta' ('Well, (pause) well, when I say that I don't know, it's that I feel bad answering the question'). So Kincannon is correct in doubting the truth of these 'I don't know' answers; nevertheless, these answers represent Montano's method of preserving his Miranda right not to talk to the police, and Kincannon's challenging repetitions of these refusals must be interpreted as a way of subverting the suspect's attempts at not incriminating himself.

The appellate court makes mention only of the repeated statements by Montano to the effect that he would 'not like to talk about this' or would 'not like to talk any more', which are clear-cut invocations of his Miranda rights. The court does not, however, pay much attention to the pattern of Kincannon's responses to the 'I don't know' answers. Kincannon's behaviour with respect to the 'I don't know' statements is just as coercive as his interrogating behaviour in its other forms.

The discussion above deals with Kincannon's behaviour while he is serving as interpreter for Breuker and the suspect. However, once he is alone with Montano, he becomes solely and completely a police interrogator. Most insidious, perhaps, is his manipulation of his official interpreting role to further his more important goals as interrogator. Specifically, Kincannon appeals to Montano's Hispanic ethnic identity and the fact that he is a Spanish speaker as a way of 'claiming common ground', since he, Kincannon, is also a Spanish speaker, as opposed to Breuker who is not. He capitalises on his ability to communicate with Montano in Spanish, using it as a way of trying to induce him to open up to him, in Spanish, now that Breuker is no longer present. Extract 5 presents Kincannon's discourse strategy for persuading Montano to begin making admissions of guilt to him:

Extract 5

1   Kincannon   Umm, y al, al traducir y a hablar con usted y también con el o...con
2   Bruce, ¿Okay?, umm, yo sentí que usted más o menos quiere hablar, pero

3		tenía problemas en hablar con un, una persona que no le entiende muy
4		bien.
5		(Umm, and while, while translating and talking with you and also with
6		the oth . . . with Bruce, Okay, umm, I felt that you more or less want to talk,
7		but you had problems in talking with a, a person that doesn't understand
8		you very well.)
9	Montano	Um hum.
10	Kincannon	Okay?
11	Montano	Um hum.
12	Kincannon	¿Había un problema en hablar con Bruce porque él no, no sabía hablar
13		castellano?
14		(Was there a problem in talking with Bruce because he, he didn't know
15		how to speak Spanish?)
16	Montano	No. Sino que no quiero hablar más.
17		(No. It is just that I don't want to talk more.)

Clearly, Kincannon's ploy does not work. Montano did not say much to Breuker because he did not want to implicate himself in the murder. It was not because Breuker was not a Spanish-speaker. And even though Kincannon is speaking in Spanish to Montano, Montano still resists his attempts to pry information from him. He keeps referring to how bad he is feeling, and how he would rather not talk about his 'problem'.

Kincannon then tries another strategy, one which has been used by other interrogators and which the courts have ruled in prior cases to be fundamentally coercive: the appeal to religion and conscience. The full text of the interrogation demonstrates how Kincannon the interrogator brings up the subject of the 'errors' that Montano may have committed in the past, and alluding to the 'problem' that he had had that night, links it to Montano's Catholicism and to the fact that he himself is a Catholic. Kincannon manages to get Montano talking about his religious training as a youngster, about his love for God, the consequent need for repentance when one has erred, and the danger of going to hell if one does not confess one's sins. The appellate court (Court of Appeal 1991, p. 14) quotes from case law to justify finding fault with Kincannon for using this strategy:

[A] state law enforcement officer conducting an interrogation of one accused of crime may not use his own or the suspect's personal religious beliefs as a tool to extract admissions of guilt . . . [para.] Religious beliefs are not matters to be used by governmental authorities to manipulate a suspect to say things he or she otherwise would not say.

Manuals on criminal interrogation such as Aubry and Caputo (1980, p. 198), however, teach interrogators to use the theme of religion, if the suspect is religious, in order to play upon his or her emotions. The appeal to religion is intended to make the suspect feel the moral seriousness of the crime, and to bring about a guilty conscience in him or her.

The appellate court singles out other discourse strategies as well, ones that are used by Kincannon and Breuker alike, which contribute to the coerciveness of the interrogation: their use of 'recurring themes', for example, specifically, that Montano should 'overcome his unwillingness to talk about aspects of the crime', and that he should 'agree to talk at a later time' (Court of Appeal 1991, p. 15). The court refers to the interrogation as constituting 'relentless questioning', whose intended purpose was to give the suspect the clear impression that the questioning would not end until his will broke.

The court is quite accurate in its interpretation of how the interrogation was conducted. Kincannon was more guilty of such behaviour than was Breuker: he was more insistent on getting Montano to talk. What, specifically, did the court find objectionable in the style of questioning? Upon examining the data we see that every time Montano said that he did not want to talk about his problem, or about what had happened earlier in the evening, Kincannon would ask him, 'When will you want to talk about this?' 'Tomorrow?' or else he would question him on his reasons for not wanting to talk at that moment. At other times he would change the subject, trying to give Montano the impression that he was complying with his desire not to talk further about the events of the evening. But then within one or two turns at talk, Kincannon would switch back to the topic of what had happened that night, and the serious problem that the suspect had. Thus, it became abundantly clear to Montano that Kincannon in his interrogation, and Breuker when he conducted the questioning, were not giving up on finding out the details of the crime. In discourse analytical terms, each police officer in his own right would 'recycle' the topics of interest to him: the murder, and the suspect's involvement in it. Similarly, the subtheme of blood is recycled several times: that the victim's blood was found on the suspect's shoes, in his pants, on the knife whose handle bore his fingerprints. In the language of professional criminal interrogators, this is an approach known as 'constant repetition of one theme', and consists of 'repeating the same questions or line of questioning over and over again' (Aubry and Caputo, 1980, p. 210).

This recurrent pattern of recycling topics, through the mechanism of changing the topic whenever the suspect invokes one of his Miranda rights but then abruptly dropping that topic and shifting back to the true topic of interest to the interrogator, is one of the tactics for what has been called by police interrogator experts the strategy of 'keep the talk going' (Van Meter and Bopp, 1973, chapter 7). As Van Meter and Bopp (1973, p. 94) point out, in their advice to the police, 'An interrogation goes along only as long as the interrogator can keep it going. It is up to you to keep the conversation flowing'.

Conclusions

Manuel Hernández Montano's first-degree murder conviction was reversed by the California Court of Appeal in 1991.[5] In their ruling, the judges referred to the 'flagrancy of the official misconduct', and considered the illegality to have a 'quality of purposefulness'. The judges' principal rationale for reversing the conviction was the goal of deterring improper police conduct (Court of Appeal 1991, p. 17).

From a discourse perspective, the two police officers in this case had engaged in 'extensive badgering and softening up' of the suspect, to use the accusatory terminology of Montano's defense attorney. These are lay terms for the discourse phenomena of topic recycling, repetition, appeals to common ground (for example, shared religious beliefs), and concern for the interlocutor's positive face needs (including expressions of empathy and sympathy).

The case of Manuel Hernández Montano has to do with police violation of the Miranda rights. While the defense attorney and appellate court were in agreement on how the police interrogators effectuated their misconduct, they seem to have overlooked one important element in this instance of police wrongdoing, and that is that one of the police interrogators was not properly executing the role that he had been delegated with, namely, that of legal interpreter. As I explain elsewhere (Berk-Seligson, 2000), legal interpreters are supposed to adhere to a set of norms required by their profession, yet it is an open question whether in all the documented criminal cases in which the police have served as interpreters, the police have abided by those norms.

The police detective assigned the role of interpreter in the Montano interrogation flagrantly ignored the guidelines of legal interpreting. At the same time, he became an active participant in helping the designated interrogator coerce a confession from the suspect. He in effect became an interrogator. Such shifts in footing have been noted in other sociolegal settings where interpreters are at work (Berk-Seligson, 1999b; Berk-Seligson and Trinch, 1999).

The case of *The People* v. *Montano* demonstrates the dangers of using the police as interpreters during interrogations. The danger is that the police interpreter will not remain in interpreter footing, but will shift back and forth between interpreter and police interrogator. The potential for this to happen is particularly great because, as in other situations involving legal interpreters, the suspect or defendant may assume at the outset that the person who has been assigned to help him or her understand what the interrogator is asking, is actually trying to help him or her in a broader sense and is taking his or her side (Berk-Seligson, 1990, 2000; Morris, 1999). Thus, to play the role of interpreter when one really considers him/herself to be in police detective footing, is one way of subverting the Miranda rights. It is a way of seducing a suspect into talking. To be a bilingual police officer assigned the role of interpreter at an interrogation is to give oneself a great advantage as a detective, and that is the enhanced ability to manipulate the detainee. This advantage puts the Miranda rights in greater jeopardy than usual, for a police detective who is in the footing of interpreter might easily turn out to be a wolf in sheep's clothing.

Notes

1 In recent years, several high-profile cases of police brutality at the time of arrest, all of them involving African-American detainees, have reached trial courts in the USA – Rodney King in Los Angeles, and Abner Louima in New York City, being perhaps the most widely known.
2 A limited-English speaker is one who lacks proficiency in English but has some ability to use English.
3 Goffman (1979, p. 173) explains his notion of footing as 'the multiple senses in which the self of the speaker can appear, that is, the multiple self-implicated projections discoverable in what is said and done'. And so, 'a change in footing implies a change in the alignment we take up to ourselves and others present as expressed in the way we manage the production or reception of an utterance' (Goffman, 1979, p. 5).
4 'Oprah' is a reference to the immensely popular television talk show hosted by Oprah Winfrey, in which people are invited to reveal their most intimate problems, or confess having engaged in socially stigmatised behaviour, to millions of TV viewers.
5 On being convicted by the trial court, Montano was sentenced to life in prison without possibility of parole. In appealing the conviction on the basis of improper police conduct during his interrogation, his defense attorneys requested that the conviction be reduced to second-degree murder and that his sentence be adjusted accordingly.

References

Aubry, A. S. Jr and Caputo, R. R. (1980) *Criminal Interrogation*. Springfield, Ill.: Charles C. Thomas.

Berk-Seligson, S. (1990) *The Bilingual Courtroom: Court Interpreters in the Judicial Process*. Chicago: The University of Chicago Press.

Berk-Seligson, S. (1999a) 'The Impact of Court Interpreting on the Coerciveness of Leading Questions', *Forensic Linguistics*, vol. 6(1), pp. 30–56.

Berk-Seligson, S. (1999b) 'Off-the-Record Legal Interpreting: Court Interpreters in an Advocacy Setting', Plenary talk given at the 4th Biennial Conference of the International Association of Forensic Linguists, Birmingham, United Kingdom, 1999.

Berk-Seligson, S. (2000) 'Interpreting for the Police: Issues in Pre-Trial Phases of the Judicial Process', *Forensic Linguistics*, vol. 7(1), pp. 213–38.

Berk-Seligson, S. and Trinch, S. L. (1999) 'The Transformation of Domestic Violence Narratives in Pre-Trial Interviews: The Unanticipated Shifting of Roles of the Court Interpreter', Paper presented at the annual meeting of the American Association of Applied Linguistics (1999), Stamford, Connecticut, and the XVII National Conference on Spanish in the United States (1999), Coral Gables, Florida.

Bromwich, M. R. (1999) 'Miranda Endangered', *The New York Times* 7 December.

Brooks, P. (2000) *Troubling Confessions: Speaking Guilt in Law and Literature*. Chicago and London: The University of Chicago Press.

Brown, P. and Levinson, S. (1979) 'Universals in Language Usage: Politeness Phenomena', in Esther N. Goody (ed.), *Questions and Politeness: Strategies in Social Interaction*. Cambridge: Cambridge University Press.

Cotterill, J. (2000) 'Reading the Rights: A Cautionary Tale of Comprehension and Comprehensibility', *Forensic Linguistics*, vol. 7(1), pp. 4–25.

Court of Appeal of California (1991) *California Reporter*, no. 277, p. 327.

Davidson, B. (2000) 'The Interpreter as Institutional Gatekeeper: The Social-Linguistic Role of Interpreters in Spanish-English Medical Discourse', *Journal of Sociolinguistics* vol. 4(3), pp. 379–407.

Goffman, E. (1979) *Forms of Talk*. Philadelphia: University of Pennsylvania Press.

Greenhouse, L. (2000) 'Justices Reaffirm Miranda Rule, 7–2; A Part of "Culture"', *The New York Times*, 29 June, pp. 1 and 18.

Inbau, F. E., Reid, J. E. and Buckley, J. P. (1986) *Criminal Interrogation and Confessions*. Baltimore: Williams & Wilkins.

Morris, R. (1999) 'The Gum Syndrome: Predicaments in Court Interpreting', *Forensic Linguistics*, vol. 6(1), pp. 6–29.

Perl, E. S. (2000) 'It Feels So Good to Confess', *The New York Times*, 6 July.

Roy, C. B. (2000) *Interpreting as a Discourse Phenomenon*. Oxford: Oxford University Press.

Russell, S. (2000) "Let Me Put it Simply . . . ": The Case for a Standard Translation of the Police Caution and its Explanation', *Forensic Linguistics*, vol. 7(1), pp. 26–48.

Schegloff, E. A., Jefferson, G. and Sacks, H. (1977) 'The Preference for Self-Correction in the Organization of Repair in Conversation', *Language*, vol. 53, pp. 361–82.

Shuy, R. (1997) 'Ten Unanswered Language Questions about Miranda', *Forensic Linguistics*, vol. 4(2), pp. 175–96.

Shuy, R. (1998) *The Language of Confession, Interrogation, and Deception*. Thousand Oaks, London, and New Delhi: Sage Publications.

Van Meter, C. H. and Bopp, W. J. (1973) *Principles of Police Interrogation*. Springfield, Ill.: Charles C. Thomas.

Wadensjö, C. (1998) *Interpreting as Interaction*. New York: Longman.

Yeschke, C. L. (1997) *The Art of Investigative Interviewing: A Human Approach to Testimonial Evidence*. Boston: Butterworth-Heinemann.

Cases cited

Dickerson v. *United States* [2000] No. 99–5525.

Miranda v. *Arizona* [1966] 384 US. 436.

People v. *Montano* [1991] No. A045323, Court of Appeal of California, First Appellate District, Division Four, 226 Cal. App. 3d 914.

Part III

The Language of the Courtroom I: Lawyers and Witnesses

9
'Just One More Time...': Aspects of Intertextuality in the Trials of O. J. Simpson

Janet Cotterill

Multiple versions and multiple voices in forensic narratives

Narratives produced in forensic settings are essentially multi-perspectival and multi-voiced. By the time a case reaches the courtroom, it has potentially been subject to a large number of retellings in a variety of contexts, including police interviews, grand jury and plea-bargaining sessions as well as pretrial indictment and arraignment hearings.

Repetition is therefore a critical and defining feature of forensic narratives, to a large extent explaining the protractedness of both police interviews and courtroom testimony. In police interviews, many witnesses and particularly suspects are questioned repeatedly, with interviewing and interrogation strategies such as the cognitive interview technique promoting re-elicitation of the crime narrative. Witnesses and suspects are re-interviewed to check both the internal consistency of their accounts and also to verify that their stories match with those of their fellow witnesses. The 'Account' phase of the PEACE mnemonic, whose principles govern many police interviews (see Russell, this volume for further discussion), encourages officers to pursue repetition of narratives through varied elicitation strategies as a means of uncovering any evidential inconsistencies in the various versions of events:

P   Plan and prepare;
E   Engage and explain;
A   Account – obtain a first account of events, suspending belief and disbelief. *Review the account, picking a topic, probing and summarising it. Attempt to uncover any anomalies or inconsistencies and get the detained person to commit to or compound any apparent lies he may have told. Move on to the next topic and repeat the process, finally challenging the first account;*
C   Closure, in a polite and positive manner;
E   Evaluate.

(My emphasis)

The result is a complex set of interlocking narrative versions of the crime event and its circumstances created by a large and potentially conflicting group of narrative voices.

The courtroom, too, is the site of repeated and multi-voiced narratives. Should the case proceed to trial, the defendant and witnesses can expect to repeat their stories on several further occasions. However, the constraints of courtroom interaction are such that the narrative account which is elicited in court may bear only a passing resemblance to the base version recorded in any foundational police interview or statement. Stygall (1994, p. 123) discusses how pieces of testimony in court are broken down into non-sequential fragments during witness examination by the process of direct and cross-examination. The result of this legal dynamic is a fragmented and disjointed narrative account; as Gewirtz (1996, pp. 7–8) explains:

> neither side is allowed to keep its perspective uninterruptedly before the decision-maker until its overall story can be fully presented. Instead, immediately after one side elicits a witness's story, the opposing side cross-examines, thereby introducing the opposing side's perspective even as the first side's story is unfolding...one side's narrative is constantly being met by the other side's counter-narrative (or side-stepping narrative), so that reality is always disassembled into multiple, conflicting and partly overlapping versions.

With each witness, the prosecution and defence narratives are interwoven, on up to four or more occasions, in the following alternating sequence:

Direct examination $\rightarrow$ Cross-examination $\rightarrow$
Re-direct examination $\rightarrow$ Re-cross-examination $\rightarrow$
(Further re-direct examination etc...)

One of the reasons for such a high degree of repetition is the need to test the quality of the account presented. The adequacy of narrativised versions of crime events, both in terms of completeness and consistency, is challenged on many occasions and in a variety of contexts. Narratives must be both internally consistent and must demonstrate consistency between versions in order to optimise their credibility and plausibility in the eyes of the judge and/or jury (Bennett and Feldman, 1981; Jackson, 1995).

Not only are narratives produced and reproduced repeatedly throughout the pretrial and trial process, they are also produced by a variety of narrative voices. Many witnesses may present testimony relating to the same micro-event in the original crime story, and this testimony may concur to a greater or lesser degree with previous versions (see Maley and Fahey, 1991). In terms of interactional properties, it is possible to identify three basic types of narrative: *spontaneous*, *prompted* and *elicited*. Dynamically, these three types of narrative demonstrate differing degrees of intervention and influence by the non-teller as the narrative type becomes increasingly dialogic. In spontaneous, monologic narratives, topic and narrative focus is essentially speaker-controlled, with a commensurate reduction in speaker autonomy as the degree of elicitation progressively increases.

Narratives produced in power-asymmetric contexts, for example in medical, educational and other institutional settings, tend towards the prompted and elicited end of this spectrum. In the forensic context, the process of elicitation in police interviews and adversarial courtroom witness examinations has a much more purposive function than in the average casual conversational context. Both parties have a vested interest in the outcome of the narration process, because the accounts presented form part of a chain of forensic narratives extending back to the original police interviews and forwards to potential future appeal proceedings. This process of narrative evolution and co-construction gives the final accounts produced in court a significant degree of authorial complexity, since they are usually a version 'not only of the events that have given rise to the legal proceedings in the first place, but as well a narrative of the previous proceedings (charging, sentencing, arguments in lower courts...)' Maley (1994, p. 47).

The dialogic process of elicitation responsible for producing these narratives has a significant impact on the shape and content of the final account. In the courtroom context, one of the most dominant of the narrative voices is that of the lawyer, who possesses the power as well as the means – through a variety of elicitation strategies – to influence both the form and the content of the account produced by the witness. A number of researchers on courtroom language, *inter alia* Harris (1984, 2001), Woodbury (1984), Drew (1992) and Luchjenbroers (1997), have written about the extent to which the question-and-answer model of testimony elicitation within the adversarial system, which prioritises the use of closed and controlling question forms, has the effect of constraining the witness' freedom to present narrative testimony, thereby preventing them from 'telling their own story'. Courtroom narratives may best be characterised as dual-authored texts, using 'author' in Goffman's (1981) sense, with the emphasis on the voice of the lawyer as the primary and authoritative teller, rather than that of the witness.

In this chapter, I extend this sense of dual-authorship to include the presence of a further narrative voice, that of evidence given by the same witness in an earlier hearing. In many respects, intertextual references to previous proceedings are commonplace in the courtroom, since witnesses are frequently questioned about sections of their police interviews or statements when they appear in court. However, the data presented in this chapter add an additional layer of dialogism and heteroglossic potential to the already complex picture presented so far. In the O. J. Simpson case, the fact that a nine-month criminal trial preceded the civil action allowed both sides (though as we will see, it was predominantly a cross-examination strategy) in the civil trial to exploit the existence of a protracted and explicit prior account of events. This chapter will focus on some of the ways in which voices from the criminal trial may be seen to have left discernible echoes and traces in the evolving civil trial narrative.

I will begin by briefly discussing the nature of intertextuality in forensically-oriented narratives.

Intertextuality in forensic narratives

Intertextuality, a term coined by Kristeva (1980), and originally used in a literary context, concerns the extent to which any single text incorporates and/or acknowledges its interaction with other texts, both past and future, paradigmatic and syntagmatic. The Bakhtinian notions of heteroglossic potential and dialogic connectivity (Bakhtin, 1981, 1986) are central to the adversarial legal process, since, as we have seen, each part of the (re)constructive process of the crime narrative is potentially the site of influence from previous interviews and hearings and, equally significantly, has an eye on potential future appeal proceedings.

The intertextuality which is the focus of this analysis occurs at a relatively localised level; as such it is concerned not with the broader social voices and discourses which shape courtroom interaction more generally, but rather with what Fairclough (1992, p. 104) has termed *manifest intertextuality*, where other specific texts are '"manifestly" cued by features on the surface of the text, such as quotation marks'. Such a phenomenon has also been referred to as 'projection' (Fuller, 1998), or 'extra-vocalisation' (White, 1998), whereby a prior discourse is directly re-presented, without recontextualisation, as semiotic content in a future text.

As Fairclough (1992, p. 119) states, two important considerations in this process of representation (or re-presentation) are '(i) to what extent the boundaries between representing and represented discourse are clearly marked, and (ii) to what extent represented discourse is translated into the voice of the representing discourse'. A third issue, concerning the extent to which the represented discourse is *appropriated* by the representing discourse is the primary focus of this chapter.

I will draw on data from the 1994/5 criminal and 1996 civil trials of O. J. Simpson, where Simpson was accused of killing his ex-wife and her male companion. In particular, I will focus on the testimony of Robert Heidstra, a key timeline witness who testified in both trials, exploring the potential for manipulation of this preceding version. Although this chapter adopts a case-study approach, involving the analysis of a single witness' testimony, the narrative intertextuality discussed here is a more widely observable phenomenon in the data.

Before embarking upon the analysis of Heidstra's *micro*-narrative, however, it is first useful to consider the degree of convergence in the *macro*-narratives constructed in the two trials of O. J. Simpson.

Macro-narrative congruence between the criminal and civil trials

In the criminal trial, the prosecution case centred around Simpson's allegedly aggressive nature and his previous history of violence towards his ex-wife. The prosecution claimed that Nicole Brown Simpson had been murdered as a result of Simpson's jealousy about her relationships with other men. In their reconstruction of events, they argued that the murder of the second victim, Ron Goldman, had been unplanned, and that he had simply had the misfortune to be at Nicole's house at the time the murderer arrived.

Since the criminal burden of proof rests with the prosecution, Simpson's defence were not obliged to construct an alternative version of events, simply to challenge the prosecution macro-narrative account as unreliable. The defence account comprised four such challenges, as summarised by Hastie and Pennington (1996): the 'O. J. Simpson story', which placed Simpson elsewhere at the time of the murders; the 'real killers' narrative, which suggested potential alternative perpetrators; the 'rush to judgement' story which portrayed various LAPD investigative officers as racist, lacking in integrity and unprofessional; and finally the 'bungling criminal investigators'' narrative, which told of incompetent and unethical criminologists, responsible for mishandling and cross-contaminating forensic evidence.

Following O. J. Simpson's acquittal in October 1995, the families of the two victims filed a civil suit against Simpson, which began almost exactly a year later in October 1996. In terms of macro-narratives, the prosecution and defence cases were broadly similar, since they were dealing with the same crimes and circumstances. It might therefore be reasonable to assume that the same witnesses would be called at the two trials. However, this was not the case, as I will illustrate.

The first important difference concerned the *number* of witnesses called to construct the crime narrative. In the criminal trial, no fewer than 126 witnesses had been called over a nine-month period. In contrast, the civil trial involved 94 witnesses, still a significant group of narrative voices, but one which represented a reduction of a quarter in the number of individuals giving evidence between the two trials. This discrepancy is to some extent explained by the greater financial constraints of the civil trial, where the families of the victims and Simpson himself were responsible for the respective prosecution and defence costs. However, perhaps more significant than this straightforwardly quantitative difference is the fact that only half of the witnesses who testified in the civil action had previously given evidence in the criminal trial, a surprising statistic given that the two cases concerned the same basic crime event.

There are also some interesting differences in terms of the degree of witness overlap between the respective prosecution and defence cases. The prosecution used just over half (54%) of the same witnesses to construct their civil-trial version of the crime narrative. In their case, the main areas of change related to the family of the victims (reflecting the civil nature of the action) and a number of witnesses who were brought in to refute Simpson's civil testimony, including his ex-girlfriend and an expert on domestic violence. The presence of Simpson's testimony was of course a significant difference between the two trials, as he had previously declined to testify in his criminal trial. Finally, the prosecution's police and forensic testimony remained similar in content, although, as prosecutor Daniel Petrocelli later explained, a strategic decision was made to call fewer police officers in the civil trial:

> Their [the defence's] goal was to try the case of the Los Angeles Police Department and keep attention off their client [Simpson]. The last thing we wanted to do was to serve up a full menu of police witnesses and give the defence weeks of counterattacks in out case-in-chief. We decided we would use a minimum of individuals to lay out the police evidence, and would keep it tight. There would be no duplication, no two cops telling the same story.
>
> (Petrocelli, 1998, p. 397)

In contrast, the defence were more consistent in their choice of witnesses, using two-thirds (62%) of the same witnesses in the construction of their civil case. The defence's civil case was very much based on the same issues as its criminal counterpart had been, focusing predominantly on police corruption, incompetent handling of the forensic and DNA evidence, resulting in a reasonably high proportion of the same witnesses being called to testify. Where the witnesses were different, they were mainly in the form of additional LAPD officers, in an attempt to support the claims of incompetence and corruption, and photographic and scientific experts, reinforcing the allegations of mishandling and contamination of forensic evidence.

In terms of macro-narrative congruence, therefore, it seems that the prosecution in the civil trial attempted to accentuate the human dimension of the case, whereas the defence prioritised its scientific foundations. This provides an interesting correlation with the type of legal proceeding, with the prosecution case mapping on to the more victim-impact focused civil proceedings.

I will now move on to a micro-analysis of the testimony of one of the 58 witnesses who testified in both the criminal and the civil trials, Robert Heidstra, and will discuss some of the ways in which both prosecution and defence made reference to his prior criminal trial testimony.

Intertextual echoes and traces in the civil trial testimony of Robert Heidstra

Robert Heidstra's trial testimony was significant both to the prosecution and the defence, insofar as it helped to establish the exact timing of the attacks. In the criminal trial, he was originally intended to have been a prosecution witness, but was dropped by the prosecution and was instead called by the defence, under subpoena. By the time of the civil trial, however, Heidstra had switched sides and gave evidence for the prosecution. Heidstra testified that, whilst walking his dogs on the night of the murders, he had heard Nicole's Akita dog barking continuously and had gone to investigate. He overheard an argument, but continued on his way, assuming that 'if these two guys have an argument, it's nothing more than that. It's like an argument. I said, well, that's it' (Civil trial testimony, 25 October 1996). In the remainder of the chapter, I will explore the some of the ways in which the lawyers from both sides incorporated Heidstra's criminal trial testimony into their civil trial questioning of the witness.

Because Heidstra had previously testified in the well-publicised criminal trial, becoming, like many witnesses, a minor celebrity, there was some important groundwork for the prosecution attorney to do with respect to Heidstra's neutrality and credibility. The following exchange between Heidstra and the prosecuting attorney, Petrocelli, represented an attempt to neutralise Heidstra's perceived celebrity status which could potentially have tainted his direct examination testimony:

Extract 1

```
 1  Q  Okay. Sir, after the – you testified in the criminal trial, right?
 2  A  I did, yes.
 3  Q  Okay. And the verdict came down sometime in October of last year?
 4  A  Yeah.
 5  Q  Okay. Now, since that time, have you made plans to write a book about
 6     your observations?
 7  A  Yes, after the verdict.
 8  Q  Okay. Have you sold your book?
 9  A  No. No takers.
10  Q  Nobody interested?
11  A  Guess not.
12  Q  You have not received any money at all?
13  A  Not at all, not one penny.
14  Q  And basically, the book that you are writing is about the observations
15     you made?
16  A  Right. Exactly.
17  Q  And did you write any of that book before you testified at the trial?
18  A  No, never.
19  Q  Okay. Thank you.
```

(Civil trial direct examination, 25 October 1996)

In this extract, the lawyer plays up Heidstra's apparent lack of financial motivation to testify and his failure to capitalise on his criminal trial appearance in the intervening year between the criminal and civil trials. In this way, Heidstra is portrayed as a reliable witness and his evidence as credible and by beginning his examination of the witness in this way, the prosecutor,

Petrocelli, attempts to preempt and to some extent circumvent a potential defence challenge during cross-examination.

Apart from implicit references such as that in Extract 1, the prosecution made relatively few references to Heidstra's criminal evidence overall, preferring to reconstruct his narrative as far as possible from scratch. With this witness, the prosecution presumably decided to 'cut their losses' because he had been a relatively poor witness on the stand at the original trial.

In contrast, the defence exploited his prior testimony extensively, basing much of their cross-examination on his criminal trial evidence a year earlier rather than relying on his civil trial direct examination testimony from earlier that same day, a more typical cross-examination dynamic.

Some references to the witness's prior evidence were more explicit than others; on some occasions his criminal trial appearance was simply alluded to in a relatively unspecific way, as in the Extract 2 between Heidstra and defence attorney Baker.

Extract 2

1   Q   And you previously testified that you began to go into that alley at 10:30
2   to   10:35?
3   A   Yeah, 10:35.

(Civil trial direct examination, 25 October 1996)

Here, no explicit reference is made to the fact that his prior testimony emanated from the criminal trial.

There were also more direct uses of the criminal trial testimony in Heidstra's civil cross-examination, however. Defence attorney Baker used such a strategy during his cross-examination of the witness, in relation to his recall of the colour of a vehicle which he claimed to have seen near the crime scene. Establishing the colour was crucial as identification evidence, since Simpson had been driving a white Bronco that night. Seemingly incontestable evidence from an even earlier text did actually exist, in the form of a police interview conducted with Heidstra on the night of the murder; in this interview, Heidstra repeatedly refers to a 'large white vehicle' (Schiller and Willwerth, 1997, p. 206). Heidstra's direct examination testimony, reproduced below as Extract 3, is entirely consistent with this description:

Extract 3

1   Q   (BY MR PETROCELLI) Did the car that you saw that evening look
2   like the one in the photo?
3   A   It was – it resembled a car like this, yes. For sure, I couldn't say exactly
4   this car, but it resembled the size of the car.
5   Q   And the color?
6   A   White.

(Civil trial direct examination, 25 October 1996)

Rather than use either preexisting text, however, Baker chose instead to invoke Heidstra's *criminal trial* testimony, where the witness was much less certain in his identification and description of the vehicle (lines 6–18 represent the intertextual portion taken from Heidstra's criminal trial testimony):

Extract 4

1   Q   (BY MR BAKER) *Now, one other thing: You testified, did you not, that the color was*
2   *light or white?*
3   A   *No. It was definitely white, sir.*
4   Q   Let me just get your – 36324.
5   (BY MR PETROCELLI) One second, Mr. Baker. Okay.
6   (MR BAKER, Reading)
7   'Q   Did that car make a turn, or did it go up Dorothy, or what did it do?'
8   'A   It made a turn.'
9   'Q   Which direction did it go?'
10 'A   A right turn and went south.'
11 'Q   Are you sure that vehicle went south?'
12 'A   Sure, sure.'
13 'Q   Would that be towards Wilshire Boulevard?'
14 'A   Towards Wilshire Boulevard.'
15 'Q   *What color was the color?*'
16 'A   *Very light color, white or light.*'
17 'Q   *White or light?*'
18 'A   *It was white or something.*'
19 Q   (MR BAKER TO HEIDSTRA) *Does that refresh your recollection, sir?*
20 A   *It was white, definitely white.*
21 Q   *So it wasn't white or light?*
22 A   *No, it was white.*
23 Q   *It wasn't white or light?*
24 A   *It was white.*
25 Q   Thank you.
26 (MR BAKER) Nothing further.

(Civil trial cross-examination, 25 October 1996)

Baker's first question (in line 1) relates not to the actual colour of the vehicle, but the content of Heidstra's criminal testimony – '*You testified, did you not, that the color was light or white*'. The witness treats the question as one which relates predominantly to the second part of the question, the colour of the vehicle, however, and provides only a cursory 'no', meaning 'it wasn't light or white', elaborating further that '*it was definitely white, sir*'. However, this allows the cross-examining attorney to interpret this 'no' response as a 'no' to his original question, that this was *not* the content of his testimony. He is able to directly challenge this implied assertion by invoking Heidstra's criminal trial testimony.

In a sense, this places the witness in a no-win situation; if he admits that he did indeed testify that the vehicle was 'light or white', which he is virtually compelled to do given the existence of the criminal trial transcript, then he appears unreliable both in terms of his recall (an unfavourable characteristic for an eyewitness) and as far as the actual evidential value of his testimony is concerned, since he cannot be certain about the colour of the vehicle. However, if he acquiesces and admits that this was indeed his testimony, then his assertion in line 3 that '*it was definitely white, sir*' appears inconsistent at best and deceptive at worst. By using the criminal trial transcript in this way, and particularly by quoting in direct speech rather than using paraphrase, thereby employing an explicitly 'manifest' form of intertextual reference in Fairclough's terms, cross-examiner Baker is able to exploit a potential discrepancy in Heidstra's testimony and to portray this as symptomatic of Heidstra's more general unreliability as a witness.

In any case, Heidstra's criminal trial testimony does him no favours in the credibility stakes; initially he is only able to provide a disjunctive reply to the colour question (lines 15 and 16), stating that the vehicle was a '*very light color, white or light*'. The criminal trial direct examination lawyer's attempts to repair this vague response with his more specific '*white or light?*' (line 17) only results in a further hedged, and even less precise, response – '*it was white or something*' (line 18).

Despite the fact that, in the resumed cross-examination (lines 19–26), Heidstra disregards the question '*does that refresh your recollection sir?*' (line 19) insisting that the vehicle '*was white, definitely white*' (line 20), and resists the attorney's challenges – '*no, it was white*' (line 22), '*it was white*' (line 24), the power of his original (and best?) testimony in the criminal trial is undeniable. I will revisit the issue of an evaluative primacy effect below.

In the process of using prior testimony in attempts to ensnare the witness, the civil trial cross-examination also provides an opportunity for the criminal evidence to be subtly altered. Some recent work has focused on the production process and subsequent status of trial transcripts. Although transcripts are designed to be (and are largely considered to be) verbatim written reproductions of the oral event, there is of course considerable potential for variation between the original event and the written product. Not only is it possible for even experienced court reporters to introduce errors into their transcriptions, the mode of representation is essentially problematic. As Walker (1990), Eades (1996) and Tiersma (1999) have all pointed out, the transformation of a dynamic speech event into a written representation necessarily involves the elimination of most prosodic, non-verbal and paralinguistic features of the original, such as hesitations, gestures and intonational contours. This is not simply due to the constraints of the medium, but is also because such features are not considered of significance to the envisaged 'end-user', typically a legal audience of appeal judges, trial lawyers and law-school students. Despite the paucity of the reproduction, the transcript stands as an autonomous and authoritative text, as Tiersma (1999, p. 177) notes, 'the transcript of proceedings . . . becomes the definitive record of what occurred', with what was actually said both largely irrelevant and invariably irretrievable.

The availability of such a 'stripped-bare' version of the witness' criminal trial testimony, combined with the dynamic constraints of witness examination, both work to the advantage of the cross-examining lawyer, since in reinstating the spoken-ness of the written transcript through an in-court performance, it is potentially possible for the lawyer to introduce deleterious prosodic and paralinguistic features which were not originally produced by the witness and, conversely, to neutralise positive features which were produced but which were not recorded in the trial transcript. This gives the cross-examining lawyer a great degree of artistic licence in his reenactment of the exchange which is reinforced by his relative interactional freedom in the courtroom. Furthermore, and perhaps more significantly, there is the somewhat ironic fact that the only person present at both the original proceedings and the current reenactment is the witness himself. Not only is he precluded from 'playing himself' in the reanimation of the transcript, but he is also prohibited from challenging the authenticity of the lawyer's performance.

In terms of content as well as delivery, the cross-examining lawyer is able to employ selective editing in his 'reproduction' of Heidstra's testimony in Extract 4, above. In this way, not only is the testimony replayed as a decontextualised extract, it is also possible for him to edit out sections which are 'unhelpful' to the point under construction. Hence the following question, which occurred in the criminal trial and which would have come between lines 18 and 19 above if it had been reproduced, is omitted in the civil trial replay:

Extract 5

1 Q Did you see that car very clearly?
2 A I could clearly see it.

(Criminal trial direct examination, 12 July 1995)

Had this final question appeared in the civil trial rerun, it may have reinstated some of Heidstra's dented credibility, and would surely have diluted the impact of his apparently indecisive testimony.

This strategy is, in evidentiary terms, somewhat akin to a prosecutor being able to make reference to a defendant's prior crimes, misdemeanours and convictions but not his acquittals and mistrials, in other words, anything you say (in a previous hearing) really may be used in evidence (against you), to echo the Miranda warning. Although in the extract above, the implications are presumably not grave, it would be easy to imagine a context where the consequences could be infinitely worse. The interactional constraints of courtroom questioning are such that the witness/defendant would be relatively powerless to defend himself, having to rely instead on an eagle-eyed lawyer to spot the discrepancies between the two versions. It should be noted that there was not a single objection raised by the defence during Heidstra's civil trial cross-examination.

In Extract 4 above, there was the implicit suggestion by the cross-examination that the witness's first version of events, as expressed in his criminal testimony, had a greater intrinsic truth value than any subsequent version. This appears to be a common implication, a kind of 'I have to take your first answer', in the parlance of the quiz show host, which appears throughout the cross-examination data. The status of the transcript as the definitive version extends to the *content* of the witness' testimony as well as the *form*. I will illustrate this point with reference to a final set of extracts from Heidstra's civil trial cross-examination.

A point of dispute in Heidstra's testimony concerned the exact time he had been in the vicinity of the crime scene. As he was a time-line witness in both trials, establishing the exact route and timing of his evening walk was of crucial importance as Simpson had an extremely narrow window of opportunity within which he could have committed the murders.

Cross-examiner Baker's opening gambit, in the form of a reasonably straightforward declarative tag question, is vehemently denied by Heidstra:

Extract 6

1   Q   Now, when you got to the place where you were parallel to Nicole's,
2   that was at 10:40, right?
3   A   No, no, no. It was before that.

(Civil trial cross-examination, 25 October 1996)

As prosecutor Petrocelli would later recount in his post-trial memoirs:

Reconstructing his [Heidstra's] movements and adding up the time each took, rather than simply accepting his estimates, I put the time at between 10.35 and 10.40. Baker used Heidstra's criminal trial testimony ('It must have been in that time exactly when I came to the alley. Exactly. Around that time') in an attempt to make him move closer to 10.45, which would make the timing tighter.

(Petrocelli, 1998, p. 396)

Baker's reaction to this denial in the following turn was once again to invoke Heidstra's criminal testimony, which was apparently at odds with his negative response in line 3, above. This has the effect of suggesting that the witness is either unreliable or is lying, and is all the more powerful for the jury by using Heidstra's own testimony, apparently presented in his own 'voice', to reinforce the suggestion:

Extract 7

1   Q   Let me read what you said in the criminal trial, please, at 36504, lines 5
2   through 19. *And I'll omit the objections. See if I can refresh your*
3   *recollection a little bit, Mr. Heidstra.*
4   'Q   So now that we're clear, Mr. Heidstra, is there any doubt in your mind

5   that you were in that alley, and was walking parallel to Bundy, on the
6   night of June 12, 1994?'
7   'A   No doubt. I'd never forget that.'
8   'Q   Any doubt in your mind that when you stopped behind that house, it
9   was approximately 10:40, any doubt?'
10 'A   *No. No doubt about it.'*

(Civil trial cross-examination, 25 October 1996)

By implying in lines 2 and 3 that he is reintroducing the criminal testimony as an *aide-mémoire* for the witness, Baker implies an altruistic rather than a coercive motivation. Baker also helpfully offers (in line 2) to *'omit the objections'*, potentially altering the transcript and therefore the testimony. Again, interestingly, this produces no objections from the defence.

Unfortunately for him, Heidstra has no defence when faced with his prior testimony, and simply claims a lapse of memory, producing the following credibility-damaging exchange:

Extract 8

1   Q   Now, does that refresh your recollection?
2   A   I don't recall that at all, sir. Unfortunately, it's too late.

(Civil trial cross-examination, 25 October 1996)

Heidstra, a native speaker of French, produces the potentially damaging ambiguous comment, *'Unfortunately, it's too late'*, which presumably means that the events occurred too long ago for him to remember. Whatever the precise meaning, the cross-examining lawyer is content to leave its nuances unexplored.

In the final question-and-answer sequences of this segment of testimony, Baker is understandably happy to oblige when he is then asked to repeat the damaging extract (in line 3 below), and he further reinforces the primacy of Heidstra's criminal testimony over his current claims by getting him to agree that *'our memories are usually better closer to the event'* (lines 4/5):

Extract 9

1   Q   Well, I take it a year or so ago, your memory may have been just a
2   little clearer about the event after the passage of time.
3   A   Repeat it again.
4   Q   Be happy to. All I'm saying is that our memories are usually better
5   closer to the event.
6   A   Sure. Sure, I understand.

(Civil trial cross-examination, 25 October 1996)

Conclusion

In this chapter I have attempted to illustrate some of the ways in which trial lawyers, particularly during cross-examination, are able to exploit more or less convergent versions of witnesses' narratives originating earlier in the legal process. Although I have taken quite an unusual instance of 'manifest intertextuality', insofar as relatively few cases lead to both a criminal and civil trial, such a phenomenon is observable throughout the texts produced in the adversarial legal system, from police interviews to appeal proceedings.

These findings are in many respects speculative and exploratory. Despite this, the analysis presented here is perhaps a preliminary step towards a more detailed illustration of the complexity of narrative voices and versions which permeate the legal process. Both the crime and its resulting narrative representations are multifaceted and multiperspectival events. However many voices contribute to this process of reconstruction, it is ultimately true that the final and definitive voice belongs to the jury, whose job it is to sift through the versions presented to them and arrive at a sound and satisfactory verdict.

References

Bakhtin, M. M. (1981) *The Dialogic Imagination: Four Essays*, trans. C. Emerson and M. Holquist, M. Holquist (ed.). Austin: University of Texas Press.

Bakhtin, M. M. (1986) *Speech Genres and Other Late Essays*, trans. V. W. McGee, C. Emerson and M. Holquist (eds). Austin: University of Texas Press.

Bennett, L. and Feldman, M. S. (1981) *Reconstructing Reality in the Courtroom*. London: Tavistock.

Drew, P. (1992) 'Contested Evidence in Courtroom Cross-Examination: The Case of a Trial for Rape', in P. Drew and J. Heritage (eds), *Talk at Work*. Cambridge: Cambridge University Press, pp. 470–520.

Eades, D. (1996) 'Verbatim Courtroom Transcripts and Discourse Analysis', in H. Kniffka (ed.), *Recent Developments in Forensic Linguistics*. Frankfurt: Peter Lang, pp. 241–54.

Fairclough, N. (1992) *Discourse and Social Change*. London: Polity Press.

Fuller, G. (1998) 'Cultivating Science', in J. R. Martin and R. Veel (eds), *Reading Science: Critical and Functional Perspectives on Discourses of Science*. London: Routledge, pp. 35–62.

Gewirtz, P. (1996) 'Victims and Voyeurs: Two Narrative Problems at the Criminal Trial', in P. Brooks and P. Gewirtz (eds), *Law's Stories: Narrative and Rhetoric in the Law*. New Haven: Yale University Press.

Goffman, E. (1981) *Forms of Talk*. Oxford: Blackwell.

Harris, S. (1984) 'Questions as a Mode of Control in Magistrates' Courts', *International Journal of the Sociology of Language*, vol. 49, pp. 5–28.

Harris, S. (2001) 'Fragmented Narratives and Multiple Tellers: Witness and Defendant Accounts in Trials', *Discourse Studies*, vol. 3(1), pp. 53–74.

Hastie, R. and Pennington, N. (1996) 'Perceptions and Decision Making: The Jury's View: The O. J. Simpson Stories: Behavioral Scientists' Reflections on *The People of the State of California* vs. *Orenthal James Simpson*', *Colorado Law Review*, vol. 67, University of Colorado Press.

Jackson, B. (1995) *Making Sense in Law: Linguistic, Psychological and Semiotic Perspectives*. Liverpool: Deborah Charles Publications.

Kniffka, H. (ed.) (1996) *Recent Developments in Forensic Linguistics*. Frankfurt: Peter Lang.

Kristeva, J. (1980) 'Word, Dialogue and Novel', in J. Kristeva, *Desire in Language*. Oxford: Oxford University Press.

Luchjenbroers, J. (1997) '"In Your Own Words ... ": Questions and Answers in a Supreme Court Trial', *Journal of Pragmatics*, vol. 27, pp. 477–503.

Maley, Y. (1994) 'The Language of the Law', in J. Gibbons (ed.), *Language and the Law*. London: Longman, pp. 11–50.

Maley, Y. and Fahey, R. (1991) 'Presenting the Evidence: Constructions of Reality in Court', *International Journal for the Semiotics of Law*, vol. IV (10), pp. 3–17.

Petrocelli, D. and Knobler, P. (1998) *Triumph of Justice: The Final Judgment on the Simpson Saga*. New York: Crown Publishers.

Schiller, L. and Willwerth, J. (1997) *American Tragedy: The Uncensored Story of the Simpson Defence*. New York: Avon Books.

Stygall, G. (1994) *Trial Language: Discourse Processing and Discursive Formation*. Amsterdam: Benjamins.

Tiersma, P. (1999) *Legal Language*. Chicago: Chicago University Press.

Walker, A. G. (1990) 'Language at Work in the Law: The Customs, Conventions and Appellate Consequences of Court Reporting', in J. Levi and Walker, A. G. (eds), *Language in the Judicial Process*. New York: Plenum Press, pp. 203–46.

White, P. (1998) 'Telling Media Tales: The News Story as Rhetoric', unpublished PhD thesis, University of Sydney.

Woodbury, H. (1984) 'The Strategic Use of Questions in Court', *Semiotica*, vol. 48(3/4), pp. 197–228.

10

'Evidence Given in Unequivocal Terms': Gaining Consent of Aboriginal Young People in Court[1]

Diana Eades

Introduction

In an unusual and headline-making court case in Brisbane in 1995, three Aboriginal boys were prosecution witnesses in a committal hearing in which six police officers were charged with the unlawful deprivation of their liberty. The case was somewhat of a role-reversal: in Australian criminal proceedings police officers participate usually as prosecution witnesses, while Aboriginal participants are generally defendants (that is, the accused).

This chapter presents part of a detailed study of the cross-examination of the three Aboriginal boys, which examines the linguistic strategies used by the two defence counsel to manipulate and construe the evidence of the three boys. These strategies succeeded in the magistrate accepting the defence's construction of these victim-witnesses as criminals with 'no regard for the community', and the reinterpretation of the alleged abduction as the boys voluntarily giving up their liberty while the police took them for a ride, both literally and metaphorically. My sociolinguistic study of the cross-examination in this case takes up Conley and O'Barr's call to linguists to focus on what they see as 'the most important theoretical issue in law and language: the use of linguistic methods to understand the nature of law and legal power' (1998, p. 6). The major focus of this chapter is on the lawyers' particularly effective exploitation of the Aboriginal tendency to use 'gratuitous concurrence' – namely freely saying 'yes' in answer to questions regardless of whether or not the speaker actually agrees with the proposition.

The 'incident'

The incident had occurred some time after midnight on 10 May 1994, when the three boys, who were then aged 12, 13 and 14, were taken by the six police officers in three separate vehicles from a shopping mall in the Fortitude Valley area near the downtown area of Brisbane, Australia. The boys were told to get in the police cars, but they were not charged with any offence, nor were they taken to any police station. They were driven out of town and left about 14 kms away in an industrial wasteland in Pinkenba near the mouth of the Brisbane River, from where they had to find their own way back to the Valley. According to police, the young people were 'taken down to Pinkenba to reflect on their misdemeanours' (ABC *Four Corners*, 8 March 1996).

Following investigation of the boy's complaints, the police officers were charged that they had unlawfully deprived each of the boys of 'his personal liberty by carrying him away in a motor vehicle against his will'. In February 1995, the boys were prosecution witnesses in the committal hearing, which was the first stage in the trial process against the police officers.[2] There was considerable public interest in this case as it involved such serious allegations against the police officers, and the committal hearing was attended by a large contingent of reporters as well as onlookers.

Most of the four-day hearing consisted of evidence from the three boys, which included lengthy cross-examination by each of the two defence counsel who represented three of the police officers. The case centred on the issue of whether or not the boys had got into and travelled in the police cars against their will: no doubt was ever raised that they were approached and told to get in the police cars, nor that they were taken to the industrial wasteland and abandoned there. The defence case was that the boys 'gave up their liberty' and that 'there's no offence of allowing a person to give up his liberty'.[3]

The witnesses

The boys had grown up in extended Aboriginal families in southern Queensland. Two of them had spent most of their lives in a rural Aboriginal community a few hours drive northwest of Brisbane (Cherbourg) and the oldest had spent most of his time in Brisbane. At the time of the alleged abduction they were not regularly attending school, and they perhaps could be described as 'part-time street kids': sometimes staying with different relatives in Brisbane and Cherbourg, and other times staying in the city or Valley, sleeping in disused buildings, and meeting friends in parks and pin-ball arcades. Each of the boys had a criminal record, which included such offences as unlawful use of a motor vehicle, theft, and break, enter and steal.

Although these boys were 'streetwise', and much was made of this in the media as well as in cross-examination, they were not 'interview-wise'. Having grown up in Aboriginal families and communities, most of their interaction with non-Aboriginal society was in schools, where they had not been regular or successful participants.[4] Although they were speakers of quite a 'light' (or acrolectal) variety of Aboriginal English, they had had little chance to develop bicultural competence, which is essential to successful participation in the legal system (see Eades, 1992, 1994). That is, they were using Aboriginal ways of communicating which involve significant cultural differences from mainstream English, and which disadvantaged them in the interview situation, as we will see below. Elsewhere (see Eades, 1993, 1996) I have argued that perhaps the most important features of light varieties of Aboriginal English are pragmatic. For example, even where phonology and grammatical patterns differ little from other varieties of Australian English, speakers of light Aboriginal English often use much more silence than others. Silence in Aboriginal English is seen as a valuable and positive part of interaction, and is not taken as an indication that something is wrong, or that the speaker is evasive, lying or ignorant (see Eades, 1994, 1996). The legal implications of such a difference in the use of silence should not be underestimated. O'Barr (1982, p. 99) points out that silence in response to an accusation in court can be 'interpreted by the court as an admission of [its] truth', and that this has happened frequently in America.

Aboriginal young people and the criminal justice system

The Pinkenba case needs to be understood in the light of ongoing police control over the movements of Queensland Aboriginal people in various ways since British invasion and settlement in the early nineteenth century. Central to this control have been two processes:

1   the 'pivotal role' of police in the removal of Aboriginal children from their families and kinship groups under 'protective' legislation from the 1860s for over a century (HREOC, 1997, p. 44);
2   the current 'overpolicing' of Aboriginal young people in public places, which has resulted in their being 41 times more likely to be in juvenile correctional institutions than a non-indigenous young person, and 26 times more likely to be in police custody.

(HREOC, based on 1995 statistics)

It is not difficult to see this extreme overrepresentation of indigenous young people in police custody and detention as an extension of the earlier official removal policies and practices (See for example Cunneen, 1994). Cunneen (1994) and Cunneen and White (1995) argue that this process of criminalisation, which clearly discriminates against Aboriginal young people, results to a considerable extent from the way in which police exercise their discretionary power (for example in deciding whether to arrest, use diversionary measures, or to issue a caution).

Not surprisingly, Aboriginal people do not accept this situation, and there is an ongoing struggle between police and Aboriginal people. In the Pinkenba incident, yet again Aboriginal young people in a public place are being singled out for police attention, and yet again Aboriginal young people are removed by police. But unlike so many of these earlier occurrences, Aboriginal complaints about this police action were not ignored: through the Aboriginal Legal Service and the Criminal Justice Commission these complaints were heard and investigated. The struggle between Aboriginal people and the police moved from the streets into the courtroom, where the major weapon is undoubtedly language. Before we examine some of the specific details of how language was used in this courtroom struggle, we will look briefly at issues concerning child witnesses, as well as the conversational pattern known as *gratuitous concurrence*, and its significance generally for Aboriginal witnesses.

Child witnesses

In Australian law, anyone under the age of 18 is defined as a child (Bowen, 1995), and accused persons under 18 are dealt with in Children's Court. Suggestibility, that is, being easily led in cross-examination, is of particular concern with child witnesses. In reviewing the literature on the evidence of children in court, Thompson (1999, p. 679) reports that a number of researchers have found that 'children are more susceptible to leading questions than adults', that 'children can be misled more easily than adults' (p. 681), and that the 'extent of the child's suggestibility is determined in large measure by the behaviour of the interviewer' (p. 683). See also Brennan (1995) on the language used in the cross-examination of child witnesses.

Actually the boys would have been eligible for provision as 'special witnesses' under a 1977 amendment to the Queensland Evidence Act (s21A).[5] According to this section it should have been possible for them to give evidence either out of view of the defendants, or in another room, or even by videotape. However, it seems that these provisions are rarely utilised (ABC, 1999), and they would not have provided any protection from the cross-examination. But such protection would be offered by new legislation proposed in 2000 by the Queensland Law Reform Commission in its report on the evidence of children (2000). This report recommended the amendment of the existing Evidence Act by the insertion of the following provision on the 'Improper questioning of child witnesses' (p. 8):

> The court may disallow a question put in cross-examination to a witness under the age of 18 years, or inform the witness that it need not be answered, if the question is:
>
> (a) misleading or confusing;
> (b) phrased in inappropriate language; or
> (c) unduly annoying, harassing, intimidating, offensive, oppressive or repetitive.

The second part of the provision lists a number of factors which the court needs to take into account, which include culture of the witness, as well as factors such as age and education. It is important to note that, unlike the 1977 amendment 21A discussed above, this proposed amendment on cross-examination is to apply to any witness under 18 (not 12). Further, the Commission notes that 'this provision may be equally applicable to adult witnesses' (*ibid.*), but that its reference confines it to examining issues affecting child witnesses.

Gratuitous concurrence

Compounding their situation of being child witnesses (in an adult court), the boys were particularly affected by the conversational pattern known as *gratuitous concurrence*. Liberman (1981, 1985) used this term to refer to the tendency, frequently used by Aboriginal people, of saying 'yes' in answer to a question (or 'no' to a negative question), regardless of whether the speaker actually agrees with the proposition, and at times even if the speaker does not understand the question. Liberman's work shows that gratuitous concurrence cannot be understood solely as a response to colonisation and subjugation, but is consistent with the Aboriginal tendency to keep surface harmony, and work 'behind the scenes' to deal with disagreements.

This conversational pattern, which is found in Aboriginal conversations throughout Australia, has long been recognised by people working with Aborigines in a wide range of professional and para-professional areas, such as Strehlow (1936, p. 334) and Elkin (1947, p. 176). More recent explorations of gratuitous concurrence can be found in many discussions of Aborigines and the law, including Coldrey (1987), Cooke (1996), CJC (1996) and Mildren (1997, 1999). While the examples cited in the literature until recently have been primarily with Aborigines who speak traditional Aboriginal languages, the phenomenon of gratuitous concurrence is also widely recognised by people working with Aboriginal English-speaking people in non-traditionally-oriented societies. Research with such witnesses has found that gratuitous concurrence is important to an examination of the misunderstanding and miscommunication which is common between Aboriginal and non-Aboriginal speakers of English in many lawyer interviews, police interviews and courtroom hearings (see Eades, 1992, 1994).

Thus the simple word 'yes' (or its variants, such as 'yeah' and 'mm') is crucial in legal contexts. From the legal perspective, such an answer to a question signals agreement to the proposition being questioned. But from the perspective of many Aboriginal witnesses, 'yes' *may* signal something like 'I know I have to cooperate with your lengthy questioning, and I hope that this answer will help bring the questioning to an end'. On the other hand, it *may* signal agreement to a proposition.

And once a witness in a court hearing, or a suspect in a police interview, has agreed to a proposition, then this becomes a binding agreement. To renege on such an agreement to a proposition is not just seen as contradictory or contrary, as it might be in ordinary conversation, but it *can* establish the witness or suspect as a liar, as we will see below.

My research over a number of years with speakers of Aboriginal English has found that certain factors increase the likelihood of gratuitous concurrence. These include: repeated and pressured questioning, particularly if over a lengthy period of time; lack of opportunity for the person being questioned to take control of the discourse; and pressure from the questioner, for example by shouting. These are all factors which can be found in courtroom cross-examination, as we will see.

In fact, the discourse structure of courtroom hearings seems to be conducive to the use of gratuitous concurrence. A number of studies have demonstrated that the 'majority of questions put to witnesses contain already completed propositions' (Harris, 1984), and that 'witnesses can hardly be thought to tell their stories in their own words' (Luchjenbroers, 1997, p. 501). To a considerable extent, witnesses' contributions in court are limited to providing answers to narrowly-framed questions. Gratuitous concurrence is particularly favoured by the aims and strategies of cross-examination, which generally attempts to weaken the credibility of the witness by showing either that the witness is unreliable and untrustworthy in some way, or that the witness' story is contradictory or inconsistent, or both. If a witness can be shown to give contradictory evidence in court, on any matter, then how could this witness be trusted to give reliable and trustworthy evidence against the accused?

The central cross-examination technique known as 'leading question' is obviously important here. Leading questions are a specific type of Yes–No question, but they are defined in *legal* terms, not grammatically – that is, a leading question is one which suggests a particular answer, or assumes the existence of a fact which is in dispute (Nygh and Butt, 1997). Rules of evidence limit the use of leading questions in examination-in-chief, but they are a major tool of cross-examination. While leading questions can clearly trigger gratuitous concurrence, it should be noted that this communication pattern is not limited to leading questions – it can occur in response to any Yes–No question.

A major cross-examination strategy is the use of repeated Yes–No questions to show inconsistencies in the witness's story, and leading questions are central in this process (Roberts 1998). The much-quoted evidence classic (Wigmore, 1940, p. 1367, cited in Palmer 1998, p. 45) claims that cross-examination 'is beyond any doubt the greatest legal engine invented for the discovery of truth'. But this 'greatest legal engine' for the discovery of truth is based on a fundamental legal assumption that repeated questioning is the way to test the consistency of a witness' story. Elsewhere (for example Eades, 1992, 1996), I have pointed out that this cultural assumption is not necessarily shared with Aboriginal societies.

Undoubtedly, there are now a number of legal professionals who are aware of the Aboriginal strategy of gratuitous concurrence, and who exploit it in their questioning of Aboriginal witnesses. So, if an Aboriginal witness is susceptible to gratuitous concurrence, it is not at all difficult for a cross-examining counsel to get the witness to 'agree' to conflicting propositions. An important question concerning Aboriginal witnesses, then, is: how can we know if an answer of 'yes' (or one of its variants) to a leading question in cross-examination is a genuine agreement on one hand, or on the other hand an answer of gratuitous concurrence which should not be interpreted literally?

It is obvious that we cannot know for sure what is in a speaker's mind. But we need to be alert to situations in which gratuitous concurrence is likely, or highly likely, and be certain not to rely for important decisions on literal interpretations of 'yes' answers in such situations. As we will see below, such caution should have been exercised in the Pinkenba case, but it was not.

The most recent legal publications to deal with communication with Aboriginal witnesses in court are the writings of a judge of the Supreme Court of the Northern Territory in a law journal (Mildren, 1997) and a linguistics journal (Mildren, 1999), and a report of the Queensland Criminal Justice Commission, titled *Aboriginal Witnesses in Queensland's Criminal Courts* (CJC, 1996). These publications all deal with the problem caused by gratuitous concurrence in legal interviewing of Aboriginal people (both speakers of traditional languages as well as speakers of Aboriginal English), and they see this as a type of 'suggestibility'.[6] Both the CJC report and Justice Mildren point to provisions already existing, in both common law and legislation, which could be used in such situations to disallow leading questions where a witness 'has proven to be – or is likely to be – highly suggestible' (CJC, p. 52). The CJC found, however, that this 'discretion to disallow the use of leading questions is rarely exercised by the courts' (*ibid.*).

On this point, the CJC report recommended that Queensland follow the lead of the revised Evidence Acts for both the Australian Federal Courts (Commonwealth Evidence Act) and the courts of the state of New South Wales. It recommended the amendment of the Queensland Evidence Act:

> to include a provision that a party may put a leading question to a witness in cross-examination unless the court disallows the question or directs the witness not to answer it. In determining whether to disallow the question, the court should be required to take into account, among other things, the extent to which the witness's cultural background or use of language may affect his or her answers.
>
> (CJC, 1996, p. 53)

'Yes', 'Yeah', 'Mm' and 'Yeh' answers in the Pinkenba cross-examination[7]

Turning specifically to the Pinkenba cross-examination, we find that several *specific* strategies were used to elicit agreement which appears highly likely to be gratuitous concurrence, on the central legal issue of the case (whether or not the boys got into the police cars of their free will), namely:

- complex questions in which several different propositions are questioned at once;
- pressured prosodic features such as shouting;
- witness silence being interrupted by repeated question tags;
- the timing of pauses, including adjournments.

The cross-examination in this case is riddled with apparent gratuitous concurrence. The most disturbing instances occur with DC1, the lawyer who often shouted and used much overt harassment. DC2 is, in contrast, generally quietly spoken, and playing the equivalent of the 'good cop' in the 'good cop, bad cop' strategy so clearly used by these two lawyers. He uses a number of subtle strategies to lead the witnesses to agree, in situations which are quite likely to produce gratuitous concurrence.

Example 1 occurs right at the end of the first day of the hearing. Thirteen-year-old David has been giving evidence for over two and a half hours, most of which has been in cross-examination. He has been visibly upset by the experience, even crying on a number of occasions:

Example 1 (DC2 to W1, day 1, p. 81)[8]

1   DC2   It's not that you were <u>forced</u> to go in any police car – it's the fact that you were <u>left</u> out at Pinkenba – that's what you're complaining about – isn't it? (2.0) That's right – isn't it–David – co<u>RRECT</u>?

2   W1   Yeah.
            (3.4)

3   DC2   Your worship is that a convenient time [i.e. to stop proceedings for the day]?

4   M   Yes, I was thinking about that Mr- uh- Humphrey.

Turn 1 is a typical example of the questioning style of the less-aggressive defence counsel, DC2. It questions two propositions, with the requirement for a single answer: (1) you are complaining not about being forced to go in any police car, and (2) you are complaining about being left out at Pinkenba. There is little chance for the witness to think about his answer (two seconds being quite a short silence for Aboriginal English speakers) before being pressured by repeated question tags, the final one with raised volume. These are all strategies conducive to the elicitation of gratuitous concurrence from Aboriginal witnesses. After the witness' 'yeah', which is taken as agreement to this crucial double-barrelled proposition about the central legal issue of the trial, DC2 calls for an adjournment, thereby maximising the impact of his final exchange with the witness.

It is impossible to know whether the witness did actually agree with the crucial question in turn 1 of Example 1, but we have seen above several reasons which would urge caution about giving a literal interpretation to his answer in turn 2.

On the second day of the hearing, David's cross-examination by DC2 continued. In Example 2, we see DC2 again using complex questions in which more than one proposition is being questioned:

Example 2 (DC2 to W1, day 2, p. 97–8)

1   DC2   David- let me just try to summarize if I can- what you- what you've told us. (3.1) You told us yesterday that the <u>real</u> problem wasn't anything that happened getting into the car or <u>in</u> the car- but the fact that you were left at Pinkenba- that right?

2	W1	(1.5) Mm.
3	DC2	Mm- that's the truth, isn't it?
4	W1	Mm.
		(4.3)
5	DC2	You see- you weren't de<u>prived</u> of your liberty at all- uh in going out there- it was the fact that you were <u>left</u> there that you thought was wrong?
6	W1	(1.2) (p)Yeah.
7	DC2	Eh?
8	W1	Yeah.
		(3.5)
9	DC2	You got <u>in</u> the car (2.1) without being forced- you went <u>out</u> there without being forced- the <u>prob</u>lem began when you were <u>left</u> there?
10	W1	(1.5) [Mm.
11	PROS	[With respect Your Worship- there are <u>three</u> elements to that question and I ask my friend to break them down.
12	M	Yes- just break it up one by one Mr Humphrey.
13	DC2	You got in the car without being forced David- didn't you?
14	W1	(1.5) No.
15	DC2	You told us- you've told us a ((laughs)) number of times today you did.
16	W1	(1.3) They forced me.

In turn 1, DC2 asks a complex question with a double proposition of the form 'The <u>real</u> problem wasn't X, it was Y, that right?' After a brief pause the witness agrees with 'Mm'. In turn 5, DC2 introduces legal language, actually presenting part of the charge against the officers in an expression that is quite likely to be unfamiliar to the witness, namely, 'you weren't deprived of your liberty...'. This fifth turn questions two propositions in the form 'X didn't happen to you, it was Y that you thought was wrong? The witness' answer (in turn 6) is a very short and quiet 'yeah' (erroneously transcribed in the official transcript as 'Yeah, yeah'). Turn 9 questions three separate propositions, which the witness agrees to with 'Mm'. This is the third question in this short extract in which more than one proposition is questioned, and it is not clear whether the witness' reply of 'Mm' or 'Yeah' is an agreement with all three propositions, or just one, or two of them, or whether it is simply gratuitous concurrence. After the prosecutor's request to the magistrate to direct DC2 to question one proposition at a time, we see an exchange (turns 13–16) in which the witness clearly disagrees with one of the three propositions in the turn 9 question – whether or not he had been forced into the police car – which is the most important issue in the whole case.

What this example shows is a witness appearing to freely agree to questions containing multiple propositions. When one of these multiple questions was 'broken down', and just one of the propositions was questioned, the witness did not agree to it. Further, his disagreement with the proposition comes as a complete sentence (turn 16): a relatively rare occurrence for this witness whose answers were overwhelmingly single words, such as 'yeah' and 'no'. Such a contrast should urge caution in a literal interpretation of the 'yes', 'yeah' and 'mm' answers on this point. This example shows the important role that can be played by multiple question forms in the elicitation of gratuitous concurrence. But as the next example highlights, it is only one of the factors in cross-examination conducive to the elicitation of gratuitous concurrence.

Examples 1 and 2 illustrate strategies used by DC2 to gain agreement to the crucial defence proposition: that the boys got into the police cars of their own free will. The strategies of DC1 were more aggressive, as we will see in Example 3 below. In this we see the construction of the third witness as an unreliable witness, as a result of his being easily and skilfully pressured into conflicting answers by DC1, again on the central point of the whole hearing:

Example 3 (DC1 to W3, day 3, p. 170)

1	DC1	And you <u>knew</u> (1.4) when you spoke to these six police in the Valley that you didn't have to go anywhere with them if you didn't want to, didn't you?
2	W3	(1.3) No.
3	DC1	You <u>knew</u> that, Mr (1.2) Coley I'd suggest to you, PLEASE DO NOT LIE. YOU KNEW THAT YOU DIDN'T HAVE TO GO ANYWHERE if you didn't want to, didn't you? (2.2) DIDN'T YOU? (2.2) DIDN'T YOU, MR COLEY?
4	W3	(1.3) Yeh.
5	DC1	WHY DID YOU JUST LIE TO ME? WHY DID YOU JUST SAY "NO" MR COLEY (4.4)? YOU WANT ME TO SUGGEST A REASON TO YOU MR COLEY? THE REASON WAS THIS, THAT YOU WANTED THIS COURT TO <u>BELIEVE</u> (2.1) THAT YOU THOUGHT YOU HAD TO <u>GO</u> WITH POLICE, ISN'T THAT SO?
6	W3	(1.2) Yeh.
7	DC1	AND YOU <u>LIED</u> TO THE COURT, TRYING TO, TO (1.2) YOU <u>LIED</u> TO THE COURT TRYING TO PUT ONE <u>OVER</u> THE COURT, DIDN'T YOU?
8	W3	(1.8) (p) No.
9	DC1	THAT WAS YOUR REASON, MR COLEY WASN'T IT? (3.1) WASN'T IT? (3.2) WASN'T IT, MR COLEY?
10	W3	(1.9) Yeh=
11	DC1	=YES. (2.9) BECAUSE YOU WANTED THE <u>COURT</u> TO <u>THINK</u> THAT <u>YOU</u> DIDN'T KNOW THAT YOU COULD TELL THESE POLICE YOU WEREN'T GOING <u>ANYWHERE</u> WITH THEM. THAT WAS THE REASON, WASN'T IT? (1.5) WASN'T IT?
12	W3	(0.6) Yes=
13	DC1	=Yes.

This excerpt occurs after Barry (who is sarcastically addressed by this defence counsel as 'Mr Coley') has been on the witness stand for over 90 minutes on two consecutive days, most of it being cross-examination. Turn 1 in this example puts the proposition central to the defence argument: that the witness knew he did not have to go in the police car. The witness' answer of 'No' (turn 2) is not accepted by defence counsel, so he is harassed in turn 3 until he does agree (in turn 4). Of course, we cannot know what is in the witness' mind, but we can see the ideal situation for gratuitous concurrence, increased when defence counsel begins shouting angrily in turn 3. The contradictory answers given by the witness in turns 2 and 8 on the one hand, and turns 1, 6, 10 and 12 on the other hand, are interpreted literally by defence counsel, to provide clear evidence that the witness is a liar (emphasised for the court with the theme of 'Why did you lie?', a frequently repeated 'chorus' throughout the cross-examination of all three boys).

However, an understanding of Aboriginal English background assumptions and ways of speaking, might well lead to a situated inference indicating that the answer of 'Yeh' in turns 4, 6, 10 and 12 are answers of gratuitous concurrence – indicating the witness' realisation that he will be harassed until he gives the answer required by his interrogator. It is clear that we cannot with confidence assume that the speaker (here Barry) intends to agree with the proposition of the question. However, as we have seen there are compelling reasons which would caution against such a literal interpretation, suggesting a strong possibility of gratuitous concurrence.

It is interesting that the question in turn 11 contains four clauses embedded in the main clause, a sentence structure which would confuse many witnesses, regardless of age, sociolinguistic background, and experience with interviews:

=YES. (2.9) BECAUSE YOU WANTED THE <u>COURT</u> TO <u>THINK</u> THAT <u>YOU</u> DIDN'T KNOW THAT YOU COULD TELL THESE POLICE YOU WEREN'T GOING <u>ANYWHERE</u> WITH THEM. THAT WAS THE REASON, WASN'T IT? (1.5) WASN'T IT?

This example shows a frequently occurring pattern in the cross-examination of all three witnesses by DC1, which seems most likely to involve gratuitous concurrence. Basically in this example, when the witness gives an answer which defence counsel does not accept, the witness is harassed until he agrees, so we have the following pattern:

1   The witness disagrees with the proposition (turns 2 and 8).
2   The witness is harassed, often through raised voice, at times shouting, and repeated questioning (turns 3 and 9 – note that DC1 shouts consistently in this excerpt from turns 3–11). This stage often includes accusations of lying, as in turns 3, 5 and 7.
3   The witness gives in and agrees with the proposition (often in a barely audible voice) (turns 4 and 10).
4   Following this conceded agreement, the witness is further harassed, often with a refrain such as 'Why did you lie?', and subject to further pressured questioning, as in turns 5 and 11. This follow-up harassing questioning generally succeeds in eliciting agreement (as in turns 6 and 12), often to a damaging explanation for the allegedly contradictory answers which have just been elicited.

Interpreting the 'Yes', 'Yeah', 'Mm' and 'Yeh' answers in cross-examination

The above examples have all raised doubt about the validity of a literal interpretation of the 'Yes', 'Yeah', 'Mm' and 'Yeh' answers (hereafter referred to generically as 'YES' answers) given by the witnesses in cross-examination. While we can never know what was in a witness' mind, the following questions need to be considered in understanding the witnesses' answers, particularly in the light of the likelihood of gratuitous concurrence, and the demonstrated suggestibility of the witnesses, as well as the fact that they were child witnesses:

1   Did the witnesses fully understand the questions, especially those which questioned more than one proposition?
2   To what extent were the witnesses' answers influenced by pressured questioning, for example repeated tag questions, and/or shouting?
3   Would the facts concerned have been better ascertained if leading questions were not used (Commonwealth Evidence Act 1995 s42)?
4   Were any of the questions 'misleading or confusing; phrased in inappropriate language; or unduly annoying, harassing, intimidating, offensive, oppressive or repetitive'? (QLRC, 2000, p. 8)

An analysis of the data in the light of such questions, and an understanding of gratuitous concurrence in interviews with Aboriginal people, led to my statement to the media that it 'would be absurd to conclude this case on the basis of a literal interpretation of answers given by the boys' (quoted in Scott, 1995). This is consistent with the prosecutor's somewhat mild response to the closing submissions of DC1 that 'differential weight' should be given (seemingly, to the answers produced in response to leading questions, although this is not entirely clear). It is also consistent with the general concern expressed by the CJC in its report the following year that if 'a witness is suggestible... there is an increased risk that judicial officers, lawyers and particularly jurors will misconstrue the significance of the answers given by the witness' (1996, p. 51).

And this misconstrual is exactly what appears to have happened. In reaching his decision, the magistrate was clearly persuaded by the closing submission of both DCs, in which they relied on the words they had put to the witnesses, and the literal interpretation of their answers of 'YES'. As the prosecutor pointed out in his final response to the closing submissions of DC1, 'all of the answers on which [the defence] rely were brought about as a result of leading questions'.

In their concluding submissions, both DCs read out passages of the cross-examination transcript, and used the boys' answers of 'YES' to make key assertions about the central issue, namely that they knew they had the right not to get in the police cars, and they freely chose to do it. For example, DC2 said: 'each of the persons who heard this statement ['hop in the car'] and acted by getting in the police car, knew that they had no obligation so to do... they knew that they didn't need to do it'. His assertion that they knew this comes from the boys' answers of 'YES' in exchanges such as we have seen in the examples in this chapter.

In a similar way, both DCs used the boys' answers of 'YES' to destroy not only their credibility and reliability, but also their moral character generally. For example, DC1 said: 'You've got to give a lot of weight to a statement "I'll lie if I think I can get away with it, and you won't know when I'm telling the truth and when I'm not"'. No such statement was ever made by any of the witnesses, although Albert did give answers of 'YES' to such propositions under the kind of pressure we have seen in the above examples (Transcript, p. 113). Examples such as this show that the consequences of answers of gratuitous concurrence in this hearing extend far beyond being interpreted as demonstrating that the boys got in the police cars voluntarily. In this example we see the consequence for the attribution of complex and damning propositions about the witness's moral character, which were never made by the witness.

The magistrate's decision was a brief statement of approximately 450 words, which included the central finding: 'They *all* knew that they had the *right* to refuse to get in to the police motor vehicle, but despite this knowledge they proceeded and got in'. About half of the statement addresses the character of the boys, in which the key points raised by the DCs, especially DC2, are echoed. The magistrate even went so far in his assessment of the characters of the boys to say: 'All three of them – by their history and their own testimony have no regard for members of the community – their property or even the justice system.' To draw this conclusion from their testimony is only possible by the ridiculously literal interpretation of the boys' answers of 'YES' to harassing questions, such as those we have seen in this chapter.

In a rare occurrence, the magistrate's decision that the case should not proceed to trial, and that all the charges against the police officers be dropped, was appealed against by the three complainants (through a close relative of each of them). This resulted in a judicial review of the magistrate's decision. The judge who carried out this review dismissed the application, thus upholding the magistrate's decision. In his Reasons for Judgement (Ambrose, 1996), he found that the boys' evidence had been 'given in unequivocal terms', actually using the word 'unequivocal' about their evidence five times in his 13-page report. Again, the only way in which the boys' evidence could be seen as 'given in unequivocal terms' is through the farcically literal interpretation of the boys' answers of 'YES' to pressured questions, as illustrated above.

The central role of language in the naturalisation of police control over Aboriginal young people

This chapter has shown how absurd it is to rely on literal interpretations of the boys' answers of 'YES' in a number of exchanges in the hearing. It has rejected the view that their evidence was given 'in unequivocal terms'. It has also rejected the view that these witnesses were freely consenting to all of the propositions put to them in cross-examination.

The outcome of this case rests on a number of assumptions which are fundamental to courtroom cross-examination, particularly:

- that facts are best ascertained through Q–A;
- that repeated questioning is the way to check the reliability of a witness' story; and
- that answers of 'YES' in cross-examination unequivocally indicate agreement to a proposition.

These assumptions, which are highly questionable and culture-specific, are not questioned in the legal process (an attempt to do so in this case was ruled out by both the Director of Public Prosecutions and the review judge). They are seen as natural and legitimate, and in this way the cross-examination process is naturalised, that is, it is seen as the commonsense way to test a witness' story.

This naturalisation of the discourse type (to use Fairclough's 1989 terms) is key to the naturalisation of the police control over the movement of Aboriginal young people. Defence counsel in this case argued in their closing submission that it was legitimate and natural for the police to act as they did in the Pinkenba incident. DC2 spoke clearly in terms of the commonsense nature of the police actions, saying:

> What are people supposed to do? I mean, what are the police supposed to do if- if they say to someone, fully cognizant of his legal rights, 'look- hop in the police car'- he decides- in accordance with his legal rights- to do so- and then they're accused of CRIME- now this is just remarkable.

This naturalisation of the police actions was facilitated by the 'consent' which was claimed to be clear from the cross-examination of the boys. But this was only 'clear' because of the naturalisation of the cross-examination process, and the successful elicitation of gratuitous concurrence.

The naturalisation of the police actions, in turn, can be seen as part of a bigger naturalisation process, namely that of the incarceration of Aboriginal people. Cunneen (1996, p. 21) argues that 'the historical and colonial relationship between the state and Indigenous peoples has taken on the appearance of a natural relationship: Aboriginal people are dealt with in a certain manner because they are "criminal"' and so it is natural for them to be incarcerated. This chain of naturalisation processes – discourse type of cross-examination, to police actions, to criminalisation and incarceration of Aboriginal people – depends to a very large extent on the manipulation of language, as we have seen in this chapter.

Conclusion

This case shows how the power of the police over the movements of Aboriginal young people does not simply exist: here we see it being 'worked for' (following Matoesian, 1993, p. 223) in the courtroom . Further, this case shows that this police power is not localised in the actions of police officers: the legal system has given its consent, accepting this as the commonsense way for police to act. This consent of the legal system has arisen from adherence to 'due process' and the rules of evidence, combined with the skillful manipulation of the boys in court, so that even they too could be claimed to be giving their consent. Central to this consent has been the farcical use of unreliable and problematic linguistic practices and assumptions, which enabled the state to legitimise police removal of Aboriginal young people.

This case casts serious doubt on the ability of the legal process, and specifically the cross-examination process, to serve the cause of justice in proceedings such as these, when members of an oppressed minority group give evidence against members of one of the most powerful groups in the state.

Notes

1   I am grateful to Tony Keyes and Victoria Anderson for assistance with aspects of this study, and to Jeff Siegel and Steven Talmy for valuable comments on the draft. All errors are my responsibility.

2   *Crawford* v. *Venardos and Ors*, Brisbane Magistrates' Court, 21 February 1995, unreported.

3   All quotations from this hearing are based on my transcription of official tape-recordings, and they follow the transcription conventions given in note 8 below. It should also be pointed out that I was in court for most of the hearing, and was able to observe the event as well as work with the tape-recording.

4   These comments are based on my research over a number of years with Aboriginal people in south-east Queensland (Eades, 1982, 1988), as well as my interviews with and observations of the three boys, separately and together, over a two-day period in June 1994 (undertaken at the request of Aboriginal Legal Services).

5   The boys' eligibility for this special witness status would have been on the grounds of cultural difference rather than their age.

6   It should be pointed out that these publications all postdate the Pinkenba case, and in fact the CJC report was commissioned following the outcry over this case.

7   I have been unable to discern a significant difference in the function of the three different variant responses 'Yes', 'Yeah' and 'Mm'. And at this stage it appears that 'Yeh' does not function differently from the other variant responses, although further analysis is needed on this point. This response, transcribed by me as 'Yeh', is pronounced with a very short vowel, and weak glottal stop, giving the connotation of a minimal positive response, for example in Example 3, turns 4, 6 and 10. Note that this form appears in the official transcript as 'Yep', possibly giving the erroneous connotation of enthusiastic

agreement. It is recorded over 100 times as the answer for W3, once for W2, and on no occasions for W1.

8   I use the following standard transcription conventions:

- underlining indicates utterance emphasis;
- CAPITALS indicate raised volume;
- (p) before an utterance indicates that it is spoken in a low volume;
- =indicates latched utterances, with no pause between the end of one utterance and the start of the next;
- a number in parentheses indicates the length of a pause in seconds, for example, (3.2);
- a square bracket [indicates both the start of an interruption and the utterance which is interrupted;
- the following abbreviations are also used in the transcripts: DC = defence counsel; M = magistrate; P = prosecutor; W = witness.
- All personal names in this chapter have been anonymised.

References

ABC (Australian Broadcasting Commission) (1996) *Black and Blue*, Four Corners TV documentary, 8 March.

ABC (Australian Broadcasting Commission) (1999) *Double Jeopardy*, Four Corners TV documentary, 19 July.

Ambrose, J. (1996) *Purcell and Ors v. Quinan and Anor*: Reasons for Judgment, unpublished Apn No. 190 of 1995.

Bowen, J. (1995) *Macquarie Easy Guide to Australian Law*. Sydney: Macquarie Library.

Brennan, M. (1995) 'The Discourse of Denial: Cross-Examining Child Victim Witnesses', *Journal of Pragmatics*, vol. 23, pp. 71–91.

CJC (Criminal Justice Commission) (1996) *Aboriginal Witnesses in Queensland's Criminal Courts*. Brisbane: Criminal Justice Commission.

Coldrey, J. (1987) 'Aboriginals and the Criminal Courts', in K. Hazlehurst (ed.), *Ivory Scales: Black Australia and the Law*. Sydney: NSW University Press, pp. 81–92.

Commonwealth of Australia (1995) *Evidence Act*.

Conley, J. and O'Barr, W. M. (1998) *Just Words: Law, Language and Power*. Chicago: University of Chicago Press.

Cooke, M. (1996) 'A Different Story: Narrative versus "Question and Answer" in Aboriginal Evidence', *Forensic Linguistics*, vol. 3(2), pp. 273–88.

Cunneen, C. (1994) 'The Police and Young People in Australia', in R. White and C. Adler (eds), *The Police and Young People in Australia*. Cambridge: Cambridge University Press, pp. 128–58.

Cunneen, C. (1996) 'Detention, Torture, Terror and the Australian State: Aboriginal People, Criminal Justice and Neocolonialism', in G. Bird, G. Martin and J. Neilson (eds), *Majah: Indigenous Peoples and the Law*. Sydney: The Federation Press, pp. 13–37.

Cunneen, C. and White, R. (1995) *Juvenile Justice: An Australian Perspective*. Oxford: Oxford University Press.

Eades, D. (1982) '"You Gotta Know How to Talk . . . ": Ethnography of Information Seeking in Southeast Queensland Aboriginal Society', *Australian Journal of Linguistics*, vol. (2)1, pp. 61–82.

Eades, D. (1988) 'They Don't Speak an Aboriginal Language, or Do They?', in I. Keen (ed.), *Being Black: Aboriginal Cultures in Settled Australia*. Canberra: Aboriginal Studies Press, pp. 97–117.

Eades, D. (1992) *Aboriginal English and the Law: Communicating with Aboriginal English Speaking Clients: A Handbook for Legal Practitioners*. Brisbane: Queensland Law Society.

Eades, D. (1993) 'The Case for Condren: Aboriginal English, Pragmatics and the Law', *Journal of Pragmatics*, vol. 20(2), pp. 141–62.

Eades, D. (1994) 'A Case of Communicative Clash: Aboriginal English and the Legal System', in J. Gibbons (ed.), *Language and the Law*. London: Longman, pp. 234–64.

Eades, D. (1996) 'Legal Recognition of Cultural Differences in Communication: The Case of Robyn Kina', *Language and Communication*, vol. 16(3), pp. 215–27.

Eades, D. (forthcoming) 'The Politics of Misunderstanding in the Legal Process: Aboriginal English in Queensland', in J. House, G. Kasper and S. Ross (eds), *Misunderstanding in Spoken Discourse*. London: Longman.

Elkin. A. (1947) 'Aboriginal Evidence and Justice in North Australia', *Oceania*, vol. 17, pp. 173–210.

Fairclough, N. (1989) *Language and Power*. London: Longman.

HREOC (Human Rights and Equal Opportunity Commission) (1997) *Bringing Them Home: National Inquiry into the Separation of Aboriginal and Torres Strait Islander Children from their Families*. Sydney: Commonwealth of Australia.

Harris, S. (1984) 'Questions as a Mode of Control in Magistrates' Courts', *International Journal of the Sociology of Language*, vol. 49, pp. 5–28.

Liberman, K. (1981) 'Understanding Aborigines in Australian Courts of Law', *Human Organization*, vol. 40, pp. 247–55.

Liberman, K. (1985) *Understanding Interaction in Central Australia: An Ehnomethodological Study of Australian Aboriginal People*. Boston: Routledge & Kegan Paul.

Luchjenbroers, J. (1997) '"In Your Own Words...": Questions and Answers in a Supreme Court Trial', *Journal of Pragmatics*, vol. 27, pp. 477–503.

Matoesian, G. (1993) *Reproducing Rape: Domination through Talk in the Courtroom*. Chicago: University of Chicago Press.

Mildren, D. (1997) 'Redressing the Imbalance against Aboriginals in the Criminal Justice System', *Criminal Law Review*, vol. 21(1), pp. 7–22.

Mildren, D. (1999) 'Redressing the Imbalance: Aboriginal People in the Criminal Justice System', *Forensic Linguistics*, vol. 6(1), pp. 137–60.

Nygh, P. E. and Butt, P. (1997) *Butterworth's Concise Australian Legal Dictionary*. Sydney: Butterworths.

O'Barr, W. M. (1982) *Linguistic Evidence: Language, Power and Strategy in the Courtroom*. New York: Academic Press.

Palmer, A. (1998) *Principles of Evidence*. Sydney: Cavendish Publishing (Australia) Pty Ltd.

QLRC (Queensland Law Reform Commission) (2000) *The Receipt of Evidence by Queensland's Courts: The Evidence of Children*. Report no. 55, part 1, Brisbane: Queensland Law Reform Commission.

Queensland (1977) *Evidence Act*.

Queensland (1992) *Juvenile Justice Act*.

Roberts, G. (1998) *Evidence: Proof and Practice*. Sydney: Law Book Company.

Scott, L. (1995) 'Aboriginal Youth Abduction Verdict "a travesty of justice"', *Australian*, 28 February.

Strehlow, T. G. H. (1936) 'Notes on Native Evidence and its Value', *Oceania*, vol. 6, pp. 323–35.

Thompson, D. (1999) 'Eyewitness Testimony', in I. Freckelton and H. Selby (eds), *Expert Evidence in Criminal Law*. Sydney: Law Book Company, pp. 647–89.

Van Dijk, T. (1993) 'Principles of Critical Discourse Analysis', *Discourse and Society*, vol. 4(2), pp. 249–83.

Wigmore, J. (1940) *Wigmore on Evidence*, 3rd edn. Boston: Little, Brown & Co.

11
The Clinton Scandal: Some Legal Lessons from Linguistics[1]

Lawrence M. Solan

It is almost impossible to think about the scandal that led to President Clinton's 1999 impeachment trial without recalling his answer to a question under oath before a federal grand jury with these words: 'It depends upon what the meaning of the word "is" is.' (Grand Jury Transcript, p. 510).[2] Clinton's political enemies were not alone in adopting that sentence as a model for how Clinton in particular and lawyers in general rely on silly, unnatural uses and understandings of language to achieve favourable results.

Throughout the proceedings Clinton distinguished between being truthful but deceptive on the one hand, and being dishonest on the other. He believed that he was on safe turf if he took care not to cross the line from one to the other. Legally, Clinton was right. The American perjury statute has been interpreted to prohibit only statements that are literally false. Yet even Clinton's supporters remained uncomfortable at watching the President proudly announce that he had been dishonest in just the right way.

This chapter will use aspects of linguistic theory to explore some significant questions that the Clinton scandal raised: Should we be so legalistic in distinguishing between lying and deceiving? Should the perjury statute be interpreted so narrowly? These questions are political. Yet, to evaluate the practical consequences of the decision, it is first necessary to understand the conceptual difficulties that arise when one tries to study these problems. As Clinton might have put it, the answers to these questions depend in part upon where the meaning of 'lies' lies.

The Clinton scandal

In American politics, each house of Congress has authority to investigate the administration, and each house uses this authority liberally when the party in control of that house differs from the party of the President. Clinton, a Democrat, was first elected in 1992. Once the Democrats lost control of Congress in 1994, Clinton was under investigation for one thing or another for the rest of his tenure in office. As Toobin (2000, pp. 9, 16) points out in his book about the scandal, most people tend to underestimate how much Clinton's enemies hated him. His casual style and licentious demeanour symbolised for them a victory of the 1960s style counter-culture that they simply were not willing to tolerate.

The largest Congressional investigation involved President and Mrs Clinton's alleged roles in a real-estate venture in Arkansas, called Whitewater, which had gone sour years before Clinton became President. Under a statute that has since expired, a special counsel, Kenneth Starr, was appointed to head the investigation. Starr had earlier been a respected conservative federal judge, but had since returned to private practice, in part litigating on behalf of the tobacco industry with which the Clinton administration was fighting a war. After years of aggressive inquiry and the expenditure of tens of millions of dollars, the Whitewater investigation produced a few convictions, but never came close to finding that the President had engaged in any wrongdoing.

At the same time, Paula Jones, a former employee of the state of Arkansas, was suing Clinton in federal court, alleging that he had harassed her sexually in a hotel room when he was governor of Arkansas. The lawsuit was funded by various conservative organisations. Ultimately, the Jones suit was dismissed because the plaintiff had no way of proving that anything that Clinton had done resulted in damage to her as a state employee, and because even if her allegations were true, they were not enough to prove the existence of a hostile work environment, which the law requires in such cases (see *Jones* v. *Clinton*, 990 F.Supp. 657, 674 (E.D. Ark. 1998)).

It was in this political atmosphere that the Monica Lewinsky scandal arose. Lewinsky had been confiding in a friend, Linda Tripp, about her relationship with the President. On a number of occasions, Tripp, who disliked Clinton, illegally taped her conversations with Lewinsky. Tripp eventually contacted Starr's office with the information. On 16 January 1998, the day before Clinton was to testify at a sworn deposition in the Paula Jones case, Starr applied to increase the scope of his investigation, claiming that Clinton may have been involved in obstructing justice in the Paula Jones case. That same day, Tripp met with Jones's lawyers and provided them with the information about Lewinsky.

At the deposition, Clinton was caught off-guard. He had no idea that Jones' lawyers knew the details about his relationship with Lewinsky, and was not prepared to deal with the questions. In fact, the deposition was more or less *only* about Monica Lewinsky, which had very little to do with any issues germane to the Jones case. The lawyers had set a trap, and Clinton fell right into it. He answered some questions evasively, others with outright lies. The most celebrated examples were his discussion of whether he had engaged in 'sexual relations' with Lewinsky.

As Judge Richard Posner points out in his book on the Clinton scandal (Posner, 1999), Clinton committed a number of dishonest acts, most of which are beyond controversy. (So did Starr; see Solan, 2001, for discussion.) However, because Clinton's relationship with Lewinsky was so tangential to the issues in the Jones case, it is unlikely that Clinton's dishonesty at the deposition would be sufficient to constitute perjury. Ultimately, Starr empanelled a grand jury to investigate the issue of whether Clinton was dishonest at the Jones deposition. On 17 August 1998, Clinton testified before that grand jury. Any false statement he made in that forum would constitute a new crime; the Supreme Court had recently ruled that it is not unconstitutional for the government to interrogate an individual about events that are not criminal, and then prosecute him for lying (see *Brogan* v. *United States*, 522 US 398 (1998)) .

Americans still argue about whether Clinton's grand jury testimony was perjured (see Solan and Tiersma, forthcoming, for discussion). In some instances, he admitted to the grand jury that the substance of what he had said at his deposition was not the truth. For example, at his deposition he was asked whether he had ever been alone with Lewinsky. He answered:

> I don't recall. She – it seems to me she brought things to me once or twice on the weekends. In that case, whatever time she would be in there, drop it off, exchange a few words and go, she was there.
>
> (Clinton deposition, pp. 52–3, quoted in *Jones* v. *Clinton*, 36 F.Supp.2d 1118, 1127 (E.D. Ark. 1999)).

To the grand jury, he conceded the following:

> Q   Let me ask you, Mr President, you indicate in your statement that you were alone with Ms Lewinsky. Is that right?
> Clinton   Yes, sir.
>
> (Grand Jury Transcript, p. 481)

Some of his grand jury testimony does not appear to be truthful either. After his deposition, Clinton met with his secretary, Betty Curry, and discussed Curry's knowledge of Clinton's relationship with Lewinsky. To most readers, it appears that Clinton was trying to give Curry a message that if anyone were to ask, Curry should say that Clinton and Lewinsky had never been alone. Clinton testified that he was trying to refresh his own recollection by quizzing Curry (Grand Jury Transcript, pp. 506–8, 582–3, 593–5).

But the most interesting cases are ones like the following:

> Q   Judge Wright had ruled that the attorneys in the Jones case were permitted to ask you certain questions.
> Clinton   She certainly did, and they asked them, and I did my best to answer them. I'm just trying to tell you what my state of mind was.
> Q   Was it your responsibility to answer those questions truthfully, Mr President?
> Clinton   It was. But it was not my responsibility, in the face of their repeated illegal leaking, it was not my responsibility to volunteer a lot of information. . . .
>
> (Grand Jury Transcript, pp. 479–80)

The testimony occurred in the context of the prosecutor's criticising Clinton for not interrupting his lawyer and correcting the following truthful, but misleading statement that the lawyer was making about Clinton's relationship with Lewinsky:

> I question the good faith of counsel, the innuendo of the question. Counsel is fully aware that Ms Lewinsky has filed – has an affidavit, which they are in possession of, saying that there is absolutely no sex of any kind in any manner, shape or form with President Clinton.
>
> (Deposition: 54, quoted in Grand Jury Transcript, p. 509)

At the time of both the affidavit and the lawyer's statement at Clinton's deposition, the statement was true. Any physical relationship between Clinton and Lewinsky had ended some time earlier. To Clinton, honest testimony includes making statements that are literally true, but lead the hearer to make false inferences.

The issue arose when, at the deposition, Jones' lawyers presented Clinton with a bizarre and broad definition of the expression, 'sexual relations', which included contact with the erogenous zones of any person 'with an intent to arouse or gratify the sexual desire of any person' (Clinton Deposition Ex. 1 quoted in *Jones* v. *Clinton*, 36 F.Supp 1118, 1121 n.5 (E.D. Ark. 1999)). Jones' lawyer never directly asked Clinton if he and Lewinsky had ever engaged in oral sex, whether either had ever touched the other sexually, or any other direct question that would have required a straightforward answer. Clinton denied having sexual relations at the deposition. At the grand jury he reiterated this position, and further testified that because they never had sexual intercourse, one would not ordinarily use the expression 'sexual relations' to describe their physical relationship, which mostly involved her performing oral sex (Grand Jury Transcript, pp. 461, 473–5, 546–51, 619). For Clinton to have told the truth, then, he must have allowed Lewinsky to perform oral sex without having touched her sexually; a possibility, but a very remote one, as commentators have pointed out (see Posner, 1999, pp. 47–8).

Subsequently, the House of Representatives voted more or less along party lines to impeach Clinton for lying to the grand jury. The proposed Articles of Impeachment relating to the Paula Jones deposition were defeated. On 12 February 1999, the Senate acquitted Clinton and he served out the rest of his term as President.

Perjury under American law

In the United States, all crimes are legislatively defined. The federal perjury statute is presented below:

> Whoever –
> (1) having taken an oath . . . that he will testify, declare, depose, or certify truly, or that any written testimony, declaration, deposition, or certificate by him subscribed, is true, willfully

and contrary to such oath states or subscribes any material matter which he does not believe
to be true . . .
is guilty of perjury and shall, except as otherwise expressly provided by law, be fined under
this title or imprisoned not more than five years, or both. . . .

(see 18 USC. § 1621)

The statute makes it a crime to testify under oath to a material matter[3] that
the witness does not believe to be true; nothing in the perjury statute
requires that a statement be literally false. Nonetheless, the Supreme Court,
in a unanimous decision, held that perjury does require proof of a false
statement. *Bronston* v. *United States* (409 US 352 (1973)) involved the prosecution of an individual who was accused of lying under oath at a bankruptcy
proceeding. Bronston's film production company was in bankruptcy, and
he was asked questions under oath about his assets. The following exchange
took place:

Q   Do you have any bank accounts in Swiss banks, Mr Bronston?
A   No, Sir.
Q   Have you ever?
A   The company had an account there for about six months, in Zurich.

(*Ibid.* at p. 354)

Everything that Bronston said was true. What he did not say is that, earlier,
he also had an account in Zurich. His failure to do so led to his prosecution
and conviction for perjury. The Supreme Court reversed that conviction,
holding unanimously that Bronston met his obligation by answering the
questions truthfully. It was up to the lawyer for the creditors to ask follow-up
questions.

To date, two scholars have written about the *Bronston* case from a linguistic perspective, and both have criticised the decision. Tiersma (1990) and
Winter (2001) both argue, in essence, that the act of lying should be seen as
a special case of the act of deception. Deception is a speech act whose effect
is to leave the listener with the impression that something is true that the
speaker knows to be false. Austin (1962) uses the expression 'perlocutionary
effect' to describe a speech act, the principal characteristic of which is to
describe the state of mind of the hearer.

There are many ways to convince people of the truth of something the
speaker knows to be false, and lying is but one. Thus, it seems unjust to punish
one form of deception as a crime, while exonerating a person who accom-
plishes exactly the same thing through different means. Philosophers have
recognised this problem. For example, Bok (1978, p. 13), in her classic book
on lying, defines a lie expansively as 'any intentionally deceptive message
which is stated'. Her intent is to distinguish lying from non-verbal forms of
deception, but not to distinguish lying from Clintonesque forms of deception.

Bronston illustrates the point well. If Bronston had said, 'no, the company
had one . . . ' instead of 'the company had one', the Supreme Court would

have affirmed the conviction. Note that Clinton was not quite as clever as Bronston. Before testifying evasively in the Bronstonian tradition about being alone with Lewinsky, he said, 'I don't know.' Bronston did not make that mistake.

Grice's (1975) theory of conversational implicature explains this dynamic. According to Grice, people employ a cooperative principle in communicating with one another. When we hear someone speak, we assume that the speaker is trying to convey new information to us, and we draw inferences accordingly. When Bronston responded to the examiner's question about Swiss bank accounts with 'my company had one...', the most reasonable inference for the examiner to draw was that Bronston himself did not, and that he mentioned the company's account only to be cooperative. Otherwise, why would Bronston have mentioned the company at all? By taking advantage of his tacit knowledge of the cooperative principle, Bronston was able to steer the examiner away from asking further questions about his own bank accounts (see also Sweetser, 1987).

Notwithstanding its literalist approach, the Supreme Court had to hedge in deciding that a statement cannot constitute perjury unless it is literally false. In a footnote, the Court considered the following hypothetical situation, which had influenced the trial court's decision to uphold the prosecution on the government's theory:

> If it is material to ascertain how many times a person has entered a store on a given day and that person responds to such a question by saying five times when in fact he knows that he entered the store 50 times that day, that person may be guilty of perjury even though it is technically true that he entered the store five times.
> ... Whether an answer is true must be determined with reference to the question it purports to answer, not in isolation. An unresponsive answer is unique in this respect because its unresponsiveness by definition prevents its truthfulness from being tested in the context of the question – unless there is to be speculation as to what the unresponsive answer 'implies'.
> (409 US at 355, n.3)

The Court presents an interesting dichotomy. On the one hand, we only punish as perjurers people who have made literally false statements. On the other hand, in deciding whether a statement is literally false, we will impose on the witness the obligation to understand the question reasonably within the context – hardly a literal act. In the case of the hypothetical, one would ordinarily understand the question as asking for the sum total of instances in which the witness has entered the store. If that is the question, then the witness who entered the store 50 times has lied when he answers with five.

But such statements are not always lies. If, needing a dollar to put in a soda machine, I ask 'Who has a dollar?', you would be entirely honest saying 'I do,' even if you have 12. Moreover, if you need a dollar and ask me how much money I have, I do not believe that I would be dishonest by saying 'I have a dollar', meaning I have at least the amount that you require, so you need not worry. However, if you were trying to find out if I had enough money in the bank to pay a debt I owe to you, I would indeed be lying if I say I have 10 dollars when I actually have 1000. Thus, literal falsity is a standard imposed after we decide which possible meaning of a question the witness understood.

Lying and deceiving

The law, then, supports Clinton's distinction between untruthfulness and deception. Unlike others who have written about this issue from a linguistic perspective, I think the legal system has made the right choice. Part of my argument depends upon linguistic analysis of what it means to lie. Much of the debate of Clinton's conduct can be seen as a battle between those who say that a lie is a lie, and those who equivocate, saying that some lies are worse than others, and if Clinton lied, he barely lied. The structure of this argument is precisely the same as the argument over whether Clinton engaged in sexual relations. Critics point to the definition, while Clinton says that people typically would not use that expression to describe what happened.

These political disagreements mirror a debate within the psycholinguistic community over the nature of word meaning. Some researchers look at the meaning of lying and other concepts in terms of a set of defining features. We will return to this perspective below. Others, following the important work of Eleanor Rosch, have argued that lying is a family resemblance category. Rosch (1975) found that people are very good at judging how good an exemplar of a category a concept is. For example, subjects ranked robins as good examples of the category bird, and ostriches as poor ones. How strongly one agrees that a particular animal is a bird depends on how prototypical a bird that animal is. Any attempt to define bird with a set of necessary and sufficient features both misses this subtlety and misses the fact that categories are often fuzzy at the margins. When does a chair become wide enough to call it a love seat? Is a lamp a type of furniture?

Coleman and Kay (1981) looked at lying in terms of prototypes. They presented subjects with a number of scenarios, and asked them the extent to which they agreed that a character in the story had lied. They hypothesised that lying contains three features: a false statement, intent to deceive, and knowledge of falsity. When all three of these are present, the lie is proto-typical, and people agree that it is indeed a lie. When none of the features are present, people agree that a statement is not a lie. When only one or two of the features is present, people equivocate. Together the features are suffi-cient, and it is necessary to have at least one of them, but none of the features is itself either necessary or sufficient. Thus, according to Coleman and Kay, lying is a family resemblance category. It has no definition. Rather, there are merely probabilities that correspond to the distribution of features present in a given situation.

Coleman and Kay's experiment varied the content of the stories they presented systematically along their three features for a total of eight stories ('true', 'intent to deceive', 'knowledge of falsity'). Subjects were asked to judge each story on a 1–7 scale, from 'very sure it is not a lie' to 'very sure it is a lie'. When all three elements were present, subjects agreed it was a lie. The mean score was 6.96. When none of the criteria were present, subjects also reached consensus. The mean score was 1.06. For the other conditions, the results were mixed. The story most relevant to the Clinton scandal is presented below:

> John and Mary have recently started going together. Valentino is Mary's ex-boyfriend. One evening John asks Mary, 'Have you seen Valentino this week?' Mary answers, 'Valentino's been sick with mononucleosis for the past two weeks.' Valentino has in fact been sick with mononucleosis for the past two weeks, but it is also the case that Mary had a date with Valentino the night before. Did Mary lie?

Just like Clinton and Bronston, Mary has made a statement that is literally true, leaves out the crucial fact, and relies on the listener's gullibly interpreting the statement in light of the cooperative principle. This story scored an average of 3.48 on the 1–7 scale.

While these results are consistent with Coleman and Kay's prototype analysis of lying, there is another possible explanation. The fact that the mean score approached the midpoint does not mean that all of the subjects equivocated. It is possible to achieve the same mean score if half of the subjects think the statement to be a lie and the other half think it to be the truth. Further inspection of the results shows that of 67 subjects who heard the story about Mary, 18 thought it was a lie (scoring a 1, 2 or 3), 42 thought it was not a lie (scoring a 5, 6 or 7), and seven subjects could not say (scoring a 4). It may be the case that people think they know criteria that constitute a lie, but disagree on the margins about whether the criteria apply.

To distinguish between these possibilities, I first presented 22 undergraduate college students with the story about Mary in an informal experiment, and asked whether they agreed that Mary had lied. Their responses approximated those of Coleman and Kay. I then asked about the following additional choice:

> I do not think that Mary lied. However, if I say that she didn't lie, I might be implying that I think Mary was being honest. I don't want to imply that Mary was being honest, so I'd rather say that she lied, even though I don't think this was really a lie.

This response received wide support, especially from those students who earlier said that Mary had lied.

As Sweetser (1987) points out, we have a rich vocabulary for dishonest conduct that we regard as socially acceptable. We speak of exaggerations, stretches, white lies, and so on. For example, newspaper reports quote Barry George, convicted of murdering BBC presenter Jill Dando, as having had the following conversation with the police: 'Do you tell lies Mr George?' George replied: 'No, exaggeration maybe, but not a lie Sir' (*Glasgow Herald*, 25 May 2001, p. 10). The sense here is the one embodied in the perjury statute: when a false statement is not material, it really isn't so bad. The problem of how to separate acceptable white lies and exaggerations from more pernicious ones has plagued theologians and philosophers for centuries, as Bok (1978) points out.

In contrast, we have very little vocabulary with which to describe acts that are dishonest, but not actual lies. The lawyer who fell for Bronston's ploy could justifiably have said: 'You tricked me by leading me to lower my guard and not see that you were creating a misleading impression.' But we do not have a large set of individual words to describe that situation.

All of this suggests an alternative explanation for Coleman and Kay's results. It may well be that people do consider defining features when using the word 'lie'. It means more or less what the perjury statute as expanded by the Supreme Court says it means: A lie is a false statement that the speaker believes to be false. Wierzbicka (1996, p. 152) proposes a definition that has just these characteristics. One can equivocate over whether articulating a set of facts from which the hearer will surely infer a falsity should count as a false statement. This explains the results without resort to prototype analysis.

A number of psychologists believe that people actually think both ways. We use prototypes in some circumstances, rules in others. Sloman (1996) argues that people employ both an associative system and a rule-based system in reasoning, and that conflicts between the two occur frequently in everyday life. Johnson-Laird (1983) also argues that we use both prototypes and defining features. A recent article by Smith, Patalano and Jonides (1998) suggests different physiological bases for the two activities, and that we employ the strategies in different circumstances. Medin, Wattenmaker and Hampson (1987) had reached similar conclusions, based on experimental evidence. They found that people prefer to rely on defining features when they do not have much information about the surrounding circumstances, but that family resemblance models are used more when we have greater information about context.

Moreover, an important study by Armstrong, Gleitman and Gleitman (1983) showed that prototype effects occur with categories such as 'bird', even though when later asked subjects do not think that a prototypical bird is any more a bird than a non-prototypical one, and disagree with the proposition that 'bird' is a graded category at all. Thus, while prototypes are part of our psychology, they do not seem to be a full explanation of how we form concepts. Fodor (1998) also takes this position.

From all of this, it appears that both Clinton and his detractors had some points. We are very competent at distinguishing between good and bad examples of a concept. Much of what Clinton did (or at least tried to do) is at most a marginal example of lying. On the other hand, we are able to identify the defining features of a concept, even if the application of those features to events in the world is sometimes fuzzy.

Should the legal system be tougher on liars?

To summarise, we can now say:

1 To convict someone of perjury, the government must prove that the defendant swore to a material fact that he believed to be false, and which was literally false. Misleading is not good enough;
2 In determining whether an answer to a question is literally false, we must decide which of a number of possible meanings of the question was the intended one, and how the witness understood the question;
3 We are uncomfortable calling a false statement about an unimportant fact, or a statement that is only slightly untrue, a lie. We use words like exaggeration. Even if we are willing to call these lies, we feel that some lies are worse than others;
4 There are clear examples of lies. When someone says something that is false, knowing that it is false, with the intent to deceive the listener, we are comfortable calling it a lie;
5 When a statement is true, but misleading, most people do not call it a lie. Of those that do, most concede that they do not think it's a lie either, but feel that 'lie' fits the story better than other words that come to mind;
6 Researchers believe that we categorise in two different ways: by defining features, and by probabilistic reasoning based on prototypes or exemplars. People are likely to equivocate and to differ in their judgements about hard cases.

In this context, there are at least three good reasons for accepting the *Bronston* approach to perjury, even if it does create serious distortions in the distribution of justice. All of them are political, but are informed by the ways in which we use and understand language.

Lenity

A principle of statutory interpretation called the rule of lenity says that when the applicability of a statute is uncertain, the system should give the benefit of the doubt to the defendant. The rule is based on concerns about fair notice to the defendant that his activities are criminal in nature, and, at least in the United States, upon the theory that it is only the legislature that can define what constitutes a crime (see Solan, 1998, for discussion of the rule and the linguistic issues it presents). If we look at Bronston's testimony in this light, lenity should govern since the statute, by its own terms, does not clearly apply. To say something true with the intention of inducing the hearer to believe something false is one way to commit a fraud – but to most of us it is not a lie, precisely because the statement was not literally false.

Moreover, legislators know how to write a statute that includes both false statements and misleading statements and omissions, but did not write the perjury statute that way. The most prominent American anti-fraud provision is probably Rule 10b-5 of the Securities and Exchange Commission. It makes it unlawful:

> (b) To make any untrue statement of a material fact or to omit to state a material fact necessary in order to make the statements made, in the light of the circumstances under which they were made, not misleading, . . . in connection with the purchase or sale of any security.[4]

Section (b) defines two kinds of fraud: statements and omissions. The definition of a fraudulent omission fits Clinton's behaviour; his defence was organised around the claim that he omitted a material fact necessary in order to make his statements made, in light of the circumstances under which they were made, not misleading. Bronston's defence was much the same.

The structure of Rule 10b-5 can help to explain the ambivalence that many people felt about Clinton's defence. On the one hand, lying is just one way of committing an act of deception. Why should those who find other ways receive no punishment? On the other, lying happens to be the only one type of deception that the perjury statute proscribes. The rule of lenity has even more force when it would have been easy enough to have stated a rule that clearly *does* include statements that are literally true, but deceptive.

Deceptive practices by lawyers

This leads to the second reason for maintaining a rather narrow law of perjury. Recall that Clinton, Bronston (and Mary) deceived by violating Grice's cooperative principle. They led their questioners astray without making a false statement. But what about the questioner? Is he being cooperative? In Bronston's and Mary's cases, the answer seems to be yes. Bronston's questioner was interested in finding assets on behalf of creditors. Mary's boyfriend wanted to know whether she was two-timing him. But Clinton's questioners, in their efforts to trap him into making a statement that could later form the basis of a prosecution or impeachment proceeding, were not much more honest than he was.

To see how, let us return to Clinton's definition of 'is'. At the grand jury, the prosecutor read to Mr Clinton the statement of Clinton's lawyer (Mr Bennett) that Lewinsky's affidavit states that 'there is absolutely no sex of any kind in any manner, shape or form with President Clinton'. Clinton responded to the document as follows:

> Clinton   Well, let me say this: I didn't have any discussion, obviously, at this moment with Mr Bennett. I'm not even sure I paid much attention to what he was saying. I was

think – I was ready to get on with my testimony here, and they were having these constant discussions all through the deposition.

But that statement in the present tense, at least, is not inaccurate, if that's what Mr Bennett meant. But as – at the time that he said that and for some time before, that would be a completely accurate statement. Now I don't believe that he was – I don't know what he meant. You'd have to talk to him, because I just wasn't involved in this and I didn't pay much attention to what being said. I was just waiting for them to get back to me. So I can't comment on or be held responsible for whatever he said about that, I don't think.

(Grand Jury Transcript, pp. 476–7, emphasis added)

The real problems with the prosecutors' conduct occurred later, when the original questioner (Mr Bittner) had been replaced by another (Mr Wisenberg). Below are Wisenberg's questions and Clinton's answer concerning Clinton's responsibility for his lawyer's remarks at the deposition:

Q   Your – that statement is a completely false statement. Whether or not Mr Bennett knew of your relationship with Ms Lewinsky, the statement that there was no sex of any kind in any manner, shape or form with President Clinton was an utterly false statement. Is that correct?

Clinton   *It depends upon what the meaning of the word 'is' is.* If is means is, and never has been, that's one thing. If it means, there is none, that was a completely true statement.

(Emphasis added)

But as I have testified – I'd like to testify again – this is – it is somewhat unusual for a client to be asked about his lawyer's statements instead of the other way around. I was not paying a great deal of attention to this exchange. I was focusing on my own testimony. And that if you go back and look at the sequence of events, you will see that the Jones lawyers decided that this was going to be the Lewinsky deposition, not the Jones deposition. And given the facts of their case, I can understand why they made that decision.

(Grand Jury Transcript, pp. 509–10)

Note that Wisenberg has inaccurately quoted the Lewinsky affidavit from which Bennett had read. The question uses the word 'was', whereas the original used the word 'is'. In all likelihood, the problem is a matter of sequence of tense. When we report past speech, we alter the tense of what we report to match the tense in the main clause of the sentence. For example, I would say, 'Bob asked me if I was going to the party', when what Bob really said is, 'are you going to the party'. But here it makes quite a difference. It is hard to blame Clinton for his legalistic response when the purpose of the question was to hold him criminally liable for not correcting a truthful statement that someone else made, and which the questioner misquoted.

There are other instances of these sorts of lawyer's tactics. For example, Clinton testified:

I prepared very well for this deposition on the Jones matters. I prepared very well on that.

(Grand Jury Transcript, p. 480)

Later, the following exchange occurred:

> Clinton   And that if you go back and look at the sequence of events, you will see that the Jones lawyers decided that this was going to be the Lewinsky deposition, not the Jones deposition. And given the facts of their case, I can understand why they made that decision. *But that is not how I prepared for it.* That is not how I was thinking about it.
>
> . . .
>
> Q   You've told us you were very well-prepared for the deposition.
>
> Clinton   No, I said I was very well prepared to talk about Paula Jones and to talk about Kathleen Willey. . . .
>
> (Emphasis added)
> (Grand Jury Transcript, pp. 510–11)

Or consider the following:

> Clinton   I believe at the time that [Lewinsky] filled out this affidavit, *if she believed that the definition of sexual relationship was two people having intercourse, then this is accurate.* And I believe that is the definition that most ordinary Americans would give it.
>
> . . .
>
> Q   But you indicated before that you were aware of what she intended by the term sexual relationship.
>
> Clinton   No, sir. I said I thought that – that this could be a truthful affidavit . . . When she used two different terms, sexual relationship, if she meant by that what most people mean by it, then that is not an untruthful statement.
>
> Q   So your definition of sexual relationship is intercourse only, is that correct?
>
> Clinton   No, not necessarily intercourse only, but it would include intercourse, I believe . . .
>
> (Emphasis added)
> (Grand Jury Transcript, pp. 473–5)

These examples contain a pattern. The questioner mischaracterises something that the witness said, and then tries to get the witness to agree with the mischaracterisation. He then can accuse the witness later of dishonesty the first time around if the witness agrees. The strategy did not work very well here because Clinton was too tough a witness. But one can only imagine what happens when lawyers engage in this kind of conduct with witnesses who are easily intimidated. Moreover, we all misspeak, and we all forget. When someone purports to be summarising what we have said, it is ordinarily in the context of being helpful, and we tend to be grateful for the help. Witnesses are not the only ones who take dishonest advantage of the cooperative principle.

The idea that the questioner holds all the cards in the legal system is not new. The substantial literature on the experience that rape victims have in court discusses the same phenomenon (see, *inter alia*, Conley and O'Barr, 1998; Taslitz, 1999, for some linguistically-oriented descriptions). Lawyers are not under oath, and sometimes abuse this position of power by their own violations of the cooperative principle, and by bullying. In fact, Clinton's grand jury testimony began with a lengthy series of questions about how

Clinton understood the oath to tell the truth (Grand Jury Transcript, p. 457). The prosecutor, Mr Wisenberg, made no such commitment, as lawyers never do in our system of justice. That is the second reason that *Bronston* was correctly decided in my opinion, and that is why witnesses have every right to testify about what the meaning of 'is' is. Witnesses are not the only ones who engage in language games; but they are the ones who go to prison for not playing them successfully.

The Problem of Judging

The third reason for accepting *Bronston* involves the behaviour of judges. As the philosopher Roy Sorensen (forthcoming) points out, in determining whether a perjury case is legally sufficient, a judge must make an all-or-nothing decision even when the case is a close call. When the system requires judges to pretend that nuances in language do not exist and that a misleading statement is just as bad as any lie, then the system provokes the judges themselves to engage in deceptive conduct. Limiting perjury to clear cases helps to protect the integrity of the system. The uncertainty in both results and explanations surrounding the Coleman and Kay study provides psychological support for Sorensen's position.

In fact, a recent Supreme Court decision shows that judges sometimes do omit significant facts to create a misleading impression. The majority of the Court recently decided not to hear an appeal of a decision requiring a town to remove a religious monument (*City of Elkhart* v. *Books*, 121 S.Ct. 2209 (2001)). A dissenting opinion, which is very unusual in such cases, argued that the monument's displaying The Ten Commandments is not necessary a statement of religion, but rather one of culture. In response, the majority pointed out: 'Even though the first two lines of the monument's text appear in significantly larger font than the remainder, they are ignored by the dissenters. Those lines read: 'THE TEN COMMANDMENTS – I AM the LORD thy God' (*ibid.* at 2210). The majority has accused the dissent of engaging in Clintonesque deception, and probably rightly so.

Conclusion

What of Clinton's fate? As mentioned earlier, he was held in contempt and forced to pay a large sum of money to both the court and to Jones' lawyers for the costs resulting from his dishonest conduct at the deposition. The state of Arkansas has suspended his license to practise law for five years. Although the impeachment failed, and a deal was struck on Clinton's last day in office to avoid a perjury prosecution, he agreed to the suspension. The theory behind this disciplinary action is that lawyers owe a special duty to the legal system to be forthright, even if their conduct is not something for which a perjury prosecution is appropriate. What a strange irony.

Notes

1 The author wishes to thank Amy Blackman and Mary Ann Buckley for their valuable assistance in preparing this chapter, and Roy Gainsburg for pointing out some important examples. This work was supported by a summer research grant from Brooklyn Law School.

2 The transcript of the President's grand jury testimony ('Grand Jury Transcript') appears in Communication from the Office of the Independent Counsel, Kenneth W. Starr ('Starr Report'), Appendices to the Referral to the US House of Representatives 453, Tab 16, pp. 456–628 (18 September 1998). Page references to 'Grand Jury Transcript' refer to the page numbers of the Starr Report Appendix.

3 This chapter does not address the issue of materiality. However, in an opinion dealing with Clinton's contempt of court, Judge Wright noted that she had dismissed the case, 'a decision that would not have changed even had the President been truthful with respect to his relationship with Ms Lewinsky . . .' *Jones* v. *Clinton*, 36 F.Supp.2d 1118, 1132 (E.D.Ark. 1999). At best, then, the materiality of Clinton's false statements at the deposition was questionable.

4 17 C.F.R. §240.10b-5 (emphasis added). There are other such provisions which contain similar language, such as Section 12 of the Securities Act of 1933, 15 USC. § 77l.

References

Armstrong, S. L., Gleitman, L. R. and Gleitman, H. (1983) 'What Some Concepts Might Not Be', *Cognition*, vol. 13, pp. 225–59.

Austin, J. L. (1962) *How to Do Things With Words*. Cambridge, Mass.: Harvard University Press.

Bok, S. (1978) *Lying: Moral Choice in Public and Private Life*. New York: Pantheon Books.

Coleman, L. and Kay, P. (1981) 'Prototype Semantics: The English Word Lie', *Language*, vol. 57, pp. 26–44.

Conley, J. M. and O'Barr, W. M. (1998) *Just Words: Law, Language, and Power*. Chicago: University of Chicago Press.

Fodor, J. A. (1998) *Concepts: Where Cognitive Science Went Wrong*. Oxford: Clarendon Press.

Glasgow Herald (2001) 'Dando Accused Denied being Liar when Questioned about Gun', 25 May, p. 10.

Grice, H. P. (1975) 'Logic and Conversation', in P. Cole and J. Morgan (eds), *Syntax and Semantics 3: Speech Acts*. New York: Academic Press, pp. 41–58.

Johnson-Laird, P. N. (1983) *Mental Models*. Cambridge, Mass.: Harvard University Press.

Medin, D. L., Wattenmaker, W. D. and Hampson, S. E. (1987) 'Family Resemblance, Conceptual Cohesiveness, and Category Construction', *Cognitive Psychology*, vol. 19, pp. 242–79.

Posner, R. A. (1999) *An Affair of State*. Cambridge, Mass.: Harvard University Press.

Rosch, E. (1975) 'Cognitive Representations of Semantic Categories', *Journal of Experimental Psychology: General*, vol. 104, pp. 192–233.

Sloman, S. A. (1996) 'The Empirical Case for Two Systems of Reasoning,' *Psychological Bulletin*, vol. 119(1), pp. 3–22.

Smith, E. E., Patalano, L. P. and Jonides, J. (1998) 'Alternative Strategies of Categorization', *Cognition*, vol. 65, pp. 167–96.

Solan, L. M. (1998) 'Law, Language and Lenity', *William and Mary Law Review*, vol. 40 (1), pp. 57–144.

Solan, L. M. (2001) 'Perjury and Impeachment: The Rule of Law or the Rule of Lawyers?', in L. Kaplan and B. Moran (eds), *Aftermath: The Clinton Scandal and the Future of the American Presidency*. New York: New York University Press, pp. 199–211.

Solan, L. M. and Tiersma, P. M. (forthcoming) Language on Trial, Chicago: University of Chicago Press.

Sorensen, R. (forthcoming) 'Vagueness has No Functions in Law', *Legal Theory* (to appear).

Sweetser, E. (1987) 'The Definition of Lie: An Examination of the Folk Models Underlying a Prototype', in D.N. Holland and N. Quinn (eds), *Cultural Models in Language and Thought*. Cambridge, Mass.: Cambridge University Press, pp. 43–66.

Taslitz, A. E. (1999) *Rape and the Culture of the Courtroom*. New York: New York University Press.

Tiersma, P. M. (1990) 'The Language of Perjury: "Literal Truth", Ambiguity, and the False Statement requirement', *Southern California Law Review*, vol. 63, pp. 373–431.

Toobin, J. (2000) *A Vast Conspiracy*. New York: Random House.

Wierzbicka, A. (1996) *Semantics: Primes and Universals*. Oxford: Oxford University Press.

Winter, S. (2001) *A Clearing in the Forest*. Chicago: University of Chicago Press.

12
Understanding the Other: A Case of Mis-Interpreting Culture-Specific Utterances during Alternative Dispute Resolution

Rosemary Moeketsi

Introduction

The South African Justice Department is faced with a critical backlog, especially in the Lower Criminal Courts, and a system of case management is being called for in order to dispose efficiently of the business of the court and to eliminate unnecessary delays in litigation. Judge Ipp (1998, p. 49), among others, proposes a 'court-annexed alternative dispute resolution' as a possible solution to the problem because 'this facility has a profound effect on reducing the number of cases coming to trial'.

Alternative Dispute Resolution (ADR), a term generally used to refer to those voluntary, structured and well-organised processes that may be used to resolve disputes without the conventional court litigation (see Faris, 1992, pp. 8–9; Mowatt, 1992, pp. 82–4; 1993, p. 787), can hardly be regarded as a totally new concept. The Sesotho[1] adage, *ntwa ke ya madulammoho* (it is normal for those who live together to be at conflict with one another), implies that conflict has always been an important part of the nation. *Kgotla* (court) has always been the place for dispute resolution. The members of a *kgotla* under the leadership of a *morena* (chief) would apply law and maintain order in accordance with traditional values and norms, in order to pacify the striving parties and to reconcile them to each other (Moeketsi, 1999c, p. 22).

Similarly, ADR methods are essentially a procedural option available in settling certain disputes; they are supportive of the court system and there should therefore be no undue competition between the two (see Stein, 1998, pp. 59–61; Faris, 1992, pp. 7–12; Omar, 1996, p. 126; Moeketsi and Mollema, 2001, pp. 80–2). Because ADR rests on the foundation that 'settlement is better than judgement' (Mowatt, 1988, p. 729), the procedure is basically consensual, confidential and casual when compared to the almost stilted and public courtroom litigation. It is not surprising then that this method is fast becoming the way to go because of its practical advantages over litigation. Furthermore, we note that an increasing number of untrained and inexperienced interpreters are being recruited to facilitate discourse where, in multilingual and multicultural South African hearings, the disputants almost invariably come from different language and cultural groups.

This chapter, thus, acknowledges how the problems encountered by the Justice Department have a direct impact on the use (or misuse) of African languages. Because languages are not isomorphic in nature, the chapter also explores the strategies employed by an ill-qualified interpreter in transferring messages across languages and cultures in the semi-legal and semi-formal setting of ADR. Reference will be made to an arbitration hearing which took place in January 2001 where the claim was brought by an ex-employee of a building company on the grounds of unfair dismissal.

The Commission for Conciliation, Mediation and Arbitration (CCMA)

There are many organisations in South Africa that provide professional services in alternative dispute resolution, but this chapter will confine itself to the CCMA, a statutory body established in terms of the Labour Relations Act, 66 of 1995. Although the CCMA is funded by the public, it is independent. Its supreme policy-making body, the Governing Body, comprises a chairperson, a director, three representatives from the State, organised labour and organised business. Its objective is to 'facilitate the transformation of the pre-1996 Labour relations system by promoting an expedited, integrated, uniform, high quality, low cost and simple dispute resolution service for the parties' (http://www.ccma.org.za/glossary_of_terms_6th.htm: p. 14). This objective is in line with what has been identified by scholars far and wide as the advantages of ADR (Faris, 1992, p. 8; Cohen, 1992, p. 126; Mulligan, 1992, p. 100; Stein, 1998, p. 59 and Mowatt, 1988, p. 729, to name a few). In the words of Nurney (1998, p. 54), ADR 'appears to be the favoured option ... owing to its perceived speed, neutrality, flexibility and finality'. Omar (1996, p. 126) the then Minister of Justice concurs that '[ADR] mechanisms are more speedy, more effective, more officious [sic], less cumbersome, less expensive and often less abrasive'. Stein (1999, pp. 27–31) eloquently encourages lawyers 'not to fear the process'. He lists some 21 reasons for ADR, ranging from its being cost-effective to its ability to enhance ongoing relationships.

Although the CCMA performs several labour-related functions, its main business is to conciliate and arbitrate workplace disputes. Examples of the labour disputes commonly addressed include dismissals, wages, working conditions, workplace changes and discrimination. These are cases that deal with an issue in the Labour Relations Act or the Employment Equity Act.

The case

On and about 29 February 1999, XYZ Precast Company[2] was engaged in extending its building and therefore had trenches dug everywhere and workers were busy all day. While the security company employed by XYZ Precast were patrolling the premises, they discovered a length of about four metres of cable hidden in a dark isolated part of the building. The cable had been dug out and cut from where it would have been used in the electrification of the section under construction. The patrolmen then sprinkled sodium biphosphate on the cable with the hope that whoever hid the cable there, would return for it. This powder, available from a special unit of the South African Police Service, leaves brown indelible marks on any human body part that comes into contact with a surface treated in this way. The marks, which fade only after two weeks, become darker when the affected body part gets moist, which means that the more the victim tries to wash them off, the more prominent they become.

Two days after the cable had been treated with the salt, it had indeed disappeared from where the security people had seen it. The patrolmen then started the search for their culprit – anybody with brown spots on their hands. Peter M[3] who subsequently came to work with his left hand in bandages, became their prime suspect. After a thorough inspection of his hands, an incisive interrogation by some XYZ managers and a subsequent internal inquiry, Peter M was summarily discharged from his duties. He then, in accordance with Section 191(1) read with (5)(a) of the Labour Relations Act, 66 of 1995, took the case for arbitration to the CCMA on the grounds of unfair dismissal.

Arbitration, the CCMA style

Arbitration has been identified by Faris (1992, p. 7; 1994, p. 336) as one of the 'primary processes of ADR', the others being negotiation and mediation. Arbitration is a voluntary process where the parties to a dispute jointly refer their dispute to a third party of their choice – the arbitrator – for a final decision. *Consensual adjudicative arbitration* is where the parties agree to allow the arbitrator to give a final decision on the matter. In contrast, in *non-adjudicative* arbitration, the arbitrator may only make recommendations (Faris, 1994, pp. 337–8).

A distinction is further made between the following types of arbitration (Faris *et al.* 1999, pp. 47–8):

- expedited arbitration, the conventional mode which resembles litigation except that the process is expedited by relaxing the rules of evidence and allowing the arbitrator a more active role (see Mulligan, 1992, pp. 99–100);

- documents-only arbitration, where there is no need for an arbitral hearing;
- quality arbitration, where the arbitrator, an expert in a particular issue in dispute, for example drugs, may smell, touch or taste a powder and be able to determine accurately that it is, say, cocaine. There is usually no need for a hearing because the quality arbitrator's word is the deciding factor;
- final-offer arbitration, where arbitration is made on the basis of the most reasonable of the last offers made by each disputant.

At the CCMA, arbitration is conducted according to CCMA rules which prescribe, among other things, that a caller requesting arbitration should have been involved in an unsuccessful prior conciliation meeting. This caller should also have served the other parties to the dispute with the referral documents of a dispute to arbitration. Disputes are arbitrated by appointed commissioners who have jurisdiction to do so. The Commission keeps a record of any evidence given in an arbitration hearing and any arbitration award or ruling. These records, in the form of audio tapes, were cordially provided by the CEO of the CCMA for the purpose of this and ongoing research. Permission was also granted to observe proceedings, interview commissioners and interpreters, and to peruse relevant literature in the CCMA library.

In the matter between Peter M and XYZ Precast, Peter M was represented by an official of NEHAWU, a registered union to which he belonged. This was done in accordance with the CCMA rule governing representation at arbitration, and based on S138(4) read with S140 of the Labour Relations Act 66. The respondent was represented by one of their company attorneys, although 'lawyers are not normally allowed to represent parties in arbitration over dismissal disputes' (http://www.ccma.org.za).

Commissioner S presided and an interpreter was available to transfer messages to and from the complainant's Sesotho and English, the language of communication at the CCMA. The matter of the South African languages used in judicial settings has been dealt with in Moeketsi (1999a, pp. 125–8 and 1999b, pp. 1–2); suffice it to say that none of the interlocutors had English as their first language, they all spoke different varieties of English, a common speech behaviour in the multilingual South Africa where there are 11 official languages. The commissioner, himself Indian, spoke Indian-English. Peter M's representative, a Mosotho, spoke African-English. The lawyer representing the respondent, as well as his four witnesses, spoke Afrikaans-English.

Aspects of interpreting

At the time of writing this chapter, the CCMA had recently undertaken a project called 'Operation Wipe-Out', the purpose of which was to dispose of a backlog of 6000 cases, and for this function extra personnel had to be acquired. Thirty experienced commissioners were contracted from the other eight provinces of the country and 12 interpreters were recruited for this task. Some interpreters came from magistrates' courts, some from the liquidated Independent Mediation Service of South Africa, and the others were freelancers. The interpreter serving in this case was one of the recruits on a three-month contract. He had no experience in interpreting except for two days of training on 14 December 2000 and 12 January 2001. The training was provided to the group of 12 recruits by an experienced CCMA interpreter, an erstwhile court interpreter with a total of 22 years' experience, who is himself studying for a BA in Court Interpreting at the University of South Africa. However, this new interpreter is a para-legal officer with an illustrious career as a trade unionist specialising in representing non-English-speaking African employees during ADR. Therefore, the CCMA was not foreign to him, neither was the bilingual arbitration hearing. It is, however, noted that being bilingual does not necessarily make one a good interpreter (Moeketsi, 1999a, p. 101; Robert and Taylor, 1990, p. 75; De Jongh, 1992, p. 119), as is evident from the following opening stages of the arbitration hearing in the matter between Peter M and XYZ Precast.

This discussion identifies the following two distinct phases of the hearing where different interpreting strategies were used: in the initial phase where the disputants presented their opening statements, the Commission was addressed in English and interpreting done into Sesotho. In the second phase, during examination and cross-examination of the applicant who spoke in Sesotho, interpreting was done into English.

Phase one: opening statements

Example A: initial phase

1	Commissioner	Good afternoon. We're here to hear the arbitration in the matter between
2		Peter M and XYZ Precast, case reference GA64954. It is the 30th of
3		January 2001. This is Commissioner S presiding.
4	Interpreter	Re tlo mamela kgang ena, ne? e mahareng a [Shuffle of papers. Voice in the
5		background: 'Peter M'] Peter M le [Interp, aside, asks: Le mang? Answer
6		from behind: 'XYZ Precast'] Ja. Re tlo mamela kgang ena.
7		(lit. We've come to listen to this dispute, OK? which is between [Shuffle of
8		papers. Voice in the background: 'Peter M'] Peter M and [Interp, aside,
9		asks: With whom? Answer from behind: 'XYZ Precast'] Yes. We've come
10		to listen to this dispute.)
11	Comm.	We'll commence by hearing brief opening statements from both parties.
12	Interp.	Re tla utlwa ka bokgutshwanyane feela hore mabapi le taba ena, hore na ho
13		lona le le babedi, ho buiwa eng.
14		(lit. We'll hear just briefly in connection with this matter, what, between the
15		two of you, is being said).
16	Comm.	I'll ask the applicant to make an opening statement first.
17	Interp.	Re tla utlwa he hore wena ya tlisitseng Peter M hore na o bua o reng ka

18		kgang ena.
19		(lit. We'll hear, then, what you, who has brought Peter M, what you say
20		about this matter).
21	Rep.	Ja, I'm actually representing Mr Peter M.
22	Interp.	A re o emetse wena, mothaka enwa.
23		(lit. He says he is representing you, this guy).
24	Rep.	In a matter between himself and XYZ Precast.
25	Interp.	Ke taba e mahareng a hao le XYZ.
26		(lit. It is a matter between you and XYZ).
27	Rep.	Peter M is in fact a shop steward. He belongs to our trade union, COSATU.
28	Interp.	Hantlentle Peter M ke shop-steward . Ke wa COSATU, trade union ya rona
29		(lit In fact, Peter M is a shop steward. He is of COSATU, our trade union).
30	Rep.	Yes, the following day there were allegations of theft by the management of
31		this company, that Peter has stolen a cable. This is the manager who called
32		himself a friendly person.
33	Interp.	E, the following day Peter a qoswa ka boshodu ke ba managemente hore
34		o utswitse kheibole. Ke menenjara ya itseng yena ke motho ya ratang batho.
35		(lit. Yes, the following day Peter was accused of theft by the management,
36		that he has stolen a cable. It is the manager who said he is a person who
37		likes people).
38	Rep.	This manager was the chairman of the case and he said that he had nothing
39		against Peter M. He promised to be impartial.
40	Interp.	Menenjara enwa ke yena ya neng a tshwere ditaba; o itse ha a na niks, ha
41		a na letho kgahlanong le Peter. O itse ha a no nka mahlakore, o tla ba
42		mahareng.
43		(lit. This manager is the one who presided over the matter. He said he had
44		nothing, he had nothing against Peter. He said he won't take sides; he will
45		be in the middle.)
46	Rep.	The management of the company then held a caucus, and 15 minutes later
47		they came back and marked his hands with pens.
48	Interp.	Ba khampani yaba ba tshwara puonyana e nyenyane. Ka mor'a 15 minutes
49		ba kgutla mme ba makha matsoho a hae ka dipene.
50		(lit. Those of the company then held a brief speech. After 15 minutes they
51		came back and marked his hands with pens).
52	Rep.	They took him to the office and told him they had no option but to suspend
53		him with pay until they hear about the DNA test.
54	Interp.	Ba mo isa ofiseng ba re ha ba na monyetla o mong ntle le hore ba mo emise
55		mosebetsing feela ba ntse ba mo lefa ho fihlela ba utlwa ka tsa test ena ho
56		thweng ke DNA.
57		(lit. They took him to the office and said they had no opportunity but to stop
58		him from working, however still paying him, until they hear about this test
59		called the DNA).

At the beginning of the hearing, the interpreting into Sesotho occurs mainly at the lexical level and most of the techniques used by the interpreter have been identified in translation studies as 'universal features' (Baker, 1993, pp. 243–7; 1996, p. 181ff). *Omission* is the most common of the transgressions by this interpreter. His lack of experience and proper training, coupled with his endeavours to cope with an information overload or to deal with menacing technical terms (see Moeketsi, 1999a, p. 163; Moeketsi and Mollema, 2001, p. 38) could be the reasons he failed so dismally to convey the source message in its entirety in the target language. The most serious omission occurs at the very beginning of his task, from lines 4 to 10.

Although the greeting (line 1) is an integral part of the African discourse, the interpreter neglects to convey it in the target language, at line 4, and this oversight may be enough to render his general communicative competence questionable. In Sesotho, for instance, *'Dumela!'* (lit. Say yes!), the most basic form for 'Hallo!, Good afternoon!', and its response *'E! /Ahe!'* (lit. Yes!), are culturally used to ascertain and confirm that the person about to be addressed is indeed capable of speech and is in fact interested in the imminent conversation. This form of greeting has its origin in the traditional behaviour where the Basotho would walk long distances to the mines of South Africa or to other places to seek employment. On the way they would meet other travellers (*diparolanaha*: lit. those who split the land open (Moeketsi, 1993, p. 39; Moletsane, 1993, pp. 60–7) who had to acknowledge that they were indeed human beings with whom a conversation could be carried out. In the Sesotho culture, the greeting is so essential it is almost an imperative conversation opener.

Despite the typically serious nature of dispute-resolution hearings, the interpreter's general demeanour at this initial stage as well as the 'key' of his discourse, that is the 'tone, manner or spirit in which [his] act is done' (Hymes, 1974, p. 57), in his usage of the hedge, *'ne?'* (line 4) (lit. OK?) convey an inappropriately casual attitude. This attitude underlies a large portion of his discourse; for example, he does not know the names of the disputants, even though these names formed part of the commissioner's source message. He does not bother to utter the name of the respondent even after having been told what it was. He simply acknowledges the name with a 'Yes' (line 9). He neglects to provide the case reference, the date of the hearing and the name of the presiding commissioner. He omits the words 'commence', 'opening' (line 11) and 'first' (line 16) which explain, albeit to only to an extent, the procedure to be followed in the hearing.

The next lexical strategy, *direct transference* (Kruger, 2000, p. 159) of English concepts into the Sesotho discourse is done for a variety of reasons. In the first place expediency seems to be the only reason for the interpreter's rendering of easily interpretable terms such as *the following day* (line 33) and *15 minutes* (line 48) as they occurred in the English source text. Secondly, English concepts that do not have cultural, and thus linguistic, equivalents in Sesotho have been transferred in English, for example, *shop-steward* (line 27) and *trade union* (line 27). This has, nevertheless, been done without any inconvenience to the target audience because these terms are commonly used in labour matters to which all the participants are accustomed. Thirdly, foreign concepts that are totally beyond the interpreter's comprehension have also been transferred directly, for instance, *the DNA test* has been rendered as *test ena ho thweng ke DNA* (lit. this test called the DNA) (lines 55/6). In the fourth instance direct transference has been possible by means of grammatical rules. Phonological adjustments have been effected in *kheibole* (cable)(34) and *khampani* (company)(48). Other English words have been morphologically adapted into Sesotho by means of, for instance, the insertion of the suffix *-ng* to form the locative *ofiseng* (in the office)(54), and the prefix *ba-* in the formation of the possessive *ba managemente* (of the manage-ment)(33). Fifthly, code-switching is regarded in this discussion as another form of direct transference of lexical items where '*they marked his hands with pens*' for instance was transferred as *Ba **makha** letsoho la hae ka dipene* (49) although there is a better Sesotho word for 'mark' (*tshwaya*).

This strategy of transferring challenging concepts as they occurred in the source utterance is in line with Venuti's (1995, p. 20ff) 'resistancy, resistance or foreignisation' translation technique which suggests that some foreign aspects of a source message be retained in order to give the target audience an 'alien experience' and to allow them to 'recognise the linguistic and cultural differences of foreign [source messages]' (1995, p. 42).

Lexical simplification is the next strategy used extensively. The interpreter exploits the semantic relationship of hyponymy and employs super-ordinate terms in the interpretation of culturally unknown terms. The word '*caucus*' (46), which conventionally refers to a political party meeting, was interpreted as *puonyana e nyenyane* (lit. a very brief speech); *puisano* (discussion), would have been a more appropriate hypernym because 'caucus' could be regarded as a specific lexical item the meaning of which is included in the more general 'discussion' (Crystal, 1985, p. 150).

In some cases the interpreter merely uses *approximations* of unusual concepts. The word 'arbitration'(1) which is crucial in qualifying the business of the hearing, has been interpreted simply as 'dispute' (7). Although there appears to be an adequate relationship of hyponymy between 'dispute' and 'arbitration' in the sense that arbitration amounts to hearing a dispute in order to grant a decision, in the context of ADR it may be useful to interpret arbitration so accurately that a clear distinction is made from related concepts such as negotiation and mediation. Negotiation is a private and voluntary discussion on a matter of disagreement between two conflicting parties in order to first listen to the other party's perspective and to then come to an agreement. Mediation on the other hand is 'assisted negotiation' (Stein, 1998, p. 61) because an objective, neutral third party assists the disputing parties in reaching a mutually acceptable resolution to their dispute (Moeketsi and Mollema, 2001, pp. 74–5). In arbitration, the third party is more actively involved in that he/she may grant the final decision.

The meaning of the word 'hear' (1) as used in the context of 'arbitration' has shifted beyond 'to perceive with the ear; to listen to'. The word refers to a judicial act of listening to, assessing and ultimately granting a decision. The interpreter neglected this polysemic quality of 'hear' in his use of *mamela* (listen to) (4,6). A modern Sesotho word *sekaseka* would have been a more appropriate interpreting of 'hear (judicially)'. The phrase 'allegations of theft' (30) would normally imply affirmed statements without proof, but it has been interpreted as 'Peter was accused of theft' (35) (*Peter a qoswa ka boshodu*). The word 'option' (52) which is more of a 'choice' (*kgetho*) has been interpreted as *monyetla* (54) (opportunity) (57).

This strategy of approximation unfortunately resulted in misinterpreting the source message and thus providing a disservice to the disputing parties and actually misrepresenting the Commission record. Although Gile (1995, p. 49) acknowledges that the interpreted message is 'an approximation, at best', the interpreter should always strive at 'message equivalence' (De Jongh, 1992, p. 61).

Explication was used with relative success. The word 'applicant' (16) in the source message was paraphrased by means of more general words, 'you, who has brought Peter M' because indeed the applicant did have a representative who provided the opening statement on his behalf. The word 'friendly' does not quite occur as an adjective in Sesotho, thus the clause 'I am a friendly person' (32) was explained by means of 'I'm a person who likes people' (36/7). The concept of *chairman* (38), which does have a Sesotho linguistic equivalent, viz. *modulasetulo* (one who sits on the chair) was rendered by means of an apt explication, *ya tshwereng ditaba* (40) (one who presides over the matter), and elsewhere by a compound noun *motshwaramarapo* which explains the function of 'having the reins'.

'To suspend with pay' (52/3), an expression that is alien to Sesotho culture where labour relations are solely between employer and employee without any involvement of third-party trade unions, was efficiently paraphrased as *Ba o emisitse mosebetsing feela ba ntse ba o patala* (lit. They have stopped you from working, however, they still pay you).

Repetition, a form of explication, (Kruger, 2000, pp. 159–61) was used extensively. This repetition, *Ke ne ke se na niks, ke se na letho* (lit. I had nothing, I had nothing) was used in transferring 'I had nothing' (40), probably to correct the unnecessary use of an Afrikaans word, *niks* (nothing) where an equivalent is available in Sesotho. Where 'impartial' (39) was interpreted as *Ke se ka nka mahlakore, ke be mahareng* (I should not take sides, I should be in the middle), near-synonymous expressions were repeated.

Another interesting feature occurs at line 22 where the interpreter suddenly interprets in the third person. We also detect serious discriminatory undertones in his use of 'this guy' (23) in reference to Peter M's representative, a non-lawyer African addressing the hearing in English. The interpreter also wrongly alters the focus from the commissioner to Peter M who is, strictly speaking, not an active part of the discourse at this stage.

If one regards culture in its broadest sense as a way of life of any society, then the CCMA as an ADR institution may be seen as having its own culture. The commissioners, interpreters and other professionals working in

ADR are privileged élites with knowledge and power; they also have the responsibility to act ethically. Disputes are heard according to pre-determined processes; discourse participation as well as role relations are determined by the CCMA rules. There is likely to be a shared set of values and beliefs generally regarded as accepted and desirable within the society of the CCMA. Nonetheless, at the initial stage of this arbitration hearing, the interpreter failed to adopt the practices and general behaviour in the source culture and then transfer them to the culture of the applicant. As a result, several important procedural issues remain unknown to the applicant, such as the essence of the greeting at the beginning of the arbitration hearing; why the date was mentioned and why S introduced himself as the presiding commissioner.

Phase two: cross-examination

This section of the discussion concentrates on the second phase of the hearing during the cross-examination of the applicant where Sesotho discourses were interpreted into English. We note that interpreting at this stage is markedly at a syntactical level and stylistic modification is also prominent. There is a strong tendency towards disambiguation.

The following decontextualised discourses by Peter M are used in order to show how the interpreter falsified the source message mainly by inserting additional information. For instance, *Ke tswile kae maobane?* (lit. Where did I go out, yesterday?) was rendered as 'Which gate did I use to leave the premises the previous evening after work', with the inclusion of 'gate' and the descriptive phrases 'to leave the premises' and 'the previous evening after work'.

Ke ba bolelletse hore ha ke tsebe letho (lit. I told them that I did not know anything) was rendered as 'I told them that I knew nothing about the cable', where 'about the cable' may be regarded as 'framing information' (Gile, 1995, p. 55) that links the present utterance to the rest of the evidence.

In *A re o ne a tla dropa case ena, jwale e se e tsejwa ke batho ba bangata* (He said *to me that if he could,* he would drop this case, but *it is unfortunate that* it was already known by other people) the addition of the highlighted sections depicts the interpreter's emotional involvement with the source message.

This interpreter also made a dismal attempt at the use of euphemisms. According to the evidence adduced, one of the Company managers, who had claimed to be 'a friendly person', had suggested that Peter M admit to handling the cable. Peter M would have to testify that he had 'gone to urinate and came back to remove the cable that happened to be on his way'. The interpretation of *urinate* was the miserable 'I went to the loo, to loo, to urinate'. For Basotho and most African cultures, the language used with reference to sex organs, sexual acts, excretion, urine and certain other natural bodily functions, is taboo and may thus not be used explicitly. Euphemisms are used instead (Moeketsi and Swanepoel, 1997, p. 127). In this case the initial 'I went to the loo' did not explain the action of urinating. When 'to loo' sounded wrong, the interpreter then abandoned the euphemism and used the culturally tabooed, explicit word 'urinate'. In subsequent discourses *to pass water* was used.

This interpreter later acknowledged a bias in favour of Peter M based on his (the interpreter's) own background, where he represented uneducated, non-eloquent African employees in ADR cases of unfair dismissals and other labour injustices. Although the interpretation of this latter part was helpful in expediting the process, the interpreter falsified the source message. Interpretation, especially in legal settings, is still a subservient activity that is supposed to reproduce someone else's original discourses. Wallmach (2000, p. 245), in her discussion of gender metaphors that abound in discourses on translation, refers to the tag 'les belles infidèles' used to describe translation in eighteenth-century France. Literally translated, the tag means 'the beautiful unfaithful'. According to this expression, if translations (like women) were faithful, they were probably ugly, and if they were beautiful they were likely to be unfaithful. This expression has obviously survived several centuries and has transcended the domain of translations into interpreting where it has captured a cultural parallel between the issues of fidelity and the controversial role of an interpreter as a cultural broker.

Ethical matters

In the following excerpt the interpreter's partiality is so pronounced that his behaviour is in fact unethical and unprofessional:

Example B

1	Commissioner	OK, what relief is sought by the applicant?
2	Interp.	O ne o batla tefo e jwang; hore ho etsahale jwang; hore o thuswe jwang? Ke
3		hore jwanong o batla hore jwalo ka ha o tlisitse nyewe mona o tlo kopa
4		thuso; o batla thuso e jwang?
5		(lit. What kind of payment do you want; what should happen; how should
6		you be helped? In other words, now that you have brought a case here to
7		come and ask for help, what kind of help do you want?)
8	Complainant	Actually ke ne ke sa batle thuso, ke ne ke batla nnete, wa bona, because, as
9		a e beile , Mr . . . . [interrupted]
10		(lit. Actually, I do not need help, I just want the truth, you see, because, as
11		he has stated it, Mr . . .)
12	Interp.	Ha o nkutlwe hore ke reng . . .
13		(lit. You don't hear what I say . . .)
14	Compl.	Ke a utlwa . . .
15		(lit. I do hear . . .)
16	Interp.	O tlile mona o tlo kopa thuso. Jwanong, akere wena o tswile mosebetsing?
17		Jwale wena o tlile mo o tlo batla thuso. Ke batla hore o nkutlwisise hantle.
18		O batla hore commissioner a o thuse ka eng?
19		(lit. You have come here to ask for help. Now, is it not that you are out of
20		work? Now, you have come here to ask for help. I want you to understand

21		me well. What do you want the commissioner to help you with?)
22	Compl.	A shebe hore ke tejetswe ka tsela e jwang, ka hobane nna ke ipona ke se
23		molato.
24		(lit. He must find out how I have been dismissed, because I don't see myself
25		as guilty).
26	Interp.	I don't think we understand each other. However, I will try . . .
27	Comm.	Just say exactly what he has said.
28	Interp.	He says he wants you to investigate the matter and find out whether he was
29		dismissed fairly. That's what he said.
30	Comm.	OK. And if I find that he was not fairly dismissed, what does
31		he want me to do for him?
32	Interp.	Jwale o re commissioner, haele hore yena o fumana hore o tejetswe
33		unfairly,ka tsela e sa tshwanelang, ha ba mosebetsing ba o tebetse ka tsela
34		e fosahetseng, o batla hore yena a o thuse ka eng?
35		(lit. Now, the commissioner says, if he finds that you were unfairly
36		dismissed, in an improper way; if your employers dismissed you in a wrong
37		way, what do you want him to help you with?)
38	Compl.	Nna vele akere ha ke sebetse, ke tlile mo hore a nthuse ke kgutlele
39		mosebetsing.
40		(lit. Indeed I do not work; I have come here that he should help me go back
41		to work.)
42	Interp.	Reinstatement.

The commissioner's utterance (1) is a common mistake by presiding officers to misdirect their utterances to the interpreter and thereby misinterpret and confuse the interpreter's role. The interpreter's response shows his under-standing of the situation. He redirects the commissioner's question to the complainant. However, the interpretation is a glaring explication of the source message fraught with additions, repetitions and simplifications. The phrase 'the relief sought' (1) has been rendered as 'kind of payment'; 'what should happen'; 'help' (5/6).

Utterance 8(10), a denial by the complainant that he needs help, conveys how divergent and inconsistent conversations can be because of the different world-views of the participants, in this case the complainant's ignorance of the purpose of the arbitration hearing. At (12) the interpreter speaks out of turn because the interlocutors were the commissioner and the complainant. This is an intrusive display of the power inherent in the interpreter who actually belongs to both worlds, that of the CCMA and that of the lay com-plainant. Despite the complainant's claim that he does understand, the interpreter insists on explaining at (16) that the complainant needs help and that he should tell exactly what kind of help he desires.

The aggression with which the interpreter offers his services could be likened to the Brazilian translation concept, 'cannibalism', initially a form of resistance but later a metaphor 'expressing a philosophy by means of which the minority culture instead of rejecting the powerful foreign "other", accepts it, "eats" or appropriates it . . . absorbs it, transforms it and derives nourishment from it' (Wallmach, 2000, p. 252). No wonder that, when the complainant ultimately gives in to the pressure, and states at (22) the kind of help he requires, this is disregarded by the interpreter who then turns to the Commissioner at (26) to claim a breakdown of communication. The result is that utterance (22) remains uninterpreted. The commissioner, who had allowed 'a private conversation' between the interpreter and the complainant to continue over six turns between (12) and (25), only now joins the discourse, and, at the invitation of the interpreter. He requests the interpreter 'to say exactly what [the complainant] said'. The interpreter's (27) is a mere summary of which neglects to convey the source message in its entirety. The omission of 'actually, I do not need help', a crucial part of (10), is later explained by the interpreter as 'a deliberate eradication of contradictory utterances'. However, the omission of this part of (24/5), viz., 'because I don't see myself as guilty' is an unfortunate exclusion of important information.

At (30) the discourse deteriorates again as the Commissioner insists on addressing the interpreter and sending him as a messenger to find out certain facts from the complainant. The interpretation of 'not fairly dismissed' at (35–7) has been interpreted three times in one sentence as 'unfairly dismissed', 'in an improper way', 'dismissed in a wrong way'. This behaviour has been observed throughout the hearing where the interpreter had desired to correct of all his code-switching into English or Afrikaans.

The interpretation of 38–9 is one of the worst cases where the summary mode has been used to interpret a piece of discourse comprising two sentences by means of a single word which does not even attempt to do justice to the source.

Conclusion

Although this chapter has used a single case-study, interpreting across cultures is a complex undertaking compounded in South Africa by 'serious deficiencies resulting from linguistic and cultural prejudice' (Kaschula, 1995, p. 9). For the fact that interpreters, especially in judicial and similar settings, are employed to be faithful to the source message, they should be provided with a comprehensive education and training, as a matter of urgency, so that they are barred from having to invent new utterances, and sometimes even to betray the source. This case has shown how the interpreter often takes the role of cultural mediator and then interprets 'expressions, intentions, perceptions and expectations of each cultural group to the other' (Taft, 1981, p. 53), in his attempt to establish and balance the communication between them. Interpreting should not be a subjective activity where the interpreter misunderstands the duty to 'facilitates communication to the best of his/her ability'.

Furthermore, it is evident that the inexperienced and untrained interpreter in this case misread the relatively flexible procedure during ADR and believed that his personal, though unprofessional, 'assistance' would expedite the settlement of the dispute. The final decision was granted against the applicant.

Notes

1 Sesotho is one of the 11 official languages of South Africa spoken as a mother-tongue by 7.7 per cent of the population. It is also the national language of Lesotho.
2 The name of this company has been anonymised throughout the chapter.
3 All names have been anonymised in order to protect identities.

References

Baker, M. (1993) 'Corpus Linguistics and Translation Studies: Implications and Applications' in G. Francis and E. Tognini-Bonelli (eds), *Texts and Technology: In Honour of John Sinclair*. Amsterdam: John Benjamins, pp. 233–50.

Baker, M. (1996) 'Linguistics and Cultural Studies: Complementary or Competing Paradigms in Translation Studies?' in A. Lauer, H. Gerzymisch-Arbogast, J. Haller and E. Steiner (eds), *Ubersetzungswissenschaft im Umbruch: Festschrift fur Wolfram Wilss zum 70. Geburtstag*. Tubingen: Gunter Narr Verlag, pp. 9–19.

Bowen, D. and Bowen, M. (eds) (1991) *Interpreting – Yesterday, Today and Tomorrow*. Binghamton: State University of New York.

CCMA <http://www.ccma.org.za>

Cohen, C. (1992) 'Mediation: Giving Law a Human Face', *De Rebus*, February, pp. 126–8.

Crystal, D. (1985) *A Dictionary of Linguistics and Phonetics*. Oxford: Basil Blackwell.

De Jongh, E. M. (1992) *An Introduction to Court Interpreting: Theory and Practice*. New York: University Press of America.

Faris, J. A. (1992) 'Reconciling Alternative Dispute Resolution (ADR) and Judicial Dispute Resolution', *Codicillus*, May, vol. 33 (2), pp. 7–12.

Faris, J. A. (1994) 'Exploring the Alternatives in "Alternative Dispute Resolution"', *De Jure*, vol. 1(27), pp. 331–40.

Faris, J. A., Hurter, E., Kelbrick R.A. and Cassim, F. (1999) *Civil Procedure Module 1: Only Study Guide for CIP101–D*. Pretoria: University of South Africa.

Gile, D. (1995) *Basic Concepts and Models for Interpreter and Translator Training*. Amsterdam: John Benjamin Publishing Co.

Hymes, D. (1974) *Foundations in Linguistics: An Ethnographic Approach*. Philadelphia: University of Philadelphia Press.

Ipp, D. (1998) 'Case Management and Court-Annexed Alternative Dispute Resolution', *Consultus*, May, pp. 49–50.

Kaschula, R. H. (1995) 'Cross-Cultural Communication in the Eastern Cape with Particular Reference to Law Courts', *South African Journal of African Languages*, vol. 15(1), pp. 9–15.

Kruger, A. (2000) 'Lexical Cohesion and Register Variation in Translation: "*The Merchant of Venice*" in Afrikaans', unpublished doctoral thesis, Pretoria: University of South Africa.

Kuper, M. (1996) 'How Does AFSA Function?', *Consultus*, November, p. 125.

Moeketsi, R. H. (1993) *Bokgeleke ba Basotho* (Aspects of Basotho Folklore). Pretoria: Kagiso Publishers.

Moeketsi, R. (1999a) *Discourse in the Multilingual and Multicultural Courtroom: A Court Interpreters' Guide*. Pretoria: Van Schaik Publishers.

Moeketsi, R. H. (1999b) 'Redefining the Role of the South African Court Interpreter', *Proteus*, vol. 8, nos 3–4, Summer-Fall <http//:www.najit.org/proteus/v8n3-4/moeketsi_v8n3-4.html>

Moeketsi, R. H. (1999c) *Court Interpreting 1: Only Study Guide for CIN101–4*. Pretoria: University of South Africa.

Moeketsi, R. H. and Mollema, N. (2001) *Court Interpreting 11: Only Study Guide for CIN201–8*. Pretoria: University of South Africa.

Moeketsi, R. H. and Swanepoel, C. F. (1997) *Souther Sotho: Only Study Guide for SSE302–5*. Pretoria: University of South Africa.

Moletsane, R. I. M. (1993) *Liparola-thota*. Maseru: Longman.

Mowatt, J. C. (1988) 'Some Thoughts on Mediation', *South African Law* Journal, November, vol. 105(4), pp. 727–39.

Mowatt, J. C. (1992) 'The High Price of Cheap Adjudication', *South African Law Journal*, vol. 109, pp. 77–86.

Mowatt, J. C. (1993) 'Some Thoughts on a Mediation Profession', *South African Law* Journal, vol. 110, pp. 787–95.

Mulligan, K. (1992) 'Alternative Dispute Resolution: An Emphasis on Expedition', *Businessman's Law*, vol. 21, pp. 99–102.

Nurney, S. (1998) 'Dispute Resolution in International Contracts: English Arbitration?', *De Rebus*, April, pp. 53–7.

Omar, A. M. (1996) 'AFSA: The Need for Alternative Dispute Resolution', *Consultus*, November, pp. 126–7.

Robert, R. and Taylor, M. (1990) 'Development of Legal Interpreter Education in New Jersey', in D. Bowen and M. Bowen (eds), *Interpreting – Yesterday, Today and Tomorrow*. Binghamton: State University of New York, pp. 70–80.

Stein, G. (1998) 'The Mediation Groundswell', *De Rebus*, April, pp. 58–61.

Stein, G. (1999) 'Dispute Resolution: Why Lawyers Should Encourage and Not Fear the Process', *De Rebus*, January, pp. 26–31.

Taft, R. (1981) 'The Role and Personality of the Mediator', in S. Bochner (ed.), *The Mediating Person: Bridges Between Cultures*. Cambridge: Schenkman, pp. 53–88.

Venuti, L. (1995) *The Translator's Invisibility: A History of Translation*. London: Routledge.

Wallmach, K. (2000) '"Get Them Lost Just as in the Narrow Streets of the *Casbah*": Metaphors of Resistance and Subversion in Translation', *Hermeneus*, vol. 2, pp. 233–58.

Part IV

The Language of the Courtroom II: Judges and Juries

13

The Meaning of 'I Go Bankrupt': An Essay in Forensic Linguistics

Stan Bernstein[1]

Introduction: 'I go bankrupt'

The principal objective of an individual's filing a petition with a US bankruptcy court is to discharge his personal liabilities. As an essential part of this process, the debtor must also file a detailed schedule of his creditors by name and last known address and the amount of each creditor's claim (the 'debtor's schedule') when he files his petition. Within a few days, the clerk of the court then sends a formal notice of the filing of the bankruptcy case to each creditor on the debtor's schedule. The notice also advises each creditor that if she wishes to preclude her claim from being discharged – assuming that the claim is based upon fraud – she must file a timely complaint for a determination of dischargeability (a 'dischargeability complaint'). If, however, the debtor fails to schedule the creditor, then that creditor's claim cannot be discharged. There is an important back-door exception to this rule: if the unscheduled creditor gets notice or acquires actual knowledge, by whatever informal means ('actual notice'), of the debtor's case in time to file a dischargeability complaint, and the creditor fails to satisfy the deadline, then her claim is also discharged.

This chapter will discuss a case in which the debtor, Robert Dunning, a native speaker of English, testified that he, in fact, gave adequate notice to his largest creditor, Steven Kim, that he had filed his bankruptcy petition.[2] This occurred during a telephone call to Kim, lasting less than three or four minutes. Dunning testified that he told Kim, 'I filed [for] bankruptcy.' If the debtor were reasonably proficient in using correct English grammar, he would have said colloquially, 'I've gone bankrupt', or 'I went bankrupt.' Only if the debtor understood and used the formal terminology of the Bankruptcy Code would he have said, 'I've filed a bankruptcy petition.' And only a very precise lawyer, speaking in the most formal and extended register, would have said, 'On behalf of our client, I filed his petition for relief under chapter 7 of the Bankruptcy Code.'

In rebuttal, Kim, a native speaker of Korean, testified (in English) that the debtor told him, 'I go bankrupt [*sic*].' Kim obviously translated what he heard into his own idiolect. In the process, the tense, aspect, mood and correct grammar of the debtor's statement was suppressed, confused or perhaps intentionally changed by the creditor. Most of the two-and-a-half-hour hearing was exhausted in trying to determine exactly what Kim understood the debtor to have meant by his statement.

This essay in forensic linguistics explores some perplexing issues in the role of language in the law within the institutional setting of a US bankruptcy case. The question is what can forensic linguistics contribute to a trial judge's better understanding of how to go about analysing what was said in the talk exchange between the parties? The prevailing bankruptcy law presupposes that the concept of actual notice in this institutional setting is not problematic at all. The simple and dispositive issue is whether or not the creditor got actual notice. This essay suggests the very concept and linguistic structure of the giving and receiving notice of an institutional fact is open-ended, rather complex, and often ambiguous. Forensic linguistics holds out the promise of more reliably describing how adequate notice actually works and may also point to a normative critique of the prevailing law on this important issue.

A primer on chapter 7 bankruptcy law for forensic linguists

The systemic function of consumer bankruptcy law is to relieve individual debtors from the oppressive burden of debts that they cannot satisfy from their present income and non-exempt assets. The implicit model at the foundation of the Bankruptcy Code is an economic exchange between an individual debtor and his creditors. (The Bankruptcy Code is the commonly used reference to the comprehensive federal bankruptcy statute, which is codified under Title 11 of the United States Code.) Under chapter 7 of the Bankruptcy Code, the debtor agrees to surrender his existing non-exempt assets to the bankruptcy trustee for liquidation in exchange for a broad form of *discharge*, or cancellation, of his personal liabilities. As a result of the discharge of all scheduled personal liabilities, the debtor is said to achieve 'a fresh start' so that he may return to economic productivity.

Historically, the Bankruptcy Code and its predecessor acts reserved a complete discharge of personal liabilities only to the 'honest but unfortunate debtor'. The corollary principle is that the *dishonest* debtor should be denied a discharge of those claims arising from his pre-petition fraudulent acts or representations provided that a defrauded creditor files a timely discharge-ability complaint (see 11 USC sub-sections 523(a)(2) and (4)). If the creditor prevails in her action, then her claim will be excepted from the scope of the debtor's discharge. This creditor will then be free to satisfy her claim by seizing and liquidating any of the debtor's post-petition non-exempt property and income.

Nevertheless, the Bankruptcy Code is also solicitous of the debtor's right to a complete discharge, and so it imposes a very tight deadline for a creditor's filing of her dischargeability complaint. That deadline is the sixtieth day after the date that the debtor is examined under oath by the trustee and any creditors at 'the meeting of creditors'. The meeting of creditors, in turn, has to be held within 20 to 45 days after the date the debtor filed his petition. This is a deadline with a very short fuse.

But under the back-up rule mentioned earlier, a creditor who was not scheduled by the debtor, but who by any informal means later gets actual notice, is held to the same deadline as the scheduled creditor. It is very important to realise that this backup rule does not require that the unscheduled creditor also get actual notice of the location of the court, the date of the petition, the number of the case, the name and address of the trustee, the name and address of the debtor's lawyer, or, most importantly, the deadline for filing a dischargeability complaint. The legal fiction is once the unscheduled creditor gets actual notice, the Bankruptcy Code imposes further 'inquiry notice' of the deadline on that creditor. The rationale for this back-up rule is to prevent unscheduled creditors who get actual notice from lurking in the bushes until the debtor's bankruptcy case is closed, and then suing the debtor in state court to collect their outstanding non-discharged claim. It should be apparent that this back-up rule creates a strong incentive for the debtor to delay giving a creditor informal but actual notice of his case until close to the deadline and to catch the creditor napping, and then for each party later on to engage in swearing contesting who said what to whom and when.

The procedural setting of the hearing

Kim missed the deadline by seven weeks. He then filed a motion for leave to file a late complaint on the ground that he did not learn about Dunning's bankruptcy case until after the deadline had passed. Kim testified that the source of his information was another creditor who told him about the case a month or so after he had received Dunning's telephone call. Attached to Kim's motion was the proposed dischargeability complaint. The debtor opposed the motion, stating that Kim got actual notice in their short telephone conversation and so was put on inquiry notice to find out the deadline and to file a complaint by that deadline. In order to resolve this dispute, the court had to determine exactly what was said during the telephone call and whether it constituted actual notice.

It should be noted at the outset that Kim's lawyer gave no indication in his motion papers that his client was not proficient in spoken English, nor that there would be any difficulty in Kim's testifying without the assistance of an interpreter on the controlling issue of whether he got actual notice. Thus, when the court began the hearing, it did not have any warning that any contested linguistic issues might have to be considered. Perhaps the court should have the presence of mind as soon as Kim began to testify to adjourn the hearing and to direct Kim's counsel to secure the services of an interpreter who could assist the creditor in testifying at the next date of the hearing. The hesitation of the court to burden the creditor with this expense was based, in large part, on the limited scope of the hearing itself and the creditor's having demonstrated sufficient proficiency in spoken English to make himself generally understood, particularly if the questions to him were presented in several different forms and if he were given considerable latitude in answering in a narrative style. The creditor's reliance on his limited proficiency in spoken English was far from optimally efficient for him to 'tell his story' with the requisite degree of clarity concerning his understanding of what the debtor told him during their brief talk exchange over the telephone. But this was a risk that Kim's counsel implicitly advised him to take.

The narrative

Kim was one of Dunning's accounting and tax clients; for more than five years Dunning prepared Kim's personal and business income-tax returns and generally served as Kim's business advisor. For the past 10 years, Kim has owned and successfully operated a gallery in Manhattan selling imported Chinese antiques, making frequent buying trips to China to support the business.

For many years, Kim and his wife have lived in Flushing, Queens, New York in which a sizeable immigrant Korean population resides. In fact, the 2000 federal census reported that in the five boroughs of New York City (Manhattan, the Bronx, Brooklyn, Queens, and Staten Island) there are over 2 000 000 immigrants and their extended families, drawn from a broad diversity of national and linguistic communities. The federal district court in Brooklyn reported that in the calendar year 1999, hearings and pre-trial depositions were conducted in over 50 languages in which official interpreters were appointed by the court or retained by one of the parties.

As their personal and business relationship developed, Dunning induced Kim to become a one-third equal partner in his broker-dealership and to assist in capitalising the firm. As friends and partners, Dunning and Kim met regularly to discuss business matters at a favourite local restaurant. Occasionally their wives joined them for dinner. By the time the broker-dealership was closed by the securities regulators a few years later, Kim and his wife had lost over $3 275 000 in funds invested through the firm. Their investments were converted by the firm. The third partner in the broker-dealership was later convicted and imprisoned for committing securities fraud against the firm's clients.

Kim testified that he and his lawyer met with Dunning and Dunning's lawyer to discuss repayment of the Kims' investments more than a year before the critical telephone call from Dunning. At the meeting, Dunning complained about the pressures he was under from his creditors. He said that he was considering filing a chapter 7 bankruptcy petition to liquidate the assets of the broker-dealership, and that he might have to do the same for himself. Dunning also admitted to having several meetings and telephone conversations with Kim over the succeeding six to nine months in response to Kim's repeated requests for repayment.

Finally, Kim began a formal securities arbitration proceeding against Dunning; he sought a $25 000 000 award, including actual and punitive damages, costs and attorney's fee, arising from the conversion of his invested funds of over $3 275 000. In response, Dunning filed his personal bankruptcy case without including Kim on the debtor's schedule of creditors. Dunning testified that he was very distraught at the time he filed his bankruptcy petition, and he could not account for why he failed to list Kim whose business and residential addresses and telephone numbers he quite clearly knew. His testimony on this point was not credible.

Kim called Dunning one last time to invite him to meet at their favourite local restaurant to discuss repayment of Kim's invested funds. Dunning immediately agreed to meet his old friend, former partner and client, but said absolutely nothing about the personal chapter 7 bankruptcy petition he had filed 10 weeks before. Within a few minutes of Kim's telephone call to him, Dunning placed an urgent call to his bankruptcy lawyer to discuss this particular situation. Acting upon the advice of counsel, Dunning called Kim back within 10 minutes of their last call, and told him for the first time that 'I filed [for] bankruptcy.' On the date of these back-to-back calls, the deadline for filing dischargeability complaints in Dunning's case was a scarce two weeks away. Dunning admitted during the hearing that he made no effort to notify Kim of the date of the filing of the petition, the case number, the location of the court, or the deadline for filing a dischargeability complaint.

The surface issues of grammar, syntax, and semantics

The grammar of what was said

The thrust of the creditor's testimony was his repeated insistence that he definitely understood the debtor to have said that he was planning to 'go bankrupt'. The important, albeit unusual, practical constraint in this case was that the creditor lacked proficiency in using the correct tense when speaking in English. Some of the ambiguity in the hearer's translation took the form of conflating the present (simple), future (simple) and past (preterit or aorist) tenses; he also had similar difficulty in expressing progressive and modal verbal phrases. He testified, with persistent prodding by his counsel and by the court, for a clearer explanation of what he heard, that 'I go bankrupt' meant to him 'I will go bankrupt', or, more precisely, 'I may go bankrupt'.

In his idiolect, the creditor subjectively understood the debtor's verbal report – 'I go bankrupt' – to mean that the debtor was reporting that either 'I [may] go bankrupt [at some future point in time, but then again I may not]' or 'I [am still considering whether to] go bankrupt, [but then again I may change my plans and once again decide not to go bankrupt].' In no permutation of what the creditor heard was the debtor's verbal report translated as 'I've gone bankrupt [by filing a petition and schedules with the court].'

To resolve the linguistic issues of (i) what was said, (ii) what Dunning, the speaker, intended Kim, the hearer, to understand, and (iii) what the hearer understood the speaker's statement to mean, the court asked a series of questions in order to test the level of the creditor's mastery of correct English grammar. Each of these questions included the term 'bankrupt' or 'bankruptcy' in a verbal phrase in the present, past and future tenses of the modal use of the verb 'to go' as in the verbal phrase 'go bankrupt'.

A well-educated native speaker of English would have had little difficulty drawing the distinctions among the proper expression of the tense, aspect and mood of these variations. To begin with, no native informant would say, 'I go bankrupt.' The closest would be to structure the verbal phrase as a present progressive, 'I am going bankrupt.' It is a parallel construction to 'I am losing my hearing.' A native speaker would not say, 'I lose my hearing.' Of course, the verb stems for 'go' are inflected in the conjugation of the third-person singular of the present tense – 'I go . . . he goes', and the verb stems are irregular in the past and prefect tenses – 'went' and 'gone', respectively. Moreover, the verb phrase for the perfect tense, 'to have gone' is also inflected in the third-person singular of the auxiliary verbal component 'to have' – as in verbal phrase 'he has gone bankrupt'. The next item in mastering this irregular verbal phrase is to resort to the contracted forms, 'I've gone bankrupt', encompassing the third person singular, 'he's gone bankrupt'. As Pinker (2000) explored so vividly in his discussion of the inflection of verb stems in the past tense, all these irregularities have to be memorised. Finally, a native speaker of English could also express the subjunctive mood in its vestigial verbal form of 'I may go bankrupt, but I haven't quite decided what I may do [or when I may do it].'

In this connection, it is worth noting that if Dunning actually used the verb 'to file' in the critical telephone call to Kim, this verb is regular in its inflected suffixes throughout its conjugations. According to Pinker, this verb adheres strictly to the default rule in the generative grammar, and avoids any of the difficulties both native and non-native speakers would have in learning the proper grammatical expressions of the tenses for this verb. But as mentioned earlier, the colloquial expression is to say, 'I've gone bankrupt', and not 'I've filed [for] bankruptcy'. The court had at least a suspicion that

Dunning may have been counselled by his lawyers to testify during the hearing that he used the formal verbal phrase, 'I filed for bankruptcy' rather than the colloquial 'I went bankrupt' or 'I've gone bankrupt' in order to take advantage of counsel's intuitive understanding of the default rule governing the verb 'to file'. If Dunning had, in fact, used the verbal phrase, 'I filed bankruptcy', with its regular inflections in all tenses, then it would make it seem less likely that Kim could have been confused by what was said. Special counsel for Dunning, retained solely for this hearing, made repeated efforts to impugn Kim's credibility on collateral issues of fact.

Mr Kim was totally at a loss to make any of these distinctions in his idiolectal conjugation and inflection of his ungrammatical verbal phrase 'I go bankrupt.' He repeatedly apologised for his inability to articulate these irregular and idiomatic distinctions. He was, nevertheless, quite adamant that he understood exactly what the debtor had verbally reported: it was very definitely not the statement, 'I have gone bankrupt.' It was the statement, 'I [may] go bankrupt, [but then again I may not have to].'

Kim insisted that Dunning did not commit himself to filing for bankruptcy relief during the acknowledged meeting between the parties and their respective counsel a year before Dunning filed his personal chapter 7 petition, nor on any later occasion when Kim pressed Dunning for payment in several later telephone conversations. All Dunning ever said during these conversations was that he was still thinking about the possibility that he might have to file for personal bankruptcy relief. Based upon this series of musings about bankruptcy, the creditor discounted the probability that the debtor would, in fact, 'go bankrupt'. Kim explained that in his experience many businessmen threaten bankruptcy when resisting payment to their creditors, and very often those businessmen never carry out their threats. It is just a way of talking, a kind of 'sales talk', which any experienced creditor is used to ignoring or severely discounting.

The creditor testified that the second telephone call was substantially the same as their prior conversations, and that was the context in which he understood the message, 'I go bankrupt.' Once the court came to understand the semantic significance of the creditor's reference to 'just sales talk', then his explanation of what he understood the debtor to have said to him during the telephone call at issue was a very plausible resolution of the contested meaning within the context of their particular relationship and past linguistic practices.

The comparative proficiency in English between the parties

Dunning was born and educated in the United States. He majored in accounting and finance as a college undergraduate, and later sat for comprehensive written examinations to become licensed by the State of New as a certified public accountant. His proficiency in spoken and written formal English was understandably quite advanced.

On the other hand, Kim was born and educated in South Korea, but he dropped out of high school. He had some limited instruction in English as a second language in high school. At the time of the hearing, Kim was about 69 years old; he had immigrated to the United States 30 years earlier at age 39. In preparing for his naturalisation as a US citizen, Kim had relied upon a cram course to pass the written citizenship examination, but he never attended any other classes to increase his proficiency in English.

Kim's limited proficiency in formal English was quite apparent as soon as he began to testify. Here, as an example, is his part of his narrative answer to a background question 'Why did you call [the debtor] on the date in question':

> Because, I had at that time a difficulty about the financing situation. So, I still had, at that time, good faith in Mr [Dunning] because we were pretty good friend, the two of us . . . When can I have back something of my – the loan I give it to you And it was a very brief and short . . . He say he have a no job and difficulties all over.
>
> So, still I had it in good faith, and well, can we get together, having a dinner, and we can work out enough, in a friendly manner.

(Transcript 63, pp. 22–5; 64, pp. 3–10)

As a close friend, tax and business advisor, and partner in a securities broker-dealership, Dunning was certainly aware of the limits to Kim's proficiency in spoken and written formal (and informal) English.

The very nature of the relationship between the speaker and the hearer justified holding the speaker accountable for the hearer's deficiency in understanding the rules for conjugating irregular verbs in English. This is a closely related aspect of overcoming any disability on the part of the creditor to understand the type of notice of the bankruptcy case in the second telephone call. It stands to reason that, based upon their long personal and professional relationship, the debtor should have developed an acute understanding of the creditor's proficiency in English. This meant that the debtor should have been fully cognizant of the limitations that the hearer had in using tenses, and what steps would have to be taken to make his own intentions clear by using additional words to underscore any important temporal aspect of his intended statement.

Bilingualism – a miscue?

As the court listened to the testimony, it was tempted to search for an explanation to account for the idiolect of the creditor. Perhaps a forensic linguist fluent in Korean could have testified about how time, aspect and mood are expressed in that language. In revising this essay for publication, the author consulted with Ms Hyung-ah Juun, a lecturer at Columbia University who teaches introductory and intermediate Korean. She advised that Korean verbs are inflected, but that the proper grammatical uses of present and past tenses in many common verbal phrases are not directly parallel to those in English. Perhaps this contributed to the creditor's difficulty in drawing the proper distinctions among tense, aspect and mood in irregular English verbs. Upon further reflection, a qualified interpreter would probably not have been sufficient for the limited issues raised in this hearing; the court would probably have to take expert testimony from a forensic linguist with a working knowledge of both Korean grammar as well as basic consumer bankruptcy concepts.

Meaning as use within a specific personal relationship

If the explicit statutory directive to the court under the Bankruptcy Code is to interpret 'notice' as is 'appropriate in the particular circumstance', then it is a minor move to consider the overall relationship between the two persons who were parties to the particular (and now contested) 'actual notice'.

The burgeoning literature in forensic linguistics stresses the importance of taking very careful note of the terms of reference used by each participant in identifying the other, whether it is in the context of an informal conversation, formal testimony in open court, or the peculiarly mixed registers in a custodial interrogation (see for example Shuy, 1998). As an index of the closeness of their personal and professional relationship, Dunning and Kim addressed the other by their first names throughout the hearing, with the practiced comfort of longtime friends. In other words, the nature and extent of the debtor–creditor relationship between these two men – the topic generally of primary interest in a bankruptcy court's determination of a contested matter such as this – was but a single aspect of their multifaceted relationship.

The practice of these two friends and business associates in meeting at a local restaurant to discuss matters of joint concern also resurfaced in the context of the debtor's verbal report that he filed [for] bankruptcy. During the first telephone call, from Kim to Dunning, the two men had quickly agreed to meet for dinner. After Dunning reached his attorney and then called Kim back, the sum and substance of that very short second call talk was, in the words of the debtor:

> I can't meet you for dinner. I was advised by my attorney not to. That I've filed for bankruptcy. And I am not obligated to pay him [sic] the money that I owe him [sic].
>
> (Transcript 39, pp. 7–10)

To clarify the record, the creditor's counsel asked a slight variation of his prior questions of the debtor concerning the second telephone call between the parties, and in this second iteration, the debtor testified:

> When I spoke to him the second time, when I called him back, to cancel the dinner, and he said – he mentioned it to me about the getting his money back, which was ninety thousand and not twenty-five million, he said that he wanted to figure out a way to get the money back. And I said that I filed for bankruptcy. I don't have to pay this money back.
>
> (Transcript 58, p. 19; 59, p. 1)

This second version of the informational content of the second telephone call is very different from the first version, and is indicative of the reason why Dunning deliberately omitted Kim from the original schedule of creditors, and why the actual notice Dunning purported to give Kim was so severely limited in its informal content. For the court had an opportunity to observe Dunning's demeanour and body language when he voiced his barely concealed anger over the sheer magnitude of Kim's claim and Kim's pursuit of recovery from him rather than from their other partner, whom Dunning blamed as the sole person responsible for the conversion of Kim's invested funds. Although why Dunning omitted Kim from his schedule of creditors is not relevant to the contested issue of actual notice, it does contribute to the court's overall assessment of Dunning's credibility of what he purported to say during the crucial telephone call.

Since under the leading appellate cases the bankruptcy court has to consider the full range and complexity of the 'particular circumstances' of the personal and business relationships between the parties in reaching its decision in a case of this type, testimony of this character is directly relevant and very revealing about the nature of these relationships.

The contribution of the philosophy of ordinary language

As Austin (1962) explained, one of the conditions for a speaker's ensuring that his intent is understood by the hearer is the speaker's obligation to 'secure the uptake' of his statement. In other words, it is the speaker's obligation to assure himself that he has, in fact, succeeded in having the hearer clearly understand what the speaker intended him to understand. If the speaker fails in this regard, then he has not 'secured the uptake'. Austin categorised this as a failure to meet the necessary conditions of felicity of a 'perlocutionary speech act'. It should be clear that in this case the debtor's verbal report was intended to serve as a notice of the fact that he had filed a bankruptcy petition. If he had clearly communicated an understanding to the creditor of that fact, then the statement would have functioned as a felicitous (or effective) performative utterance for giving notice of that fact. But by the same token, the speaker's failure to secure the uptake of what was intended to be the giving of actual notice of a pending bankruptcy case surely justifies the conclusion that the notice did not satisfy the conditions of felicity or effectiveness, and, therefore, be found as a matter of mixed issue of fact and law to have been 'inadequate'.

In a variation of 'securing the uptake', Grice (1975) introduced the principle of 'co-operative communication' in discussing the analytical differences between what is said directly and what is implied. If a 'talk exchange' is to succeed, then it has to satisfy each of four derivative maxims – Quality, Quantity, Relation (Relevance) and Manner. When we apply these Gricean maxims to the second telephone call between Dunning and Kim, we have to ask: What is the minimum informational content to giving adequate notice of the pendency of a bankruptcy case? How brief is 'brief' if the speaker is to avoid any ambiguity or obscurity in giving adequate notice?

The Gricean maxims also point in another direction: Grice's model presupposes that the gist of a talk exchange is to convey a statement to the hearer as the speaker intends that statement to be understood. Within the structure of notice of the filing of a bankruptcy case, the principle of cooperation is reduced to an absolute minimum, for the speaker's interest and the hearer's interest are diametrically opposed. The legal structure looks for that minimum, but it fails to appreciate that 'gamesmanship' creates substantial incentives to muffle the message. It also causes us to step back and ask, what is the purpose of the notice, and can that notice ever be adequate if it is limited to the lowest level and quality of information possible? If the notice requirement can be met by the simple statement that 'I have filed a bankruptcy petition', without any more information, then that creates greater incentives for the debtor to obscure the message. One should begin to see why a court would be less receptive to validating that message, when confined to its severest limit. The point of this is that every bankruptcy lawyer and judge knows that the commonest form of notice to an unscheduled creditor is to send that creditor a faxed copy of the petition itself.

Another inference that can be drawn from Grice's four maxims is that the debtor was under an implied duty to take the necessary steps to correct or override any prior use or meaning of the word 'bankruptcy' between them. In a limited sense, these two had adopted a private language or had at least adopted a linguistic stipulation concerning the use and meaning of the 'B-word'. It was, therefore, incumbent upon the creditor to make it very clear that he was no longer using the 'B-word' in the sense he had used it in their joint past – he had to eliminate any continuing reference or implication that the 'B-word' was a possible course of action, a contingent event, or a threat. To overcome that past stipulated use, he had to emphasise that he had gone ahead and finally filed a bankruptcy petition. It would not be sufficient, in light of this prior linguistic stipulation, simply to say, 'I filed for bankruptcy', in the context of a two or three-minute conversation chiefly regarding the cancellation of recent dinner plans.

It was clear to the court that the debtor made no effort, in such a brief phone call, to assure himself that the creditor understood what was being said to him, especially given the prejudice that the creditor would potentially suffer if he did not understand the communication. At a minimum, the long-term relationship between the two men necessarily provided the debtor with a very detailed and comprehensive understanding of the creditor's linguistic proficiency in English, at both the level of (i) business, investment, and tax as well as (ii) personal matters. This necessarily included a complete understanding of how each tended to use particular words, whether considered as legal, financial or business terms, for describing certain events, transactions or matters.

In a pregnant exchange Dunning made during his testimony, without any recognition of its clear implication for the issue before the court, he was asked:

> How were those [prior] conversations any different from the conversation where Mr [Kim] called you on [the date of the second telephone call]?

His answer:

> I specifically told him that I filed bankruptcy, not that I was thinking about it, but that I filed it.
> (Transcript 42: all pp. 5–10)

This answer was the 'clincher'. It forcefully demonstrated that Dunning was aware of his prior use of the word bankruptcy, and of his specific need to override that prior use by emphasising that he was no longer talking about going bankrupt or filing bankruptcy, but that he, in fact, had gone ahead and done it. When this account is compared to what he testified were his exact words, the difference is extraordinarily striking. Had he, in fact, clearly communicated this account rather than what he admitted twice to having actually said, the issue of adequate notice would have probably been decided in his favour. This, of course, begs the question concerning what should be the minimum informational content of the notice given.

The larger implications of determining 'adequate notice': an objective standard?

The state of American jurisprudence is quite unsettled when it comes to the meaning of words. One resurgent camp presses for virtually complete reliance on 'the plain language' of a statute, and by implication this orientation would extend to the meaning of 'ordinary words' used by native speakers of English. This return to 'plain language' and its first cousin, 'objective meaning' will no doubt strike forensic linguists as quaint and wholly contrary to lived experience.

But there is a risk in abandoning a standard of meaning that departs from generally well-understood statements employed in ordinary discourse. If a two-and-a-half-hour hearing had to be held in each case to determine the nature of the past relationship between the parties, their unique linguistic practices and their relative differences in proficiency in speaking English properly, the adverse practical consequence for the expeditious and orderly administration of bankruptcy cases would be self-evident. This problem becomes particularly acute in those districts with expanding immigrant populations. Next, one would have to explore the conditions in which the meaning of basic concepts and expressions used by native informants runs out at the margins of ordinary discourse.

The question then becomes: should a trial court, committed to applying an objective standard to an oral report of an event, take into consideration the linguistic proficiency in ordinary English of a person whose first language is not English? To frame the question in this manner is to introduce the practical difficulties of bilingualism in the context of a formal judicial proceeding. If an objective standard implies that the trial court must consider the meaning and intent of the person who made the oral report at issue, as it would be understood by native speakers of English in ordinary conversations, then the linguistic proficiency of the person to whom this oral report is made would be irrelevant. The person hearing the oral report would be bound by the meaning of those words as reasonably understood by a native English speaker. The only possible dispute would be limited to a determination of whether the debtor unambiguously communicated the operative words in ordinary English. And as noted above, the trial court would also tend to ignore the context in which this oral report was made, including the prior personal relationship between the two people. The rationale for adopting the objective approach is that it avoids having to hold a trial about (i) what the person addressed thought he heard, (ii) the expectations and attitudes that each of the parties brings to the conversation based upon the prior relationship between the parties, and (iii) any significant differences between the two parties in their respective proficiency in spoken English. Alternatively, the trial court could adopt a subjective standard based upon what the debtor's words meant to the person to whom they were addressed.

The court in this case, however, adopted the subjective approach without any objection from the debtor, on the implicit premise that such an approach was consistent with the purpose of the statutory provision at issue requiring the court to determine whether the creditor received 'notice or actual knowledge' of the debtor's bankruptcy filing. It may also have reflected the personal preference of the court for determining a disputed meaning within the context of the relationship between the parties. At some point the court may have conflated its concern for developing a more comprehensive, empirical and sophisticated approach to determining the meaning of the specific oral report with its concern over the inherent unfairness of the 'situation'. Perhaps this concern with fairness should not have played any part in deciding which standard the court should adopt in determining the contested meaning of an oral report. In principle, the standard arguably should be chosen on wholly *a priori* grounds, and be completely divorced from any consideration of the transactional facts or relationships between the parties.

Conclusion

By identifying many of these issues of forensic linguistics, the author does not mean to suggest that these questions were adequately introduced or even addressed during the hearing, but after reading the transcript several times over, these are the kinds of issues that on reflection were raised by this hearing. These questions all seem to point in the same direction: how should the court go about determining contested issues of meaning when the rights of the adverse parties go to the very heart of a bankruptcy case?

Forensic linguistics, defined comprehensively to include the analytical insights of the philosophy of ordinary language, appears to this author to provide a framework for unpacking the deeper issues of semantics and pragmatics now concealed in the unexamined concept of adequate notice under the Bankruptcy Code. To summarise, the proposition is that the substance of the notice given – the debtor filed a bankruptcy case – has to be completely free from any ambiguity.

When the notice is given in a verbal report to the creditor or the creditor's authorised agent, that illocutionary act – the reporting of the underlying proposition – must comply with the rules that govern 'talk exchanges'. The context in which notice of this type is given must generally be considered by the court, for if the parties have had a long and complex personal and business relationship, which gave rise to the claim itself, then the debtor (or his or her agent) must 'secure the uptake' of what the speaker intends the hearer to understand by specifically countering any prior usage of the concept of bankruptcy and by considering the hearer's proficiency in English if that would reasonably impair the speaker's securing of the uptake of his communication. In assessing the adequacy of the notice within the specific context of the communication, the court will also have to give sufficient weight to the timing of the notice, and decide whether the true purpose of giving notice was to inform the hearer of the salient fact of the pendency of the speaker's pending case with sufficient time for the hearer to review his or her remedies with counsel and to file a dischargeability complaint within the deadline or to file a timely motion to extend that deadline, or whether the timing of the notice and the manner in which it was given evidences gamesmanship on the part of the debtor to defeat the creditor's timely exercise of her remedies.

This also suggests that forensic linguists could make a very valuable contribution to a fairer and more humane administration of bankruptcy cases if they began to undertake research projects in highly structured institutional settings such as a bankruptcy court. Researchers should note that bankruptcy courts are courts of record, which means that all hearings and other proceedings are recorded either by a court stenographer or by electronic recording equipment. A majority of the urbanised districts have shifted to electronic recordings, and the tapes of these hearings are very inexpensive to obtain. It is the hope of the author that researchers in forensic linguistics will be sufficiently intrigued by the issues to consider undertaking research on such projects.

Notes

1 The author serves as a US Bankruptcy Judge for the Eastern District of New York. He also holds adjunct academic appointments teaching ethics and philosophy of law at Hofstra University, and bankruptcy law at Touro Law School. He wishes to thank Lawrence Solan, Anthony Dardis and Christopher Chow for their critical input to this chapter.

2 The author presided over the non-jury hearing that is the subject of this chapter. The names of the parties have been changed. The case number is 00–83712–288 (Bankr. EDNY). A complete stenographic transcript of the hearing in on file as docket number 25. See also, re Linzer 264 BR 704 (Bankr. EDNY, 2001) (Bernstein, Bankruptcy J.) on a related matter of written notice to the creditor's lawyer raised during the same hearing, but later decided upon briefs without further hearing.

References

Austin, J. L. (1962) *How to Do Things with Words*. New York and Oxford: Oxford University Press.

Grice, H. P. (1975) 'Logic and Conversation', in P. Cole and J. Morgan (eds), *Syntax and Semantics 3: Speech Acts*. New York: Academic Press, pp. 41–58.

Pinker, S. (2000) *Words and Rules*. New York: Basic Books.

Shuy, R. (1998) *The Language of Confession, Interrogation, and Deception*. London: Sage.

14

'If you were Standing in Marks and Spencers': Narrativisation and Comprehension in the English Summing-up

Chris Heffer

Directing the jury

> We were the ultimate fact-finders in this case. The majesty of the law was about to abdicate and cede the throne to the man on the Clapham omnibus. It was a mad notion, an awesome act of faith in the reasonableness of the common man and woman. Now there was only the judge to give us a last chance to make sense of it all and avoid some catastrophic blunder.
>
> (Grove, 1998, pp. 173–4)

The validity of trial by jury is predicated upon the degree to which jurors understand and perform their task as reasonable men and women. Stories abound, though, in both folklore and lawyer-lore, of juries bringing in 'wrongful' verdicts by failing to understand the issues in a case (Adler, 1994). These 'catastrophic blunders' then provide one of the main arsenals for concerted attacks on the jury system itself (Findlay and Duff, 1988). In this context, the judge's instructions to the jury immediately prior to deliberation are not only vital to the successful outcome of the deliberation process, but ultimately to the very defence of trial by jury. Yet, despite their importance, since Charrow and Charrow's (1979) seminal paper on jury *in*comprehension, numerous studies from within a variety of disciplines have confirmed that a majority of jurors in the United States are unable to understand most standard jury instructions (Dumas, 2000a).

Owing primarily to the Draconian Contempt of Court Act 1981, we are sadly lacking similar empirical research on British juries. Nor is it wise to extrapolate from the US studies, since both the circumstances of trial by jury and the linguistic context in which the instructions are delivered are very different in Britain. In the legal jurisdiction of England and Wales, unlike in the USA, civil cases are very rarely tried by jury and most criminal cases go before lay magistrates. Trial by jury takes place in 'Crown' Courts and is confined primarily to serious criminal cases. Furthermore, peremptory challenges to jurors, whereby prospective jury members are rejected without providing a reason, were abolished in 1986, and it is more difficult than in the States to be excluded from jury duty. All this means that both the average juror and the average instruction are likely to be different.

Regarding the context of instruction, the English judge's directions on law occur as part of his *summing-up* of the case. This meaning of 'summing-up' is not recorded in *Black's Law Dictionary* (Garner, 1999) and is often confused with the *jury summation*, or closing argument, of American lawyers. In Crown Court trials, the summing-up occurs *after* the *closing speeches* by prosecution and defence *barristers* and immediately before the jury retires to deliberate. The judge sums up the case to the jury not only by directing them on the substantive law and a number of evidential points but also by summarising the key evidence. The *directions on law* should help jurors to apply the relevant law to the facts, as in the following from my data:

> The mere fact that a defendant tells a lie is not in itself evidence of guilt. A defendant may lie for many reasons, for example to conceal some disgraceful conduct short of the offence, or out of panic or out of confusion . . . It is only if you are sure that he did not lie for an innocent reason that his lies can be regarded by you as supporting the prosecution case.
>
> (Summing-up 00)

The *summary of the evidence* should then assist them in deciding precisely what the relevant facts *are* by separating the evidential wheat from the chaff, the agreed from the disputed:

> What he says, in effect, is that he had a grievance against Mr Butcher[1] and at one o'clock in the morning he was feeling pissed off and got wound-up, and that when he's pissed off he does odd things, and therefore he walked over to the Crossways premises and stole the goods and the car. The prosecution say in the main that is true. The defence say no, it is not true for reasons that I shall remind you. The defendant says although he said those words – he does not dispute that the tape is accurate – he says he did not tell the truth on the tape but he lied.
>
> (Summing-up 94)

Most of the limited research on the English summing-up has focused on the appropriateness of this second function, and various attempts have been made to show linguistic bias in judges' summaries through semiotics (Jackson, 1995), corpus linguistics (Stubbs, 1995) and classical rhetoric (Robertshaw, 1998). In this chapter I restrict my focus to the first, *directing* function, which in most cases precedes the summarising (though a few judges interweave the two). Nevertheless, it is essential to bear in mind that the directions are part of a much larger discursive speech genre and that the summary function almost certainly influences the approach to the directions themselves.

English judges are provided with a set of *Specimen Directions* (JSB, 1999) which cover key areas of criminal and evidential law. They are similar to US 'pattern instructions' (Dumas, 2000b) insofar as they consist of a number of short texts on legal matters written to be read out to a jury. However, while

US instructions are designed to be delivered more or less verbatim, the English directions, as the Lord Chief Justice insists in his Foreword, are not meant to be used 'mechanistically': 'They are an invaluable tool – but must be a servant, not a master' (JSB, 1999). This flexible approach is made possible by the relatively lenient stance taken by the Court of Appeal, which is 'disinclined to interfere with a trial judge's exercise of his discretion' (*R* v. *Everett* 1995). Though inevitably mindful of the higher tribunal, the judge is less likely to feel constrained to use the exact words of either appellate decisions or the specimen directions.

Essentially this chapter explores the effect of this comparative discoursal freedom on the linguistic choices made by English judges during the direction phase of their summings-up, and considers the possible effect these choices might have on jury comprehension. The study is based on a corpus of 100 official transcripts of summings-up[2] amounting to just under one million words. The texts were produced by 60 judges presiding over a wide range of criminal cases in 11 Crown Courts in East Anglia over the period 1996–98.

The burden of proof

In considering judges' directions, we can pinpoint two sources of potential liberation from the shackles of statutory language inhibiting jury comprehension: the wording of the *specimens* and the judges' adaptations of those specimens in their own *versions*. We shall briefly consider the first of these sources and then concentrate on the second. Before doing so, though, we need to temporarily narrow our focus. The *direction* phases of the summings-up are extremely heterogeneous, ranging from 1000 to 14000 words and covering a wide selection of the 70 sections of the *Specimen Directions*. To ensure some degree of systematicity, we need to restrict ourselves to just one of these sections.

The obligatory but felicitous choice falls on the *proof* directions (Figure 14.1). Not only are these directions vital to the decision-making process, but since failure by the judge to give them, or giving them poorly, will almost certainly result in appeal, they are the only directions for which we have a full set of 100 versions. The specimen proof directions are the latest in a long history of attempts to avoid the twin pitfalls of legal misrepresentation and jury incomprehension. The current directions are written in relatively plain English: the sentences are short with no relative clauses or agentless passives and comparatively few subordinate clauses. Moreover, no mention is made of the troublesome legal concepts of 'presumption of innocence' or 'reasonable doubt' (Solan, 1999; Dumas, this volume), no attempt is made to define sureness, while some effort is made to engage with the jury through direct address and a rhetorical question. The implication seems to be that the judiciary are willing to rely to a great extent on the jurors' 'common sense'

Burden of proof

In this case the prosecution must prove that the defendant is guilty. He does not have to prove his innocence. In a criminal trial the burden of proving the defendant's guilt is always (see Note 1) on the prosecution.

Standard of proof

How does the prosecution succeed in proving the defendant's guilt? The answer is – by making you sure of it. Nothing less than that will do. If after considering all the evidence you are sure that the defendant is guilty, you must return a verdict of 'Guilty'. If you are not sure, your verdict must be 'Not Guilty'.

Figure 14.1 Specimen proof directions
Source: (JSB, 1999[3])

and 'knowledge of the world', the two qualities judges most frequently appeal to in their summings-up. At the same time, the third sentence of the 'burden of proof' seems to be a legal reformulation of the previous two:

In a criminal trial the burden of proving . . .

And the fourth sentence of the 'standard of proof' appears to return to more legal syntax:

If after considering all the evidence . . .

The net result is a mixed-genre text which provides a good starting point for an investigation of the judge's own versions of the specimens. The methodological problem posed at this point is how to explain the resulting variation in a meaningful fashion.

In a larger study currently in progress, I argue that lawyers before juries might be seen as divided selves torn between the need to conform to the *Weltanschauung* of the law on the one hand, and the necessity to communicate with lay people unversed in that world-view on the other. This tension can be described very effectively using Bruner's distinction between *paradigmatic* and *narrative* modes of thought (1986, 1990). In brief, the paradigmatic mode is the mode of theory, of striving for ideal logical systems of description and explanation, while the narrative mode is the mode of daily life, of striving to understand the actions and intentions of humans situated in place and time. The narrative mode develops earlier in children and dominates everyday adult reasoning, while the paradigmatic mode tends to be learnt at school and underlies the type of logico-scientific reasoning found in most academic disciplines, including the law. The prototypical textual manifestations of

Table 14.1   Key tendencies of the narrative and paradigmatic modes

Narrative mode	Paradigmatic mode
Fundamentally concerned with *human* or human-like *action* and *intention*	Fundamentally concerned with *categorisation* and *conceptualisation*
Aims for *lifelikeness*	Aims for *truth*
Applies to *particular, time-bound* cases	Applies to *universal, timeless* cases
Appeals to *shared experience*	Appeals to *universal logic*
Retrospective – relies on past experience	*Prospective* – predicts possible worlds
Personal	*Impersonal*
Evaluative	*Non-evaluative*
Dialogic	*Monologic*
Prefers *modal probability*	Prefers *logical necessity*
Tends to *oral* mode	Tends to *written* mode
Prefers *temporal* sequencing	Prefers *logical* sequencing

the two cognitive modes are the well-formed logical argument and the well-made story, but the modes can be manifested to a greater or lesser extent in *all* textual production. Indeed, Bruner argues that even judicial opinions are as much influenced by the narrative mode as by legal theory (Amsterdam and Bruner, 2000). Some of the key tendencies and contrasts of the two modes are summarised in Table 14.1.

Drawing primarily on functional grammar (Halliday, 1994) and register analysis (Biber, 1988), I suggest it is possible to associate specific linguistic forms and functions with these general cognitive tendencies, which in turn permits some degree of systematic comparison between texts along this mental divide.

Categorising and narrativising language

In this section I list a number of linguistic categories indicating a paradigmatic or narrative tendency and briefly compare their use in the proof specimens and judges' versions. Since the texts are to be seen as part of an ongoing tension rather than as static products, I describe the categories of features as 'categorising' (the principal paradigmatic tendency) and 'narrativising'. Categorising features are <u>underlined</u> while narrativising features are *italicised*. The categories are presented according to three basic kinds of meaning, or metafunctions, running throughout language: our construal of *experience*, our enactment of *interpersonal* relationships, and the creation of coherence in *text* (Halliday, 1994).

Experiential features

The law is concerned with universally applicable abstract categories, while a trial involves a specific case occurring at a specific time and place with human participants acting on, thinking about and communicating things. Features stressing the former will be categorising, those stressing the latter narrativising. Consider a fairly 'neutral' clause from the specimens:

... the prosecution must prove that the defendant is guilty

Now compare this with a markedly narrativised version from my data:

In this case the prosecution must *prove* that *Mr Singh and Mr Brown* are guilty

(Summing-up 47)

The prosecution is now identifiable as the team of lawyers *in this case*, who become the human agents of the material process *prove*, while the defendants assume human individuality by being named. This might be contrasted with a thoroughly categorising version, based very closely on the specimens:

In a criminal trial, the burden of proving a defendant's guilt is always on the prosecution

(Summing-up 77)

Here the circumstances are generalised to all criminal trials (In a). The participants are not only represented as abstract legal categories (a defendant; the prosecution), but are also removed from the principal action of the clause by being embedded in prepositional phrases (of proving...; on the...). Instead, the subject becomes the abstract burden while the predicator *is* describes an abstract relation. The trial itself is classified legally as criminal, the burden is subcategorised by the defining 'of' qualifier (of proving...) and the defendant becomes no more than a grammatical determiner of guilt. Effectively the participants and circumstances are depersonalised and decontextualised in order to assume universal application. Table 14.2 indicates *narrativising* and categorising experiential features, along with examples of each found in the judges' versions.

With respect to the specimens, the judges' versions contained both more narrativising *and* more categorising features. With regard to narrativising features, 22 per cent of the texts named the defendants or barristers in the case (category 1 above), while just over half referred deictically to *this case* and *this defendant* (2). Strikingly, there were over 100 occurrences of the verbs *say* or *tell* in the data (3) despite there being no reference to verbal acts in the specimens. These frequently occur at the beginning of the directions to refer back to the closing speeches and/or to introduce what the judge has to say:

You have been told already but *I have to say* it again ...

(Summing-up 19)

Table 14.2   Experiential features in proof directions (*n* = 100)

Feature categories	Corpus examples
Nar. 1 Naming	They, *Mr. Kabil* and *Mr. Hudar*, do not have to prove that they are innocent (S82)
2 Deictic reference to participants and circumstances	... the Crown brings *this case* against *this defendant* (S28)
3 Human agent + material/mental/ verbal process	... *she says*, and *she knows*, and it is the law ... (S07)
4 Deictic or defined reference to time or place	... you have been told it at least four times *already* ... (S51)
5 Past tense	You have got to be sure about what *happened* ... (S63)
6 Perfect or progressive aspect	The prosecution, you *have heard*, *have brought* this case ... (S98)
Cat. 7 Abstract person category	... no burden whatsoever upon a defendant ... (S36)
8 Embedding of agent, e.g. in adjunct	The burden of proof remains upon the prosecution throughout (S68)
9 Agentless passives	If you are left in any reasonable doubt, then the defendant is entitled to be acquitted (S01)
10 Abstract subject + relational process	... so the burden is on the crown (S29)
11 Legal 'Classifiers' (Halliday, 1994, p. 184)	This is a criminal trial, of course (S76)
12 Double-headed NPs (Sinclair, 1991, p. 90)	The burden of proof lies upon the prosecution (S13)
13 Genitives with abstract noun head	It is for them to establish the defendant's guilt (S35)
14 Defining 'of' qualifiers	The burden of proving the guilt or otherwise of the defendant (S72)
15 Defining relative clauses	... prove the primary facts which make up the offence which they charge against him (S85)
16 Abstract nominalisations	... referred to as the presumption of innocence (S02)
17 Generalisation of circumstances	In a criminal case ... (S40)

Note: S = Summing-up.

Reference to the trial events explains the presence of the perfect aspect (6) in half of the texts and the past tense (5) in 19 per cent of them. Many of the judges, then, show a desire to situate this formal instruction in the immediate context of the particular trial.

At the same time, several paradigmatic features excluded from the specimens reappear in the judges' versions. Defining relative clauses (15) occur 66 times, while 63 per cent of the texts use at least one agentless passive (9). Although some versions were clearly more paradigmatic than the specimens, the occurrence of 'excluded' categorising features is not explicable solely in these terms. For example, while the legally classifying <u>reasonable doubt</u> is used in 27 per cent of the versions, in many cases it has not so much a classificatory and definitional purpose (a paradigmatic concern), as a rhetorical one (a narrative concern):

> The phrase <u>beyond reasonable doubt</u>, it has been used I think in this trial, is part of the language and you will be familiar with it. Think of it like that if you want to, it comes to the same thing.
> (Summing-up 69)

Interpersonal features

The narrative mode is strongly interpersonal in nature. This is expressed primarily through features which engage the jury in the discourse and ones indicating the speaker's evaluation of the content. Compare the following two versions of the standard of proof:

> The prosecution must make *you* sure in relation to *these* counts.
> (Summing-up 52)

> *How does the prosecution prove its case, you may ask. Well, members of the jury,* that is *quite simple* – by making *you* sure of it; *nothing* less will do.
> (Summing-up 30)

In S52 the standard is set down as a statement of law, albeit one which is related to the juror (*you*) and the particular trial (*these* counts). In contrast, S30 presents the situation dialogically. A rhetorical question (*How does...*) becomes a probable question in the juror's mind (*you may ask*). An interpersonal discourse marker (*well*) is then followed by a vocative (*members of the jury*) and an appraisal of the answer (*simple*) which is intensified (*quite*). It is only then that the judge provides the informational response to the putative question. The text, then, is personal, dialogic and clearly evaluative and is designed more to persuade than inform. These and other interpersonal features are indicated in Table 14.3.

Although a number of narrativising features are included in the specimens (for example, *you, nothing*), the richness of features in the judges' versions was striking. *I* can be found in 62 per cent, and *we* in 31 per cent of the texts (1). A quarter of the judges go one step further than rhetorical questions by projecting this question on to the speech or thought of the jurors (21). Discourse markers *now* (19 per cent of texts) and *well* (10 per cent) are surprisingly common (22), as are vocatives (19) (22 per cent). Perhaps most remarkable for an essentially paradigmatic genre is the degree of evaluation: not only intensifiers such as *quite* and the synthetic negative *nothing* (23),

Table 14.3 Interpersonal features in proof directions (*n* = 100)

Feature category		Corpus examples
Nar. 18	1st and 2nd person pronouns	The first thing *I* must tell *you* which *I* am sure *you* know... (S60)
19	Vocatives	He does not, *members of the jury*, have to... (S80)
20	Rhetorical questions (and tags)	*What about the law?* (S79)... not proved, *is it?* (S41)
21	Projection of speech and thought	... you must be able to *say to yourselves, 'We are sure that he is guilty'* (S86)
22	Discourse markers	*Well now*, let us come to... (S02)
23	Intensification: quantifiers/ superlatives; synthetic negation; repetition	That is *not very good enough*; you *certainly* do not... *nothing* less will do (S26)
24	Authorial comment in disjuncts	*Simply put, I suppose,* members of the jury, suspicion is never ever enough (S47)
25	Lexical appraisal (Martin, 2000)	They are *fundamental*. They are *important* (S08)
26	Subjective modalities	... one *could* have a situation where you *may* not believe certain things... (S62)
Cat. 27	External obligation	If you are not sure, then you <u>must</u> acquit (S67)
28	Modal certainty	... proving the defendant's guilt is <u>always</u> on the prosecution (S95)

but also direct authorial comment (24) (25 per cent) and even explicit lexical appraisal, especially when indicating the *fundamental importance* (20 per cent) of the proof directions (25). Narrative mode modalities are presented as subjective judgements (26). On the other hand, the paradigmatic mode presents obligations (27) and certainties (28) as being necessitated by the objective categories of the law (the prosecution *must always*). Overall, the range and frequency of interpersonal narrative mode features in the judges' proof directions was considerable.

Textual and other features

If the development of a prototypical narrative mode text might be typified as *and then*, that of a paradigmatic mode text is more typically *if... then*. The *specimens* present an archetypal binary paradigm:

If you are sure	[THEN]	guilty
If you are not sure	[THEN]	not guilty

Table 14.4 Textual and other features in proof directions (*n* = 100)

Feature category		Corpus examples
Nar.	29 Temporal succession	I *now* turn to the most important aspect... (S06)
	30 Lexical simplification	... the burden – that is to say the *job* of... (S14)
	31 Truncated clauses	The answer is – *by making you sure of it* (S49)
	32 Explicit paraphrase	*That means the same thing as* making you sure (S61)
	33 Exemplification	... *if you think about it in this life there is*... (S22)
Cat.	34 Conditional subordinators	However, if you are not sure, if you are less than sure... (S71)
	35 Other logical connectors	... it is their duty, therefore, to prove it (S32)
	36 Binomials	You do not convict unless and until you are sure of guilt (S33)
	37 Degree-defining adverbs	You must be satisfied so that you are sure... (S73)
	38 Polarity paradigm structures	If you are sure convict, if you are not sure acquit (S64)
	39 Negative non-finite clauses and phrases	It is not for him to prove that he is not guilty (S75)
	40 Qualification of subordinate structures	If, having considered all the evidence... (S46)

Two logical relations are made explicit here: the syntagmatic relation of condition–consequence signalled by conditional subordinators like *if* and the paradigmatic relation of polarity (*sure–not sure*). These types of logical relations dominate the categorising features in Table 14.4.

The directions are ultimately a paradigmatic mode genre, so it is not surprising to find only four cases of temporal succession (29) and hundreds of cases of logical relations. As in the specimens, *if* occurs an average of twice per text. However, the judges also introduce a number of other conditional subordinators (34) typical of written legal texts, including *before* (you can convict) and *unless* (you are satisfied). What is interesting about these choices is that they tend to be conceptually negative. While expressing something which does not *happen* is typically evaluative in the narrative mode (Labov, 1972), expressing things which do not *meet criteria* is typically paradigmatic. The need to meet definitional criteria explains not only these negative constructions (38–39), but also various forms of qualification (37, 40) and even binomial constructions (36). Many of these structures are evident in the following marked example:

> ... on this indictment you <u>cannot and must not</u> convict <u>any one or more</u> of these defendants of any count on this indictment <u>unless</u> <u>in relation to</u> that defendant and that count you are sure

(Summing-up 42)

As for narrative mode textual features, paraphrase is explicitly signalled at least once in almost a quarter of the texts (32), and this can lead to lexical simplification, as in *job* for 'burden' (30). Exemplification (33) is not as common as in many of the other types of direction, but there are some cases of truncated clauses typical of oral grammar (31).

Overall, this brief analysis of linguistic features in the proof directions suggests a substantial narrativising tendency, even though the specimens have already been considerably narrativised with respect to statutory language. - Despite the monologic format of the genre, it would appear that many of the judges wish to involve the jurors dialogically in the instruction process.

Categorising and narrativising judges

Having linked linguistic features with functional characteristics of the two modes, we can now investigate the extent to which judges lean towards narrativisation or categorisation. The texts were manually analysed for the 40 feature categories (20 for each mode) and scores assigned to each. Given their frequency, personal pronouns scored half a point, but otherwise no attempt was made to weight the features and all scored one point. This applies equally to single word features like *well* and to multi-word elements like subordination structures. Given the very considerable range in text length, the resulting values were then converted into simple percentages to show the relative proportion of marked categorising and narrativising features in each text. Figure 14.2 shows an analysis of the specimen directions with numbered cross-references to the feature categories in Tables 14.3–14.4 above.

In this *case* [2] the prosecution <u>must</u> [27] *prove* [3] that the defendant is guilty. He does not have to *prove* [3] his innocence. <u>In a</u> [17] <u>criminal</u> [11] trial the burden <u>of proving</u> [14] the <u>defendant's guilt</u> [13] <u>is</u> [10] <u>always</u> [28]...<u>on the prosecution</u> [8]. *How does* [20] the prosecution succeed in proving <u>the defendant's guilt</u> [13]? The answer is – by *making* [31] *you* [18] sure of it. *Nothing* [23] less than that *will do* [30]. If [34] <u>after considering</u> [40] all the evidence *you* [18] are sure that the defendant is guilty, *you* [18] <u>must</u> [27] *return* [3] verdict of 'Guilty' [14]. <u>If</u> [34] *you* [18] are <u>not sure</u> [38], *your* [18] verdict <u>must</u> [27] <u>be</u> [10] 'Not Guilty'.

(Cat = 17 (62%); Narr = 10.5 (38%))

Figure 14.2   Analysis of the specimen proof directions

Such a presentation does not do justice to the analysis since some features (for example, agent + material process (3) or polarity paradigms (38)) extend in scope beyond the marked items. Nevertheless, it provides some idea of the coverage of the features and how the percentages were achieved. As always when applying linguistic categories, and particularly functional ones, there were a number of cases where the analysis was not straightforward. It would also be foolish not to recognise a considerable degree of subjectivity involved in the assignments. However, a high degree of error can be accommodated without seriously affecting the general patterns revealed.

The results of the analysis of the 100 proof directions enable us to divide the texts into three broad discourse tendencies, presented in Table 14.5.[4]

Table 14.5 Mode tendencies of proof directions (*n* = 100)

Tendency	No. of texts	Full-time judges (% of total)	Part-time judges (% of total)
Categorising (more than 55% categorising features)	28	22 (32%)	6 (19%)
Mixed (46–54% categorising or narrativising)	33	21 (31%)	12 (37%)
Narrativising (more than 55% narrativising features)	39	25 (37%)	14 (44%)

The results seem to confirm the high degree of narrativisation suggested by the initial analysis. Not only does the narrativising group account for almost 40 per cent of texts, but over three-quarters of the texts show a greater degree of narrativisation than the specimen directions, which fell into the categorising group at 62 per cent. As for correlations with judge type, though the figures are by no means conclusive, the full-time *circuit* and *high-court* judges seem to show a greater tendency to categorising than the part-time judges (*Recorders* and *Assistant Recorders*). Only seven of the summings-up in the corpus are given by women (a reflection of the inadequate representation of women on Crown Court benches), yet interestingly three of those rank in the top eight narrativising texts.

The degree of narrativisation found in the judges' directions can even be seen in texts which are otherwise strongly categorising:

> The prosecution *bring these charges* against Mrs. *Buckley* and before she can be convicted of any of *these offences* with which she is charged, the prosecution needs to satisfy *you* upon the evidence so that *you* are sure of her guilt. If *you* are less than sure, if *you* are left in what *you* will

have heard I am sure time and again referred to as reasonable doubt, if *you* are left in any reasonable doubt, then the defendant is entitled to be acquitted. It is sometimes said that if *you* are left in no reasonable doubt then *you* will be sure about the matter and *I hope* that expresses *precisely* the degree of sure, sureness that is required of a jury before a defendant can be convicted. If *you* are not sure, if *you* are in that reasonable doubt, acquit the defendant of those counts in respect of which *you* have that doubt.

(Summing-up 01)
(Cat.=31(65%); Narr.=16.5(35%))

That this is so can be seen by contrasting this text with the existing Californian pattern instruction on proof (Tiersma, 2000):

A defendant in a criminal action is presumed to be innocent until the contrary is proved, and in case of a reasonable doubt whether [his][her] guilt is satisfactorily shown, [he][she] is entitled to a verdict of not guilty. This presumption places upon the People the burden of proving [him][her] guilty beyond a reasonable doubt. Reasonable doubt is defined as follows: It is not a *mere* possible doubt; because everything relating to human affairs is open to some possible or imaginary doubt. It is that state of the case which, after the entire comparison and consideration of all the evidence, leaves the minds of the jurors in that condition that they cannot say they feel an abiding conviction of the truth of the charge.

(Cat. = 33(97%); Narr. = 1(3%))

None of the English texts are over 70 per cent categorising, so this text, at 97 per cent, is in a category apart. Though the English judge in (S01) above clearly has a predilection for categorising features, he nevertheless engages with the jury (*you*), makes specific reference to the context (*these charges*; *Mrs Buckley*) and expresses his perspective (*I am sure*; *I hope*). The Californian instruction, on the other hand, is unremittingly impersonal and abstract. The contrast with a narrativising example from my data is arresting:

Also *bear in mind, members of the jury*, when *you* do that consideration, that the prosecution must *prove* the defendant is guilty. He does not *have to prove* anything. *How do* they *succeed* in doing that? *Well*, that is *quite simple. You have already heard* it, but *I emphasise* it because it is of *fundamental importance*. And that is that they must *make you* sure he is guilty. *Nothing* less *will do*. It is not enough that, *'Oh, we think he may have acted badly'*, or *'I suppose he did it'*. That is *just* not enough. *You* must be sure of his guilt before *you* can convict in respect of any of *these* counts.

(Summing-up 54)
(Cat. = 5(14%); Narr. = 32(86%))

The more narrativising the directions are, the more they seem to depend for their effect on oral performance. The importance of delivery is now being stressed by US researchers (Dumas, 2000a), but it is essential to realise that the type of language used is inextricably linked with the oral/written mode distinction. It is as difficult to imagine the Californian text being communicated orally in an effective way as it would be to find the English woman judge's direction above written up in an appeal ruling.

Knowledge, belief and comprehension

The *Specimen Directions* by no means provide guidance to the judge on conveying all aspects of criminal law; most charges on a given indictment have to be explained without help, and in some cases the judges struggle to translate statutory into lay language. Others appear adept at the task. Here we shall consider one judge's attempt to bridge the gap between the paradigmatic mode of the law and the narrative mode of everyday life.

The female Recorder is explaining the offence of handling stolen goods. She begins with reference to the indictment, of which the jury have a written copy:

> *Let me just move on then* to the offence of handling, because *you need to consider* the definition of that. That is *a bit more complicated* and *I will go through rather more slowly with you.* (I have to find the right page.) A person handles stolen goods if otherwise than in the course of stealing, knowing or believing them to be stolen, he dishonestly receives them. *Now*, that is the offence which is handling *here.*
>
> (Summing-up 14)

Although preceded by a narrativising prefacing structure, the charge itself is highly legal and paradigmatic. The judge then tries to interpret this law to the jury through progressively narrativising techniques. First she paraphrases the charge in terms of the jury's decision-making task:

> What *you* would have to be satisfied *in this case . . . was* that the defendant *received* them, *took* them into his control *as it were.* And that at the time that he *took* them into his control (he *received* them) he *knew* they were stolen or *believed* they were stolen.
>
> (Summing-up 14)

Then she begins an explicit paraphrase of a potentially confusing distinction:

> *You* can appreciate the difference between knowledge and belief. When it comes to knowledge *of course that means* you have direct knowledge of the actual theft and therefore for that reason you *know* they are stolen.

Finally she introduces two highly narrativised examples:

> If for example *you were standing in Marks and Spencers and you watched a shoplifter steal and then ten minutes later you took the goods from the shoplifter* you would receive them knowing that they were stolen. If on the other hand *you were* not *in Marks and Spencers when the shoplifters stole that elegant hat and you were outside in The Crown and Robe and somebody came up to you and said, 'Look what I have just nicked from Marks and Spencers',* you do not have direct knowledge of it but you have the belief based on what you have been told. So that is the distinction *if I can put it that way.*
>
> (Summing-up 14)

There is no *logical* or *legal* need for the judge to mention a particular department store, the length of time that passes, the elegance of the hat, the local pub or what the shoplifter said. Yet the narrative mode can convey far more than the simple denotation of the words used. Marks and Spencers, for example, is no mere shop but a British institution (albeit a faltering one) while local pubs are central to British social life. Simply put, by particularising in this manner, the judge is both showing solidarity with the jurors and making the explanations of law more relevant to their shared everyday experience. This example shows a potentially functional marriage of our cognitive 'odd couple'. The overall structure is paradigmatic, as it must be given the nature of the direction, but the judge tries to breathe back life into the law through careful use of narrativising features.

There is, however, a sting in the tail of this account of a marriage of modes, for there is a very fine line between knowledge and belief. While our Recorder in S14 above suggests that even if the thief makes a self-declaration the handler still only has 'belief', the Assistant Recorder in S71 seems to have a more catholic view of knowledge:

> Or you may be said to **know** it if you are told that they are stolen by somebody who has got first hand knowledge, somebody who is themself a thief or has seen it being stolen himself.
>
> (Summing-up 71) (emphasis added)

Clearly one judge's *knowledge* is another judge's *belief* and in this judicial discrepancy lies a danger in judicial discretion.

Directing the judge

How, then, should judges be directed to instruct juries? The answer from this study would appear to be 'not too strictly'. For it seems that a combination of linguistic tolerance on the part of the Appeal courts, specimen directions written in relatively plain language and the encouragement of linguistic discretion leads to actual directions which are far more 'listener-friendly' than equivalent US directions. This conclusion, though, needs to be qualified in at least two ways. Firstly it holds primarily for the proof directions. Many of the other lesser-used directions are still highly categorical both in the specimen and in the judges' actual texts, perhaps confirming that the guidance given by the specimen directions is a crucial ingredient in the communicative cocktail. Secondly, the means of characterising text developed here is both in its methodological infancy and highly subjective in many ways.

If the conclusion *is* a valid one, it suggests that narrativisation in broad Brunerian terms might be a significant factor in aiding lay comprehension of directions which are essentially paradigmatic in nature. Several of the strongly categorising features identified here, such as embeddings, nominalisations and some types of passive, have been frequently recognised as impediments to comprehension (Tiersma, 1999). On the other hand, some of the suggestions made by US researchers to improve comprehension of pattern jury instructions – such as 'road maps', paraphrase, examples and brief narratives (Dumas, 2000b) – are already being implemented by many English judges as a natural result of following the narrative mode. The sole existing survey of English jurors (Zander and Henderson, 1993) is encouraging in this respect. Of the 7300 respondents to the jury questionnaire, only 6.4 per cent claimed to find the judges' directions on law 'fairly' or 'very' difficult (1993, p. 216), compared to 9 per cent who found the evidence itself difficult to understand (1993, p. 206) and 35 per cent who found it difficult to remember the evidence in trials of more than one week (p. 209).[5] On the face of it, these results would seem to suggest that English judges are performing their task reasonably well, though, as Jackson (1995, p. 427) cautions, 'What the judge tells the jury may indeed be understood, but understood in a different sense from that intended'. In any case, what is desperately needed is a relaxation of the Contempt of Court laws to allow more jury research into this issue.

Assuming that there *is* a connection between narrativisation and improved comprehension, we must ask whether the benefits which would appear to accrue from a more communicative context of instruction outweigh the inevitable increase in subjectivity, and thus possible misdirection, that results from greater judicial discretion. In this respect, I believe we need to take into account that the *de jure* function of the directions belies their *de facto* purpose of persuading the jury. As long as juries are not accountable for, or obliged to motivate, their decisions, they are under no real obligation to follow the judge's guidance on the law – the judge must *persuade* them to do so. Indeed, the type of narrativising processes found in the English judges' directions are more typical of persuasive genres than instructional ones (Biber, 1988).

The fundamental question for research of the English summing-up as a whole, then, is whether the comparative linguistic freedom granted Crown Court judges leads to too uneven a playing field and too much potential abuse, or whether an experienced and well-trained Crown Court judge might function as a Virgil to 12 bewildered Dantes unexpectedly finding themselves in the 'wood of wilderness, savage and stubborn' that is the law for most laypeople. As the judges themselves perennially say to the jury in their summaries of the evidence, *it is for you to decide*.

Notes

The transcripts from which I constructed the corpus of summings-up were very kindly made available to me by Anne Perkins and Janet Cotterill.

1 All specific names and places in the data have been anonymised with the exception of 'Marks and Spencers'.
2 No private recording of any kind is permitted in English courts. However, my analyses are supported by extensive ethnographic study of the summing-up.
3 For brevity and clarity, the notes with sub-directions are not included.
4 The 'Mixed' group might be seen as a buffer zone to account for errors in analysis. It should be remembered that the percentages bear absolutely no relation to absolute values.
5 The figures on understanding and remembering the evidence suggest that the summary function of the summing-up may also be indispensable, providing the judges do succeed in clarifying and reminding.

References

Adler, S. J. (1994) *The Jury: Trial and Error in the American Courtroom*. New York: Random House.

Amsterdam, A. G. and Bruner, J. (2000) *Minding the Law*. Cambridge, Mass.: Harvard University Press.

Biber, D. (1988) *Variation across Speech and Writing*. Cambridge: Cambridge University Press.

Bruner, J. (1986) *Actual Minds, Possible Worlds*. Cambridge, Mass.: Harvard University Press.

Bruner, J. (1990) *Acts of Meaning*. Cambridge, Mass.: Harvard University Press.

Charrow, R. P. and Charrow, V. R. (1979) 'Making Legal Language Understandable: A Psycholinguistic Study of Jury Instruction', *Columbia Law Review*, vol. 79(5), pp. 1306–74.

Dumas, B. (2000a) 'Jury Trials: Lay Jurors, Pattern Jury Instructions, and Comprehension Issues', *Tennessee Law Review*, vol. 67, pp. 701–42.

Dumas, B. (2000b) 'US Pattern Jury Instructions: Problems and Proposals', *Forensic Linguistics*, vol. 7(1), pp. 49–71.

Findlay, M. and Duff. P. (eds) (1988) *The Jury Under Attack*. London: Butterworths.

Garner, B. (ed.) (1999) *Black's Law Dictionary*, 7th edn. St Paul, Minn.: West Publishing Co.

Grove, T. (1998) *The Juryman's Tale*. London: Bloomsbury.

Halliday, M. A. K. (1994) *An Introduction to Functional Grammar*, 2nd edn. London: Edward Arnold.

Jackson, B. S. (1995) *Making Sense in Law*. Liverpool: Deborah Charles Publications.

JSB (Judicial Studies Board) (1999) *Crown Court Benchbook: Specimen Directions*. London: JSB. Available online at http://www.cix.co.uk/~jsb/specdir/index.htm.

Labov, W. (1972) *Language in the Inner City*. Philadelphia: University of Pennsylvania.

Martin, J. (2000) 'Beyond Exchange: Appraisal Systems in English', in S. Hunston and G. Thompson (eds), *Evaluation in Text: Authorial Stance and the Construction of Discourse*. Oxford: Oxford University Press, pp. 142–75.

Robertshaw, P. (1998) *Summary Justice*. London: Cassell.

Sinclair, J. (1991) *Corpus, Concordance, Collocation*. Oxford: Oxford University Press.

Solan, L. M. (1999) 'Refocusing the Burden of Proof in Criminal Cases: Some Doubt about Reasonable Doubt', *University of Texas Law Review*, vol. 78(1), pp. 105–47.

Stubbs, M. (1995) *Text and Corpus Analysis: Computer-assisted Studies of Language and Culture*. Oxford: Blackwell.

Tiersma, P. M. (1999) *Legal Language*. Chicago: University of Chicago Press.

Tiersma, P. M. (2000) <http://www.tiersma.com/JURYINST/COMPARE.HTM>
Zander, M. and Henderson, P. (1993) *Crown Court Study*. Royal Commission on Criminal Justice, Research Study no.19. London: HMSO.

Case cited

R v. *Everett* (1995) Criminal Law Review 76. Court of Appeal.

15

Reasonable Doubt about Reasonable Doubt: Assessing Jury Instruction Adequacy in a Capital Case

Bethany K. Dumas

Introduction

Proof beyond a reasonable doubt has long been the standard in US criminal cases, while *preponderance of the evidence* is the standard in civil cases. A large body of research documents the problems jurors face as they wrestle with the language of jury instructions that attempt to clarify such concepts as *reasonable doubt*, seldom defined in jury instructions (see for example Tanford, 1990; Charrow and Charrow, 1979; Steele and Thornburg, 1988; Tanford, 1991; Tiersma, 1993, 1995; Lieberman and Sales, 1997). It is clear that the instructions are usually, perhaps always, confusing to jurors and that jurors' questions about their instructions are generally not answered. This article traces the history of a capital case in Texas in order to summarise problems with *reasonable doubt* and other language in the jury instructions that were identified by testifying linguists.[1]

Most researchers who have explored standards of proof in criminal cases have concluded that the *proof of reasonable doubt* standard itself – *proof beyond a reasonable doubt* – is a fair standard, if we can just get the language right.[2] This article examines the problems inherent in such phrases as *reasonable doubt*; it draws upon previous research and also upon research and conclusions testified to by other experts who testified in the Texas case, as well as research done by defence counsel.[3]

Jacobs v. *Johnson*

Jurors serving in criminal cases in Texas must negotiate a maze of legal terms in capital jury instructions, in both the guilt/innocence phase and the sentencing phase. In one recent case, defence counsel assembled a team of experts to assess the comprehensibility of instructions, including whether jurors who sentenced Charles Bruce Jacobs to death had understood the meaning of the term *reasonable doubt*. There is no evidence that jurors understood the term as the court intended. Further, experts testified that there was a high likelihood that jurors did not understand a number of legal distinctions:

1 that Jacobs could be convicted of a *lesser included offence* (*murder* or *burglary of a habitation*);
2 that jurors needed to find that Jacobs committed a *felony offence of burglary* as well as one of *murder*;
3 that the instructions and information about special issues in the sentencing phase did not mean that jurors could not fully consider the *mitigating evidence* offered by the defence;
4 that the word *deliberately* does not mean the same thing as *intentionally*;
5 that the word *probability* means something more than a *possibility*; and
6 that the terms *criminal acts of violence*, *continuing threat*, *reasonable expectation*, and *society* have legal definitions that may be different from ordinary meanings.

The experts[4] all concluded that there was a high likelihood that jurors understood some key terms in several different ways and that they understood some terms in ways different from those intended by the Court. They were in agreement that the death sentence was imposed as a result of decisions made by jurors who had not understood their instructions.

In *Jacobs* v. *Johnson*, a case now pending in federal court, the petitioner was convicted in 1987 for capital murder in the Third Criminal District Court of Dallas County, Texas, *State* v. *Bruce Charles Jacobs*. Acting upon the jury's findings in sentencing, the trial judge sentenced Jacobs to death. The Texas Court of Criminal Appeals affirmed the conviction and the sentence. In 1996, the Court of Criminal Appeals appointed counsel to write and file Mr Jacobs' first state application for a writ of habeas corpus in the convicting district court. The petition for relief was denied.

Jacobs was convicted of the residential stabbing murder of a 16-year-old victim. A knife was found near the boy's home, where he was murdered. No prints were identified. Jacobs was identified by some witnesses as having been in the vicinity of the crime, and he was eventually arrested. At trial, the jury found Jacobs guilty of capital murder. At the sentencing or punishment phase, the jury answered two special issues affirmatively, and the trial court ruled that Jacobs should be executed.

Defence counsel questioned whether jurors had understood the complex instructions used in Texas capital murder trials. Defence counsel obtained the services of six specialists in speech, communications, rhetoric, psychology and English, all of whom prepared affidavits stating that in all probability Mr Jacobs' jurors failed to grasp certain critical issues crucial to the decision to execute him. Each expert testified that the jury instructions at issue were of supreme importance at both the guilt–innocence and sentencing phases of trial, and that Jacobs' jurors could not have adequately understood their instructions, They emphasised that common assumptions of juror comprehension of legal concepts are misplaced.

These experts presented social-science findings demonstrating that there was a reasonable likelihood that the jurors had failed to understand such concepts as *reasonable doubt* and *lesser included offence*, and also the degree to which the court's charge permitted them to consider *mitigating evidence*. Experts testified (via affidavit) that the jury instruction failure was such as to satisfy the standard for instructional error established in 1990 by the US Supreme Court in *Boyde* v. *California*, a standard that holds that a constitutional violation has occurred only if there is a reasonable likelihood that a jury has considered itself precluded from considering *mitigating evidence*.

In 1996, while Jacobs was awaiting execution on death row in Texas, counsel for Jacobs, James W. Volberding, filed a state petition for writ of habeas corpus, asking the court to issue a writ ordering his release. Of interest to linguists are two sets of the 42 claims for relief, four that have to do with the appointment and payment of expert witnesses in capital cases, and two that implicate linguistic issues.

Jacobs' lawyer claimed violation of rights to due process, equal protection, effective assistance of counsel, and also violation of the eighth amendment because his client was repeatedly denied funding for experts to assist on a vital issue (claim 13), a lack of standards by which the court of criminal appeals may determine whether an expert should be appointed (claim 14), a failure to require appointment of experts in state habeas corpus proceedings (claim 15), and failure to determine compensation of attorneys and experts (claim 18) (because denial of funding suggested that the linguistic claims were not taken seriously by the court).

The six experts all had experience as expert witnesses and had published on language and law issues. All provided their time (at reduced hourly fees), knowing that counsel did not have advance approval of their fees. Counsel attempted to obtain advance authorisation from the Court, then filed a motion for expert fees. The requests were denied; no expert witnesses were paid for the 50+ hours they collectively spent on the case. In his writ of habeas corpus, counsel noted that 'convincing specialists to accept a case without promise of payment is difficult' and lamented that:

> [b]ecause the Court has refused payment, the result has been a loss of credibility, by me in this case, but also by other defence lawyers seeking to obtain expert opinion in other cases, realizing and their experts learning, that funding is difficult to come by in Texas capital cases.

Claims 23 and 24 state that social-science evidence demonstrates that the jury instructions used in the sentencing phase failed to explain the concept of *mitigating evidence*, thereby violating Jacobs' rights to a fair trial, due process and equal protection, and his right not to suffer cruel and unusual punishment as guaranteed by the fifth, eighth and fourteenth amendments of the US Constitution. It was also claimed that such evidence demonstrates that the jury instructions used in the sentencing phase failed to define the key terms *deliberately, criminal acts of violence, probability, continuing threat* and *society*, thereby further violating Jacobs' rights to a fair trial, due process and equal protection, and also his right not to suffer cruel and unusual punishment as guaranteed by the fifth, eighth and fourteenth amendments of the US Constitution.

At trial, the guilt/innocence phase instructions (Appendix A) were fairly lengthy. The sentencing instructions (Appendix B) were brief, though complex. In the sentencing instructions, jurors were told that they were required to answer two questions or special issues and that the State had to prove each issue beyond a reasonable doubt. They were further told they might not answer either issue 'Yes' unless the jury 'unanimously concurred'. The court further instructed that the jurors might not answer either issue 'No' unless 'ten or more jurors concurring shall individually sign the special verdict'.

Jurors were told that if they answered both questions 'Yes', then Jacobs would automatically be sentenced to death. If the jury answered either question 'No', then he would be sentenced to life in prison. The charge allowed the jury to 'take into consideration all of the facts shown by the evidence admitted before you in the full trial of this case, and the law as submitted to you in this charge, and the charge heretofore given to you by the Court'. Special Verdict No 1. asked:

> Do you find from the evidence beyond a reasonable doubt that the conduct of the defendant, Bruce Charles Jacobs, that caused the death of the deceased, Conrad Harris, was committed deliberately and with the reasonable expectation that the death of the deceased would result?

Special Verdict No. 2 asked:

> Do you find from the evidence beyond a reasonable doubt that there is a probability that the defendant, Bruce Charles Jacobs, would commit criminal acts of violence that would constitute a continuing threat to society?

Linguistic issues

The experts were asked to review the jury instructions and also copies of the verdict sheet from the guilt/innocence phase and the issues and recommendation sheet used by the jury in the sentencing phase, as well as the notes from the jury to the judge and his responses. These texts provided the basis for their individual analyses.

As noted above, several legal terms were at issue in this case – *reasonable doubt, mitigating evidence, deliberately, criminal acts of violence, probability, continuing threat* and *society*. Testimony was offered about these terms. In addition, some experts gave an overall assessment of the jury instructions.[5] The opening paragraphs of the affidavit submitted by Carolyn R. Miller articulate the perspective from which each expert appeared to speak:

> My analysis is guided by social theories of meaning . . . [that] hold that meaning is not in the language itself or in the intention of the speaker but is derived from convention, linguistic context, social context, and some general cognitive strategies. Meaning is thus a social negoti-ation based on mutual experience with the world and with interpretive conventions – a basis that cannot guarantee perfect agreement. The application of experience and convention in any given situation is influenced by many factors in the situation and the ways participants understand the situation. There can there be no compelling or necessary interpretation.
>
> Interpretation by jurors in the context of a court at law is a particular situation about which some generalisations can be made. In a courtroom, jurors are strangers and novices; they are relatively inexperienced and lack authority. In contrast, the judge is in every way the authority. Jurors will defer to those who are more experienced, those who belong there, and especially to the ultimate authority of the judge. When an interpretive problem arises, it is reasonably and likely for a juror to defer to the judge and to look to the judge for guidance, whether direct or indirect. It is not reasonable for a juror to rely on some independent interpretation or on common meanings. The context provide by the judge thus becomes especially important.
>
> Much of language comprehension in any context is guided by indirection and implicature. Thus, what the judge does *not* say, as well as what he or she does say, is significant to jurors and is likely to influence their interpretation, so also the order in which the judge presents things to jurors is naturally and legitimately taken by them as significant. The judge is not merely a legal and civic authority; he or she is an interpretive authority.
>
> (Affidavit of Miller on 25 September 1996, at pp. 2–3)

Several problems with the instructions are immediately apparent. Critical terms are undefined; jurors are left to guess the meanings of vital words; and there is no explicit option permitting jurors to sentence Jacobs to life without parole. In particular, there is no definition of the terms *mitigating circumstances* or *deliberately*. It is likely that the jurors in Jacobs' trial failed to understand that the law permitted them to consider and give effect to the mitigating evidence offered by Jacobs' lawyers in the punishment phase. It is also likely that the jurors failed to understand that the term *deliberately* used in the first special punishment issue had special legal significance that meant far more than *intentionally*. The defence position in *Jacobs* is that social-science evidence is both appropriate and necessary if the assessment of juror comprehension is to be other than a guessing game. At the request of defence counsel, experts directed their analyses and conclusion to consideration of the following issues (not all experts discussed all issues):

1   the meaning of *reasonable doubt*;
2   the concept of a *lesser included offence*;

3   the requirement that the jury find Jacobs guilty of the *felony offence of burglary*;

4   whether jurors would have understood that they could consider *mitigating evidence*;

5   the meaning of *deliberately* (does it mean the same thing as *intentionally*?);

6   the meaning of *criminal acts of violence*;

7   the meaning of *continuing threat*;

8   the meaning of *reasonable expectation*; and

9   the meaning of *society*.

The terms most often discussed were *reasonable doubt, lesser included offence, felony offence of burglary*, and *mitigating circumstances*. The first three were particularly important during the guilt/innocence phase of the trial; *mitigating circumstances* was particularly important during the sentencing phase of the trial.

In addition to discussing the meanings of terms, experts also discussed syntactic complexity and general vagueness or ambiguity. One affidavit, that of the author, began discussion of the concept of a lesser included offence by pointing out that some sentences are generally confusing; she quoted an example, then suggested a revision. Here is the original language:

> Unless you so find beyond a reasonable doubt, or if you have a reasonable doubt thereof, you will acquit the defendant of capital murder, and next consider whether or not he is guilty of the lesser included offence of murder.

In her affidavit, Dumas suggested that the paragraph presents serious comprehension problems for both lexical and syntactic reasons:

> First, it contains the archaic word 'thereof,' a word that few ordinary citizens are completely comfortable with. Second, it contains difficult and nonparallel syntax ('Unless you so find beyond a reasonable doubt, or if you have a reasonable doubt thereof'). Third, it does not spell out explicitly what the options are. Fourth, it does not define the term 'lesser included offence,' and that term (like the term 'reasonable doubt') is not defined either in the definitions section of the instructions or anywhere else. The simplest way to illustrate clearly the problems is to examine a rewritten version of the paragraph, one that replaces all the problematic words with more ordinary words and replaces all the confusing syntactic constructions with simpler one:

>> If you do not find beyond a reasonable doubt that the defendant committed capital murder, as defined above, then you must acquit the defendant of capital murder. Next, you must consider whether or not the defendant has committed the lesser included offence of murder. A lesser included offence is one which is composed of some, but not all elements of a greater offence, here capital murder. Capital murder is the intentional causing of the death of an individual in the course of committing or attempting to commit the offence of burglary of a habitation. Murder is the intentional causing of the death of an individual.

>> (Affidavit of Bethany K. Dumas on 1 October 1996, at p. 4)

Like Dumas, Miller found that problems with the instructions arose as much from the syntax of the sentences in which confusing terms was used as from the lack of a clear definition In discussing *reasonable doubt*, Miller also suggested a revision:

> The central problem is that the sentence . . . can easily be read in two opposing ways because in everyday English, 'or' can be understood in two senses, a disjunctive sense and an inclusive sense (see standard style guides such as Fowler's or Morris and Morris). Here, according to the sentence on the previous page ('you must find not only . . . but also . . . '), the disjunctive sense is meant, that is, either condition *alone* is supposed to be sufficient to acquit the defendant of capital murder:
>
>> If you do not believe from the evidence beyond a reasonable doubt [A] that the defendant entered the habitation of Holly Kuper, if he did, with the intent to commit theft,
>
> or
>
>> [if you do not believe . . .] [B] that after entering the habitation of Holly Kuper, if he did, he committed theft, then you will acquit . . .
>
> In order to acquit, a juror has to be willing to say, 'I don't believe he did both A and B', which is equivalent to 'I believe he did not do both A and B.' In other words, the defendant must pass only one test of reasonable doubt in order to be acquitted.
> But the disjunctive 'or' is not the most likely or the easiest to extract from this sentence. The inclusive 'or' is functionally equivalent to 'and,' and in the sentence . . . requires both conditions for acquittal.
> . . .
> Here, in order to acquit, a juror would have to be willing to say, 'I don't believe he did either A or B,' or 'I believe he did either A nor B.' Understanding the 'or' as inclusive requires the defendant to pass **two** tests of reasonable doubt, rather than only one of two and thus changes the conditions on his acquittal.
> . . .
> The following rewritten version spells out the disjunctive nature of the 'or' and, by foregrounding the potential for acquittal rather than possible actions of the defendant, strengthens the presumption of innocence. Because the negative form of the belief clause is necessary in order to retain the burden of proof on the prosecution, the strong separation between this clause and the two clauses about the defendant's actions help prevent the migration of the 'not' to these clause.
>
> You will acquit the defendant of capital murder if you do not believe from the evidence beyond a reasonable doubt that at least one of the following statements is the case:
>
> (1)   The defendant entered the habitation of Holly Kuper, if he did, with the intent to commit theft;
> (2)   After entering the habitation of Holly Kuper, if he did, the defendant committed theft.
>
> (Affidavit of Miller on 25 September 1996, at pp. 3–6)

Additional comments were made about the term *reasonable doubt* by Ronald R. Butters, who focused on the syntactic complexity of the instruction and suggested that in the instructions *reasonable doubt* could be read as synonymous with *reasonable certainty*; he suggested that it would have been helpful to replace *reasonable doubt* with *high degree of certainty*, suggesting indirectly that jurors who read *reasonable doubt* as synonymous with *reasonable certainty* may in effect substitute the civil standard preponderance of the evidence for that of *reasonable doubt* (Affidavit of 18 September 1996, at pp. 2–3).[6]

When the case experts considered *lesser included offence*, some of them concluded that while there was the possibility of misunderstanding the instruction because of the confusing ways in which the court used the term *reasonable doubt*, the Court had made it clear that the jury could find the defendant guilty of *noncapital murder* (Affidavit of Butters at p. 3) (but see discussion by Dumas, above). However, Miller pointed out that 'the order in which the jury [was] asked to make its determinations [might] be prejudicial against acquittal for capital murder' (p. 6):

> A juror, especially one with any predisposition to convict, may well be induced by the order of decisions to convict on the capital murder charge, because this decision is presented first and because once this section of the instructions is considered, the other two sections will seem repetitive and redundant and thus hardly worth considering carefully on their own merits. I consider this inducement to be *very possible*.
>
> If the decisions were given in reverse order, from least to most serious, the effect would be reversed and the presumption of the instructions would be for innocence on the most serious charge. If the jurors considered felony burglary first and then murder and found the defendant innocent of either charge, they would be required to stop their deliberations at that point, and consideration of the more serious charges including capital murder could never (as it properly should not) occur. On the other hand, a jury finding the defendant guilty of either felony burglary or murder could find such a conviction both legally and psychologically sufficient and not find any emotional need to convict on capital murder.
>
> (Affidavit of Miller at p. 7; emphasis added)

The concept of the felony offence of burglary was difficult for jurors; they sent two notes to the judge requesting clarification. They first asked: 'Does "felony" in the definition of burglary include, in this case, any other felony?' The judge's written response was: 'I do not understand exactly what you are asking me.' They then asked: 'On page 1, the definition of burglary states it is entering a habitation with intent to commit a felony or theft. The jury's question is whether a burglary occurs if defendant intends to commit a felony other than theft?' The judge replied: '[Y]ou have been given all of the law you are entitled to. I can not answer your question under the law.'

It is well-established that US jurisprudence seeks to avoid the arbitrary or capricious imposition of the death penalty. Thus, factors of aggravation and mitigation are generally of paramount importance in the sentencing phase of a capital case (*Gregg* v. *Georgia*, discussed in Tiersma, 1995). The issue of mitigating circumstances was perhaps the most important of the issues after that of *reasonable doubt*. It is crucial, for it underlies the possibility of:

> an individualised determination on which jurors are permitted to consider and give effect to any possible mitigating evidence. Because jurors need to unanimously determine that a mitigating factor exists, a single juror can conclude that something about the defendant or the

crime constitutes a sufficiently persuasive reason to vote for imprisonment, thus precluding imposition of the death penalty.

(Tiersma, 1995, p. 9)

All of the experts Butters, Luginbuhl, Miller, Dumas and Levenbook (note 4) found it unlikely that the jurors would have perceived that they could consider *mitigating circumstances*. Their reasoning varied, but all noted that the special verdicts may be read as 'preventing the jury from directly weighing any and all mitigating circumstances against any and all aggravating circumstances' (Butters at p. 5). James Luginbuhl put it most strongly:

> [T]he purpose of mitigation is to enable to jury to make an individualized decision, to come to a conclusion for that particular defendant whether he/she should be sentenced to life or death. The instructions used in *Jacobs* never give the jury that opportunity, because they specifically restrict any consideration of mitigation to whether either of the special circumstances exist. There is no allowance for the jurors to consider whether the defendant deserves the death penalty.
>
> (Affidavit of Luginbuhl on 16 September 1996, at p. 3)

Thus, expert testimony suggested strongly that linguistic analysis could be used to identify specific problems in the instructions given to jurors in the *Jacobs* case – and that those problems could be remedied by rewriting the instructions.

Conclusion

The *Jacobs* experts all concluded that there was a high likelihood that jurors were confused about the meanings of key terms and that they sometimes understood terms in ways different from those intended by the Court. They were in agreement that the death sentence was imposed by jurors who did not understand their instructions. Such a scenario clearly undercuts extremely important constitutional rights and violates the very foundations of the US criminal justice system.

This article has traced the history of a case, now pending in federal court, in which jurors' decisions, based upon a faulty understanding of relevant law, led to a death sentence. It has described briefly some of the problems inherent in such phrases as *reasonable doubt* when they are not adequately defined for jurors in capital cases. It is clear from expert testimony in this case and other research that there are enormous problems in comprehensibility with the capital instructions at issue in this case. Research on issues of comprehensibility should continue, and lawyers should continue to bring these issues to the attention of the judiciary. If we as a society are serious in our attempt to safeguard important constitutional rights in our criminal justice system, we must continue our joint effort to improve the comprehensibility of jury instructions.

Appendix A: charge of the court (guilt/innocence phase)[7]

A person commits the offence of capital murder if he knowingly or intentionally commits the offence of murder, as hereinafter defined, and while intentionally committing such offence, he was in the course of committing or attempting to commit the offence of burglary of a habitation, as that offence is hereinafter defined.

A person commits the offence of murder if he intentionally causes the death of an individual.

Our law provides that a person commits the offence of burglary if, without the effective consent of the owner, he enters a habitation with intent to commit a felony or theft.

. . .

A person acts intentionally, or with intent, with respect to the nature of his conduct or to a result of his conduct when it is his conscious objective or desire to engage in the conduct or cause the result.

A person acts knowingly, or with knowledge, with respect to the nature of his conduct or to circumstances surrounding his conduct when he is aware of he nature of his conduct or that the circumstances exist. A person acts knowingly, or with knowledge, with respect to a result of his conduct when he is aware that his conduct is reasonably certain to cause the result.

Before you would be warranted in convicting the defendant of capital murder, you must find from the evidence beyond a reasonable doubt not only that on the occasion in question the defendant was engaged in the commission or attempted commission of the felony offence of burglary of a habitation owned by Holly Kuper, as defined in this charge, but also that during the commission or attempted commission of burglary of habitation owned by Holly Kuper, if any, the defendant intentionally caused the death of the deceased, Conrad Harris, by stabbing or cutting said Conrad Harris with a knife, with the intention of thereby killing him. Unless you find from the evidence beyond a reasonable doubt that the defendant, on said occasion, specifically intended to kill the said Conrad Harris when he stabbed or cut the said Conrad Harris, it he did stab or cut him, you cannot convict him of the offence of capital murder.

If you do not believe from the evidence beyond a reasonable doubt that the defendant entered the habitation of holly Kuper, if he did, with the intent to commit theft, or that after entering the habitation of Holly Kuper, if he did, he committed theft, then you will acquit the defendant of capital murder.

Now, if you find from the evidence beyond a reasonable doubt that the defendant, Bruce Charles Jacobs, did in Dallas County, Texas, on or about the 22nd day of July, 1986, then and there intentionally cause the death of Conrad Harris, an individual, by stabbing or cutting the said Conrad Harris with a knife and the defendant intentionally did cause the death of the said Conrad Harris while the said defendant was in the course of committing or attempting to commit the offence of burglary of a habitation owned by Holly Kuper, then you will find the defendant guilty of capital murder, as charged in the indictment.

Unless you find beyond a reasonable doubt, or if you have a reasonable doubt thereof, you will acquit the defendant of capital murder, and next consider whether or not he is guilty of the lesser included offence of murder.

If you find from the evidence beyond a reasonable doubt that on the 22nd day of July, 1986, in Dallas County, Texas, the defendant did knowingly cause the death of Conrad Harris by stabbing or cutting him with a knife, but you have a reasonable doubt as to whether the defendant intentionally killed Conrad Harris as the term 'intentionally' has been defined herein, then you will find the defendant guilty of murder, but not capital murder, regardless of whether you find from the evidence beyond a reasonable doubt that the defendant was then and there in the course of committing or attempting to commit the offence of burglary of a habitation owned by Holly Kuper.

If you should find from the evidence beyond a reasonable doubt that the defendant is either guilty of capital murder or murder, but you have a reasonable doubt as to which offence he is guilty, then you should resolve that doubt in the defendant's favor, and in such event, you will find the defendant guilty of the lesser offence of murder.

Unless you so find a reasonable doubt, or if you have a reasonable doubt thereof, you will acquit the defendant of murder.

If you do not find from the evidence beyond a reasonable doubt that the defendant is guilty of capital murder or murder as defined in this charge, then you shall acquit the defendant of capital murder and murder and next consider whether or not the defendant is guilty of the felony offence of burglary of habitation.

Now, if you find from the evidence beyond a reasonable doubt that on or about the 22nd day of July, 1986, in Dallas County, Texas, the defendant, Bruce Charles Jacobs, did knowingly or intentionally enter a habitation without the effective consent of Holly Kuper, the owner thereof, who had a greater right to possession of the habitation than the defendant, with the intent to commit theft or did commit theft, and the said entry was without effective consent since no assent in fact was given by the owner or a person legally authorized to act for the owner, then you will find the defendant guilty of burglary of a habitation.

Unless you so find beyond a reasonable doubt, or if you have a reasonable doubt thereof, you will acquit the defendant of burglary of a habitation.

Our law provides that a defendant may testify in his own behalf if he elects to do so. This however, is a privilege accorded a defendant, and in the event he elects not to testify, that fact cannot be taken as a circumstance against him. In this case, the defendant has elected not to testify, and you are instructed that you cannot and must not refer or allude to that fact throughout your deliberations or take it into consideration for any purpose whatsoever as a circumstance against the defendant.

You are instructed that if there is any testimony before you in this case regarding the defendant's having committed offences other than the offence alleged against him in the indictment in this case, you cannot consider said testimony for any purpose unless you find and believe beyond a reasonable doubt that the defendant committed such other offences, it any were committed, and even then you may only consider the same in determining the defendant's state of min, or knowledge of motive, if any, in connection with the offence, if any, alleged against him in the indictment in this cause, and for no other purpose.

You are further instructed that mere presence at the scene of a crime is no evidence of guilt.

You are further instructed that under our law, no evidence obtained as the result of an illegal arrest shall be admissible in evidence against the defendant. The Texas law, as applicable in this case, concerning when an officer may arrest a person without a warrant is set out below.

Any peace officer may arrest, without warrant:

1   persons found in suspicious places and under circumstances which reasonably show that such persons have been guilty of some felony or breach of the peace, or threaten, or are about to commit some offence against thee law, or

2   where it is shown by satisfactory proof to a peace officer, upon the representation
     of a credible person, that a felony has been committed, and that the offender is
     about to escape, so that there is no time to pursue a warrant, such peace officer
     may, without warrant, pursue and arrest the accused.

Probable cause must exist before a peace officer may arrest a person without a warrant.
Probable cause exists where, at that moment, the facts ad circumstances within the
knowledge of the arresting officer and of which he has reasonable trust worthy
information would warrånt a prudent man in believing that a particular person has
committed or is committing a crime.

Unless you believe beyond a reasonable doubt that the arrest of the defendant was
lawful, then all evidence obtained as a result of that arrest must be disregarded by you
and not considered for any purpose.

The evidence obtained as a result of the arrest is as follows:

[List deleted.]

A grand jury indictment is the means whereby a defendant is brought to trial in
a felony prosecution. It is not evidence of guilt nor can it be considered by you in
passing upon the issue of guilt of the defendant. The burden of proof in all criminal
cases rests upon the State throughout the trial and never shifts to the defendant.

All persons are presumed to be innocent, and no person may be convicted of an
offence unless each element of the offence is proved beyond a reasonable doubt. The
fact that Bruce Charles Jacobs has been arrested, confined, or indicted for, or otherwise
charged with the offence gives rise to no inference of guilt at his trial. In case you
have a reasonable doubt as to the defendant's guilt after considering all the evidence
before you, and these instruction, you will acquit Bruce Charles Jacobs.

You are the exclusive judges of the facts proved, of the credibility of the witnesses
and the weight to be given their testimony, but the law you shall receive in these
written instructions, and you must be governed thereby.

Appendix B: charge of the court (sentencing phase)

By your verdict returned in this case you have found the defendant, Bruce Charles
Jacobs, guilty of the offence of capital murder, which was alleged to have been committed on or about the 22nd day of July, 1986, in Dallas County, Texas. It is necessary
now for you to determine, from all the evidence in the case, the answers to certain
questions called 'Special Issues' in this charge.

The burden of proof is on the State to prove each issue submitted to you beyond
a reasonable doubt. If the State does not prove an issue beyond a reasonable doubt
or if you have a reasonable doubt thereof, then you shall answer the issue or issues
'No'.

SPECIAL ISSUE I
Was the conduct of the defendant that caused the death of the deceased committed
deliberately and with the reasonable expectation that the death of the deceased
would result?

SPECIAL ISSUE II
Is there a possibility that the defendant would commit criminal acts of violence that
would constitute a continuing threat to society?

You are instructed that you may not answer either issue 'Yes' unless the jury unanimously concurs, and, in such event, the special verdict is signed by your foreman. You may not answer either issue 'No' unless ten or more jurors concurring shall individually sign the special verdict. However, if the jury unanimously concurs in answering 'No' on either issue, the special verdict shall be signed only by the foreman.

The punishment for the offence of capital murder in this state is death or confinement in the Texas Department of Corrections for life.

You are further instructed that if the jury returns an affirmative finding on each of the two issues submitted, this Court shall sentence the defendant to death. If the jury returns a negative finding on either issue submitted, the Court shall sentence the defendant to confinement in the Texas Department of Corrections for life.

You are instructed that in answering the special issues, which you will show in your verdict, you may take into consideration all of the facts shown by the evidence admitted before you in the full trial of this case, and the law as submitted to you in this charge and the charge heretofore given to you by the Court.

You are further instructed that in determining the punishment in this case, you are not to discuss among yourselves how long the defendant will be required to serve any sentence imposed.

The law allows the defendant to testify in his own behalf, but a decision on his art to remain silent during any part of the trial is not a circumstance against him. I instruct you not to consider, discuss or even refer to such silence on the part of the defendant during your consideration of the special issues in this case.

You are further instructed that your verdict shall be arrived at by due deliberation and not by drawing lots or by any other means of chance.

You are the exclusive judges of the facts proved, the credibility of the witnesses and the weight to be given the testimony, but you are bound to receive the law from the Court, which is herein given you, and be governed thereby.

Notes

1 I am grateful for assistance from the following individuals, who provided information or feedback as I completed this chapter: James W. Volberding, Esq.; The Honourable Dennis H. Inman, US Magistrate Judge, Eastern District of Tennessee; and Jean Moore, Instructor, University of Tennessee College of Law Library.

2 That assumption has been challenged recently by a lawyer/linguist who questions whether *proof beyond a reasonable doubt* 'is the best way to promote the values our system of criminal justice claims to venerate' (Solan, 1999, p. 105; see also Simon and Mahan, 1971 and 1999). Solan suggests that 'standard reasonable doubt instructions focus the jury on the defendant's ability to produce alternatives to the government's case, and thereby shift the burden of proof to the defendant' (p. 105). This chapter examines only the problems inherent in such phrases as *reasonable doubt* when they are not defined for jurors.

3 James W. Volberding, Esq. generously shared copies of relevant case documents with the author.

4 Dr Ronald Butters, Professor of English, Duke University; Dr Barbara Levenbook, Professor of Philosophy, North Carolina State University; Dr Carolyn R. Miller, Professor of English, North Carolina State University; Dr Bethany Dumas, Associate Professor of English, University of Tennessee; Dr James Luginbuhl, Professor of

Psychology, North Carolina State University; Dr John N. Wall, Professor of English, North Carolina State University.
5 Relevant portions of the instructions, standard in capital cases in Texas, are included in the Appendices; readers may wish to read those instructions before reading the rest of this chapter.
6 See Dumas 2000b for a detailed discussion of problems in defining the term *reasonable doubt*.
7 Introductory and concluding paragraphs have been omitted, as have definitions for the terms 'enter', 'building', 'habitation', 'theft', 'appropriation', 'appropriate', 'property', 'deprive', 'effective consent', 'owner', 'possession', 'felony' and 'individual'.

References

Charrow, R. P. and Charrow, V. R. (1979) 'Making Legal Language Understandable: A Psycholinguistic Study of Jury Instructions', *Columbia Law Review*, vol. 79, pp. 1306–74.
Dumas, B. K. (2000a) 'US Pattern Jury Instructions: Problems and Proposals', *Forensic Linguistics: The International Journal of Language and the Law*, vol. 7(1), pp. 49–71.
Dumas, B. K. (2000b) 'Jury Trials: Lay Jurors, Pattern Jury Instructions, and Comprehension Issues', *Tennessee Law Review*, vol. 67(3), pp. 701–42.
Lieberman, J. D. and Sales, B. D (1997) 'What Social Science Teaches us about the Jury Instruction Process', *Psychology, Public Polity, and Law*, pp. 589–644.
Simon, R. J. and Mahan, L. (1971) 'Quantifying Burdens of Proof: A View from the Bench, the Jury, and the Classroom', *Law and Society Review*, vol. 5(3), pp. 319–30.
Simon, R. J. and Mahan, L. (1999) 'Probability Statements of Sufficiency of Proof in Criminal and Civil Trials', in W. F. Abbott and J. Batt (eds), *A Handbook of Jury Research*. Philadelphia: American Law Institute–American Bar Association Committee on Continuing Professional Education, Section 19, pp. 1–11.
Solan, L. M. (1999) 'Refocusing the Burden of Proof in Criminal Cases: Some Doubt about Reasonable Doubt', *Texas Law Review*, vol. 78, pp. 105–47.
Steele, W. M. and Thornburg, E. G. (1988) 'Jury Instructions: A Persistent Failure to Communicate', *North Carolina Law Review*, vol. 67, pp. 77–119.
Tanford, J. A. (1990) 'The Law and Psychology of Jury Instructions', *Nebraska Law Review*, vol. 69, pp. 71–111.
Tanford, J. A. (1991) 'Law Reform by Courts, Legislatures, and Commissions following Empirical Research on Jury Instructions', *Law and Society Review*, vol. 25, pp. 155–75.
Tiersma, P. M. (1993) 'Reforming the Language of Jury Instructions', *Hofstra Law Review*, vol. 22, pp. 37–78.
Tiersma, P. M. (1995) 'Dictionaries and Death: Do Capital Jurors Understand Mitigation?', *Utah Law Review*, vol. 1, pp. 1–49.

Cases cited

Boyde v. *California*, 494 US 370, 110 S. Ct. 1190, 108 L. Ed. 2d 316 (1990).
Gregg v. *Georgia*, 428 US 153, 49 L. Ed. 2d 859, 96 S. Ct. 2909 (1976).

16
Discipline and Punishment in the Discourse of Legal Decisions on Rape Trials

Débora de Carvalho Figueiredo

Introduction

This chapter investigates the pedagogical role played by the discourse of English legal decisions on rape trials. This analysis owes a lot to the work of Michel Foucault, in particular to his book *Discipline and Punish* (1991) which traces the evolution of criminal justice systems from Medieval *torture* to Enlightenment's *punishment* to modern *discipline*. Foucault argues that until the late eighteenth century, punishment was frequently the public spectacle of torture: prisoners would be flogged, put on the pillory and even executed in open squares. From then on, however, the entire economy of punishment began to change: torture disappeared as a public spectacle, punishment became the most hidden part of the penal process, and the body ceased to be the only target of penal repression. The body began to be exposed to new techniques that aimed to render it 'docile', in other words able to be subjected, used, transformed and improved. In Foucault's words, 'these methods, which made possible the meticulous control of the operations of the body, which assured the constant subjection of its forces and imposed upon them a relation of docility-utility, might be called *"disciplines"'* (1991, p. 137; my emphasis).

Foucault argues that while the ancient forms of penality, such as torture and death addressed the *body* of the condemned, modern forms of penality, for example, incarceration, address their *soul*. It is over the souls (subjectivities) of men and women that the microphysics of judicial power is exercised.

The reform of criminal law (from torture to punishment to discipline) introduced a new economy of the power to punish, which was then rendered more regular, effective, constant and detailed, and which began to operate at a lesser cost. The idea was 'not to punish less, but to punish better; to punish with an attenuated severity perhaps, but in order to punish with more universality and necessity; to insert the power to punish more deeply into the social body' (Foucault, 1991, p. 82). In short, a move from *coercion* to consent.[1] As punishment became hidden, it left the realm of everyday perception and entered that of abstract consciousness; Foucault points out that in the modern economy of criminal justice systems it is the certainty and the reach of punishment, rather than its spectacle, which must render punishment effective and discourage crime. To achieve this internalisation of the power to punish, discipline is vital; individuals must be docile, amenable to subjection, to the subtle grip of disciplinary power.

Disciplinary power is realised through three basic instruments: (1) *hierarchical observation*; (2) *normalising judgement*; and (3) *examination* (*ibid.*). Applying this to the judicial discourse on rape, we can say that all of the three instruments of disciplinary power are present in legal decisions – judges have the hierarchical right to observe the social and sexual behaviour of women and men; they judge human behaviour, categorising some actions as 'abnormal' or 'criminal' (outside the social pact), and others as 'acceptable' or 'excusable' (within the social pact); and to arrive at these categories, judges rely on expert evaluations (made by doctors, psychiatrists and probation officers). According to Foucault, *examination* is the most important technique of discipline. Examination leads to the documentation of people, enabling on the one hand individual descriptions, and on the other hand the compiling of statistics and generalisations. As I will argue in this chapter, the judicial discourse of legal decisions relies both on medical and psychiatric examinations to classify, instruct and discipline rape defendants and rape complainants.

The pedagogical function of legal decisions

In modern times, it is no longer necessary to discipline exclusively the body. Now that forms of surveillance and control have been individually internalised (mainly through discursive practices), the object of discipline and punishment is the *soul*, conceptualised in terms of the psyche, subjectivity, personality, consciousness and individuality (Smart, 1983). Discourse plays a crucial role in the discipline of subjectivities and consciousnesses. Women, for instance, are discursively trained to police and control their own behaviour and the behaviour of others, without the need for coercion or external surveillance (Lees, 1997). For those who have difficulty internalising the habits of self-surveillance and self-correction (non-conformists, rule-breakers) there are several panoptic and disciplinary mechanisms to supervise, discipline and rehabilitate individuals. One of these mechanisms is the rape trial.[2]

According to Foucault, different discourses transformed areas such as sexuality and crime into objects of scientific knowledge and targets for institutional practices. Applying his view to rape trials, we can interpret the discursive practices of judges, for instance, as tools in a complex pedagogy of behaviour constructed and realised through legal discourse, a pedagogy which aims to supervise, discipline, educate and control the way men and women behave socially and sexually. From this viewpoint, no legal trial and legal sentence are the judgement and punishment of an isolated individual; the discourse of lawyers, prosecutors and judges also represents the social-cultural evaluation of human behaviour, the setting of examples, an attempt to recompose normality and restore the social pact.

In trial proceedings and legal decisions we can see two forms of penality at work: *the penality of the law* – legal rules, the opposition of 'legal' and 'illegal' acts and so on etc – and *the penality of the norm* – the trial represents a space for a broader form of pedagogy, which works by setting examples to be followed, by attempting to homogenise, normalise, bring 'offenders' back to the social pact (through rehabilitation) or exclude them from society (through condemnation) (Foucault, 1991).

In short, the restorative and educational roles of legal punishment could extend to those who have broken not legal but moral or cultural rules. Take rape complainants, for instance. They have not been charged with a criminal offence, and therefore cannot be the object of direct penal punishment (for example, loss of money or of freedom). However, during the rape trial the victim's body is exposed in a representational form, the events are reenacted, details are discussed, an atmosphere of the circus (of a spectacle) is created. If we interpret the rape trial as a pedagogy of sexual behaviour, as I am doing in this chapter, we can argue that the discourse of rape trials has 'side-effects' which reach far beyond the confines of the courtroom. Seen as a symbolic event, a rape trial establishes for the defendant and the complainant, as well as for men and women in general, the forms of behaviour which guarantee social and legal protection, and those which lead to exposure and punishment. Fear of symbolic punishment is enough to prevent many women from reporting a rape (Hall, 1985; Adler, 1987; Edwards, 1996). Their silence indicates that women have internalised the notion that they should learn to avoid male violence and to keep quiet about it (see Bumiller, 1991).[3]

To illustrate the argument that the judicial discourse on rape is inserted within a complex pedagogical process, I will discuss in this chapter a very specific type of legal decisions: reported appeal decisions. In what follows, I will briefly describe and delimit the texts I have analysed. A *reported appellate decision on a rape trial* (or *reported decision*) is a type of text where gender relations and power relations overlap. Reported appellate decisions (or RADs for short) are the decisions reported from the higher courts and published in official law reports, which form the basic units of what lawyers call 'case law' (Radford, 1987). In order to situate these texts, I will point out exactly where they fit in a sequence of judicial procedures: a crime or felony is initially judged by a first instance court, presided over by a single judge, and sometimes a jury (in the British legal system, these courts are the Magistrates' Court or the Crown Court). In this first level the defendant may be considered guilty or not guilty; if found guilty, he/she will be sentenced. If the first instance verdict and sentence is unsatisfactory for the defendant, he/she may appeal to a higher court (in England, the Divisional Court of Queen's Bench, Crown Court or Court of Appeal). The Court of Appeal, which judges appeals on more serious cases (for example, rapes), and where three judges typically sit, will produce a new decision entitled 'appellate decision', maintaining or altering, partially or entirely, the previous decision. The most important of these decisions are then published in law reports.

For organisational purposes, three sections follow dealing with functions of a custodial sentence of rape; interdiscursivity (the 'discourses of man' and legal discourse); and the control of the body (bio-power). All the excerpts used as illustrations were taken from appeals published in the Criminal Appeal Reports (Sweet & Maxwell) and the All England Law Reports (Butterworths) between 1987 and 1998. The excerpts are individually numbered, each number representing one reported appeal decision. The words or sentences highlighted in italics within each excerpt are the ones I wish to focus on as they better illustrate the pedagogical role of legal decisions (although these italics do not reflect the emphasis of the originals).

Functions of a custodial sentence for rape

From the point of view of the British criminal justice system, a sentence of imprisonment given to a rapist serves five basic functions: (1) to punish the offender; (2) to serve as a warning/deterrence (example); (3) to protect women and society; (4) to reflect the gravity of the offence; and (5) to reflect public repugnance at the offence (against the breach of the social pact). Each of these functions is made explicit in the words of the judges quoted below:

  1 The imposition of a custodial sentence, it is submitted, is required to *mark the gravity of the offence, to emphasise public repugnance for such offences, to serve as a warning to others, to punish the offender and for the protection of women and girls.*
     [Attorney-General's Reference (no. 3 of 1993) (W) [1994] 98 Cr.App.R. 85 – stranger rape – community service sentence increased to 2 years imprisonment]

  2 An offence of this nature, it is submitted, should attract a more substantial sentence *to reflect both its gravity and the aggravating features; to act as a deterrent to the offender and others; and to reflect public repugnance*
     [Attorney-General's Reference (no. 35 of 1992) (David Vernon Taylor) [1994] 15 Cr.App.R.(S) 233 – stranger rape – 4-year sentence increased to 6]

Nowadays, modern penalities are traversed by disciplinary examinations. The legal punishment is a correction, a therapy, an attempt at normalisation; the judicial process is supposed to measure, assess, diagnose, cure and transform individuals. The transformation of individuals is achieved through the redemptive nature of the penalty, and the restoration of normality is partly achieved through the examples set out by legal punishment. The following excerpts illustrate legal decisions where judicial and medical discourses joined forces to advocate the reformative function of imprisonment:

3 Nine years' detention in a young offender institution for rape of a widow aged 100 by a boy aged 16 at the time of the offence reduced to seven years.

   A *social inquiry report* commented that there was no doubting the appellant's remorse for his victim's suffering and the deep shame which he was currently experiencing . . . The doctor expressed concern about the 'self damaging potential which his ruminations may cause', and recommended *professional counselling, together with guidance and support*. Although his potential for dangerousness needs to be examined, the psychiatrist thought he could not be regarded as a serious danger within the community.

   [McIntosh (1994) 15 Cr.App.R.(S.) 163 – stranger rape – 9-year sentence reduced to 7]

4 Nine years upheld for the rape of a 16-year-old prostitute with false imprisonment and violence.

   The psychiatrist says under a sub-paragraph headed 'Insight': '[The applicant] tended to blame the index offence on the cannabis and alcohol he has used on the night [in question]. However, he did take responsibility for the offence and is seeking an explanation for what has taken place. He seemed genuinely confused that he has committed this offence [and] . . . *specifically stated that he wanted to participate in a programme for sex offenders'.*

   [Masood (1997) 2 Cr.App.R.(S.) 137 – prostitute rape – 9 years upheld]

5 The psychiatrist concluded his report by saying: 'Mr Low must be considered at high risk of further offending behaviour in the light of that which is stated above. As such he forms *a high priority candidate for treatment of sex offenders in prison. Mr Low recognises the need to address his offending behaviour . . .* '

   [Low (1998) 1 Cr.App.R.(S.) 69 – stranger rape – life sentence – parole period reduced from 10 to 7 years]

The examples above illustrate how the disciplines (especially through the technique of examination) transformed the individual into a 'calculable man', someone who can be analysed and controlled through a collection of files, records and individual information. The appellants were analysed and diagnosed as potential candidates for psychiatric or psychological treatment. The examples also illustrate the view of the prison as a place for 'reeducation' and 'reintegration'. The excerpts imply that the trial process has achieved one of its pedagogical functions – the judicial requirement for appellants to express remorse, accept responsibility and recognise their offending behaviour (even though we have no evidence to indicate that the appellants' remorse and admission of responsibility is genuine).

Example and warning

In this chapter, rape trial proceedings and legal decisions on rape are being interpreted as part of a pedagogy of gender behaviour. This pedagogy has a twofold aim: to deter or warn potential rapists from committing the offence of 'rape', and to instruct women (both rape complainants and women in general) about the dangers of going against social and sexual 'normality'.

The disciplinary powers at work in rape trial proceedings represent a system of *'infra-penalities'* (Foucault, 1991) – they define and repress areas of behaviour (such as the social and sexual behaviour of women) that have escaped the reach of written laws and statutes. For instance, women who have many sexual partners might be defined as 'promiscuous', 'impure' or 'imprudent' by legal and medical discourses. Consider Excerpt 6, for instance. In this particular case, the defendant claimed that the victim's 'notorious' sexual past led him to believe she was consenting to sex.[4] Below is the appeal's judge's opinion about the complainant's 'promiscuity':

> 6 In our opinion, *this was a case near the borderline. Clearly the complainant was prepared to have intercourse with a number of different men,* but we do not think that the mere fact that *she was suffering from some venereal disease* is necessarily evidence of *substantial promiscuity* . . . Nevertheless, although *we have not found it easy to reach a decision on this appeal,* in the end we do not think that the 'evidence of *sexual promiscuity'* of the complainant was 'so strong or so closely contemporaneous in time to the event in issue as to . . . reach the border between mere credit and an issue in the case'.
> [**Brown (1989) 89 Cr.App.R. 97 – acquaintance rape – appeal dismissed – 7 years upheld**]

In the example above, the judges dismissed the appeal and upheld the prison sentence because they did not find sufficient evidence of promiscuity in the complainant's behaviour. The judicial conclusion, then, is that she 'was prepared to have sexual intercourse with a number of different men'; however, her promiscuity was not 'substantial', and as the appellant was not alleging he mistook her promiscuity for consent, it was not possible for the judges to allow the appeal. In spite of that, in many parts of the RAD the judges point out the complainant's promiscuous lifestyle:

> [the counsel for the appellant alleged that] *not only had she had sexual experience with men to whom she was not married but that she had done so casually and with little discrimination. It was, of course, in any event fundamental to such a submission that there was a factual basis for suggesting sexual promiscuity in this case'*), and at one point they question the way she reacted to the attack (*'in the present case the complainant did not seek help from her boyfriend when the appellant, on her evidence, was forcing her away from the club. She did not shout out to her friends who were there at the time and who saw what was happening. She did not complain to the taxi-driver the following morning when she was picked up at the appellant's home'*.

The fact that the appeal was denied occupies a secondary position in relation to the larger picture occupied by the judgmental, disciplinary description of the woman.

If on the one hand a 'notorious' reputation is often used in court as a way of discrediting the rape complainant and as a kind of excuse for rape, a women who can present her reputation as unimpeachable is more likely to see her assailant convicted of rape. That is the case of young virgins and elderly women, frequently depicted as 'genuine victims' especially when they resist the attack physically (on the importance of clear, strong resistance to characterise lack of consent in rape trials, see Ehrlich, 1998), and of married women who forgive their abusive partners, frequently defined as noble or 'remarkable' (Figueiredo, 2000).

In Extract 7 below, we have an illustration of the binary view of women on the basis of their sexual behaviour: the complainant is described as a 'genuine victim' because she is, in the judge's own words, *'a girl from a good home and was well brought up'*, rather than *'a hussy who was only too anxious to nip into bed with [the defendant] in this extraordinary circumstance'*:

> 7　A 14-year-old girl visited London for the first time from her home in Durham . . . She lost her way back to King's Cross station and was accosted by the appellant who offered to assist her; but in fact he took her back to his flat, plied her with drink and then raped and buggered her. She had never taken alcohol before and was *a virgin*.
>
> The story he [the defendant] told the jury was very involved. If the jury were to accept what he said, far from being *a girl from a good home and was well brought up*, she was *a hussy who was only too anxious to nip into bed with him in this extraordinary circumstance*, namely that she was far from home not knowing where she was and where on earth she was going to go the following morning. We have looked very carefully at the evidence which he gave. *It is just as improbable a story as one could read, even in fiction*
>
> [Kabariti (1991) 92 Cr.App.R. 363 – stranger rape – appeal dismissed – 12 year's imprisonment upheld]

The two excerpts below illustrate modes of feminine behaviour and lifestyle presented by appeal judges as 'appropriate' – an elderly widow who tries to resist the burglar who rapes her; a woman who forgives her sexually abusive former partner:

> 8　Fifteen years' imprisonment upheld for the rape of *an elderly widow* by a *burglar*.
>
> The appellant broke into a house occupied by *a widow aged 78* who lived alone. *With considerable bravery, she hit him with a wooden banister which she kept hidden under her pillow.*
>
> [Thomas (1995) 16 Cr.App.R.(S.) 686 – stranger rape – 15-year sentence upheld]

> 9　Six years' imprisonment for the rape of a former partner reduced to five years.
>
> However, it seems to us that Mrs E. is *one of those remarkable women who is prepared to forgive*, and has forgiven, that which was done to her by somebody whom she loved and probably still does love.
>
> Accordingly, some mitigation must be seen in that one factor. It is not provided by anything which this appellant has done; it is provided by *the forgiveness of his victim*.
>
> [Hutchinson (1994) 15 Cr.App.R.(S.) 134 – marital rape – 6-year sentence reduced to 5]

Definitions and descriptions such as the ones above serve to point out 'correct' forms of behaviour and to repress 'inadequate' ones. To achieve its pedagogical ends, the criminal justice system relies both on forms of legal punishment (loss of money, freedom or life) as well as discipline (social exposure, loss of social value/respect, discrimination). The rape trial proceedings represent an arena where women can be personally disciplined through public exposure, loss of social repute, shame, and humiliation, or indirectly disciplined through the setting of examples of 'proper' and 'improper' modes of behaviour.

In the following section, I will argue that the judicial discourse makes use of other social discourses to attribute responsibility and causality, and to define 'victims' and 'villains' in a rape case.

Interdiscursivity: the 'discourses of man' and legal discourse

In his genealogical analysis of history, Foucault (1991) investigates the interplay between the structuring of the social domain and the multiplicity of discourses emanating from the human sciences (Smart, 1983, p. 66). One of the areas of the social domain which was structured and influenced by the discourses of the social sciences was the criminal justice system. The social sciences, or 'the sciences of man', as Foucault calls them, resulted from the disciplines as a whole new corpus of knowledge, techniques and 'scientific' discourses which became entangled in the mechanics of legal punishment. The sciences of man provided legal punishment with a hold on the condemned's soul: an assessment and a description not only of what criminals do, but also of who they are, will be, may be (Foucault, 1991).

A trial is no longer concerned merely with establishing the truth of a crime and its proper punishment but, as Smart contends (1983, p. 72):

> It constitutes a context within which there occurs an assessment of normality and the formulation of prescriptions for enforced normalisation. A series of subsidiary authorities have achieved a stake in the penal process; psychiatrists, psychologists, doctors, educationalists and social workers share in the judgement of normality, prescribe normalising treatment and contribute to the process of fragmentation of the legal power to punish.

The human sciences of psychiatry, psychology, gynaecology, pedagogy and criminology all have the same roots: the procedures of individualisation, of measurement, diagnosis and treatment of individual bodies, introduced by the disciplinary methods of the 18th and 19th centuries. Discipline and its tools (psychiatric and medical expertise) have penetrated the penal process, from investigation and judgement to punishment (Smart, 1983, p. 72).

The mingling of the trial process with sciences such as psychology and psychiatry has apparently purified and cleansed legal proceedings from their hard, cold and impersonal nature. In fact, what it has done is to transfer power from one site to another, or better, to integrate different sites of power, thus making them stronger. Fairclough (1995) claims that when one expert system relies on another to construct its discourse, this reinforces its power structure. By resorting to scientific discourses, judicial discourse also increases its power by endowing itself with extra scientificity and rationality.

The excerpt below illustrates the intimate link between psy-discourses and legal discourse:

10 A *social inquiry report* commented that there was no doubting the appellant's remorse for
   his victim's suffering and the deep shame which he was currently experiencing. It stated

he had attempted suicide. Also before the Court was *a report from a consultant psychiatrist who noted that the appellant was the youngest of six children in the family, an over-protected child showing early neurotic signs, devastated by his mother's death when he was 12*. Thereafter he showed general signs of delinquency, instability and a tendency to drug taking and alcohol abuse. He led an increasingly criminal lifestyle, chaotic, nomadic, much of it nocturnal, finding greater security in the criminal fraternity than within his family circle. *The offence itself appeared to the psychiatrist* to be 'out of character'. His mental profile did not indicate the need either for violence or a habitually aberrant sexual lifestyle. *The rape occurred at a time of chaos, insecurity and humiliation with life when, it was said, his judgements, control and perceptions were very severely reduced by drug and alcohol intake.* His remorse and regret were genuine. *The doctor expressed concern about the 'self damaging potential which his ruminations may cause', and recommended professional counselling, together with guidance and support.* Although his potential for dangerousness needs to be examined, *the psychiatrist thought he could not be regarded as a serious danger within the community.*

[McIntosh (1994) 15 Cr.App.R.(S.) 162 – stranger rape – 9-year sentence reduced to 7]

In the example above, the use of psychiatric expertise helps legal discourse to establish a relation of causality between the defendant's psychological profile and lifestyle (drug abuse, emotional problems) and his crime. Excerpt 10 is a classic example of the use of social-work discourse and psychiatric discourse as a support for a more 'humane' legal decision. The social and psychiatric profiles give support to a paternal judicial view of the appellant, depicting him as a young man 'to be pitied' and helped, and thus reducing his sentence by two years.

The diagnostic assessments present in penal judgement extend not just to the defendant, but also to the complainant (she too is evaluated by doctors and psychiatrists to establish the physical evidence of the rape, her 'trauma', her profile):

11 That was evidenced by *a psychiatric report* from Dr Jasper dated January 19, 1993, which was before the learned judge. Dr Jasper examined the victim on four occasions prior to the offender being sentenced ... *She found that the victim was then suffering from a post-traumatic stress disorder* which, she said, includes: '*symptoms of flashback (re-experiencing the event), intrusive thoughts and images relating to the traumatic event, nightmares, acute disturbance, depression, anxiety and irritability, all of which Sarah has experienced since the rape*'.

[Attorney-General's Reference (no. 3 of 1993) (W) [1994] 98 Cr.App.R. 85 – stranger rape – community service sentence increased to 2 years imprisonment]

12 Fifteen years' imprisonment for rape of an elderly woman by an intruder in her home reduced to 13 years.

The appellant broke into the home of a woman aged 74 in the early hours of the morning. He pressed a knife at her throat, and threatened to kill her. The woman resisted and the appellant attacked with some violence and raped her. The appellant told the victim that he had AIDS. *The woman was subsequently admitted to hospital suffering from depression.* Sentenced to 15 years' imprisonment.

On March 18, 1992, *she was admitted to hospital after taking an overdose of sleeping tablets and anti-depressants.* The medical report before the judge and before this Court indicated that *she was suffering at that time from depression,* although it is right to say that there were

causes other than, and in addition to, this appalling experience which contributed to that depression.
[Guniem (1994) 15 Cr.App.R.(S.) 90 – stranger rape – 15-years sentence reduced to 13]

In the two extracts above, the judges borrowed from psychiatric and medical reports to describe the traumatic effects of the rape on the victims and to depict them as 'genuine' victims and their assailants as 'true' rapists.

In the modern style of legal punishing, other 'discourses of man' share with the juridical discourse the responsibility of evaluating, categorising, educating and punishing both offender and victim. The legal power to educate, discipline and punish has been fragmented and divided among magistrates, 'psy' experts, educators, social workers, prison personnel, and so forth. As Lees points out, 'power is not a possession, as radical feminists have argued, but is seen as embedded in the discourses of medicine, law, psychology and the social sciences' (1997, p. 12).

The control of the body (bio-power)

The final section of this chapter deals with the use of the judicial discourse on rape as a way of better controlling the bodies of women. With the creation of the disciplines, especially the disciplinary mechanism of examination, the body became the object or target of new forms of power exercised with the help of scientific (for example, medical) knowledge.

The examination, and the process of documentation that accompanied it, allowed the constitution of the individual as an analysable, describable object. The disciplinary technique of examination was also vital for the surveillance, control and punishment of individuals.

The new individual created by the processes of examination and documentation is, as already pointed out, a calculable man (*sic*). According to Foucault, a mastery of the body and knowledge of its forces constitutes 'a political technology of the body'. That technology is diffuse and cannot be located in a particular institution or state apparatus. What the institutions and apparatuses do is to operate 'a micro-physics of power' (1991, p. 26), in other words, they observe, analyse and document the human body (thus functioning as a laboratory to enlarge the knowledge about the body), and supervise and discipline the uses we put our bodies to (thus fulfilling an educational function).

The judicial discourse on sexual crimes is one vehicle through which power over the body is exercised. Male and female bodies are diagnosed, treated and imprisoned during or as a result of a rape trial; women are depicted and judged as being constituted by their sex; female virginity and reputation, or unfaithfulness and promiscuity, all marked in the body, are protected or disciplined to safeguard women's social worth and social norms. In the discourse of rape trials, the body is a main target of legal and microforms of power (the penality of the law and the penality of the norm). To illustrate this view, I will discuss the links between the discourse of rape trials and pornography.

Descriptions of female bodies and of rapes as pornography

One example of institutional examination and control of the body is the descriptions of female bodies found in rape trials and legal sentences on rape cases. Reported appellate decisions on cases of rape vary in the way they describe the event and the complainant: some are discreet and almost laconic, while others give detailed and graphic accounts of the rape.

If some appellate decisions are laconic about the details of the rape, the same cannot be said about the trial, where every single detail of the event and of the victim's body is scrutinised and debated. In the opinion of the American legal scholar Catherine MacKinnon (1987), rape trials and pornography share a common link: both publicly portray and evaluate the female body. The victim's testimony during the trial has also been compared with a pornographic vignette: the details of male penetration can give pleasure as with other pornographic materials.[5]

In rape trials, as in pornographic texts, the events are constructed in fine detail (including for example, where the woman was touched, who removed her knickers, if she had a period or not). During most rape trials the complainant is forced to describe minutely which parts of her body were assaulted, and in which ways; these descriptions, which would embarrass women even in private circumstances, are particularly humiliating when given in public, in front of an audience. The paradox is that the very use of language to describe the sexual parts and functions of a woman's body is sufficient to render her unrespectable in the courtroom, as will be evidenced in the excerpts below. Giving evidence in court can be interpreted as a way of 'shaming' the complainant, of exposing her to public scrutiny and contempt, of disciplining and punishing her (Lees, 1997). And the graphic details of female bodies are not restricted to courtroom discourse. The detailed (and probably distressing) descriptions of the rape given by rape complainants, plus evidence from medical examinations, also find their way into legal decisions, as we can see in the extracts below:

13   *He then began an act of intercourse with her. She objected, and took her hands away from his buttocks where she had had to place them. She took her hands away to wipe her mouth, and then she tried to put her hand between his body and hers. He said to her, angrily, that she must put her hands back on his buttocks. She did so, and he put his penis back in her mouth. While it was there he kept thrusting; because of the force of his thrusting she choked and began to, as she described it, 'urge' – or, as one would suppose she meant, 'retch'. He asked her why she was doing that. She replied that he had 'pushed it too far back'. He continued with what he was doing, albeit not pushing as far back as he had before. Throughout the whole of this episode the knife was at the nape of her neck.*

He then stopped, withdrew his penis from her mouth and said, 'Get on the bed'. She lay on the bed. He told her to get on her front and instructed her to kneel, and put her head down and her hands behind her back. She obeyed. With her kneeling in that position he put his penis into her vagina. She could feel the knife in the region of her neck the whole while. He continued the act of sexual intercourse. She did not co-operate and he said to her, 'You can do better than that. If you help me you will live, if you don't you will die; I am going to die tonight anyway'. So she did something to appease him.

Although he was to continue the intercourse for some little time, that is a sufficient description of the events for the purposes of this case.

[Kowalski (1988) 86 Cr.App.R. 338 – marital rape – 4-year sentence reduced to 2]

Extract 13 presents detailed descriptions of the rape. In it the judges seem a little embarrassed by their lengthy description (*'Although he was to continue the intercourse for some little time, that is a sufficient description of the events for the purposes of this case'*), which does not happen in the following excerpt:

14   *On March 7, 1996 he went to see his doctor to discuss a referral to the marriage guidance organisation know as Relate. The complainant came home shortly after he did and saw him come into the house with a carrier bag. When she came into the house, he grabbed her by the throat and he pushed her down on the sofa. He pushed her face into a cushion, so that she was frightened that she was going to suffocate. He held her down with a tea towel across the back of her neck. She asked him not to kill her or to hurt her. He then said that he would not hurt her so long as she kept quiet and did not struggle. He said that he wanted to 'fuck her' and that it was going to last a few hours as he 'made the most of it'. He then took off most of his wife's clothing. She removed her own necklace and she hid her broken glasses down the back of the sofa for fear that he would strangle or cut her. He then took stockings which he had purchased out of the carrier bag and made his wife put them on. He ripped the remainder of her clothes. He then penetrated her against her will. He forced her to go into the kitchen with him to fetch some wine from the refrigerator. He placed cushions on the floor, forced her to kneel on all fours and then penetrated her again. He forced her to perform oral sex, holding the back of her head and threatening to hurt her. He told her that he was thinking of tying her up. He hit her with a tea towel. He then took her upstairs, saying that he was going to 'defile her little nest'. He then attempted to penetrate her whilst holding her against the bedroom door. He took her into the bedroom, forced her to put the stockings on with a suspender belt and forced his penis into her mouth. He then penetrated her again.*

[Michael H (1997) 2 Cr.App.R.(S.) 339 – marital rape – 5 years upheld]

Extract 14 is the one which most resembles pornography, evidenced in the mentions of *erotic lingerie* (stockings and suspender belt), an *erotic scene* (the cushions on the floor, the wine, the language used by the assailant), the threat of *'bondage'* (*'he told her he was thinking of tying her up'*), and finally *the threats and the use of violence* (he tried to suffocate her, he hit her with a tea towel, he threatened to hurt her and to tie her up), which conjures up *a sado-masochistic scenario* (this feature is present in the two excerpts).

The distressing experience of giving evidence in court, the frequent practice of character assassination carried out by defence lawyers and even by judges, and the fear of having the most intimate details of one's life publicly discussed, laughed at or even enjoyed as erotic material, are indications of what awaits women who file a complaint of rape, and probably leads many of them to keep quiet about male sexual violence.

Final remarks

In this chapter, based on a Foucauldian view of the criminal justice system, I have interpreted the judicial discourse on rape as part of a pedagogy of sexual behaviour. From this perspective, rape trials serve several educational aims: they discipline and punish the individual offender; they set 'proper' and 'improper' modes of behaviour both for the offender and other potential offenders; they serve as warnings to people in general. The warning function extends the discourse of rape trials and of legal decisions beyond the confines of the courtroom and even of the legal environment; the judicial discourse on rape serves as warning and example both to those directly involved with the trial (offender and victim) and to women and men in general.

The educational aim of judicial discourse is furthered by the help of several 'discourses of men', such as the discourses of psychiatry and psychology. Foucault claims that the legal power to punish has been fragmented and divided among several disciplines which, through the techniques of observation, judgement and examination, help to categorise people as 'normal' or 'abnormal', 'criminal' or 'innocent', amenable to rehabilitation or beyond recuperation. The discourses of medicine, psychiatry and psychology also help to add scientificity to legal discourse, somehow purging it of its harsh and cold punitive character. The idea is that the legal right to punish is not merely about retribution and revenge, but that it also encompasses a humane view of criminals.

The disciplinary techniques of observation, judgement and examination present in rape trials also serve to strengthen the hold over the body, and to increase its docility and its usefulness. The bodies and minds of rape victims are scrutinised to determine relations of causality and responsibility, to assess the seriousness of the rape, and to portray the complainant either as a 'genuine' or as a 'non-typical' victim. In this process, the bodies of women are trapped in minute and embarrassing descriptions that resemble pornography, descriptions which also serve as warning to other women of the symbolic exposure a rape complainant goes through.

Notes

1   Fairclough (1989, pp. 3–4) points out that power is exercised through *coercion* of various sorts (including physical violence), or through the manufacture of *consent* or at least acquiescence to it. Power relations depend both on coercion and consent to varying extents. Ideology is the primary means of achieving consent, and the favoured vehicle of ideology is discourse.
2   Lees (1997, p. 87) contends that the role of trial processes in policing female behaviour (especially of the sexual kind) has not yet been fully appreciated. In her words, 'through court procedures, women who do not behave in a stereotypical "feminine" way, or women who speak out about male violence, render themselves open to such disciplinary techniques which are laid bare in the court drama'.

3 According to Foucault (1991, p. 106), the modern transformation of the art of punishing into a 'technology of representation' means that the sign of the penalty and its disadvantages must be more lively than of the crime and its pleasures. However, rather than decreasing due to the severity of the law, sex crimes and cases of domestic violence are on the increase (see Temkin, 1987; Edwards, 1996). This might lead some people to conclude that the symbolic message of legal punishment is not getting through. Others, like myself, may conclude the opposite: the pedagogical aims of rape trials and of other discourses on rape are being successfully achieved. Indeed, in the view of some theorists (Connell, 1987; MacKinnon, 1989; Walby, 1990, in Matoesian, 1993), rape and sexual violence constitute a social structure to control women. The discourse of the law, in tandem with a host of other private and public discourses, is still based on myths about sexuality and discriminatory classification systems, which leads some men to see violence as acceptable, and many women either to accept violence as part of their lives or to be too frightened and ashamed to report it.
4 In Adler's (1987) study of 50 rape cases tried at the Old Bailey, applications from the defence to cross-examine a rape complainant about her past sexual history were denied by the judges only in 25 per cent of cases. In addition to that, to 'assassinate' a woman's character in court, defence counsel do not have to rely exclusively on the judge's authorisation to question her about her past sexual life; they frequently resort to innuendo and insinuations to stain the complainant's character (Temkin, 1987; Adler, 1987; Matoesian, 1993).
5 On the use of trial transcripts as pornographic reading, see Sampson (1994) and Lees (1997).

References

Adler, Z. (1987) *Rape on Trial*. London: Routledge & Kegan Paul.
All England Law Reports (1993) 2 All ER. London: Butterworths.
Bumiller, K. (1991) 'Fallen Angels: The Representation of Violence against Women in Legal Culture', in M. A. Fineman and N. S. Thomadsen (eds), *At The Boundaries of Law*. New York: Routledge, pp. 95–111.
Edwards, S. (1996) *Sex and Gender in the Legal Process*. London: Blackstone Press.
Ehrlich, S. (1998) 'The Discursive Reconstruction of Sexual Consent', *Discourse and Society*, vol. 9(2), pp. 149–71.
Fairclough, N. (1989) *Language and Power*. Harlow: Longman.
Fairclough, N. (1995) *Critical Discourse Analysis: The Critical Study of Language*. Harlow: Longman.
Figueiredo, D.C. (2000) 'Victims and Villains: Gender Representations, Surveillance and Punishment in the Judicial Discourse on Rape', unpublished doctoral thesis, Universidade Federal de Santa Catarina, Florianópolis, Santa Catarina, Brazil.
Foucault, M. (1991) *Discipline and Punish* (Alan Sheridan, trans.). London: Penguin (original work published 1975).
Hall, R. (1985) *Ask Any Woman: A London Inquiry into Rape and Sexual Assault*. Bristol: Falling Wall Press.
Lees, S. (1997) *Ruling Passions: Sexual Violence, Reputation and the Law*. Buckingham: Open University Press.
MacKinnon, C. (1987) *Feminism Unmodified: Discourses on Life and Law*. Cambridge, Mass.: Harvard University Press.

Matoesian, G. (1993) *Reproducing Rape: Domination Through Talk in the Courtroom.* Chicago: The University of Chicago Press.

Radford, L. (1987) 'Legalising Women Abuse', in H. Jalna and M. Maynard (eds), *Women, Violence and Social Control*, London: Macmillan–now Palgrave Macmillan, pp. 135–51.

Sampson, A. (1994) *Acts of Abuse: Sex Offenders and the Criminal Justice System.* London: Routledge.

Smart, B. (1983) 'On Discipline and Social Regulation: A Review of Foucault's Genealogical Analysis', in D. Garland and P. Young (eds), *The Power To Punish.* London: Heinemann, pp. 63–83.

Temkin, J. (1987) *Rape and the Legal Process.* London: Sweet & Maxwell.

Cases cited

The Criminal Appeal Reports (1988) 86 Cr.App.R. London: Sweet & Maxwell.

The Criminal Appeal Reports (1989) 89 Cr.App.R. London: Sweet & Maxwell.

The Criminal Appeal Reports (1991) 92 Cr.App.R. Part 1. London: Sweet & Maxwell.

The Criminal Appeal Reports (1994) 15 Cr.App.R.(S). London: Sweet & Maxwell.

The Criminal Appeal Reports (1994) 98 Cr.App.R. Part 1. London: Sweet & Maxwell.

The Criminal Appeal Reports (1995) 16 Cr.App.R.(S). London: Sweet & Maxwell.

The Criminal Appeal Reports (1996) 1 Cr.App.R.(S.).Part 1. London: Sweet & Maxwell.

The Criminal Appeal Reports (1997) 2 Cr.App.R.(S.). Part 1. London: Sweet & Maxwell.

The Criminal Appeal Reports (1998) 1 Cr.App.R.(S.). Part 1. London: Sweet & Maxwell.

Index

Aboriginal English, 163–4 *et* Ch. 10
    passim
ADR (Alternative Dispute Resolution),
    196 *et* Ch. 12 *passim*
AIDA (Action-implicative discourse
    analysis), 78
ambiguity, 12–13
appellate decisions, 260 *et* Ch. 16 *passim*
arbitration, 198–9

bankruptcy court, 213 *et* Ch. 13 *passim*
burden of proof, 230–1

child witnesses
    Aboriginal children, 164–5 *et* Ch. 10
        passim
    in police interviews, 97–105
Clinton scandal, 180–3 *et* Ch. 11
    passim
coaching undercover targets, 16
coercion
    during courtroom cross-examination,
        162 *et* Ch. 10 *passim*
    during native-speaker police
        interviews, 22–30
    during non-native speaker police
        interviews, 132–40
comprehensibility
    of legal language, 47–8
    of lexis, 46–7
    literacy levels and, 56
    of jury instructions, 38–9, 228 *et*
        Ch. 14 *passim*, 246 *et* Ch. 15 *passim*
    of US immigration documentation,
        36, Ch. 3
    of warning labels, 54 *et* Ch. 4
        passim
    Plain English, 65, 69
    pre-supposition, 57
    syntactic complexity, 41–6
    technical jargon, 57
    use of symbols, 60–2
confessions, 21, 23, 24 *et* Ch. 2
    passim

conversational strategies, 13–18
    blocking exculpatory statements,
        14
    camouflaging, 13
    the contamination principle, 14
corpus linguistics, 93
courtroom interaction, 147 *et* Ch. 9,
    Ch. 10 *passim*
courtroom narratives, 147–9
courtroom questioning
    in the O. J. Simpson trials, 151–2
    of Aboriginal juveniles, 169–76
cultural differences
    exploitation of in the courtroom,
        165–76
    exploitation of in undercover
        operations, 15
    interpreting cultural taboos, 205–6

deception, 186–9
document design, 40–1, 58
domestic disputes, 75 *et* Ch. 5
    passim

expert witness
    the linguist as, 3 *et* Ch. 1, Ch. 2,
        Ch. 3 *passim*, 249–54 *et* Ch. 15
        passim
    neutrality, 6–8
    testimony vs consultancy, 5–8, 18

FBI undercover operations, 12–13
FDA (Food and Drug Administration),
    66–8
footing, 127, 134–40

gratuitous concurrence, 166–8
    et Ch. 10 *passim*
Gricean implicature, 57, 185, 190,
    222–3

illocution, 19, 117, 226
immigration, textual barriers to, 36
inferencing analysis, 11

interpreting, 111 *et* Ch. 7, Ch. 8,
    Ch. 12 *passim*
  ethics during Alternative Dispute
      Resolution, 206–8
  ethics of police officers as
      interpreters, 133–40
  in Alternative Dispute Resolution,
      199–209
  interpreter strategies in police
      interviews, 120–4
  turn-taking dynamics in police
      interviews, 118–20
interruption, 14–15
intertextuality, 147 *et* Ch. 9 *passim*

jury instructions
  and jury deliberations, 228 *et* Ch. 14
      passim
  comprehensibility in capital murder
      case, 246–54 *et* Ch. 15 *passim*
  narrative vs paradigmatic modes,
      231–42 *et* Ch. 14 *passim*

lying, 186–9

Miranda rights, 127 *et* Ch. 8 *passim*
  subversion of, 131

narrative mode of reasoning, 231–2
non-native speakers of English, 36, 38
    et Ch. 7, Ch. 8 *passim*
  Aboriginal English speakers in court,
      163–76
  gratuitous concurrence, 166–76
  proficiency in English during hearings,
      217–21, 224–5 *et* Ch. 13 *passim*
  subversion of Miranda rights, 131

PACE (Police and Criminal Evidence
    Act), 19, 20, 112
  PACE Codes of Practice, 113
paradigmatic mode of reasoning, 231–2
PEACE mnemonic, 112, 113, 147
perjury, 183–6
perlocutionary effect, 184, 222
police emergency calls, 75 *et* Ch. 5
    passim
  call-takers as gatekeepers, 84–7
  interactional structure, 76–7
  openings, 78–9

police interviews/interrogations, 21,
    24–7 *et* Ch. 6 *passim*
  in Customs and Excise, 111 *et* Ch. 7
      passim
  procedure for conducting, 19, 20,
      29–30, 112–13
  role of interpreters, 111 *et* Ch. 7
      passim
  so-prefaced questions, 91 *et* Ch. 6
      passim
  tape-recording, 19, 33, 114
  with children, 97–105, 108–9
product liability warnings, 54
    et Ch. 4 *passim*
  adequacy, 55–8

rape cases
  appellate decisions, 260 *et* Ch. 16
      passim
  construal of victims and defendants,
      265–7
  police interviews with suspects,
      105–8
reasonable doubt standard, 240, 246
    et Ch. 15 *passim*
response analysis, 10–11
rule of lenity, 189–90

scripting undercover targets, 16
speech act theory, 48–9, 184, 222–4
statements, 19, 21, 27–30
summings up, 229–30 *et* Ch. 14
    passim

topic analysis, 9–10
transcripts, accuracy, 8, 156–7

US Immigration and Naturalization
    Service, 35 *et* Ch. 3 *passim*
US Senate impeachment hearings
  President Bill Clinton, 180 *et* Ch. 11
      passim
  Senator Harrison A. Williams, Jr, 14

'verballing' of suspects, 19
verbatim records, 20, 23, 30

warnings, 48–9 *et* Ch. 4 *passim*
  bilingual, 59–60
  pragmatics, 62–4